MONKS AND MONASTERIES
OF THE
EGYPTIAN DESERTS

MONKS AND MONASTERIES OF THE EGYPTIAN DESERTS

Revised Edition

Otto F.A. Meinardus

The American University in Cairo Press
Cairo • New York

CONTENTS

PREFACE

People who live in Egypt have a different understanding of the desert from those who live in Europe or America. In some parts of the world the desert has become a testing ground for nuclear energy, but here in Egypt it is still considered by many a blessing of God. The desert has provided, from time immemorial, a testing ground for the souls of men. Go to the desert for food and drink and you will find a barren waste. Go there to listen to the voice of God and you will receive insight, understanding and wisdom. The desert is silent, apart, different. It conveys a picture, waterless and featureless, yet overwhelming to the senses.

I have visited various deserts in Egypt, the Desert of Scetis (Wâdî 'n-Natrûn), the desert of the Wâdî 'Arabah, the desert of al-Qalamûn, and the desert of Maryût. Here I discovered people who awakened my interest. Some of them were very ordinary people, others appeared strange, yet there were others again who radiated a love, a concern and a spirituality that could only have resulted from the impact of the desert. Thus I repeated my visits, spending days and nights with those whose life was formed by the desert. It is to them that this volume is dedicated, for they were the people who provided the impetus to study the many books written by and about them.

The importance of a study of this kind in the middle of the twentieth century lies in the fact that now, as in the days of old, the Coptic leaders, the patriarch, the metropolitans and the bishops are recruited from among the desert monks. It is no oversimplification to say that the state of the monasteries reflects the state of the Church.

Since the days of Anbâ Kîrillus VI (1959–1971) the monastic movement in Egypt has experienced an unprecedented renaissance, which has exerted a profound influence upon the spiritual vitality of the Church. In the 1960s the Sunday School Movement, led by Anbâ Shenûdah, inspired educated young men to forsake the worldly pleasures and to join the desert fathers. Many of these young ascetes have since been promoted to the episcopacy. The number of monks has significantly increased. New cells, spacious conference centres and guest rooms, as well as extensive agricultural projects, have not only altered the outward appearance of the monasteries, but also given the Church a new purpose.

Thirty years ago, when I set out to gather material for the first edition of *Monks and Monasteries of the Egyptian Deserts*, the overwhelming majority of the monks were fifty years of age or older. Today, the majority of monks are academically trained young men between twenty-five and forty. In the past, a certain anti-intellectualism characterized the piety of the desert fathers, reflecting to some extent the tradition of their founders. St. Macarius the Great was a camelherd; St. Macarius of Alexandria was a small shopkeeper; St. Apollo was a goatherd, while St. Paphnutius and St. Pambo were illiterate. Today the desert monks are recruited from the academic professions: many of them were engineers, pharmacists, physicians, chemists, architects, agricultural engineers, etc.

The following statistics show the numerical increase of monks over the past twenty-five years:

Monastery	1960	1986
Dair Anbâ Antûnîûs	24	69
Dair Anbâ Bûlâ	22	40
Dair al-Barâmûs	20	83
Dair Abû Maqâr	12	105
Dair Anbâ Bishoî	12	115
Dair as-Surîân	28	55
Dair al-Muharraq	70	50
Dair Anbâ Samwîl	20	46
Dair Abû Mînâ	6	30
Dair Mârî Girgis	–	25
Dair Anbâ Bakhûm	–	12

In addition to two new monasteries in Upper Egypt which have been officially recognized (Dair Mârî Girgis at al-Riziqât and Dair Anbâ Bakhûm at Edfu), a number of formerly abandoned monasteries in Upper Egypt have been repeopled with monks.

The most significant change to the monastic life was effected by the construction of desert roads leading to the monasteries, thus lifting the desert fathers out of their geographical isolation. The original places of withdrawal from the world, protected by miles of impassable desert sand, have now become popular pilgrimage sites that can be reached in a few hours by car or bus. On certain holidays, literally hundreds of visitors descend upon the desert monasteries, and youth groups gather there for spiritual retreats and conferences. For the first time in their sixteen hundred years of history, the desert monasteries are woven into the fabric of the parish churches of the cities, towns and villages.

It is not surprising that this ecclesiastical renaissance has coincided with numerous extraordinary spiritual events and religious occurrences.

There were the spectacular apparitions of the Holy Virgin in spring 1968 in the Church of the Holy Virgin at Zeitûn, and in spring 1986 in the Church of St. Dimiana in Shubra, Cairo. In September 1975 an unusually bright light, witnessed not only by the monks but also by numerous visitors, appeared above the cave–church of St. Paul the Theban in Dair Anbâ Bûlâ. The translations of the relics of St. Mark in 1968 and of St. Athanasius in 1973 from Venice to Cairo were important demonstrations strengthening the Christian identity. The discovery of the relics of St. John the Baptist and the prophet Elisha in the Dair Abû Maqâr in November 1978, the discovery of the incorruptible remains of Anbâ Yûsâb (1735–1826) in Dair Anbâ Antûnîûs, and the blood–miracle of St. Bisada in Dair Anbâ Samwîl in December 1976 provided spiritual support that increased the religious fervour of the monks.

Perhaps the most remarkable aspect of Coptic monasticism over the past thirty years has been the move towards renewed ascetic practices, especially those which in the past led to a high degree of self–mortification and the withdrawal from the world of the senses. The monks have imposed such a strict spiritual discipline of prayer and work that one concludes that their lives are governed by the rules of St. Pachomius or St. Benedict rather than by the *Apophthegmata* of the early fathers.

This volume ought to be read and considered merely as an introduction to the subject. This means that I do not claim in any way to have exhausted the literary sources, for many documents, manuscripts and books were not accessible to me. Furthermore, my whole undertaking suffers from the fact that I am neither a church-historian nor a Copt. This means that, like so many Westerners, I have written about something in which I am not personally involved. Moreover, I have limited myself merely to a study of the inhabited monasteries. A thorough study of Coptic monasticism from its beginnings to the present day, in all its various forms and expressions, requires such a profound knowledge of Coptic archaeology, history and theology that it would seem to me to be the work of a team, rather than that of an individual.

As to the historical veracity of the material presented, it might be helpful to point to the utter subjectivity of what is commonly understood to be "History". Historical writings describe events which others remember and project upon paper. Therefore, it is always difficult to distinguish later between projected memory and projected imagination, realizing that imagination is one of the creative aspects of our mind. I do not claim to be the judge to determine where actual history ends and imagination commences. This every reader will have to do for him- or herself. I have presented some material of the history of the Coptic monasteries, but I do not vouch for its historical veracity. Each monastery has been dealt with separately so as to enable the reader to trace the history of the monastery throughout the centuries. This method has inevitably produced some repetition as well as some arbitrary selections of material, especially in the case of the four monasteries of the Wâdî 'n-Natrûn.

For easier and more consistent reading, all dates in the text have been converted into those of the Christian era, Anno Domini. In Egypt there are four calendar systems in use: the Coptic, the Islamic, the Julian-Gregorian and the Gregorian. The Muslim era commences on 15 or 16 July, 622. This date does not exactly coincide with the date of Muhammad's migration from Mecca to Medina, for it was fixed by 'Umar in such a way that the year begins in Muharram. The Coptic church begins its era on 29 August, 284, which is termed the "Era of the Martyrs" (A.M.) and which commemorates the martyrs who suffered and died for the Christian faith during the Diocletian persecution. According to reckoning by the Gregorian Calendar, the Coptic Year begins on 11 September, or on 12 September in Leap Years. Thus the "Era of the Martyrs" marks the official beginning of Coptic history. The Julian-Gregorian Calendar is used by the Greek Orthodox. For immovable feasts, the date is according to the Gregorian reckoning, but for the movable feasts of Easter, Ascension Day and Pentecost the Julian Calendar is followed. The Gregorian Calendar resulted from a correction of the Julian Calendar by Aloysius Lilius and was introduced into the Western church by Pope Gregory XIII in 1582.

Twenty-five years ago the first edition of *Monks and Monasteries of the Egyptian Deserts* appeared. This second, revised edition is an attempt to bring up to date some of the developments that have changed this once obscure movement of oriental Christianity into a dynamic institution within the Coptic church. Because of lack of space, several chapters of the first edition have had to be either shortened or omitted in order to include relevant new material.

I wish to express my sincere thanks to The American University in Cairo Press, which has made this second revised edition possible.

Otto Meinardus
1989

In this second printing of the revised edition, I have taken the opportunity to add a new chapter on monasticism in the Fayyûm and to make a few other minor changes in the text.

Otto Meinardus
1992

GLOSSARY OF
ECCLESIASTICAL TERMS

Abûnâ	father, address for a monk or a priest
Amîn ad-dair	the head of a monastery
Anbâ	saint, bishop, archbishop, pope
Apophthegmata	a terse, pointed saying embodying an important truth
Archimandrite	the superior of a monastery, archpriest
Catholicos	the head of the Armenian–and since 1959 of the Ethiopian–Orthodox churches
Chrism	oil mixed with balm, used for sacramental anointing
Chrismation	application of the chrism, sacramental unction
Ciborium	canopy raised above the altar
Cross Nimbus	a bright or golden disk with a cross surrounding the head of Jesus Christ
Dair	monastery
Epiphany tank	a deep oblong basin about 2 or 3m by 2.25m, sunk in the floor, nowadays boarded over. Formerly used for the service of Blessing the Water on the feast of Epiphany
Feretory	a shrine, often richly adorned, for the relics of saints
Gynaekion	a place for women in the church
Haikal	the sanctuary with its altar
Hegoumenos	archpriest
Jacobites	Syrian Orthodox Christians
Lakan	a shallow rectangular basin sunk in the floor (in modern churches a small movable copper tank) used for the service of foot-washing on Maundy Thursday and the feast of SS. Peter and Paul, and for Blessing the Water on the feast of Epiphany
Laura	an aggregation of detached cells tenanted by recluse monks under a superior
Mâr	holy, saintly
Martyrium	place where the relics of a martyr are kept, or the church built above the tomb of a martyr or in honour of a martyr
Melkites	the "King's Men", or Greek Orthodox Christians, today Greek Catholics

Metropolitan	an archbishop heading a metropolis or a large area
Narthex	a vestibule or portico stretching across the western end of a church
Oeconomus	the monk responsible for the administration and economy of a monastery
Pallium	a scarf of red silk on which are marked three crosses, measuring about four by two metres (also known as *omophorion*)
Qasr	keep or tower for the defence of a monastery
Qummus	archpriest or hegoumenos
Selim (sullam)	vocabulary, list of words, scales
Skene	hut or tent
Theotokos	Godbearer, title of the Holy Virgin since the Third Ecumenical Council of Ephesus in 431
Xenodochos	the monk responsible for visitors and guests

THE COPTIC MONTHS

Tût	September 11–October 10
Bâbah	October 11–November 9
Hâtûr	November 10–December 9
Kîhak	December 10–January 8
Tûbah	January 9–February 7
Amshîr	February 8–March 9
Barmahât	March 10–April 8
Barmûdah	April 9–May 8
Bashons	May 9–June 7
Baûnah	June 8–July 7
Abîb	July 8–August 6
Masrî	August 7–September 5
Nasî*	September 6–September 11

* The month of Nasî has six days, if the following year is a leap year.

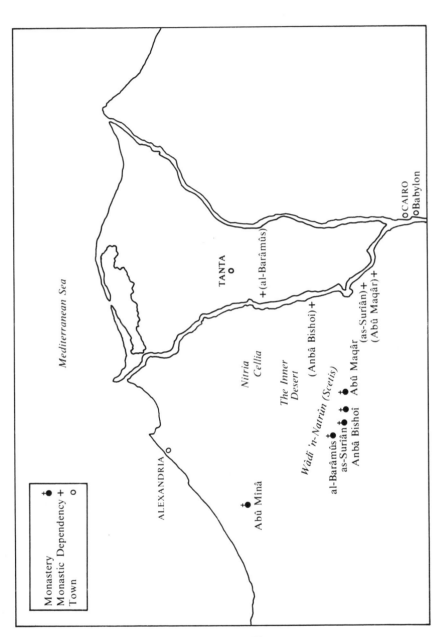

Map I: Lower Egypt

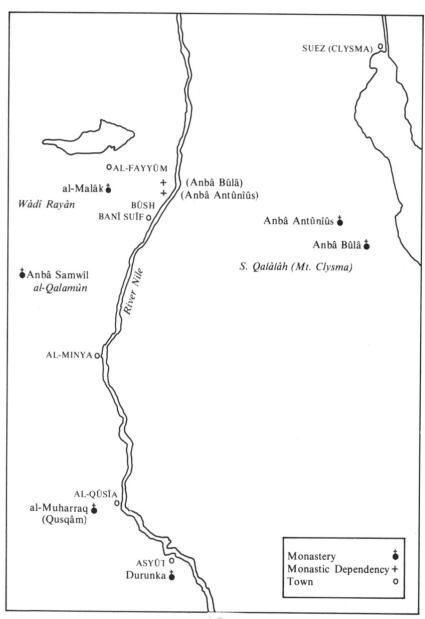

SUEZ (CLYSMA) o

o AL-FAYYÛM

al-Malâk 🕆   +   (Anbâ Bûlâ)
                     +   (Anbâ Antûnîûs)
Wâdî Rayân   BÛSH
              BANÎ SUÎF o   Anbâ Antûnîûs 🕆

                                   Anbâ Bûlâ 🕆

🕆 Anbâ Samwîl   S. Qalâlâh (Mt. Clysma)
al-Qalamûn

AL-MINYA o

AL-QÛSÎA
al-Muharraq 🕆 o
(Qusqâm)

              ASYÛT o
              Durunka 🕆

Monastery	🕆
Monastic Dependency	+
Town	o

Map II: Middle Egypt

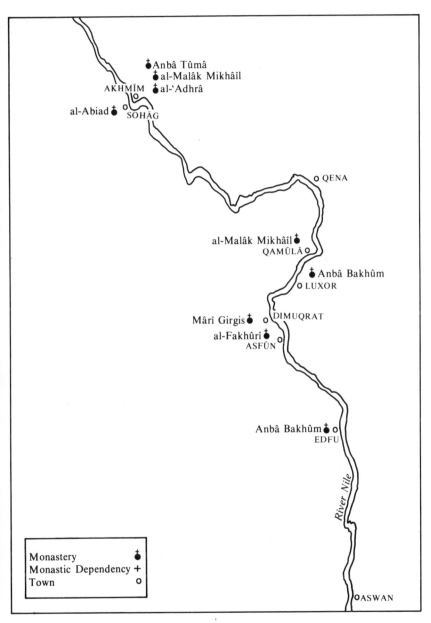

Map III: Upper Egypt

1

ST. ANTONY
THE ASCETE

St. Antony (Anbâ Antûnîûs) is the prototype of Coptic asceticism in particular and of Christian monasticism in general. The life, the attitudes, the words and works of this great hermit of the desert have influenced, and still influence, the lives of the desert fathers, be they anchorites or coenobitic monks. It is fortunate and also important for the development of Coptic and Christian monasticism that a man of the stature of St. Athanasius, bishop of Alexandria, turned his attention to the writing of a biography of St. Antony. His *Vita Antonii* was purposely addressed to the West, where it produced a lasting influence. Theologians like St. Jerome and St. Gregory Nazianzen show acquaintance with St. Athanasius' *Vita*, and the demand for information about the great hermit, especially by the Western church, must have prompted Evagrius, about twenty years after the saint's death, to translate the Life of St. Antony into Latin. By the end of the fourth century the life of the saint was read even in faraway Gaul. In Book VIII of his *Confessions*, St. Augustine relates how he was stirred by the reading of the life of St. Antony. "For I hear of Antony, that coming in during the reading of the gospel, he received the admonition, as if what was being read was spoken to him: 'Go sell all that thou hast, and give to the poor, and thou shalt have treasure in heaven, and come and follow me'... and by such oracle he was forthwith converted unto Thee." It was this divine command that moved not only St. Antony but also St. Augustine. As a matter of fact, we find that the desert movement, early Catholic scholasticism, and the practical concern of Christian charity as expressed by St. Francis of Assisi were all inspired by the same word.

The Life of St. Antony

The following *Vita Antonii* was related to me by a monk of the Monastery of St. Antony. It seems to be much more relevant to understand the mental image which a monk has of his patron–saint, than to add another biography to the large number of translations, abbreviations or condensations that are available.[1]

"It is somewhere about here where our Anbâ Antûnîûs was buried. Though we don't know where exactly, but I am sure, he is here in the monastery. Every now and then we are told by the Bedouins, who are around the monastery, that they see him and Anbâ Bûla (St. Paul the Theban), walking on the walls (of the monastery). This is at night time, and they are carrying their lanterns, as they go up and down the wall. And we are glad that they are here. Anbâ Antûnîûs was a friend, a good friend of Anbâ Bûlâ, and his monastery is just across the mountain ... Before Anbâ Antûnîûs came here he lived in the Nile valley. He came from a good family, and they had plenty of money.[2] When he was still a young man, his father and his mother died. He was a Christian, and he went to church. But when his parents died, he was more prepared to receive the glorious news of our Lord Jesus Christ. One day, he heard the gospel being read, and he felt as if it were spoken to him, that he should sell all that he had and give it to the poor people.[3] And so he gave away all he had, except a little which he kept for his sister. But some time later, when he was in church again, he decided to put his sister into a convent, that she might be with the holy women. There were many monks living in caves at that time. And Anbâ Antûnîûs went to see one of them. He wanted to live with him, but the monk refused to let him come near. So he lived all by himself. This is near Kuraimât, where the supply-trucks turn in. Here, Anbâ Antûnîûs lived and began his life as a monk. Many villagers came to be healed and to talk to him. Some of them stayed with him, and there (at Dair al-Maimûn) began the first monastic community. He also went to Alexandria to fight the heretics. After that, he came here, where he used to have a little garden with palm trees. He stayed around here the rest of his life. But when people heard where he was, they even came here to see him, and so he left the spring and his garden, and he went up to the cave, which is about an hour's walk from here—up on the mountain. But even there people came to see him, but many people stayed here at the foot of the mountain, and so this settlement became larger and larger, as more and more peasants settled down here. Before he died, he told them that nobody was to know where they buried him, and to Anbâ Athânâsîûs he left his cloak and to Anbâ Sarâbîûn (Serapion) he left a sheepskin. There are some people in France who say they have his bones, but he is here.

"Only a few years ago (1950) Abûnâ Hazaqîâ (Ezekiel) asked Abûnâ Mitîâs (Matthias) to get a certain book from the Church of St. Antony (within the monastery). As Abûnâ Mitîâs went into the sanctuary he forgot to pay his respect to the saint and to ask his intercession. Then he felt somebody patting his shoulder, and Abûnâ Mitîâs trembled, and everyone could see how pale his face was as he came out of the church and told them his experience. 'Anbâ Antûnîûs is always there,' Abûnâ Hazaqîâ said. 'As you enter our church, you must show respect and devotion to him.' There are many monks here who have had similar experiences, who have seen him and who have also felt him."

Regarding the bodily remains of the saint there is no unanimity as to their later history and location. As has been shown by the testimony of our monk, the inhabitants of the monastery claim to have the body of St. Antony for themselves.

The Influence of St. Antony

Before turning our attention to the monastery that bears his name, it might be well to consider the influence that St. Antony wielded and which has had such far reaching effects on his contemporaries and on the generations which followed him. His name became associated with a new way of life leading to salvation. His disciple Anbâ Makârîûs (St. Macarius), who stayed with Anbâ Antûnîûs at least twice, established Antonian monasticism in the Desert of Scetis (Wâdî 'n-Natrûn), where several thousand monks imitated and even surpassed the rigour and austerity of their founder. Anbâ Ammûn, the father of Nitrian monasticism, was inspired by Anbâ Antûnîûs just as Anbâ Ishaq and Anbâ Pelusian upheld the Antonian tradition at Mount Clysma (now known as the South Qalâlâh range of mountains).

Hilarion, the originator of Palestinian monasticism, derived his ascetic enthusiasm from the great hermit. Born in 291, near Gaza, he had made a pilgrimage to the South Qalâlâh for the purpose of learning the angelic life from St. Antony. After staying two months with him, he could no longer endure the crowds that came so frequently to visit the hermit. On his return to his native land, Hilarion lived in a tiny cell near Gaza for fifty years. Within a few years of his death, laurae and monasteries were to be found in all parts of Palestine.

Johannes Cassianus (360-435) visited the East with his friend Germanus. He entered a monastery in Bethlehem, but his desire to visit the Egyptian hermits of the Desert of Scetis inspired him to leave Palestine. For seven years he lived with the Egyptian fathers of the desert. Afterwards he went to Constantinople, where he became a pupil of St. John Chrysostom. He then proceeded to Marseille and founded a monastery where the Egyptian rule was followed. Nearby, St. Honoratus founded the Monastery of Lerinum (Lerins) in 400 where, until the introduction of the Benedictine rule in the seventh century, the Egyptian system was followed.

Soon after St. Antony's death, people from all over the Levant came to Egypt. St. Epiphanius, bishop of Constantia in Cyprus, visited Egypt and, after his return to Palestine, became hegoumenos of a monastery which he founded near Eleutheropolis in Judaea. St. Basil the Great, bishop of Caesarea and founder of many monastic institutions in Asia Minor, derived his knowledge of monasticism from the monks and hermits of Syria and Egypt, whom he visited. Monasticism, like Christianity, was introduced into Ethiopia from Egypt. In 480, Anbâ Aragawi, who is said to have received his habit from St. Pachomius, founded the celebrated monastery at Debra Damo. With him came eight other monks from the Monastery of St. Antony and together they are known in the Ethiopian church as the "Nine Saints". In 385, St. Hieronymus (Jerome) travelled in company with two Roman ladies, Paula and her daughter Eustochium, to Palestine. They continued their journey to Egypt where they visited the monasteries of the Desert of Scetis. On returning to Palestine they settled in Bethlehem where Paula founded four monasteries, three for nuns and one for monks. It was the latter monastery over which Jerome presided and where he was engaged in most of his literary work.

The part played by early Egyptian monasticism in the conversion of England is a matter that has still to be determined. "It is more than probable," writes Stanley Lane-Poole, "that we are indebted to the remote hermits for the first preaching of the gospel in England where, till the coming of St. Augustine, the Egyptian monastic rule prevailed. But more important is the belief that Irish Christianity, the great civilizing agent of the early Middle Ages among the northern nations, was the child of the Egyptian church." The Irish Stowe Missal, which is the oldest missal of the Irish church, refers to the Egyptian anchorites of the fourth century. The text, which is in four columns, and consists mostly of single words, reads in the second column of folio 32 verso: *pauli—antoni—et ceterorum patrum heremi sciti.* The list of the saints of Egypt appears between the *Memento etiam domine* and the *Nobis quoque peccatoribus* of the Canon.

Apart from the direct influence of Egyptian monasticism upon European Christianity, it might be well to mention only briefly some of the Egyptian saints who are given special veneration in Europe. St. Verena the Theban (Upper Egypt) had followed St. Maurice to Switzerland where she suffered martyrdom during the Diocletian persecution. Her relics are venerated at Zurzach in Aargau. Some of these relics were translated to Cairo in 1986 where they repose in the Cathedral of St. Mark. St. Victor (Buqtur) is venerated in Geneva, where his relics were taken at the end of the fifth century, and SS. Felix and Regula, who are commemorated on September 11, also belonged to the Egyptian Legion of the Thebaid. The two saints suffered martyrdom and are the object of veneration in Zürich.

2
DAIR ANBÂ ANTÛNÎÛS

The Beginnings of the Monastery

It is now generally assumed that the Monastery of St. Antony (Dair Anbâ Antûnîûs) was built in the reign of Julian the Apostate, between 361 and 363.[1] A few years after the death of the great hermit, his followers settled in the place where their master had lived and died. The original settlement consisted only of the most essential buildings. The monks lived in solitary cells, within walking distance of a communal worship centre where the Divine Liturgy was celebrated and where the monks took part in a common meal. Things changed as the fervour of the ascetics declined. The monks began to associate themselves in closer relationship for the purpose of safety, convenience and mutual fellowship. Thus the communal or coenobitic character of the Antonian life evolved. The hermit retreated from his mountain cave to a separate cell within the framework of the monastic community, still living, however, a separated and highly ascetic life. It is interesting to observe that this mode of asceticism has prevailed to this day.

At present, there are no anchorites living in the Wâdî 'Arabah or in the South Qalâlâh range, although some monks may visit the mountain cave of their master for special prayer, meditation or ascetic exercises, returning to their monastery within a few hours or a day or two. However, Mrs. Winifred Holmes writes that in 1956 she saw a hermit at St. Antony's: "A mysterious figure in tattered dusty robes, a rough Tau[2] and a scarf wound round his head, who appeared suddenly in church during the long services beginning with Maundy Thursday. He seemed dazed and exalted, perhaps a little strange as he stumbled in and wandered up into the choir, and gazed with amazement at the bishop in his panoply and glory, sitting on the

5

bishop's throne before the narthex. I was told that he was a solitary who lived in the desert outside the walls. He was treated with great deference by the senior monks, whom I saw speaking to him outside the church. He looked to me about sixty, but much aged by his hard and solitary life."[3]

When Arius confronted the Christian church with its first great theological controversy,[4] the monks were· faced with theological and philosophical problems. We read in the *History of the Patriarchs*[5] that "the people continued for a long time to communicate in caves and deserts and in the fields in all the provinces of Egypt as far as the Thebaid, for the Arians, who were friends of the prince,[6] were spread over every place."

Egyptian monasticism remained loyal to its Alexandrian See. A pro-Arian attempt to suppress Orthodoxy, launched by the Emperor Valens, culminated in an edict for the expulsion of the orthodox. It is difficult to determine to what extent St. Antony's monastery was affected by this internal persecution. One thing, however, is certain: the monasteries in the Desert of Scetis and the Fayyûm remained strongholds of Orthodoxy.

The Monastery of St. Antony served as a place of refuge for some monks of the Desert of Scetis. These monasteries underwent several sacks during the fifth century, and we read in the *Ethiopian Synaxarium* that John the Short escaped to the Red Sea. "When the Barbarians came to the desert of Scete to plunder the houses of the monks, and to slay the monks, this Saint Abba John went to the Monastery of Saint Abba Antony in the desert of Kuelzem by the Red Sea, not that he was afraid of death, but he said: 'I go that a pagan may not come and kill me, and go to Sheol because of me, I do not wish to be in a state of ease and for that pagan to suffer punishment of my account'."[7]

On account of the decisions reached at the Council of Chalcedon,[8] the Egyptian church separated from the rest of Christendom. The confusion produced in Egypt by the decisions of the Council of Chalcedon was to have later consequences. The Byzantines or Melkites as they were called, accepted the decisions of Chalcedon, and there was naturally friction between them and the Egyptians who rejected these decisions.

Copts and Greeks

A note in Butler's *Arab Conquest of Egypt* asserts that in 615 the Melkite Patriarch St. John the Almoner (609-620) supplied a certain Anastasius, hegoumenos of St. Antony's monastery, with large sums of money and ordered him to buy up captives taken by the Persians.[9] Therefore, Melkite monks must have inhabited the monastery in the seventh century, for it is unlikely that John the Almoner would have sent money to a Coptic abbot. It is true, however, that St. John "held the monastic system in the greatest reverence, and that he was the more profuse in his liberality to different monasteries."[10] He gave Christian concern to all in need. He established hospitals for the sick, and fed 7,500 of the poor every day.

Leroy, whose evidence comes from ancient manuscripts, states that "ses premiers occupants furent non des monophysites, mais de moines grecs (melkites)." Around 790 some Coptic monks, disguised as Bedouins, entered the monastery to steal the bodily remains of St. John the Short of the Wâdî 'n-Natrûn, who had found shelter at St. Antony's sometime in the fifth century and who had died there.[11] The *Ethiopian Synaxarium*[12] tells how, during the days of Anbâ Yûânnis IV (777-799), the body of St. John the Short was brought back to Scetis. The monks of the Monastery of St. Macarius went to Mount Clysma to retrieve the body, but when they arrived, "it was not possible for them to fulfil their mission for the moment, for the body of the saint was guarded by the Melkite Chalcedonians who dwelt in the sanctuary." Then, "the judge from among the Arabs said to the Melkite bishop who sat in the sanctuary: 'Make all your men get out of the church, for I wish to enter the church myself and stay here this night.' The bishop did as the judge commanded, and the Coptic monks made ready their beasts outside the town and entered by night and took the body and returned to the desert of Scetis."

Some of the Coptic monasteries did occasionally change their ecclesiastical allegiance, as is evident from the following observation by Maqrîzî. During the patriarchate of Anbâ Murqus II (799-819), the patriarch of the Melkites, who was well educated in medicine, went to Baghdâd to heal one of the caliph's concubines. After she was cured, the caliph ordered that the monasteries of the Melkites, which had been occupied by the Copts in Egypt, were to be returned.[13] It is likely that the two Red Sea monasteries were affected by this announcement. The Copts may have taken possession of the monasteries only to surrender them again shortly afterwards to the Melkites.

From the Eighth to the Fourteenth Century

It is difficult to know whether the Monastery of St. Antony underwent the same fate as that of the monasteries in the Desert of Scetis in the eighth or ninth century. During the patriarchate of Anbâ Mîkhâîl I (744-768) there were tribes "in mountains in the eastern part of Egypt, from Bilbais to al-Qulzum and the sea, consisting of Muslims who were called Arabs. And there were among them more than thirty thousand horsemen, and they had chiefs in command of them."[14] About this time, Orthodox monks went to the Monastery of St. Antony. Anbâ Mînâ entered the monastery, after he had left his wife, and became a friend of Anbâ Mîkhâîl who ascended the patriarchal throne in 743. Then both Anbâ Mînâ and Anbâ Mîkhâîl left St.

Antony's and went to the Monastery of St. Macarius where they became disciples of Anbâ Abrâm and Anbâ Girgis.[15]

During the patriarchate of Anbâ Quzmân III (920-932), Mînâ made a tour with his friend, Buqtur, and penetrated into the lands of Ethiopia, where they presented themselves to the metropolitan to ask him for money. When he refused, they wrote a counterfeit letter, as if from the patriarch, which caused a great deal of internal dissension in Ethiopia and eventually led to insurrection.[16] Though this incident is of little importance to the history of the monastery, it shows that the monastery at Mount Clysma had some relationship with the Ethiopian church in the tenth century.

After two hundred years of internal tension and intrigue, Egypt was finally conquered by the Arabs in July 640. The survival of Christianity in Egypt was due largely to the influence of the monasteries, and the security of the latter was due in some degree to their remoteness in the desert. Yet few passages in the annals of Egypt are more agreeable reading than those which tell of the extremely friendly relations that prevailed between some of the Coptic abbots and the caliphs, and the delight which the latter took in visiting the monasteries.

There were times when the Church appears to have been left in peace, but again there were periods of fierce persecution, distress and trouble. Al-Hâkim's persecution and the destruction of some three thousand churches between 1000 and 1017 caused many Christians to flee to the desert.

The eleventh century brought a number of disasters to Egypt.[17] An earthquake laid waste many cities, a pestilence caused much suffering and a rebellion by the Kurds and the Turks inflicted every kind of misery. This was followed by famine and unexampled suffering. Peace was partially restored to Egypt when Nasr ad-Dûlah, the leader of the Turks, was defeated. The remains of his army, however, invaded the Thebaid, where they pillaged the monasteries of St. Antony and St. Paul the Theban and put to death many of the monks. When Nasr ad-Dûlah was slain these calamities ceased.

About one hundred years after the sack by the Mamelukes, the Monastery of St. Antony was restored and in Coptic hands. During the patriarchate of Anbâ Murqus III (1166-1189), a certain Murqus ibn Qunbar went over to the doctrine of the Melkites, but afterwards returned to that of the Jacobites. After that he again went over to the Melkites and then returned to the Jacobites, but this time he was not received.[18] Threatened with excommunication by the patriarch, this "filius Elkonbari" submitted to the Coptic church and subsequently was sent to the Monastery of St. Antony. There he was compelled to have the hair of his head shaved, and to prove his good faith by swearing on the body of the saint.[19]

A letter of the twelfth century from Abûnâ Mîkhâîl to the hegoumenos Theodore contains a petition for the hegoumenos to accompany him to the Monastery of St. Antony. "Now it is many days since I came to the service and sought means to go to Apa Antonius; and the... have not been able to bring me (thither)... But I humbly beg, for God's sake, that thou come and that we go to Apa Antonius and lay our faces one to another, perhaps we shall be held worthy to lay our bones there. I think that they will be preparing the caravan on the sixth Sunday and we (will) go thither, if it be God's will, on the seventh. We will take the litter (?) and mount thereon, both together."[20]

During the patriarchate of Anbâ Yûânnis VI (1189-1216), the monastery was inhabited by Coptic monks and supplied the Ethiopian Abunate. The story leading to the consecration of Abûnâ Ishaq is reported by Renaudotius.[21] The patriarch consecrated a certain Kilus, bishop of Fuwah, for the Ethiopian church. After having served for four years, Kilus was charged with the murder of the treasurer of the Metropolitan church. On bare suspicion of having purloined a golden staff of great value, Kilus had caused the priest to be seized, and scourged to death. Kilus had to leave the country and Ishaq of St. Antony's monastery succeeded him.

Abû Sâlih, writing in the beginning of the thirteenth century, says: "This monastery possesses many endowments and possessions at Misr. It is surrounded by a fortified wall. It contains many monks. Within the wall there is a large garden, containing fruitful palm trees, and apple trees, and pear trees, and pomegranates, and other trees besides beds of vegetables, and three springs of perpetually flowing water, with which the garden is irrigated and which the monks drink. One feddan and a sixth in the garden form a vineyard, which supplies all that is needed, and it is said that the number of the palms which the garden contains amounts to a thousand trees, and there stands in it a large well-built qasr... The monastery possesses property also in Itfîh. There is nothing like it among the other monasteries inhabited by Egyptian monks. It is the possession of Jacobite monks."[22]

It is quite uncertain if the monastery at Mount Clysma sustained any damage as to its inmates or influence during the period of the Black Death in the middle of the fourteenth century which ravaged the monasteries in the Wâdî 'n-Natrûn and caused them to be deserted. The monastery was included among the renovation projects executed by the Coptic church during the twelfth and thirteenth centuries. The wall-paintings in the Church of St. Antony belong to the thirteenth century, being the work of the sons of Ghâlib (1232-1233).[23] The next reference comes to us from a Syriac manuscript which tells how a certain hegoumenos, Constantine of the Monastery of the Syrians, being dissatisfied with his post because of the insults and dangers from the monks, fled to the Monastery of St. Antony.

As he departed, he took with him the book of Mâr Ishaq and a silver cross. He had intended to return these belongings to Scetis, but he died at Mount Clysma and the objects remain there to this day.[24] This took place during the patriarchate of Anbâ Kîrillus III (1235-1243).

During the reign of Anbâ Yûânnis VII (1271-1293), a venerable old monk of St. Antony's monastery, saw in a vision a glorious angel who said: "Within three days, Anbâ Ghabrîâl will be taken from us and he will be led to Alexandria to ascend the patriarchal throne." When the old monk came out of his cell, he met Anbâ Ghabrîâl and related to him his vision. Then one day the magistrate of the town of Entafih came to the Monastery of St. Antony with a letter from the king instructing Anbâ Ghabrîâl to report at once so that he could be consecrated to the patriarchate in Alexandria. They seized him against his will and took him to the city of Alexandria with great ceremonies. The bishops accompanied him and all the people rejoiced on behalf of the future patriarch. That day, Anbâ Ghabrîâl ordained a metropolitan of Jerusalem, bishops and priests and deacons. At this time, St. Antony appeared to him and said: "Your death is approaching and within a year and a half you will be judged by God, and you will receive eternal life."[25]

European Pilgrims Rediscover the Monastery

Probably the first of the European travellers to mention the desert of the Thebaid as the abode of monks and hermits was the Venetian pilgrim Marino Sanuto who passed through Egypt in 1320.[26] He mentions the "triangular pyramids which are said to have been Joseph's granaries". Two leagues from them he locates the ruins of the city of Thebes. "Adjoining this is the wilderness of the Thebaid, where in the days of old there was a multitude of monks." In the first part of the fourteenth century, Ludolph, parish priest of Suchem, in the diocese of Paderborn, visited Egypt on his pilgrimage to the Holy Land. He mentions the monasteries: "Likewise in the Egyptian deserts there stand at this day so many cells and hermitages of holy fathers, that in some places, I believe, for two or three German miles there is one at every bow-shot. At the present day very many of them are inhabited by Indians, Nubians and Syrians living under the rule of St. Antony and St. Macarius... In this desert there is a place beneath an exceeding tall and narrow rock, wherein St. Antony used to dwell, and from out of the rock there flows a stream for half a stone's throw, until it is lost in the sand, even as running water flows into the snow and is seen no more. This place is visited by many for devotions and pleasure, and also by the grace of God and in honour of St. Antony many sicknesses are healed and driven away by the fountain."[27] In his description of his travels to the Orient in 1346, Fr. Niccolo di Poggibonsi refers to the cave and the

Monastery of St. Antony. According to his account, however, the Monastery of St. Antony was situated two miles beyond the Pyramids.[28]

On 5th Ter, the Ethiopians commemorate Anbâ Mattâ I (1376-1408), the eighty-seventh patriarch of Alexandria. Before his consecration to this office, he lived at the Monastery of St. Antony: "And at the monastery was a certain righteous monk whose name was Jacob, and he saw a vision in which it seemed that a shining angel came unto Abba Mattâ and embraced him, and gave keys into his hands. And when Abba Jacob awoke, he told this to Abba Mattâ who straightaway, because he hated empty praise, wandered round the country from city to city. One day, whilst Abba Mattâ was officiating in the office of the Eucharist, he saw our Lord Christ sitting upon the altar, and he lay in the paten like a little child. And at the time when he broke the offering, he stood up for a long time with his hands stretched out and covered with blood, and he continued to weep abundantly, and he was afraid, and he told this vision to no man. Then Abba Mattâ fetched some iron nails, and drove them into his knee every Friday until a worm came out therefrom."[29]

In 1395, Ogier VIII, Seigneur d'Anglure, came to the Holy Land and Egypt during the period of the Crusade of Nicopolis. With a number of French pilgrims he visited the Monastery of St. Catherine and then went to the monasteries of St. Antony and St. Paul. "The Monastery of St. Antony," Ogier noted, "was even more beautiful than that of St. Catherine. Its inhabitants numbered one hundred monks – most holy, goodliving, charitable, benign and self-denying Christian Jacobites."[30]

Twenty-six years later, in May 1421, Ghillebert de Lannoy, who was both a traveller and a diplomat, sailed with seven pilgrims to Egypt in order to visit the Monastery of St. Catherine. Instead of continuing his travels to the Holy Land, Ghillebert returned to Cairo and sailed up the Nile for two days to the Church of St. George. From here he crossed the Arabian desert to the Monastery of St. Antony. St. Antony's was inhabited by fifty Jacobite monks, who were circumcised Christians. Ghillebert describes the beautiful palm-garden, the many fruit trees and the castle-like building built round a spring which came out of the rock.[31]

In 1433, Philipp, the last Count of Katzenellenbogen crossed the desert of al-'Arabah. He too noticed the rich vegetation and the springs in the Monastery of St. Antony and proceeded to the Monastery of St. Paul.[32]

In 1436, a German pilgrim of Schleswig by the name of Dettlof Schinkel visited the Monastery of St. Antony, where he inscribed his name, his coat-of-arms and the date of his arrival. It was the custom for pilgrims to add their coats-of-arms to their names as can be seen in the refectory of the Monastery of St. Catherine.[33]

By the beginning of the fifteenth century, the desert of St. Antony had become an attraction for pilgrims. The Spanish pilgrim Pero Tafur (1435-39) notes: "The pilgrims had to return that night to sleep at Jericho and to go the next day to Quarantana, where our Lord fasted. But I arranged with a Moor to take me to the desert of Arabia, three leagues further on, where St. John preached, and where the first hermit, St. Antony, as well as other holy fathers, retired to live, and from there I returned to the Dead Sea."³⁴ Of course, Pero Tafur never visited the Monastery of St. Antony, but identified the wilderness of the Jordan Valley and its hermits with St. Antony.

Maqrîzî, writing between 1419 and 1441, listed the Monastery of al-'Arabah as the ninth in his catalogue of the eighty-six monasteries in Egypt. To reach this monastery, he says: "One travels for three days by camel, for it is located between the Eastern mountains and the sea of al-Qalzam. All kinds of fruits are planted in the monastery, and, furthermore, it has three springs of running water. It was built by St. Antony and the monks of this monastery fast throughout their whole life. Their fasting lasts until the evening when they do take food, except for the great fast and the Bermûlât, when their fasting lasts until the rise of the stars."³⁵ Usually Holy Week falls in the month of Barmûdah.

Neither Felix Fabri (1484), nor his travelling companion, Bernhard von Breydenbach, visited the Wâdî 'Arabah. Bernhard comments only that: "Also by going up the Nile, one soon comes to the deserts of Aran and Saran and Scetis, of which mention is made often in the Lives of the Fathers, and here are seen to-day the deserted monasteries of the holy fathers Antonius, Macarius, Paul the first hermit and many others... In these places in former years, many Greek monks used to reside, who are known by the general term *calogeri,* but all this is lacking in these days, when former charity is growing cold."³⁶

At the Council of Florence in 1439, the Coptic church was represented by a delegate, John, hegoumenos of the "celebrated Monastery of St. Antony". He travelled to Florence, but arrived late and the Greek delegates had already departed. However, a decree was issued for the reunion of the Copts with the other churches. The desert father from Mount Clysma signed the Act of Union (uniting Latins, Greeks and Jacobites) which for a few days, at least, united the whole of Christendom.³⁷

In the middle of the fifteenth century, the monastery supplied the ninety-first patriarch, Anbâ Ghabrîâl (1466-1474).

On one of my own visits to the Church of St. Antony, Abûnâ Mitîâs al-Antûnî gave a detailed account of the destruction of the library at the end of the fifteenth century. At that time, the monks employed Bedouins as gardeners, servants, etc. One night the Bedouins killed all the monks, and took possession. Smoke stains remain as a solemn reminder for it was in the Church of St. Antony that the Bedouins established their kitchen, lighting their fires with the ancient scrolls and documents of the Antonian library.[38]

We do not know exactly when the monastery was devastated, but Jean Thénaud, visiting the Monastery of St. Catherine in 1512, remarks that the Monastery of St. Antony was occupied by Syrian monks, and that the monastery had been destroyed and its monks killed some seven years before.[39]

Between 1517 and 1520, Leo Africanus, known as al-Hassan ibn Muhammad al-Wezaz al-Fasî, visited Egypt. In his *History and Description of Africa*, he mentions that "among the monasteries of Egypt those of Saint Antony, Saint Paul and Saint Macarius are the principal. The first lieth in Troglodytica right over against Sait upon a hill, where St. Antony was said to be beaten by diuels, the second (St. Paul's monastery) is seated not far from this, in the middest of a desert."[40]

In the history of the Monastery of the Syrians we read that Anbâ Ghabrîâl VII (1525-1568) assisted in the rebuilding of the monastery. At that time, sixty-three monks inhabited Dair as-Suriân, and of these twenty were sent to Dair Anbâ Antûnîûs, while another group of ten monks helped in the reconstruction of Dair Anbâ Bûlâ.[41] Belon du Mans may well have been the first traveller to refer to the monastery after its restoration by Anbâ Ghabrîâl VII. However, his testimony, written in 1539, is most unreliable. He says of St. Catherine's, with shameless exaggeration: "Nous voyons aisément les montagnes où est situé le monastère de Saint Antoine, ou de Saint Macaire." An anonymous Spanish Franciscan who visited Egypt in 1555 merely mentions the desert of the Thebaid, which was once inhabited by SS. Antony and Paul and many other hermits.[42]

After the restoration of the monastery, an Ethiopian community lived with the Egyptians in the Monastery of St. Antony. Francesco Alvarez (1520) talks about Ethiopian pilgrims to Jerusalem, who came from Deboroa to Suachin, a journey which they accomplished in fifteen stages. From Suachin they went to the monastery where St. Antony the Hermit lived.[43] Forty years later an Ethiopian monk, who called himself the small son of the sons of Takla Haymanot, wrote a book on penance. The colophon states that this volume was written in 1561 in the Monastery of St. Antony.

Seventeenth- and Eighteenth-Century Travellers

It is beyond the scope of this account to record in detail the impressions and experiences of the men who ventured to the Red Sea desert by camel caravan with guides and guards, food supplies and guns. Still, it is interesting to compare their notes and thus to evaluate the size and importance of the monastery.

In 1520, a Portuguese mission travelling through Egypt and Ethiopia passed by the Monastery of St. Antony. Dom Franciscus merely mentions the monastery which they reached after eight days of travel from the valley of the Nile.[44]

In 1626, Frater Bernardus carved his name in large block letters into the wooden haikal-screen of the Church of St. Antony. "Frater Bernardus a Ferula Siculus de observantia primus visitator Catholicus, sub die 31 decembris 1625, 11 januarii 1626, 31 januarii 1626."[45] The Franciscan friar Bernardus also visited the Monastery of St. Paul. The date is clearly 1626 and not 1726 as Jullien has maintained [46]

The next traveller to leave information about the monastery was Fr. J. Coppin in 1638. His view of the "Cophites" is anything but sympathetic, regarding them as the most absurd and erroneous sect that had separated itself from the Latin church by following the heresies of Dioscorus and Eutyches, holding at the same time to many Judaistic ceremonies. Coppin witnessed a Coptic service in which the priests apparently recited in Syriac. Modern authorities believe that the Coptic language was used. In his description of the church, Coppin mentions a Greek influence, especially evident in the icons.

After the celebration of the Divine Mysteries, he joined the monks in their meal of lentil soup. Previously three hundred monks had inhabited the monastery, though their cells had now been destroyed. Coppin only saw sixty-two cells.[47] One of these had been given to his colleague, Fr. Agathangelus, O.F.M. Coppin gives its height as four feet, its width five feet and its length seven feet. Coppin and his party then climbed the mountain to the cave where St. Antony had spent so many days of his life.

The purpose of his mission was an attempt by the Latin church to unite the Coptic church with the See of Rome. Fr. Agathangelus stayed at the monastery for a period of four months, conducting doctrinal discussions and giving spiritual conferences. "Two out of fifteen monks were reconciled to the Church... The prospect of the reconciliation of the Coptic church, was, however, wrecked by the evil conduct of the Latin residents in Egypt, and of the Consul of France in particular." In 1637, Fr. Agathangelus left in despair for Ethiopia, where in the following year he was martyred.[48]

It is difficult to ascertain exactly when the Franciscan missionaries concentrated their efforts on the Monastery of St. Antony. The visits of the Frs. Bernardus, Cassien and Agathangelus may be regarded merely as preparatory to the work that was to be undertaken in the fourth decade of the seventeenth century. Until recently a Franciscan Terra Santa Cross could be seen above the entrance to the Church of St. Mark.

The Franciscans used the Monastery of St. Antony as a language school to prepare missionaries to the Orient. A letter written by Fr. Andrea d'Arco to the *Propaganda* on 23 February, 1639, suggests that the *Propaganda* pay the monastery forty scudi annually, so that two or three Franciscans could reside there and study Arabic. One of the students was Fr. Gerard of Milan, whose description of the monastery is quoted in *MS. Della Minoritica Riforma:* "One is pulled up by a windlass in order to enter the monastery, because the doors are very high on account of their fear of wandering robbers. The monastery is large, but rather old and dilapidated. It is beautifully situated, and it is surrounded by a mountain. There is an abundance of water, many palms as well as olive trees and other fruits." Fr. Gerard "was hospitably and warmly received by the monks, who were very poorly dressed, and whose clothes were patched up according to the ancient manner, – they appeared like beggars... They ate vegetables and rice, and they drank water, and they ate only once a day; on fasting days they ate after sunset. From the monastery one can see the shores of the Red Sea, as well as the place where St. Paul, the first hermit, used to live."[49] Fr. Santa dalle Pieve di Sacco of Padua wrote to the secretary of the *Propaganda*, on 1 March, 1639, informing him that Fr. Gerard had gone to the Monastery of St. Antony to learn Arabic. A letter written by Fr. Antonius de Virgoletta to the *Propaganda* (18 April, 1639), requests the authorities to send new missionaries either to the Monastery of St. Macarius or to the Monastery of St. Antony, so that they could learn the Arabic language within seven or eight months.[50]

The result of this strategy is evident from reports sent from Egypt to the ecclesiastical and secular authorities in Europe. Fr. Sylvester of St. Aignam reported in 1651 that the Patriarch had permitted him to preach in Coptic churches,[51] and Fr. Johannes Baptista of St. Aignam sent a detailed account of the mission of the Capuchins to the French minister Colbert. He records that since 1630, the fathers had often preached in Coptic churches and that they had absolved many Copts, including priests and monks.[52]

In the account of their travels, Monceaux and Laisné observe that many Europeans had visited the Monastery of St. Antony, from which they had removed many valuable manuscripts. "One must not expect to get any at all from the Monastery of St. Antony and the Monastery of St. Macarius, for they have all been carried off by the Venetians, the English and the Flemish, who were interested in them before us."[53]

On 3 October, 1672, Johann Michael Wansleben arrived at the Monastery of St. Antony, after passing by the village of Bûsh. "The monastery enclosed another one which years ago was inhabited by the Ethiopians, which now, however, is completely ruined. The monastery, built in a large square, is surrounded by a weak and ruined wall which is incapable of offering any protection. The wall has no door, and everyone who wants to enter the monastery is pulled up by a pulley. The circle of the walls is very large and encloses 600 feddans or 2,400 *arpens de terre.* The cells are extremely small and poorly made of yellow sand and without wood, without symmetry, order and any paint. They are so small and so low that one can easily touch the ceiling, and because of this smallness, the monks cannot even stand up in their rooms. Their refectory is a very dirty and dark place. Only for visitors, the monks have an apartment which is fairly large and which has two adjoining rooms.

"There is a great abundance of water, clear like crystal and cool, but very salty. This water has its source in the Mount Qalzam behind the monastery.[54] The monastery has three churches. The main church is of St. Antony which is the oldest one. It is the only thing in the whole monastery that was spared from the rage of the Arabs. The church is decorated with paintings which are very antiquated and extremely simple. The smoke of incense which is burnt there every day has rendered the pictures almost as black as a chimney. Near this church is that of SS. Peter and Paul which has a small steeple and a small handbell. The third church is in the garden and is dedicated to a lay-member called Mark.

"The rule obliges them to give up marriage, all carnal desires and the relationships to their parents. They are not to possess anything; they are to live in the desert, to abstain from meat and wine. They are obliged to sleep on the ground, except the superiors and the sick. They are bound to recite the Canonical Hours, and before retiring at night they prostrate themselves 150 times. They have never more than one meal a day, except on Saturdays and Sundays, when they have two meals. While they are not permitted to eat meat in the monastery, they are allowed to eat it outside the monastery walls. As for fish they rarely eat it because of the great distance between the Nile and the monastery. They do not obtain any fish from the Red Sea because they do not have the instruments for fishing and, in addition, all roads to the Red Sea are dangerous because they are inhabited by Arab thieves. The monks do not engage in studies, and they seem to be satisfied with the reading of devotional books, the *Synaxarium, The Paradise of the Fathers* and others.

"In the tower or keep there is the library with three or four cases full of ancient Arabic and Coptic manuscripts. Most of these manuscripts were worthy to be placed in a royal library."[55] Wansleben mentions three books in particular—a Coptic grammar, a Coptic-Arabic dictionary, and a work by Ibn al-'Assal. After spending two weeks at the monastery, he departed on 17 October in the direction of Banî Suîf and Bûsh.

In 1692, twenty years after Wansleben's visit, de Maillet called on the Monastery of St. Antony.[56] Like Wansleben, de Maillet observed in the neighbourhood of St. Antony's monastery the ruins of another monastery as well as numerous caves. He too referred to the Dependency at Bûsh. His description of the monastery is very similar to Wansleben's. The following year, de Maillet, in a letter dated 17 September, 1693, pointed out to the antiquarian J.P. Rigord, *Commissaire de la marine* at Marseille, the usefulness of drawing up a general map of Egypt and the advantage of making a visit to the libraries of St. Antony and St. Macarius.[57] (The first maps with correct placings of the monasteries appeared in the first half of the eighteenth century.)

The next traveller to visit the Monastery of St. Antony was Fr. Antoine-Marie Nacchi, S.J., who became general superior of the missions in the Levant in 1746. He wrote to the general of the Jesuits in Rome from Cairo on 20 May, 1698. "Having been in Egypt in the ancient Monastery of St. Antony I saw also a room full of ancient manuscripts, but I am not able to use them because they are written in the Egyptian and Coptic letters, which language is lost, which I think could show and recover the fine memory, but what is lacking is the Oedipus of the Sphinx".[58]

In 1714, Paul Lucas, instructed to do so by Louis XIV, travelled through the lands of the Levant.[59] He visited the Fayyûm, the Thebaid and the Monastery of St. Antony.

In 1716, an anonymous person made a sketch of the Antonian monastery which he dedicated to Nicholas, bishop of Exeter. This sketch, which Pococke discovered in a manuscript map, was included in his *Description of the East.*[60]

On 23 May, 1716, Frs. Claude Sicard and J.S. Assemani departed from Old Cairo on their visit to the Red Sea monasteries.[61] Travelling south along the Nile, they turned into the desert at Banî Suîf and arrived at the monastery on 28 May. On their arrival, they were greeted by the hegoumenos who conducted them to the church for prayers. After that, they were welcomed by the fifteen monks and offered wine and coffee. Fr. Sicard noticed two churches, twenty or thirty feet long, one being dedicated to SS. Peter and Paul, and the other to St. Antony. He also saw the smaller church dedicated to St. Mark.

There were thirty cells, which were separated from each other, and arranged in little streets. The cells and the streets offered Sicard the impression of a little town located in the desert. Like the other visitors he comments on the luxuriant garden and the brackish water. His companion, Assemani, secured some of the monastery's books for the Vatican library.

Fr. Sicard engaged in numerous theological debates with the hegoumenos of the monastery who was the "superieur general" not only of

the Monastery of St. Antony, but also of that of St. Paúl. After visiting the
Monastery of St. Paul, Fr. Sicard climbed up to the cave of St. Antony
where he celebrated Mass. On the trip down, Fr. Sicard engaged again in
theological debates in an attempt to fulfil his mission.

The efforts of Fr. Sicard and other missionaries of the various Latin
orders to convert the monks of the Monastery of St. Antony led Anbâ
Yûsâb, bishop of Girga and Akhmîm, to write some thirty-one articles in
defence of the Coptic faith. Yûsâb, who lived for many years as a monk at
the Monastery of St. Antony, was consecrated in 1791.[62]

On 9 April, 1730, Tourtechot de Granger arrived at the monastery. He
saw twenty-eight cells, the refectory and two small and obscure churches.
Granger also mentions the Church of St. Mark the Hermit which had two
altars. There were twenty-five monks, of whom twelve were priests.[63] Their
provisions came from the village of Bûsh.

Richard Pococke did not visit the Monastery of St. Antony personally,
but he relates a description given him by one of the monks who was staying
in a monastery in the Fayyûm. "The patriarch is head of the convent of St.
Antony, I know not whether it is always so, or that the patriarch being
chosen from there, might have presided over this convent, and continue to
do so; he has a deputy there. There are three other persons who have a
share in the government of the convent, four more that are priests, and
twenty-three that are lay monks. The deputy they call Rubeti, the three next
Gumous, the priests Keshiesh, and the others Ruban... They have three
springs of water running into the convent, that are a little salt. And it is
probable that in these convents are the only bells in Egypt."[64]

In the latter part of the eighteenth century the monastery underwent
several changes. In 1766 the Church of St. Mark was rebuilt and in 1733
Lutfallah Shâkir restored the Church of the Apostles, otherwise known as
the Church of SS. Peter and Paul. In 1783, Ibrâhîm Gawharî renovated the
walls of the monastery. The building activity within the monastery walls no
doubt attracted visitors to come and see the many renovations. An
Armenian graffito on the north wall of the Church of the Holy Virgin
informs us that in 1765, the Doctor of Theology, Sarqis of Hadjen (Sarquis
vartabed hagentsi), was in the monastery.

Coming from the Fayyûm and travelling via Bûsh and Itfîh, Nicholas
Savary arrived at Mount Qalzam in 1777, where he entered the monastery
by a pulley. His observations are similar to his predecessors'. He speaks of a
canal through which the water runs from the mountain to the monastery.
"The water is a little salty but satisfies the needs of life. The monks exhibit a
great admiration for the cave of St. Antony which is obscurely hidden in
the mountain."[65]

To this day, the monks refer to the hardships experienced in 1805 when persecution fell upon the monks of the monastery and when the caravans ceased to come from Bûsh. A few years of Muhammad 'Alî's rule, however, apparently restored order to the desert.

Nineteenth- and Twentieth-Century Travellers

Writing in 1817, Count de Forbin makes only a passing reference to the monasteries of St. Antony and St. Paul. "A few Coptic monks inhabit these two convents. Lofty walls afford protection from the incursions of the Bedouins, as well as from the tigers which swarm in those dreary solitudes. An aqueduct, much impaired, conveys some brackish water to irrigate their garden, some trees and leguminous plants."[66]

In 1834, a Russian traveller, Avraam Norov, visited Egypt and went to the Monastery of St. Antony on the western bank of the Nile at Bûsh, which served as an intermediate station between the Nile valley and the monastery near the shore of the Red Sea. Norov describes the Red Sea monastery as being situated on a high rock, surrounded by a high wall with one window only, through which the traveller is lifted up with a rope fastened to a board or to a basket. However, Norov did not visit the monastery himself.[67]

On 13 March, 1839, Dr. Tattam and his step-daughter, Miss Platt, were hospitably received by the monks of the Monastery of St. Antony. Dr. Tattam was permitted to examine the library, where he found a selim, similar to one he had procured in Cairo; two copies of the Pentateuch; two of the Minor Prophets; one of Job; one of Isaiah; and a copy of the Revelation and the New Testament. None of these books was he able to obtain. He brought with him a letter of introduction from the patriarch, which the monks respectfully kissed, both before and after reading it, and one of them stuck it in his turban. After visiting the library, Dr. Tattam went through "the two pretty gardens, which are well irrigated by means of furrows; and there are two large cisterns within the walls to receive the water that descends from the mountain immediately above."[68]

Sir Gardner Wilkinson went to the Monastery of St. Antony in 1843. "It is about seventy-six or seventy-seven miles from the Nile and the road presents nothing worthy of remark until you reach that building. It is inhabited by Copts and their principal saint is St. George of Cappadocia, but their patron saint is St. Antony of the Thebaid... Dayr Antonius is seventeen or eighteen miles from the sea and it may be considered the principal monastery in Egypt, and its importance is much increased since the election of the patriarch has been transferred to it from those at the Natron lakes..." Sir Gardner tried in vain to learn something about the dictionary for Coptic and Arabic, which Wansleben had seen and identified as having been written by Ibn al-'Assâl, which he had valued at thirty crowns.[69]

Then in 1850, the Russian archimandrite, Porphyrius Uspensky, who had travelled to the East looking for valuable manuscripts, came to Egypt, where he conceived the idea of a union between the Russian Orthodox church and that of the Copts. He believed that he had discovered that the Coptic creed was not heresy and that a union of the two churches was quite possible from a theological point of view.[70] Accompanied by the abbot of the monastery, Qummus Dâûd, (the future patriarch, Cyril IV), Porphyrius visited the Monastery of Mount Clysma. In his book he relates that the buildings are grouped together in the north-west corner. In addition to the narrow, gloomy and untidy cells of the monks scattered without order, the main buildings are the cathedral church with the adjoining Church of St. Antony, the vestry and the library in the crenellated tower, the dining hall, a store-house three stories high, a little house for the patriarch, an isolated church dedicated to St. Mark in the north-east corner of the garden and a well.

In the Church of St. Antony under the three steps that lead into the passage before the altar, there is the grave of St. Antony. "But the monks are not sure themselves, whether this grave contains the relics of the saint or not... Adjoining the south-western part of this church is a little chapel, quite dark, in the name of the four beasts.[71] In the lower, northern part of the garden, stands the Church of St. Mark, who according to the reckoning of the Copts, lived five hundred years ago... A coffin of the Abyssinian Bishop Mark is shown there. He alone came back from Ethiopia, all the rest had died and were buried there."[72] A graffito on the west wall of the Church of St. Antony testifies to Porphyrius' visit.

In July 1851, Cardinal Gugliemo Massaia, O.F.M., travelled by camel in the company of a young monk and three others to the Wâdî 'Arabah. The purpose of the visit was to "liberate" a certain young man named Michelangelo, who apparently lived as a prisoner in the monastery. Michelangelo, a young Copt, had studied in Rome and had become a pupil of the Congregation of Propaganda. On his return to Cairo he was supposedly taken prisoner by some Coptic monks and sent to the Monastery of St. Antony. Cardinal Massaia, passing through Egypt on his way to Ethiopia, heard about this young man and decided to investigate. The hegoumenos of the monastery, Qummus Dâûd, was in Ethiopia at the time, preaching against the activities of the cardinal, who had previously conducted a mission in that country.

On arriving at the monastery, the cardinal assumed the false name of George Bartorelli, and was introduced to Michelangelo, who was much distressed. The young Italian-speaking Copt-Catholic confessed to the cardinal that he had not received the Holy Sacrament for two years.

The cardinal then visited the churches and the various buildings including the library in the qasr. Here he saw four or five baskets containing valuable books in Coptic and Arabic, though he was told that a great deal of the library treasures had been bought by a Frenchman. Then he went to the refectory, which was still being used by the monks. Near the Church of St. Antony he noticed a small room where the monks and servants bathed before saying Mass. This was referred to as the Place of Purification. He was also shown the cell of Anbâ Andarâûs, at that time bishop in Ethiopia, whose name was written in English and Italian on the door of his room. The cardinal spent the night in what he called the Sepulchre of St. Antony, a crypt which was the cleanest place, and also the best place to converse with Michelangelo.

The cardinal was told by the monks that the water in the spring of St. Antony had been blessed by the saint, and thus had the power to purify the souls and minds of those who drink from it. But experience had taught them that drinking the water without a certain medicine added to it could be disastrous. This medicine had to remain in the water for a period of three days, otherwise the person drinking from the spring would be changed into a woman. The cardinal promised to obtain some medicine from Cairo, provided they would permit Michelangelo to accompany him, and then to return to the monastery with the promised medicine. Then Cardinal Massaia and Michelangelo left the monastery, and went to Banî Suîf, where Michelangelo contacted the French consulate.[73]

That the monastery has played an important part in the general history of the Coptic church can be seen from the large number of patriarchs who have come from Mount Clysma. The leadership of the Antonian monastery is especially noticeable during the seventeenth, eighteenth and nineteenth centuries. Twelve Antonian monks ascended the patriarchal throne, and for almost three hundred years they determined the history of the church. Anbâ Murqus VIII (1796-1809) was patriarch when Napoleon invaded Egypt. The next patriarch, Anbâ Butrus VII (1809-1852), also came from the mountain of Clysma. More important however, was Qummus Dâud, who after only two years of service in the monastery was elected hegoumenos. He is known as "the Reformer of the Church" or Anbâ Kîrillus IV (1852-1861). His principal improvements were to education. As hegoumenos he founded a school at the dependency at Bûsh. His life as patriarch is one of the fullest and most fascinating biographies that the Coptic church has provided and it is very likely that this dynamic personality did not die a natural death.

In May 1859, the monastery was visited by Callinicus, the eightieth Greek Orthodox patriarch of Alexandria, who had ascended the patriarchial throne just a year prior to his visit. A graffito on the north wall of the Church of St. Antony informs us that the patriarch travelled in company of Gabriel of Hiero—.

In 1873, Greville J. Chester went to the Antonian monastery. At the time of his visit, travellers were still being pulled up by rope and basket, though not many travellers could have visited the monastery in those days, for Chester states explicitly that it had not been called upon by more than one or two Europeans in his generation. He saw three churches besides the new Church of al-'Adhrâ. About the Church of St. Mark he says that it is dedicated to a brother of that name, who lived in the monastery in ancient times, and whose body is preserved in the church. In the qasr, he was shown the library, which consisted of some books which deserve examination, an ancient Ethiopian shield of hippopotamus hide, a cross, a very ancient bronze lamp and a silver–mounted umbrella which was held over the silver gospel case on the occasion of the annual procession to the cave of St. Antony.[74] In the second half of the nineteenth century the monks kept a register of visiting tourists. Fr. Jullien records that in June 1871, the monastery was visited by Colonel Pindy and his officers, and that an Englishman called on the monks in January 1875.[75]

When Dr. Georg Schweinfurth visited the monastery in 1876 and again in 1877, he records that only very seldom had European travellers called on the monks, and he bemoans the fact that those who did visit the monastery scratched their names on the walls, without any consideration of the valuable wall-paintings of the Church of St. Antony and that neither Greek patriarchs nor Russian archimandrites were any exception to the rule. Dr. Schweinfurth adds that the monastery spreads over six hectares and is enclosed by a wall which is 1120 metres long. The altitude of the monastery is 410 metres above the level of the Red Sea. He was not shown the library, and, therefore, concludes that the monastery did not possess one. He describes the well with its salty water to which a stranger has difficulties in getting accustomed. He maintains that every traveller ought to visit the cave of the saint, though he adds that there is little to attract one's attention.[76]

In November 1883, Fr. Michel Jullien, S.J., rector of the College of the Holy Family in Cairo, accompanied by Mgr. François Sogaro, Apostolic Vicar of the Coptic Catholic Church, and Fr. Luigi Korrat and Mr. Sante Bonavia visited both monasteries of the Thebaid. Travelling via Bûsh, where the party visited the dependency, Fr. Jullien followed the caravan route to the monastery, and arrived there after several days of desert travel. After having been welcomed by the monks in front of the monastery, they entered it by pulley and were introduced to the hegoumenos, an old monk of seventy years. Then, Fr. Jullien describes how he went up to the ten to twelve-metre high walls, while discussing theology with the monks, for this had been one of the main purposes of his journey. Following his visit to the churches Fr. Jullien retraced the steps of Fr. Sicard by ascending the mountain of Clysma in order to visit the cave of St. Antony.

In November 1901, the monastery was visited by an extraordinary party of diplomats. With a letter of recommendation from the patriarch, Anbâ Kîrillus V, Georges Cogordan, French ambassador to Egypt, Auguste Boppe, Lovier Taigny and Leon Ouerry went via Banî Suîf to the desert monastery, where they arrived on 25 November. Cogordan recalled the popularity and the fame of St. Antony in France during the Middle Ages, and presented the monastery with a large case containing an exact reproduction of the painting of St. Antony by Velazquez which Boppe and Taigny had brought from France. This picture was placed in the Church of St. Antony, where it still hangs.

By this time the monastery had regained momentum and was inhabited by forty-one monks of whom thirty were hieromonks.[77] The monks celebrated their offices three times a day, at four o'clock in the morning, before midday and before sunset only. Cogordon inquired about the library, but was told of its destruction by the Bedouins. At the end of his visit, Cogordan visited the cave of St. Antony.

In February 1904 Agnes Smith Lewis and her sister, Mrs. Margaret Dunlop Gibson, contracted with Sulaimân Mûsâ, a young Copt from the Fayyûm, to take them with every possible comfort to the two monasteries in the Thebaid. They obtained permission to visit the Monastery of St. Antony from the hegoumenos who resided in Bûsh. The ladies were not pulled up by a rope and windlass like other visitors, but entered through a small narrow door, which was usually opened only once a year, or when the patriarch visited the monastery.[78] As they stepped across the threshold, Agnes Smith Lewis writes: "We had the unique feeling that we were breaking the tradition of sixteen hundred years." The visitors were shown the churches and were allowed to examine some manuscripts. They found Coptic and Syriac Bibles, as well as recent publications of the patriarchal press and books from the American Presbyterian Mission. Two ancient copies caught their special attention, one was the *Didascalia Sanctorum Apostolorum* in Arabic, the other was a copy of the romance of Barlaam and Josaphat.

At four o'clock on the same day, they climbed Mount Clysma and visited the cave of St. Antony. "One wriggles with difficulty into a circular chamber nearly filled with an altar of rock and earth, on which the guide had placed a taper, to the right of this is a hole where the saint slept." The party returned just before sunset. They left the monastery at seven-thirty in the direction of the Red Sea, and camped in the Wâdî 'Arabah so as to be ready for the following day's journey to the Monastery of St. Paul.

On 13 March, 1928, Johann Georg, Duke of Saxony, and Professor Sauer started on their expedition to the Monastery of St. Antony. Travelling in a sixteen horse-power Renault, they drove south of Cairo along the Nile to Kuraimât and from there eastwards into the Wâdî 'Arabah. Because of several flat tires and other mishaps, the distinguished party arrived at the monastery late at night and on foot. The following morning the duke visited the Church of St. Antony where he attended the celebration of the Divine Liturgy. He decided the church had been built in the seventh century and believed the monks' story that St. Antony's tomb lay in the western part of the church. According to Johann Georg, the destruction of the monastery took place in 1517,[79] rather than in the end of the fifteenth century. It might be well to substantiate the traditional date for the destruction of the monastery by a colophon of 1506 belonging to a gospel in the Vatican Library. "...The monastery of our holy father Antûnîûs, known as the Monastery of al-'Arabah in the desert of al-Kulzum inhabited by monks, was vacant without residents, ravaged by the Arabs, and this book was then taken from the hands of the Arabs, who then ravaged the place utterly."[80] After leaving the Church of St. Antony, the duke went to the Church of SS. Peter and Paul which he decided had been built in the seventeenth century. From there he went to a church which had been started by Anbâ Kîrillus in or around 1859, but which had not been completed. For this reason the church had not been named after a saint and the church was being used to dry olives. The fourth church, dedicated to St. Mark, is only vaguely mentioned by the duke. In the qasr he discovered several icons. Upon request, the hegoumenos Abûna Surîân al-Antûnî, presented him with the most valuable icon of the whole collection, a thirteenth-century painting of the Blessed Virgin Mary. The day before, he had received a T-staff of olivewood.

At the time of this visit the monastery was inhabited by eighteen monks, though the Duke was told that eighty monks stayed at the dependency in Bûsh. His final judgment, however, is interesting: even if Dair as-Surîân was artistically more advanced and richer in treasures, the Monastery of St. Antony was the wealthiest monastery he had seen in the Orient.

In September 1929, Marcus Simaika completed the cataloguing of the manuscripts and books at Dair Anbâ Antûnîûs and stipulated that they might be studied only in the library and that under no circumstances were they to be removed.

In 1930 and 1931, the Byzantine Insitute of America sent two winter expeditions to the monastery to study the archaeology and the history of the place. The expeditions were composed of Professor Thomas Whittemore, the architect Oliver Barker, the artist Netchetailor, the photographer Kazazian and Professor Piankoff. In addition to identifying and photographing the wall-paintings in the Church of St. Antony, Professor Whittemore photographed the famous fourteenth-century Difnâr in the monastery library.[81] The findings, based on an exhaustive examination *in situ*, were to be published. So far I have not been able to locate the results of this expedition.

One of the first visitors to reach the monastery by automobile via Suez–'Ain Sukhnah–Za'frânah was Fr. A. Chaine, S.J., who wrote a report of his trip in the magazine *Le Rayon*, which is published in Cairo. At the time of his visit, in 1936, the monastery was inhabited by thirty-five monks. The monastery seemed to him a little monastic village, in which the spirit of hospitality was overwhelming.[82]

In the same year, H. Romilly Fedden travelled to the monastery. His valuable observations are set down in his monograph, *A Study of the Monastery of St. Antony.*

H.V. Morton describes his visit to the Monastery of St. Antony in 1937 in his book *Through Lands of the Bible.* "When Father Antony and I approached the church door, I saw a row of slippers standing outside the church as if it were a mosque, and therefore I removed my shoes. I found that this was expected of me whenever I entered this church. We passed into the narthex which led into one of the strangest and most primitive churches I have ever seen, even in Coptic Egypt... The whole church had once been covered with frescoes. The dome bore blackened traces of paintings all over it and the south wall still carried a series of scratched and almost invisible saints, standing stiffly under a continuous arcade. But the most interesting features of the church were the ancient painted crosses visible in those places where the plaster had fallen away. These are obviously old and very beautiful. Each cross is about twelve inches high, Greek in shape, and is surrounded by a conventional wreath. Above the arms of the cross are the Greek letters ICXC, and beneath the arms, NIKA, the well-known Greek monogram meaning "Jesus Christ the Conqueror". Each cross is painted a deep shade of red, on a cream ground, and the wreath is green... I was anxious to pick away a small piece of plaster to see the lower letters more clearly, but no sooner had I touched it with my nail than a monk came up and said politely that the last time someone had attempted to do such a thing a thunderbolt had killed him." From the Church of St. Antony, Morton went to the library. "After wrestling for some time with a difficult lock, Father Antony opened the door of a room where hundreds of volumes stood entombed in wooden book-cases. What a depressingly uninviting sight a library can be when it belongs to people who rarely read a book and take no interest in them. The volumes were packed tightly together as if by the relentless hand of a charwoman, and books for which no place could be found on shelves were harshly tucked away on top and wedged in anywhere. They looked, indeed, as forbidding as a lawyer's library, and the air of the room was stuffy with paper and parchment which have been locked away for months on end."[83]

On 10 April, 1956, a party of five Catholic priests, namely Frs. Giacomo Rock, Stanislav Perovic, Tarcisio de Piano, Egidio Sampiere and Gabriele Giamberardini, went from Ma'adi in a southerly direction to Kuraimât, and from there to the Wâdî 'Arabah. In the monastery Abûnâ Sîdârûs al-Antûnî showed them the churches, the garden and the spring. Fr. Gabriele asked Abûnâ Sîdârûs about the three monastic virtues: poverty, obedience and chastity. "As to poverty, if anyone were to offer you a hundred pounds, would you take them?" "I would accept the whole basketful; and as to obedience, I am independent, if I have the fancy to become a Catholic, I'll become a Catholic; and as to chastity, if I want to get married, I leave the monastery, I am independent." When the group of priests inquired about the library, the librarian refused to show it, diplomatically pointing out that the library key was with the bishop in Bûsh. Fr. Gabriele had heard from the late Yassâ 'Abd al-Masîh in Cairo, that the monastery library consisted altogether of 2171 volumes, of which 1662 were manuscripts and 509 printed books.[84]

Then Abûnâ Sîdârûs took the visitor to Abûnâ Buqtùr, regarded the saintliest monk of the monastery, and to Abûnâ Kîrillus, a young priest, who has published several books. Abûnâ Barsûm took them to the cave of St. Antony where they took measurements of the tunnel and the inner cave.[85]

On 30 August, 1958, the Apostolic Internuncio H.E. Mgr. Silvio Oddi visited the monastery with a group of priests.

Until the beginning of the twentieth century, the only contact that the monastery had with the outside world was the monthly camel caravan that supplied the desert monks with food and necessities from the dependency at Bûsh in the Nile valley. The journey from Kuraimât to the monastery took between three and four days. From Kuraimât one travelled along the camel path passing the well of Araiyidah after ninety kilometres and the well of Bûiât after another twenty-two kilometres. To this day, this route is followed by the supply trucks which have supplanted the more romantic camel caravans.

The Monastery Today

Since the construction of the Suez–Râs Gharîb road in 1946 by Shell, the monastery has become much more accessible. A motorist can drive the 334 kilometres from Cairo to the monastery within five to six hours. A few gallons of petrol separate it from golf courses and *maisons de coiffure.* Each year the silence around the monastery is more broken. The Egyptian magazine *Images* impresses its urban readers with a description of: "Une excursion pour votre Week-End: Les Monastères de la Mer Rouge!" The Automobile Club d'Egypte has published an *Itinéraire de l'excursion du Caire au Monastère de Saint Antoine* prepared by Major-General Rifa'at al-Gawharî. The camel caravan has been replaced by jeeps and trucks, and the day will not be far distant, when helicopters and aeroplanes will disturb the peace and the quietness of the air which surrounds the place. On 6 January, 1955, Captain W.F. Judd of TWA introduced this possibility by landing with a Cessna 170 at St. Antony's.

Between 1953 and 1958, 370 foreigners visited the monastery, but very few Egyptians made the journey. This has changed now, however. On a holiday weekend in 1985, there were more than a thousand visitors at the monastery. A visit to St. Antony's has become a popular family excursion. Quarters for men and women have been constructed within the walls. A kiosk at the gate sells pictures, souvenirs, leather crosses and devotional literature.

The monastic life at Mount Clysma consists of community worship, that is the celebration of the Divine Liturgy; the Canonical Hours; private devotions in the cells which take the form of meditation and contemplation; and manual work in the garden, kitchen, bake-house, or library.

Between November and April, the Divine Liturgy is celebrated three times a week on Sunday, Wednesday and Friday mornings in the Church of St. Antony. The church and the old south wall are older than the rest of the monastery, which was built in the sixteenth century. The church existed in the fifteenth century as the Bedouins' smoke stains testify. Although Johann Georg places the edifice in the seventh or the eighth century, a later date is more realistic. The Gothic graffiti on the walls of the church must have been put there between the fifteenth and sixteenth centuries, while the paintings of the warrior-saints fall into the period of the restoration of the church by the sons of Ghâlib in 1232-1233. The walls show two layers of paint, indicating that the paintings were possibly restored by an Italian artist in the sixteenth century. These paintings were cleaned in 1930 by Professor Whittemore.

The paintings can be divided into five sections, as follows:

The haikal: Christ as Pantocrator; the angels; the Enthroned Christ; the Sacrifice of Abraham; Abraham and Melchisedek; Jeremiah; Elijah; Isaiah; Moses; David; Daniel; St. Mark; St. Athanasius; St. Severus of Antioch; St. Dioscorus; St. Peter of Alexandria; St. Theophilus.

The passage in front of the haikal: The myrrh-bearing women (namely: Mary Magdalene; Mary, mother of James; and Salome); Christ and two women saints; St. Mercurius; Jacob; Isaac; Abraham; three unidentified saints; Nebuchadnezzar; St. George; St. Michael and St. Gabriel.

The nave: The monks: St. Isaac; St. Paul the Simple; St. Samuel; St. Bishoî; four unidentified monks; a bishop; Anbâ Moses; two monks blessed by Christ; a monk with an angel; four unidentified monks and one unidentified female saint; two unidentified monks.

The narthex: St. Arsophonius; St. Thuan; two monks blessed by Christ; a warrior-saint; St. Claudius; St. Victor; St. Menas; St. Theodore; three warrior-saints and (?) St. George.

The small chapel located at the south-west corner of the church: two angels; Christ between the Virgin and St. John the Baptist, and the Cross adored by the angels. These wall-paintings are well preserved.

The wall-paintings of the seven warrior-saints in the narthex have attracted the attention of many visitors. The saints are portrayed with their respective martyria. The badly damaged picture showing a saint turned towards the left and riding a white horse is St. Claudius. The small church below the right foreleg of the horse is his martyrium. The saint with an almost round face and wearing a crown is St. Victor. The edifice below the left foreleg of the horse is the Bath–Martyrium of St. Victor. The warrior-saint (almost completely destroyed), who rides towards the left is St. Menas, and his martyrium is below the hind legs of his horse. The two warrior-saints on the north wall are SS. Sergius and Bacchus with their martyria. The warrior-saint on the north of the choir is St. George and the church below the horse is his martyrium. Only St. Theodore is shown without his martyrium.

The church has three haikals, which are dedicated to St. Mark (north), St. Antony (centre), St. Athanasius (south). Icons of Christ, the Holy Virgin, the Resurrection, St. George, St. Michael and St. Mercurius are attached to the choir-screen; icons of St. George, St. Michael, St. Paul the Theban and St. Antony, St. Gabriel, the Holy Virgin, and St. Mercurius decorate the nave-screen.

During the summer months from April to October, the Divine Liturgy is celebrated in the Church of the Holy Apostles just to the east of the Church of St. Antony. Built on the foundations of an older church, the present church was restored by Lutfallah Shâkir in 1733. The Church of the Apostles, or the "Summer Church" as the monks refer to it, has three haikals. The northern haikal is dedicated to the Holy Virgin, the central haikal to the Twelve Apostles and the south haikal to St. Antony. The icons attached to the northern haikal-screen represent the Falling-Asleep (Dormition) of the Holy Virgin; St. Michael; St. Gabriel; the SS. Peter and Paul. The icons and pictures fastened to the choir-screen are those of St. George; the Holy Virgin; St. Victor; the Nativity; Anbâ Kîrillus IV; St. Athanasius; St. Paul the Theban and St. Antony; St. Thecla; the Baptism of Christ; St. George; St. Mercurius; the Holy Sepulchre at Jerusalem, and St. Stephen. The icons and paintings on the nave-screen represent Abraham sacrificing Isaac; the Crucifixion; St. Barsûm; St. George, and Anbâ Shenûdah. Furthermore, there is one painting that has attracted the attention of many visitors: it shows St. Antony with his pig.

According to the story, St. Antony visited France. The king, hearing about the many miracles of the saint, asked him to come to his court. His son had been born with a pig's head, and so could not be heir to the throne. St. Antony, after his audience with the king, saw a sucking pig born blind in the court yard, and he was moved with compassion. He restored the sight of the young pig and, in gratitude for this kindly deed, the mother sow promised him all he wanted. The story continues that St. Antony only had to touch the prince, and the pig's head turned into a human head.

On the south wall of the choir stands a glass feretory with the bodily remains of Anbâ Yûsâb al-Abah, metropolitan of Girga and Akhmîm (1735–1826). Many miracles are attributed to him. He was a monk at St. Antony's and one of the most outstanding theologians and apologists during the patriarchate of Anbâ Yûânnis XVIII. He was a prolific author and wrote thirty-one expositions on the doctrines of the Coptic church. His body did not decompose and numerous votive offerings are placed in the casket. He is commemorated on 24 January.

For fifteen days during Lent, the monks celebrate the Divine Liturgy in the Church of St. Mark, who was apparently a disciple of St. Antony. The southern haikal is dedicated to St. Mercurius or Abû Saifain, the central haikal to St. Mark and the northern haikal to St. Theodore the Martyr. The icons in the church portray St. George; the Holy Virgin; St. Mark the Evangelist; St. Paul the Theban and St. Antony. For centuries the church has attracted the piety of the Bedouins and the peasant pilgrims, because of the miracles associated with the relics of St. Mark which are kept in the wooden feretory on the north wall of the church. It is said that the oil in the lamp hanging over the feretory has a therapeutic effect, when applied in cases of rheumatism, rheumatic fevers and the like. The modern iconography in this church was executed in the neo-Coptic style by Maher Fayek in 1981.

On the wooden feretory of St. Mark there is a graffito with the following text: 'Ubi celebratur quadrigenta diebus et ulta' (Here the mass was celebrated forty and more). The church was previously connected with the Catholic church and this was attested by the Latin Terra Santa Cross which used to adorn the entrance to the church. This cross has recently been removed.

The Church of the Holy Virgin on the second floor of the storage building is used during the fasting period prior to the Feast of the Assumption of the Holy Virgin. This church has one haikal. Noteworthy is the beautiful eighteenth century haikal-screen with ivory inlaid cross designs.

The Chapel of St. Michael is located on the top floor of the keep. The haikal-screen is seventeenth–century, though the church is considerably older.

The new Church of SS. Antony and Paul with its five domes and two tall bell-towers is used for the daily celebration of the liturgy, by the ever increasing number of visitors.

The library and museum are situated in the north-eastern part of the monastery. Noteworthy are some of the icons, e.g. a triptych of the Baptism with the Holy Virgin and St. John; a Byzantine Elëusa (Vladimirskaja) with Ge'ez text from the sixteenth century; the Holy Virgin and Child with the Ethiopian Negus Lebna Dengel (1508-1540) and Queen Sabla Wangel. The silver chalices belong to the nineteenth century, while the three glass chalices are medieval. Among the processional and hand crosses is the Cross of St. Takla Haymanot. The liturgical vestments belonged to Anbâ Kîrillus IV (once Abûnâ Dâûd al-Antûnî) and Anbâ Yûsâb al-Abah of Girga and Akhmîm. The librarian is Abûnâ Samwîl al-Antûnî.

In April 1979, Anbâ Shenûdah III visited the monastery. New directives were issued which have been carried out in the meantime. Among the new architectural developments are a subterranean water tank; a water tower; the restoration of old cells and the building of new ones; two new guest houses for about 150 men and 150 women; a new gate in the western wall; workshops and the installation of two new generators, and a cell for the pope.

The spring of St. Antony supplies the monastic community with sufficient water for use.[86] Situated in the southern part of the monastery, it provides about 100m³ daily. The temperature is constant at about 23°C and, in spite of a small percentage of phosphorus, it is a sweet and excellent drinking water. East of the spring of St. Antony another spring, named after St. Mark, was recently discovered. St. Mark is said to have healed the blind with this water.

The monastery walls enclose an area of eighteen feddans, of which ten belong to the garden. The walls, like those of the Wâdî 'n-Natrûn monasteries, are ten to twelve metres high, and surmounted by a *chemin de ronde* (sentinel walk) between one and two metres wide. The old walls may go back as far as the tenth century while the new ones were built by Anbâ Kîrillus IV, in 1854. The walls, on which one can walk around the whole monastery, though with some difficulties here and there, are about two kilometres in length. It takes almost an hour to complete the tour. From the walls one looks down into the monastery which looks like a typical Egyptian village with mud brick houses, narrow streets, numerous churches, gardens, palm trees and water channels.

In 1976 Abûnâ Yustus al-Antûnî died. For many years he had lived as a hermit in the monastery, and performed many miracles so he was regarded as a saint while still alive. His cell has since been torn down and replaced by the guest house for men. East of the main entrance, inside the wall, there is a souvenir kiosk selling coloured pictures of Abûnâ Yustus. His relics repose in a wooden feretory in the passage between the Church of St. Antony and the Church of the Holy Apostles.

The leadership of the monastery is in the hands of Anbâ Diusqûrus and the amîn ad-dair Qummus Ruwais al-Antûnî. There are forty monks of whom ten go out to serve churches in Egypt and overseas. In addition, there are twenty-five novices.

The Caves of the Thebaid

The Eastern desert and the Red Sea mountains have long been a retreat for ascetics. Palladius reports about Possidonius the Theban who lived "by the side of Porphyrites". This must have been towards the end of the fourth century, for the same Possidonius lived with Palladius in Bethlehem, where they met St. Jerome (340-420), "who was exceedingly well versed in the art and practices of grammar, and he was greatly skilled in the Latin language, but he possessed the vices of envy and evil-eyedness."[87]

The Wâdî 'Arabah, in which the Monastery of St. Antony is located, is full of archaeological sites. Numerous caves have been discovered recently and bear witness to the fact that the cave-life of the ancient desert fathers was practised, here in the Eastern desert, in the Thebaid. Cells in the vicinity of the Wâdî Natfîh, the Bîr Bakhît, and the Wâdî Ghanâbah[88] prove that the anchorite life was apparently just as popular there as in the Wâdî 'n-Natrûn. We know from the *Vita Antonii* that, when the great hermit withdrew from his original cell at Pispir, he did not stay in the desert, but went up to the mountain of Clysma and discovered a remote cave in which he lived the rest of his life.

As one ascends the mountain of Clysma, one passes the cave of St. Paul the Simple, who lived in close proximity to his celebrated master, and who was one of his most faithful disciples. Palladius says that he had been

married to a beautiful but wicked woman who left him after committing
adultery for a long time. Having surprised her in the act of adultery, Paul
praised God and said: "It is good, truly she is not accounted mine by me.
By Jesus, henceforth I will not take her again... I will become a monk." St.
Paul went immediately to St. Antony But his age (he was eighty) was
against him. St. Antony compelled him several times to leave his cave and
to return to his village. But St. Paul persisted, and after four days of fasting,
St. Antony said to him: "Behold, thou hast become a monk, and henceforth
thou must live by thyself so that thou mayest receive the temptations of the
devils." The solitary life gave St. Paul the Simple the gift of healing and of
casting out devils, a power in which he even surpassed his teacher. The
remains of his cave, apparently man-made, are a silent witness to this
faithful contemporary of the great hermit. About five metres east of this
cave, Abûnâ Shârûbîm wrote St. Antony's name in Arabic by placing small
rocks on the slope. A hundred metres on, one reaches a small terrace, and
St. Antony's cave. From here there is a magnificent view over the Wâdî
'Arabah, though one cannot see the Red Sea as some travellers claim. The
monastery is obscured by a hill.

A wooden table serves as an altar in the cave. This was taken up to and
into the cave in parts, and was put together on the spot. Three icons, two of
Christ and one of St. Antony, were placed in the cave in 1960. On the south
wall of the cave are numerous medieval graffiti indicating that travellers in
years past visited it. Among these graffiti is the name of Fr. Bernardus,
1626, as well as a date of 1641 without a name.

The cave is in four parts: a terrace, a tunnel, a cave and a balcony. The
tunnel (at ground level thirty-four centimetres wide and at breast height
ninety-eight centimetres wide) connects the terrace with the cave. The
balcony is located about three metres below the terrace. It is here that the
saint used to make his palm-leaf baskets. Once a year on 30 January, a
service is held in the cave.

3
DAIR
ANBÂ BÛLÂ

The Monastery and its Saint

The Monastery of St. Paul the Theban,[1] or Dair Anbâ Bûlâ, was founded to commemorate the first hermit of whom we have any knowledge. Information about the monastery's history is extremely sketchy, because it has always existed in the shadow of St. Antony's. It is more isolated than St. Antony's and has never attracted the ecclesiastical and popular attention that the Monastery of St. Antony has. This is partly because Anbâ Bûlâ has never played a dynamic inspirational role in Coptic tradition.

The geographical isolation of the monastery, its mountainous and rocky surroundings, made it difficult for travellers to visit it. Furthermore, the monastery is about one-seventh the size of St. Antony's and its source of wealth in the Nile valley is just a fraction of that of its sister monastery at Mount Clysma. In spite of its old age and its long tradition, it has been treated rather like a step-child. St. Antony's fame travelled from shore to shore; St. Macarius' ascetic enthusiasm inspired literally thousands to follow him into the Wâdî 'n-Natrûn; St. Pachomius saw in his life-time the fruits of his energetic labour and discipline. St. Paul the Theban, though he was the first of the desert monks, the prince of anchorites, left no rules to be followed, no theology to be studied, only a cave. And it is around this cave, the first known cave of Christian asceticism, that the Monastery of St. Paul was built.

Like St. Antony of Mount Clysma, St. Samuel of Mount Qalamûn or St. Macarius of the Wâdî 'n-Natrûn, St. Paul of the South Qalâlâh mountain is regarded as healer and protector, helper and sustainer of the local population, which consists exclusively of a few Bedouins who roam through the desert with their sheep, goats or camels. St. Antony made a more profound impression upon the history of the Christian church than St. Paul, but the Bedouins prefer to pray to Anbâ Bûlâ for assistance in ill-health and trouble, because as they say: "He is so much more ready to receive the prayers of the poor, and thus responds so much more quickly than Anbâ Antûnîûs, and, of course, that is all that matters."

We do not know a great deal about St. Paul the Theban, and what we know comes to us through the writings of St. Jerome. This account has been severely criticized because of the stress it lays on the miraculous, and Hardy goes even so far as to say that "in spite of St. Jerome's story of St. Paul, who is at best a symbolic figure and at worst a pious fraud, St. Athanasius[2] is correct in telling us that Antony was the first to withdraw to the desert."[3] This contradicts the testimony of the History of the Holy Fathers as compiled by Palladius in 420 AD,[4] where we find the same critical assertions "how there were many who contradicted this opinion and who asserted with firmness that Mâr Antony was the first and the prince of them all... but if we wish to learn the whole truth we shall discover that it was not Mâr Antony who was the first that dwelt in the desert, but the blessed man Mâr Paulus. For I myself have seen the disciples of Mâr Antony who buried him, and they it was who related unto us the history of the man Paulus the anchorite." One thing seems certain, and that is that the tradition that a hermit called Paul was the first anchorite to inhabit the desert (although another tradition assigns this honour to St. Antony), must have been based on fact.

At the south wall of the cave-church of Anbâ Bûlâ stands a modern marble feretory which can be illuminated by a fluorescent light tube hanging above it, though the monks told me that they light it only once a year at Christmas. The inscription on the tomb reads: "Born in Alexandria in the year 228, died in the year 343."[5] Standing in front of the feretory of the saint, Abûnâ Damîan al-Bûlî, one of the monks now living at the monastery, told me the following story:

"Our Anbâ Bûlâ was a young man when the Christians were persecuted,[6] and these persecutions were most severe at Alexandria. His parents had died while he was still a young man,[7] and so like St. Antony he lived with his sister. But they had trouble, and so he left the city and all the worldly things and came out here to live. He used to live here all by himself, and the wild animals would stay with him in his cave, and there was no trouble between the lions and the other wild animals and Anbâ Bûlâ. The crows that lived in the mountains fed him, and he prayed all his life. Then one day Anbâ Antûnîûs went to visit him. At that time, Anbâ Antûnîûs was an old man too, and the walk across the mountains is not an easy one. But the Lord was good to them, and Anbâ Antûnîûs followed the animals and the wild beasts and the crows and he found the cave of Anbâ Bûlâ. Once a year some monks from Dair Anbâ Antûnîûs still come over here on the feast-day of Anbâ Bûlâ to celebrate the Divine Liturgy. On the feast-day of Anbâ Antûnîûs, two of our monks go over to Dair Anbâ Antûnîûs. Anbâ Bûlâ made a great impression upon Anbâ Antûnîûs, and they became great friends and both of them were fed with heavenly food. Then, one day, Anbâ Bûlâ died, and Anbâ Antûnîûs, was there at the time. But he did not know what to do, and so he prayed and sang psalms. And as he meditated about the loss of his friend, there came two big lions and Anbâ Antûnîûs was frightened. But the lions wagged their tails. They had been sent by God to dig a grave with their paws. You see these lions on all the holy icons of Anbâ Bûlâ. And Anbâ Antûnîûs took Anbâ Bûlâ and placed him in the grave, and prayed, and thanked God. Anbâ Antûnîûs then took the tunic of palm-leaves which Anbâ Bûlâ used to wear, and he wore it on special days and feasts."

The monks of Dair Anbâ Bûlâ were more fortunate with their patron-saint than those of Dair Anbâ Antûnîûs. Anbâ Bûlâ's tomb, which is located in the south-eastern part of the South Qalâlâh plateau, served as an inspiration. Young men from the Nile valley and the Delta flocked to the Red Sea desert in imitation of the first hermit. There is a tradition, however, that claims that the bodily remains of Anbâ Bûlâ were transferred to Constantinople in 1240, thence to Venice in 1381, and, at a later date, to Budapest. For it was under the patronage of this desert hermit that the monastic order of the Paulines was founded in Hungary sometime in the fifteenth century.

The Monastery of St. Paul was founded about the same time, perhaps a little later, than that of Anbâ Antûnîûs. Johann Georg's suggestion that the monastery was organized at the beginning of the fifth century is probably the most plausible. Butcher[8] informs us that the monastery was restored by Emperor Justinian (483-565) and inhabited by Melkite monks.

The Early Pilgrims

The monastery must have been well known by the sixth century, for Antoninus Martyr,[9] a native of Placentia, visited the shrine between 560-570. "Then we (Antoninus and his travelling companion, John) came through the desert to the cave of the blessed Paul, which is named Syracumba, near a fountain, which up to the present time waters the whole place."

An isolated Ethiopian reference informs us that Ghabrîâl ibn Turaik, the seventieth patriarch, was banished and spent three years at the monastery, where he is supposed to have written *al-Hawi al-Kabir*.[10]

Abû Sâlih the Armenian, writing at the beginning of the thirteenth century, mentions the monastery. By that time it had become totally dependent upon St. Antony's. "Within the desert is the Monastery of St. Paul. It stands on the bank of the Salt Sea, and between it and the Monastery of al-Jummaizah there is a journey of two days through the desert. Monks in priests' orders and deacons come from the monastery of the great Antony to the monastery to celebrate the liturgy in it by turns. It stands in the Wâdî 'Arabah, near the pool of Miriam, and it is near Mount Sinai, but divided from it by the passage over the Salt Sea."[11] Falling into the same period is a manuscript from which Evelyn White quotes.[12] This document asserts that Dair Anbâ Bûlâ belonged to the Syrians at some point. "Let the Syrian brethren who come after us to this monastery know that in the convent of Abba Paulus, beside the Monastery of Mâr Antonius, which belonged to the Syrians like this, there are many Syriac books still. But because of what was to come, the Syrians were driven out, thence the Egyptians took it..."

Before he died, Ogier de Saint-Cheron, first seigneur d'Anglure, had resolved to perform a devout pilgrimage to the Holy Places, including the Monastery of St. Paul the Theban. He set out in 1395, with a group of French pilgrims, and after visiting the Monastery of St. Antony, they marched along the Red Sea to the Monastery of St. Paul where they found sixty monks of the same habit, rite and piety as the brotherhood of St. Antony.[13]

In 1421, Ghillebert de Lannoy made his second pilgrimage which included the Monastery of St. Paul which was inhabited by Jacobite Christians, who were subject to those of the Monastery of St. Antony. Ghillebert also mentioned the garden with its palms in the monastery.[14]

One of the first maps to place the monasteries of SS. Paul and Antony correctly between the Red Sea and the Nile was the *Geographica* drawn by Bernhard von Breydenbach in 1486.[15]

In the first half of the fifteenth century, the Islamic historian al-Maqrîzî in his *Account of the Monasteries and Churches of Egypt* included Dair Anbâ Bûlâ as the eighth in his list of eighty-six monasteries. He mentions that the monastery is also referred to as the Monastery of the Sons of Paul, or the Monastery of an-Numur.[16] He locates the monastery in the region west of at-Tûr (Sinai) in the vicinity of a spring, where travellers stop to rest, and where the monks say that Miriam, the sister of Moses, washed herself in it when Moses camped with the Israelites in the vicinity of Clysma.

Maqrîzî's account of the saint's life is as follows: Anbâ Bûlâ came from Alexandria, and his father had left him and his brother considerable wealth. His brother began to quarrel about the money and Anbâ Bûlâ left in disgust. He came across a corpse which was about to be buried, and this made him begin to think seriously about life. He travelled through the country until he reached the spring, and he stayed there, while God looked after him. Then St. Antony passed by and stayed with him and built the monastery above his tomb. Between the monastery and the sea are three hours (of travel).[17]

In the last decade of the fifteenth century, Dair Anbâ Antûnîûs suffered severely at the hands of the Bedouins. It is probable that Dair Anbâ Bûlâ experienced a similar fate, for we read in the history of the Monastery of the Syrians that Anbâ Ghabrîâl VII (1525-1568) assisted in the rebuilding of this monastery. Of the thirty monks whom he commissioned for the task of reconstructing the monasteries in the Thebaid, ten were sent to Dair Anbâ Bûlâ.[18]

Seventeenth- and Eighteenth-Century Travellers

One of the first visitors in the seventeenth century may well have been Fr. Bernardus, O.F.M., who left his graffiti on the haikal-screen of the Church of St. Antony. It is quite likely that the three dates mentioned in his inscription refer to at least two distinct arrivals at the monastery. It is probable, therefore, that he, following the example of other pilgrims and visitors, also visited the Monastery of St. Paul and then returned to the Monastery of St. Antony. His graffiti mention dates between 31 December, 1625 and 31 January, 1626. Graffiti by this friar have not been discovered at Dair Anbâ Bûlâ, though numerous ancient graffiti can be found on the west wall of the Church of Anbâ Bûlâ.

When Fr. Coppin, who served as French consul in Damietta, Fr. Agathangelus, O.F.M., Mr. Bayart of Marseille, Mr. Antonio Messinois and two other monks had been to the Monastery of St. Antony in 1638, they decided to visit the Monastery of St. Paul.[19] The party had stayed at St. Antony's for three days, and prior to their departure into the "unknown", which they felt was inhabited by ferocious Arabs and tigers, they celebrated Mass, recommending themselves to the protection of the two desert solitaries. Having arrived safely at St. Paul's, Fr. Coppin visited the various places of interest. He remarks that the Church of St. Paul appeared to him like a basement built on the place where the saint lived for some sixty years of his life. Then, Fr. Coppin comments upon the cruciform construction of the church with its three altars in the sanctuary, of which the principal altar faced the north, while the other two altars faced east and west. Before their return to the Monastery of St. Antony, they toured the monastery and garden. The visitors concluded their stay by celebrating Mass, and then they departed for the Red Sea.

All that we know of Fr. Gerard's visit to the Monastery of St. Paul is the date (1639), and the fact that he went there from the Monastery of St. Antony.[20]

In 1692, de Maillet mentions St. Paul's cave. He saw other caves or monastic dwellings in which the hermits made penance. Mentioning the fact that the monks sleep on the floor, he says this is common practice in agricultural areas.[21] However, he did not visit the monastery.

It seems that a second devastation ruined the efforts of Anbâ Ghabrîâl, for we hear that Anbâ Yûânnis XVI (1676–1718) reconstructed the monastery in 1701, after 119 years of desolation.[22]

In 1716, an anonymous pilgrim visited the Monastery of Anbâ Bûlâ. He was probably the first traveller to sketch the monastery, and he dedicated his work to Nicholas, bishop of Exeter.[23]

There appear to be different opinions about the supposed unified headship of both the desert monasteries in the thirteenth and fourteenth centuries. Johann Georg tells us that, until the middle of the nineteenth century, one hegoumenos was in charge of both monasteries. He was told that the older monks used to live in Dair Anbâ Bûlâ, while the younger monks inhabited Dair Anbâ Antûnîûs. He decides, however, that this is just idle talk. Labîb Habashî states that the management of the monasteries was entrusted to one hegoumenos until the middle of the nineteenth century, and that the young monks had to go first to Dair Anbâ Bûlâ. Then they were transferred to Dair Anbâ Antûnîûs, until "they became old enough to return to Dair Anbâ Bûlâ."[24] Anbâ Yûânnis XVII (1727–1745), who had been hegoumenos of Dair Anbâ Bûlâ, exercised the office of headship over both monasteries. For how long, and to what an extent the monasteries shared an administration is difficult to ascertain.

About the time the anonymous pilgrim visited the monastery, Fr. Claude Sicard, S.J. went with J.S. Assemani to the Red Sea monasteries in search of manuscripts. After having stayed for some time at the Monastery of St. Antony, they departed on 29 May, 1716 for the Monastery of St. Paul which the Arabs call Dair an-Numwan, or the Monastery of the Tigers. The trip from Mount Clysma to St. Paul's took them fifteen hours, and upon their arrival at the monastery, they were hoisted up by a pulley which took them inside the monastery. When they set foot in the monastery, the monks conducted them in procession to the church, where they recited some prayers. The hegoumenos showed them the library, but the good and valuable books and the manuscripts had been removed. On the following day, which was Whitsunday, Fr. Sicard witnessed the monks' Pentecostal celebrations.[25] After the celebrations, the visitors went to the Red Sea.

We have observed that the monastery played a secondary role. Nevertheless, the monastery provided several patriarchs and bishops, who through their work entered the pages of Coptic history. One of them was Anbâ Yûânnis XVII, the 105th patriarch, who succeeded Anbâ Butrus VI in 1726. John al-Mallawî had been the hegoumenos of the Monastery of St. Paul before he ascended the patriarchal throne.

On 11 April, 1730, coming from the Monastery of St. Antony, le Sieur Granger arrived at the Monastery of St. Paul. He mentioned the path that connects the two monasteries, by the use of which one could reach Dair Anbâ Bûlâ in a matter of eight hours. This path is called Akabe by the Arabs.[26] Because of the wilderness around the monastery, the Copts refer to it as the Monastery of the Tigers. Granger estimates the church to be thirty-two feet long and fourteen feet wide, and says that the walls were covered with paintings of saints. The wall of one of the haikals bore a Greek inscription which he reproduced in his book. At the time of his visit, the monastery was inhabited by fourteen monks, of whom five were priests and two wore the angelic habit.

In 1737, Pococke visited Egypt, and although he did not go to the monastery, he reports that twenty-five monks lived there, that they could not marry, but that widowers were accepted. He was told that the monks only ate once a day, except on Saturdays and Sundays.[27]

Nineteenth- and Twentieth-Century Travellers

Numerous Russian pilgrims and travellers came to Egypt, though only a few have left any documentation.

In 1834-35, Avraam Norov described the Monastery of St. Paul. "It is situated on the mountain of Clysma at a distance of four versts[28] from the Monastery of St. Antony. But it is separated from it by such a high and abrupt rock that one is forced to take a circuitous way. This is why St. Antony travelled nearly two days before he reached the hermitage of St. Paul."[29] The above account makes one doubt whether Norov ever visited the monastery.

On 14 March, 1839, Dr. Tattam visited the Monastery of St. Paul. "They rode dromedaries; for it is scarcely safe to attempt riding a donkey over the broken mountain-path leading to the wild spot on which Mar Bolos is situated. It is enclosed by lofty mountains, and appears inaccessible to all but the natives of the desert, who are in the habit of going thither to demand food. The monks here possess but few religious books, or did not choose to show more. They brought out a copy of St. John's Gospel in Coptic, and a copy of the Scriptures in Latin and Arabic, 4 vols. folio. The building is in better repair than that of Mar Antonius, but not so large. The monks occasionally procure fish from the Red Sea, but at other times they live on coarse bread, soup of lentils and the fruits, which their garden produces."[30]

An interesting piece of evidence about penitential prostrations was recently brought to light by a painting by Joseph Bonomi. Bonomi, son of a famous Italian architect, was in Egypt between 1824 and 1833, and again from 1844 until his death in 1878. Louis Keimer has reproduced the painting which shows the monks of Dair Anbâ Bûlâ praying in front of two large crosses. The inscription of the painting reads: "Drawing made in the convent of Paul the Hermit in the Eastern desert about the year 1840 by Joseph Bonomi." Clearly the practice of penitential prostrations, of which Fr. Sicard spoke, was still in use.[31] The painting has been reproduced in Sharpe's *The History of Egypt.*

In 1847, the Russian archimandrite Porphyrius Uspensky went as head of the first Russian delegation to Jerusalem to establish a Russian mission in the Holy Land. Though he was not successful in this, his descriptions of the monasteries in the Thebaid are helpful. He went to the Monastery of St. Paul in 1850 accompanied by the hegoumenos of the Monastery of St. Antony and made the following observations: "The cathedral Church of St. John the Baptist with a chapel of the Archangel Michael was built in 1727 by the order of the 105th patriarch, Anbâ Yohannes, according to the Arabic inscription on the central pillar of the church. The church's best decoration is an icon of the Evangelist Mark, painted in Europe... In the north corner of the monastery is a small church dedicated to the twenty-four Elders of the Revelation. The church is entered from a parvis, to which one descends by a low flight of stairs... Next to this church, and separated from it by a wooden screen is the natural cave of St. Paul, where also the stone tomb of the saint is located... The place is low and small, it is five feet long and four feet wide... a door leads into the adjoining sanctuary. It is dark there, as in a coffin. There is no cupola above the sanctuary as the cave was left untouched. In the south-west corner of the church there is a secret flight of stairs which leads into the contiguous Church of St. Mercurius."[32]

In 1876, 1877, and 1878, Dr. Georg Schweinfurth visited the monasteries of the Red Sea desert. Schweinfurth relates his impressions of the mysterious environment of the Monastery of St. Paul in a romantic and flowery style. The outer wall has a length of 455 metres, and the pulley is in the eastern part of the monastery. The dwellings of the twenty-eight monks who inhabit the monastery are built in two parallel streets. The spring provides the monks with cool, refreshing water with a minimum of mineral content. The old church which contains the tomb of the patron seemed to have been renovated some two hundred years before. The walls of this church were covered with grotesque wall-paintings. Many of the graffiti led Schweinfurth to believe that the monastery was visited by early pilgrims.

He recognized a very ancient Gothic inscription by a certain Franz Sembacher.[33]

A few years later in 1883, Fr. Michel Jullien, S.J., travelled with a party from the Monastery of St. Antony to the shores of the Red Sea, and from there to the Monastery of St. Paul, where he arrived late at night. The visitors were pulled up by a rope to the wall. Then the party was ceremoniously received by the monks, and after this the civil reception began. The hegoumenos, Abûnâ Ya'qûb, was in charge of a group of twenty-five monks of whom nine were laybrothers, and sixteen hieromonks, ten of these bearing the title Qummus. One monk, Abûnâ Tâdrus, was nearly ninety, and had lived some sixty years in the monastery. After an agreeable night at the monastery, the day began with the celebration of Mass in the cave of St. Paul. Fr. Jullien, like Schweinfurth, comments upon the pictures on the wall of the Church of St. Paul. The drawings which represent saints and biblical characters were, according to Jullien, the work of a monk of the monastery.[34]

During the latter part of the nineteenth century, the monastery was in the newspaper headlines. After many attempts at reconciliation between Anbâ Kîrillus V and the Maglis al-Millî, the pope withdrew to Dair al-Barâmûs, while the metropolitan Yûânnis retired to Dair Anbâ Bûlâ, where he remained for five months.

In February 1904, Agnes Smith Lewis and Mrs. Margaret Dunlop Gibson visited the Monastery of St. Paul. Their guide went to Bûsh to obtain the permission from the hegoumenos which he received after a great deal of difficulty. After Anbâ Arsânîûs had given his consent, he issued a letter of instruction to the monks of his monastery, advising them to show their books to the two ladies. If any of the monks objected to the women's visit, they were to be locked up together in a room during the period of their visit. On the morning of the second day after their departure from St. Antony's monastery, the ladies entered Dair Anbâ Bûlâ by rope and windlass, being heaved up by a rope-netting which was roughly sewn around their waists. Once in the monastery, they were ceremoniously welcomed by Qummus Aqlâdîûs and some thirty monks with a service that lasted for two hours, and which was conducted in their honour with a eulogy on "our beloved sovereign Queen Victoria, and a lament over her death". Then they examined the small store of manuscripts, photographed some of the monks, and visited the other churches. At the end of their visit they were again conducted to the trap door, and sewed up in a rope-netting. "The windlass was turned, I closed my eyes, and just as I opened them to ascertain if I had begun to descend, I found myself on mother earth." On their departure, the qummus and three monks escorted the ladies down the valley.[35]

In March 1908, Fr. Fortunatus Vignozzi da Seano, accompanied by Fr. Gottfried Schilling and August Schuler, visited the Red Sea monasteries of SS. Antony and Paul, where they spent several days with the monks trying to impress upon them the importance of belonging to the Catholic church.[36]

In the late 1920s, Marcus Simaika concerned himself with the preservation of the manuscripts and books in the Monastery of Anbâ Bûlâ. This work was completed in 1929, and Marcus Simaika stipulated that none of the books were to be removed from the library.

In years gone by the monastery was inaccessible for most travellers. Fowler says: "It has scarcely ever been visited by Europeans, so that it is impossible to say what treasures, in the way of manuscripts and antiquities, might be discovered within its precincts."[37]

During his last visit to Egypt in 1930, Johann Georg, Duke of Saxony, realized his dream of visiting the Monastery of St. Paul. He travelled on the 260-ton *Argyll* from Port Tawfiq to Za'frânah and from there by camel to the monastery. On his way to the monastery, the duke chanced to meet Professor Whittemore, who had spent two days at Dair Anbâ Bûlâ studying the wall-paintings in the cave-church. On his arrival the duke visited the three churches. First, he went to the "New Church" which he decided had been built in the seventeenth century. This church was normally used for services. The icon of the Holy Virgin, which the monks attribute to the hand of St. Luke the Evangelist, was identified by Johann Georg as belonging to the latter part of the nineteenth century. From the New Church he went to the ancient Church of St. Paul which he assigned to the sixth or seventh century. His criticism of the wall-paintings–following closely the remarks of Schweinfurth and Fr. Jullien–is rather harsh. He noticed the wooden feretory of the saint, but doubts the authenticity of the monks' claims that it contained the relics of St. Paul. The third church, that of St. Mercurius, obviously did not impress the visitor. He mentions that the church had been built in a rough architectural manner, and that it was quite insignificant. After four pleasant hours at the monastery, Johann Georg left again for the Red Sea, and returned to Suez.[38]

On 12 April, 1956, Fr. Gabriele Giamberardini, O.F.M., together with his companions, left the Monastery of Anbâ Antûnîûs for that of Anbâ Bûlâ where they were hospitably received. Comparing the Monastery of St. Paul with the Antonian monastery, the party had the impression that it was more alive and better organized than the latter. While they were not permitted to enter the library of the Monastery of Anbâ Antûnîûs, Abûnâ Sulaimân al-Bûlî showed them the library of the Monastery of St. Paul, where they saw, among other volumes in Arabic and Coptic, an Arabic-Latin bible which had been printed in Rome in 1671. At the time of their visit, twenty-six monks inhabited the monastery. Among the monks whom they met was Abûnâ Sîdrâk, the hegoumenos of the monastery, Abûnâ Sâwîrûs and the young Abûnâ al-Hâbib Sulaimân. Abûnâ Damîân, whom Fr. Gabriele had met before at the Monastery of Anbâ Samwîl, dominated the situation by his personality. According to the other monks, he was described as the "Gazetta del convento", knowing everything that there is to be known:

Also, in the spring of 1956, members of the Desert Institute visited the Red Sea monasteries, studying the flora of the two Qalâlâhs and of St. Antony's, where the monks complained of fungus attacking their trees and crops. The olive trees suffered particularly from this disease. From there the botanists went to the Monastery of St. Paul, where they also visited the garden inside the monastery. And again they heard complaints. The dates were falling when unripe and the vegetables and fruits were suffering from fungus. Dr. Taeckholm enumerates the fruit trees at the Monastery of St. Paul: olives, oranges, pomegranates, figs, dates, and guavas.[39]

The Monastery Today

To reach the monastery one follows the Red Sea road as far as twenty-six kilometres south of the lighthouse station of Za'frânah. A sign points to the road to the monastery. The mountainous, rocky, and sometimes mysterious environment through which the track leads is described by Schweinfurth: "A terrible wilderness of mountainous country constitutes the immediate environment of St. Paul's. It is a precipitous cliff into the abyss, a gate of hell, more horrible than the fantasy of Dante could express it." After thirteen kilometres of almost continuous bends and sharp curves, the monastery suddenly appears from around the last corner. The road is fair, except for the last 120 metres. A steep and rocky ascent leads to the large eastern gate which is lowered only for vehicles and camel caravans. The gate at the eastern end of the south wall is used by visitors, and leads to the guest house and the other main buildings.

The monastery radiates a friendly and relaxing atmosphere, and the monks go out of their way to make the visitor feel at home. The guest house was completed in 1948 and provides nine beds. Johann Georg says that the guest house was being constructed during his visit in 1930. It must have been fairly well completed at that time, since he mentions a well furnished "salon" and a few bedrooms. Pococke remarked in 1742 that "a woman is not permitted to enter the convent". This is no longer true, but women are not allowed to stay overnight, so the monks have recently built a "ladies-rest" opposite the old gate outside the monastery walls.

No visitor to the monasteries of SS. Paul and Antony can fail to notice the desert crows that continually circle above the isolated inhabited desert areas. They nest in the mountain cliffs and crevices of the South Qalâlâh and feed on the dates of the palm trees and other eatables around the monastery. The monks regard these birds as a nuisance. Schweinfurth reports that the monks hunt the desert crows in spite of their connection with Elijah and Anbâ Bûlâ. Elijah was led by God to seek refuge by the brook Cherith, and the desert crows brought him food morning and evening, and thus his life was preserved. In St. Jerome's biography of St. Paul, Anbâ Bûlâ tells Anbâ Antûnîûs: "Truly our Lord is merciful and pitiful in that he sendeth us a meal in this way. For behold, for fully sixty years I have been in the habit of receiving from this bird (a desert crow) half a loaf of bread daily, but at thy (St. Antony's) coming, behold, our Lord hath sent unto us a double portion of food because we are his servants."

Christian iconography has never omitted the crow from the pictures of Anbâ Bûlâ and Anbâ Antûnîûs. But the desert fathers despise the birds. One late evening, talking with one of the monks, I was told the story of the "Secret of the Crows."

"Many years ago, a small wooden bowl with two tiny crows carved on it was removed from the Monastery of St. Paul; a monk had taken it, and without knowing what he had done, he had brought the charm to the Antonian monastery. As the monk, carrying the bowl, entered the gate of Dair Anbâ Antûnîûs, all the crows which had been living in the immediate vicinity of the monastery, left southwards and settled in and around Dair Anbâ Bûlâ. The monks of Dair Anbâ Bûlâ were furious and demanded the immediate return of their protective charm. When the monks of Dair Anbâ Antûnîûs complied with the demand of their brethren, the crows left St. Paul's monastery, except for two crows. Still to this day there are only two crows at Dair Anbâ Bûlâ. When these two crows have young ones, the offspring eventually turn out the parents who, in their turn, join the crows at St. Antony's."

Dair Anbâ Bûlâ has altogether four churches of which three are situated in the ancient part of the monastery. The Church of St. Paul (the cave-church) is the spiritual centre of the monastery. The sanctuary was originally built into the rock-cave, where St. Paul used to live. Here the bodily remains of Anbâ Bûlâ are preserved. The walls of the church are covered with paintings which are, generally speaking, in better condition, though of inferior artistic quality, than those of the Church of Anbâ Antûnîûs in the monastery at Mount Clysma. This ancient sanctuary differs from those in the other desert monasteries in that it has only a few graffiti by travellers and visitors. Of interest, is the Gothic handwriting of a certain Franz Sembacher who must have visited the monastery in the early Middle Ages. Descending a few steps, one enters the "Dome of the Martyrs", which is decorated with the paintings of St. George, St. Victor, St. Theodore, St.

Claudius, and St. Theodore and St. Shalabi. The paintings on the east wall of the entrance represent the "Little Strangers" of Dair al-Barâmûs: St. Maximus, St. Domitius and St. Arsenius; St. Agapius; St. Macarius; St. Samuel; and St. Apollo, while the paintings on the south wall portray St. Michael; the Blessed Virgin Mary; and St. Gabriel. Having entered the dark church, one faces to the east three haikals. The northern haikal is dedicated to the Twenty-four Elders of the Apocalypse, the central haikal to St. Antony and the southern haikal to St. Paul. The west wall of the church is covered with numerous paintings of which only some can be identified. The figures furthest to the south represent the five Archangels (Raphael, Suriel, Zaqiel, Sarathiel, the Angel of God according to *Daniel*) and Shadrach, Meshach and Abed-Nego.

The wall-paintings in the subterranean Church of St. Paul were executed by a monk around the time of the visit of the Frs. Claude Sicard, S.J. and J.S. Assemani in May 1716. Fr. Sicard writes: "The walls from the vault to the ground are covered by a very rude painting representing some stories from the Holy Scriptures... The monk who executed this painting informed us that he had never learned to paint. His work was evident proof of that. We asked him from where he had obtained his different colours, and he told us that he had extracted them from the coloured soils in the neighbouring hills." The wall-paintings, therefore, were executed before 1716 and after 1701, when John XVI began to rebuild the monastery.

The new marble feretory of Anbâ Bûlâ stands at the south wall of the church. The Divine Liturgy is celebrated in this church during the months of January, February and March, and the three haikals are used during this season interchangeably.

Close to the Church of St. Paul, almost above it, is the Church of Abû Saifain which was constructed in the latter part of the eighteenth century. It is only used once a year, during the week leading up to Lent. The church is of little interest, except for its beautiful haikal-screen with inlaid mother of pearl and ivory. The icons in the church represent St. Dioscorus; St. Mercurius or Abû Saifain; St. Macarius; St. Cyril; St. Paul the Theban and St. Antony; and the Holy Virgin.

On the third floor of the qasr is the Church of the Holy Virgin.

The Church of St. Michael is the largest church in the monastery. Situated south-west of the cave-church it serves as the main church for divine services. Fr. Jullien refers to it as the *église des moines,* and the Divine Liturgy is celebrated here from April to November. Johann Georg reckons that it was built in the seventeenth century. On entering the church, one passes through the bell-tower situated just outside the main church. The Church of St. Michael has two sanctuaries, the northern haikal is dedicated to St. Michael and the southern to St. John the Baptist. In the

Church of St. Michael, or to be precise, in the south haikal, the Divine Liturgy is celebrated from April to September on Sundays, Wednesdays and Fridays. The monks point out the painting of the Holy Virgin attached to the choir-screen. The monks attribute this painting to St. Luke the Evangelist who painted it in or around the year 40 A.D. The haikal-screen decoration is rather original in so far as the customary Twelve Apostles appear in the robes of Coptic desert monks. The northern haikal of the church, or the sanctuary of St. John the Baptist, is used from the middle of September until the middle of November. The icon of the head of St. John the Baptist on a charger on a gold background dates from 1760 and was painted by Ibrâhîm ah-Nâsikh. The other icons are of the Holy Virgin, St. Mark the Evangelist, St. Paul the Theban and St. Antony, St. George, St. Stephen, and the Mystical Supper. In the western part of the church a large new baptismal font has been installed.

The library is a small room on the north side of the Church of St. Michael. There are approximately five hundred volumes, and both manuscripts and printed books have been so stored away that one gets the impression that the library is used only on rare occasions.

In addition to the thirty-two renovated cells in the south-western part of the monastery, a new row of cells has been constructed. A kiosk selling devotional books, leather crosses, medals and pictures faces the old guest house, which the monks refer to as their 'palace'.

Dair Anbâ Bûlâ is supplied by two wells; the "Spring of Anbâ Bûlâ", as the monks refer to it, is situated in the western part of the monastery. The water issuing from the mountain crevices flows into a cemented reservoir tank, and is used for drinking and cooking. A small drain leads the surplus water into a second reservoir which is used by the monks for washing. A further drain carries off the water into a larger basin from where it is distributed for. irrigation. The other spring is traditionally associated with Miriam. The monks still refer to the spring as the "Pool of Miriam". It is situated about a hundred metres south of the monastery, but nowadays it is not often used.

In 1986, there were forty monks at Dair Anbâ Bûlâ. The head of the monastery is Anbâ Agathon and the amîn ad-dair Qummus Makarîûs-al-Bûlî. Three monks from the Dair Anbâ Bûlâ have become bishops in recent years, Anbâ Kîrillus of Balyana (1948), Anbâ Kîrillus of Nag' Hammadî (1977) and Anbâ Butrus of Ismailia (1979). Abûnâ 'Abd al-Masîh al-Bûlî lives in the Dair Malâk Ghobriâl near Sidmint al-Gebel in the Fayyûm.

In many respects, the monastic life in Dair Anbâ Bûlâ appears to be more intimate, more consolidated and also more friendly than that in many other monasteries. The relative poverty of the monastery and its smallness are no doubt contributing factors. The "corporeal presence" of their patron saint may well serve as inspiration towards homogeneity, for the original cave is in the monastery and not beyond the walls.

There are several caves in the vicinity of the monastery which at one time were inhabited. South of the monastery, between the Pool of Miriam and the south gate, is the cave of Abûnâ Buqtur al-Bûlî. According to Abûnâ Rizqallah al-Bûlî, Abûnâ Buqtur lived in this cave for forty years, about one hundred years ago. The cave is simple, having one room and a large entrance facing to the south. Debris, straw and ashes lead one to conclude that it is now used by the Bedouins who live around the monastery. About one kilometre south-west of the monastery in the Wâdî Umm Sillîma are three other caves, though none of them are inhabited by monks. There is the same evidence here that these caves are used by the Bedouins. It is advisable to employ the services of a monk to visit the caves in the Wâdî Umm Sillîma.

One last note about St. Paul's monastery: An unusual event occurred during the night of Thursday, 4 September, 1975 when several monks and visitors saw a bright light ascend from the old cave-church of St. Paul, remaining there for twenty-five minutes. This phenomenon was also witnessed by travellers on the highway between Ras Za'frânah and Ras Ghârib.

4

THE VALLEY
OF THE
WÂDÎ 'N-NATRÛN

The Wâdî 'n-Natrûn has a long history dating from pharaonic times. Caravans travelled from the Buhairah and Farâfrah oases to the Nile delta, passing the small oasis of Wâdî 'n-Natrûn. The famous group of papyri known as "The Complaints of the Peasant" prove that in the early Middle Kingdom[1] some of Farâfrah's produce was taken via the Wâdî 'n-Natrûn to be sold at Heracleopolis. Recent discoveries of a black granite bust of a chancellor of the XVIIth Dynasty of Lower Egypt,[2] a granite gateway, blocks from a lintel and jambs with cartouches of Amenemhet I,[3] at Quarat ad-Dahr, and other remains, lead one to suppose that even in the year 2000 B.C. this region was held sacred. The site in question is only five kilometres north-west of the Monastery of St. Macarius (Abû Maqâr).

According to Coptic tradition, the Desert of Scetis or the Wâdî 'n-Natrun has a Christian history going as far back as the visit of the Holy Family to Egypt. We read in the *Synaxarium* that, after visiting Basâtah and Munyat Samanûd, the family crossed the river to the west bank and then saw from afar the Gabel 'n-Natrûn. The Holy Virgin blessed it.[4] Furthermore, some Christians escaped to the Desert of Scetis during the Diocletian persecution between 304 and 311.

Evelyn White devotes a whole chapter of his monumental work, *The Monasteries of the Wâdî 'n-Natrûn,* to the topography of the ancient monastic settlements in the Western desert. Three localities west of the Delta are referred to by the early monastic fathers. In the latter part of the fourth century, Macarius the Alexandrian had four cells in the western desert.[5] "One in Scete, the inner desert, one in Libya, one in the 'Cells', and one in Mount Nitria. Two of these were without windows, and in them he used to dwell in darkness during the Forty Days' Fast, another was so narrow that he could not stretch out his legs, but another, wherein he used to receive the brethren was wide and spacious."[6] The mount of Nitria, where nitrate was found, stood about forty-five kilometres north of the present Cairo–Alexandria route rest house, or some fourteen kilometres south-west of Damanhûr, near al-Barnuji.

The Greek geographer Strabo (born 63 B.C.) accompanied the prefect of Egypt, Aelius Gallus, on his expedition to Upper Egypt in 25-24 B.C. Strabo makes one of the earliest references to the area: "Above Momemphis are two nitre-beds, which contain very large quantities of nitre, and the Nitriote Nome. Here Serapis is held in honour and they are the only people who sacrifice a sheep."[7]

Though still in the desert the mountain was situated on the edge of the Delta. It is wrong to identify the present Wâdî 'n-Natrûn with the Mount of Nitria, and the latter was the first home of Christian asceticism. Palladius visited the monks living in Nitria in 391: "Now having held converse with many of the saints, and having gone around about among the monasteries which were nigh unto Alexandria for three years, and having met about two thousand of the great and strenuous men who lived there, and who were adorned with the excellence of spiritual lives, I departed from there and came to Mount Nitria. Now between this mountain and Alexandria there lieth a certain lake which is called 'Mareotis'... Now in this mountain there are seven bakers who make bread and who minister unto them, and unto the chosen men of the inner desert, of whom there are six hundred, and also unto the people of that mountain."[8] This account suggests that some primitive form of communal fellowship existed among the monks of the Mount of Nitria.

The second settlement referred to by the ancient authorities was called Cellia, situated south-west of the Mount of Nitria on the way to Scetis, the present Wâdî 'n-Natrûn. According to Palladius, this was where Macarius the Alexandrian lived: "He was an elder in the place which is called the 'Cells', wherein I myself lived for nine years." Another well-known monk who lived in Cellia was Isaac of Cellia who is commemorated by the Coptic church on 19th Bashons. Many monks must have inhabited this region and some form of hegemonic system observed as the following quotation shows: "And when they (the monks) had come out to go to the Cells, the honorable men fell down before the priest of the Cells, and said unto him, 'Father, give our brothers orders to take us to see all the fathers'." Apparently Evagrius spent two years in Nitria and fourteen more in the Cells, living on a pound of bread a day, and a box of oil every three months.[9]

Cellia was founded in about 335. In 1981 archaeologists from Geneva University uncovered large sections of Cellia, which extended over more than one hundred square kilometres, having five 'hermitage towns', thus confirming the preparatory work of Antoine Guillaumont and Rudolphe Kasser of the French Archaeological Institute in Cairo. Hermitages and cells were built of sun-dried sand bricks held together by mineral salts. Many of the oratories were adorned with polychrome wall-paintings of crosses and floral, vegetable and animal designs. Noteworthy is a painting of a beardless, youthful Christ with cross-nimbus. Over the centuries frugal hermitages gave way to a settlement of comfortable monastic apartments.

The glory of the Mount of Nitria passed away after the fifth century, and what we know of its previous existence comes from the reports of visitors. Rufinus and Melania, and St. Jerome and Paula, are said to have visited Nitria, and their testimonies give us an insight into the ascetic lives of the fathers in that region. This settlement on the edge of the desert was easily accessible, yet its proximity to the outside world was the reason why it was abandoned. A similar fate befell Cellia. Only the most remote and isolated community survived.

The area which will concern us has been known by a number of names: Scetis, Scythis, Al-Askît, Scitium, Shiet, Shihet, Wâdî Habîb, and Wâdî 'n-Natrûn. It was about sixty kilometres from Cellia. There is no indication that Scetis was inhabited until St. Macarius ventured there and discovered the quietness that he had failed to find elsewhere. This was the area that eventually became the centre of Coptic monasticism, the region into which the great saints of the Egyptian church withdrew. St. Macarius the Great; St. Bishoî; St. John the Short; St. John Kame, and many others. Here lived the "Little Strangers", Maximus and Domitius of the Monastery of the Romans (Dair al-Barâmûs), and Moses the Black, who, influenced by the saints of Scetis, decided to follow the ascetic life. Consequently Wâdî 'n-Natrûn was for many years the bulwark of Coptic monasticism, and the residence of the patriarch.

The Wâdî 'n-Natrûn is about thirty-five kilometres long, and runs in a north-westerly direction, its south-eastern end being sixty-five kilometres north-west of Cairo. The valley is never more than eight kilometres wide; the low undulating hills running on each side of it are covered with siliceous pebbles and a few stunted bushy plants. These hills slope down to the sandy valley, the lowest point of which is about twenty-five metres below the level of the sea at Alexandria. Eight lakes lie in a line from one end of the wâdî to the other. They are all salt, containing varying quantitites of chloride and carbonate of soda, and sometimes some sodium sulphate. For some distance round the lakes, and even as far south as Dair Abû Maqâr, the sand is covered with a thick outgrowth of salt. The lakes dry up in the summer, some of them becoming completely dry, while others remain moist marshes. The salt gives the country a wintry aspect, but this illusion is rapidly dispelled by the quantities of mosquitoes which frequent the area.

For centuries, the monasteries in the Desert of Scetis could enjoy the isolation that the desert provided. The building of the Cairo-Alexandria desert road in 1936 and the rest house at Wâdî 'n-Natrûn have helped to destroy the cherished isolation of the monasteries. With this encroachment of the world on the Desert of Scetis, one may well ask whether the monastic life in the Wâdî 'n-Natrûn may not suffer the same fate as the eremitical settlements in Nitria and Cellia.

Since 1960 the General Desert Development Organization has been cultivating the desert between the Cairo–Alexandria highway and the four monasteries. The cultivated land has been divided into plots of five feddans surrounded by windbreaks and water trenches. Sprinkling irrigation was largely adopted and suitable crops, e.g. castor and alfalfa, were planted. Vegetables, watermelons and tomatoes are also grown. An elaborate system of asphalt roads connect the desert monasteries with each other and the Wâdî 'n-Natrûn rest house. In the early sixties the Supreme Council of Youth Welfare established an international youth camp in front of the gate of Dair Anbâ Bishoî, which has since been abandoned. However, the desert solitude has disappeared. Isolation from the world has been supplanted by a rapidly increasing integration in the life of the church, and, to some extent in the secular world. Pilgrims travelling by cars and buses can reach the monasteries in ninety minutes either from Cairo or Alexandria.

5
DAIR
AL-BARÂMÛS

The Foundation of the Monastery

The earliest settlement in the Desert of Scetis is the Monastery of the Romans, commonly called al-Barâmûs.[1] This is testified by Serapion in his *Vita* of St. Macarius.[2] The history of its foundation is intimately related to the two Roman saints, Maximus and Domitius. According to tradition, these two young princes, sons of the Roman emperor Valentinian,[3] arrived in Scetis, after visiting the Christian shrines in Palestine. In Egypt they met St. Macarius, who served as the priest of the desert.

Palladius, who records their encounter with St. Macarius, does not mention the names of the two princes.[4] At first, feeling that they were too weak for the rough desert life, St. Macarius tried to dissuade them. After a while, however, the two "Little Strangers" had established themselves in their cell, and it was said that the older brother had achieved perfection before he died. Three days later, the younger brother also died, "and whensoever the fathers came to St. Macarius, he used to take them to the cell of those two brethren, and say unto them: 'Behold ye the martyrdom of these Little Strangers'." A year after their death, St. Macarius consecrated the cell of the princes and said: "Call this place the Cell of the Romans." Whether Maximus and Domitius were real characters or whether they were merely legendary figures is a matter of controversy.

It is quite likely that the earliest monastic community in the vicinity of the present location of Dair al-Barâmûs existed in 340. St. Macarius the Egyptian, a disciple of St. Antony, had only recently died when Palladius visited the Desert of Scetis in 391,[5] and we are informed that the saint was thirty when he entered the inner desert, which may have been around 330.

Men who admired and imitated St. Macarius gathered around him, as they gathered round St. Antony by the Red Sea, and thus formed the first monastic community in Scetis.

It is conceivable that St. Antony urged St. Macarius to be ordained to the priesthood so as to be able to celebrate the Divine Liturgy in Scetis. The church and cells may well have been built about 340, for by the time St. Antony died in 356, the community of Scetis was well established.[6]

Heresies and Destructions

The subsequent history of the monastic communities in the Desert of Scetis[7] shows internal and external difficulties. Internally, a variety of doctrinal developments threatened the spiritual harmony of the desert experience. Even during the days of St. Macarius there were heterodox tendencies. Hierax, a monk, asserted that the institution of marriage belonged to the devil and that there was no resurrection of the body, but only of the spirit. Other controversies were more lasting. The Origenist heresy (which preferred allegorical to literal interpretations of the Scriptures) troubled the fathers of Scetis, since the views of Origen were studied[8] and accepted by some of the monks at the mount of Nitria and in Cellia.[9] Another heresy, that of the anthropomorphites, made an even greater impression upon many of the illiterate monks. Their doctrine asserted, in contradiction to Origen's views, that "the sacred Scripture testifies that God has eyes, ears, hands, and feet, as men have." Though denounced by an episcopal letter from Theophilus, the doctrines of the anthropomorphites were not extinguished. The anthropomorphite heresy was so widespread that the anthropomorphists appear to have outnumbered the liberal party by at least three to one.

Internally weakened by heterodoxy and heresy, the monks faced a greater external danger from the Barbarians. These hordes were Berber tribes, who invaded the Desert of Scetis, either from al-Kharga and Dâkhla Oases or from the Oasis of Siwa. St. Macarius had prophesied the devastation of Scetis, saying "that when you see the cells growing in numbers in the valley and when you see trees growing by the gate, when you see numerous children, then take your hide and flee... and it shall be so until the first destruction of Scetis after forty years, because they shall have satisfied their passions. Then again, Christ the King will have pity on them, He will let them return a second time and He will give them these laws and commandments. And they will obey, performing half of the commandments, and this will be until the second destruction of Scetis, because of the grandeur of their luxury. And again Christ the King will let them return for the third time and will give them also these laws and these commandments..."[10]

With the gradual institutionalization of the communities of Scetis, the monks were tempted to compromise and fall into laxity, which by their founders was considered the most pernicious sin. The Coptic *collegia pietatis* harboured the world within its walls. The very purpose of the ascetic ideal was threatened and naturally, according to traditional biblical theology, God was expected to intervene and to punish the offenders. This, according to the Old Testament, God had done before in the case of the Hebrews by using the Babylonians to destroy their capital only to permit them to return under different religious conditions.[11]

The first destruction of Scetis, no doubt involving all four monastic communities,[12] may well have been in the beginning of the fifth century, before 408. The ecclesiastical historian, Philostorgius, reports "that at the time of the Emperor Arcadius (378–408) the Mazices and Auzorians, who dwell between Africa and Libya, flocking in from the eastern parts, devastated Libya, and at the same time overran a considerable portion of Egypt."[13] One of the first martyrs of the Berber invasion was St. Moses the Black, a captain of thieves, as he is referred to by Palladius.[14] An Ethiopian, banished for insubordination, he became a robber, and murderer. After hearing of the ascetes in the Western desert, he decided to join them. He met St. Isidore and St. Macarius and lived a highly ascetic life in spite of constant temptations. Later, he was ordained to the priesthood. In some way he knew beforehand of a possible raid by the Mazices (Berber tribes from the Maghreb), and he warned his disciples, who were seventy in number, advising those who wished to escape to do so. He remained with seven other monks at the community of al-Barâmûs expecting to be martyred so that the saying might be fulfilled that "all they that take the sword shall perish by the sword". Palladius does not say how St. Moses died, which leads one to suppose that the first destruction of Scetis took place after his visit.[15] Two monks who escaped the slaughter of the Berbers, Anbâ Yuhannis Colobus and Anbâ Bishoî, subsequently founded the "central" monastic communities.

Only three or four years after the first devastation, the Berbers struck again. This is attested by Anbâ Arsânîûs who had remained in Scetis during the first destruction of the monasteries: "The world has ruined Rome and the monks of Scetis." This, however, is the only reference that places the second sack of the monasteries in the year 410.[16] Nothing is known about the loss of lives or damage done to the buildings. If destroyed, the monasteries were rapidly rebuilt and reinhabited.

A third sack occurred in 444 when the forty-nine martyrs of Scetis were slain. The monasteries then regained some prosperity, and enjoyed peace and productivity. "This was at the time of the rebuilding of the four monasteries in Wâdî Habîb, which were growing up like the plants of the field in security and guidance from God; and to their inhabitants was brought all that they needed, and they worked industriously at the building."[17] However, the monks were also preoccupied with theological differences. The *History of the Patriarchs* tells of monks referred to as Meletians who received the communion chalice many times in the night before they came to church. Anbâ Damîân (569-605) banished these Meletians.[18]

The monasteries were troubled again when the Berbers invaded the desert of Scetis for the fourth time. Apparently, during the patriarchate of Damîân, "a voice came from heaven upon that desert, saying: 'Flee! Flee!' and when the inhabitants of the four monasteries had left them, they were laid waste. When news of this reached the patriarch Damîân, he was exceedingly sad."

In all of these sacks many, if not all, of the monastic buildings were wrecked, the churches plundered, and the monks either slain or carried off as captives. The fourth raid occurred at the beginning of the reign of Anbâ Damîân, so we can assume that it happened around 570-573. By the beginning of the seventh century the monks had returned to rebuild their devastated communities. When the patriarch Anbâ Banîâmîn I (622-661) consecrated the new Church of Dair Abû Maqâr, he stopped at the Monastery of al-Barâmûs for a day.[19]

The patriarchate of Anbâ Alâksandarûs II (704-729) was a period of hardship for the monks of the Coptic church. 'Abd al-'Azîz ibn Marwân, the amir, ordered a census of the monks. After it was taken he levied a tax of one dinar on each one, the first tribute ever taken from monks, and 'Abd Allah Ibn 'Abd al-Malik ibn Marwân and 'Ubaid Allah ibn al-Hagîb, a commissioner of revenue, added a tax of one qirat to every dinar on the Copts. Maqrîzî writes: "Then again, Usama ibn Zaid at-Tanukhî, commissioner of revenues, oppressed the Christians still more, for he fell upon them, robbed them of their possessions, and branded with an iron ring the name of every monk on the monk's own hand, and the name of his convent, as well as his number; and whosoever of them was found without this brand, had his hand cut off... He then attacked the convents, where he found a number of monks without the brand on their hands, of whom he beheaded some, and others he beat so long that they died under the lash. He then pulled down the churches, broke the crosses, rubbed off the pictures, broke up all the images."[20]

Though the suffering of the Christians in Alexandria and Cairo continued, there is no evidence that the desert monasteries felt a similar strain, and a temporary calm prevailed.

However, during the patriarchate of Anbâ Murqus II (799-819), the monasteries were devastated for the fifth time. "The Arabs plundered it, and took the monks captive, and demolished the churches and the cells there. And the holy seniors were scattered in every part of the world, ... the joy of Egypt had ceased, and Wâdî Habîb, the Holy of the Holies, has become a ruin, the dwelling of wild beasts. The homes of our blessed fathers, who passed their nights in prayer, have become the resort of the owl and the dens of cruel foxes, namely this foul tribe."[21] This event occurred before 819 for the *History of the Patriarchs says:* "Before the decease of the holy father, Anbâ Murqus, the holy desert of Wâdî Habîb had been laid waste ... in consequence of this slaughter, the monks were dispersed among cities and villages and monasteries, in the various provinces of Egypt and the two Thebaids. Thus none was left in the cells of Wâdî Habîb save a few persons who chose death." Maqrîzî agrees but adds that it was part of a general persecution of the Copts: "At the time of Anbâ Murqus there was a fight between al-Amîn and Ma'mûn, then the Christians in Alexandria were pillaged and many of their homes were burnt. Also the monasteries of the Wâdî Habîb were burnt and pillaged, so that only a few monks remained there."[22]

The Monastery of al-Barâmûs shared with the other monasteries of the Desert of Scetis in the reconstruction and building programme during the patriarchates of Anbâ Ya'qûb (Jacob) (819-830) and Anbâ Yûsâb (Joseph) (830-849). At the time of Anbâ Ya'qûb, a bishop named John was ordained for the land of Ethiopia. But when the king of Ethiopia went forth to war, the bishop was driven out. Thereupon, John returned to the Monastery of al-Barâmûs where he had first been a monk. After the war, the king asked the bishop to return and he left the monastery to go back to Ethiopia.[23] This proves that the monastery must have been habitable.

The sixth sack happened during the patriarchate of Anbâ Shenûdah I (859-881). "It was in the eighth year of the patriarchate of this father, and the days of the Holy Fast (Lent) drew near, and he desired to journey to the Holy Desert in the Wâdî Habîb to accomplish the Fast and the Holy Feast of Easter. Some of the faithful counselled him not to go for fear of the marauding Arabs, for it was the time when they came down from Upper Egypt to Lower Egypt, after putting their beasts to grass, lest something should befall him through them... Now the Arabs knew the time when the strangers assembled there... and they took possession of the church of Macarius and of the fortifications and carried off all the furniture and the food and other things which were in them. On the first day of Baramûdah (27 March, 866) the Arabs went to all the monasteries and robbed all those who were in them and the people who came to them, and they drove most of them out at the point of the sword."[24] The courage of Anbâ Shenûdah inspired the monks and in spite of the real danger to life some monks remained in their monasteries and the patriarch conducted the Easter service at Dair Abû Maqâr.

The situation of the monasteries remained precarious. In Alexandria, there lived a man named Madalgah and with him "there were many people of his warrior friends who were known for their courage. When their power had grown strong, they took possession of the lands and all the property of the Church of the Martyr Abû Mînâ at Maryût, and likewise, the property of the Church of St. Macarius and they pillaged them all and devoured their cereals and divided them between them. Then the Bedouins used to lie in wait for the time when the monks went out to draw water, and they slew some of them and took from others what they found on them in the way of clothes and the underskins in which they carried water." Again during the reign of Anbâ Akhristûdulûs (1047-1079) the Lewatis occupied the desert of the Wâdî 'n-Natrûn, pillaging and wrecking the monasteries and killing the monks.[25]

From the Eleventh to the Sixteenth Century

During the patriarchate of Anbâ Shenûdah II, the monks built protecting walls. "The patriarch raised up at the Church of Abû Maqâr an excellent memorial... he resolved to build a fortified wall round the catholic church... he made in it dwelling places and elevated places in the shortest space of time, for he was labouring with the workmen as one of them." The other monasteries also fortified themselves against the Arabs.

The history of Dair al-Barâmûs is similar to that of the other monasteries for the subsequent centuries. Like Dair Abû Maqâr it served as a haven for Christians during the reign of al-Hâkim (996-1021). After the death of Anbâ Shenûdah II in 1047, Anbâ Akhristûdulûs (1047-1077), a monk from the Monastery of al-Barâmûs, was elected to the patriarchate, and according to established custom he proceeded to the Monastery of St. Macarius where he was consecrated. He found the church in a bad state and drew up a series of canons that were designed to restore order.[26] Anbâ Akhristûdulûs' brother, Ya'qûb, became abbot of the Monastery of al-Barâmûs. He performed many miracles and was regarded as a great saint.[27]

The life of the Coptic church under the Fatimids was not always easy. Yazûrî, the Wazîr and Chief Qâdî of al-Mustansir bi'llah (1029-1094), exacted many fines from the Copts on slight pretexts. Anbâ Akhristûdulûs was imprisoned on a false charge for having encouraged the king of Nubia to withhold the yearly tribute.[28] About the same time, the monasteries suffered from an insurrection within the caliph's forces. In 1069, Nasr ad-Dûlah ibn Hamdan, a Turkish leader, had gained the support of the Arabs and Lewatis Berbers who overran the Delta and made havoc of the monasteries of Wâdî Habîb. In 1073, the internal situation in Egypt was restored by the arrival of Badr al-Gemalî who subdued the Lewatis Berbers.

One of the most informative statistics about the monasteries in the eleventh century was preserved by Mawhub ibn Mansûr ibn Mufarrig.[29] He visited the Desert of Scetis in 1088 and recorded that 712 monks inhabited seven monasteries. Of these twenty monks resided in the Monastery of al-Barâmûs.

By this time the Coptic monasteries had attracted wide attention and their isolation and long history became the theme of several poets. One of the great literary figures of the tenth century was Abû 'l-Farag al-Isbahanî (897-966), who was so taken by the monasteries, their inhabitants and the monastic way of life that he wrote about them in his *Book of Songs*.[30] Maqrîzî tells us that the poet Abû 'l-Fath Mahmûd ibn al-Husain, expressed his admiration for the monks' wine and friendly hospitality.[31] Another poet who praised the wine and the intimate atmosphere of the monasteries of that time was Ibn Abû Qasim. Thus, the monasteries experienced a temporary prosperity.

In the middle of the thirteenth century, during the patriarchate of Anbâ Ghabrîâl III (1268-1271), the Monastery of al-Barâmûs was rebuilt. Anbâ Ghabrîâl joined the Monastery of St. Antony at the age of twelve. Later he went to the Desert of Scetis, where he became the "supérieur de l'Eglise de Notre Dame Marie au couvent de Saint Marmos".[32]

The patriarchate of Anbâ Yûânnis VIII (1300-1320) was disturbed by further persecution and destruction. By the order of the amirs, the churches that had existed before the Arab conquest were permitted to remain, but those erected since that period were to be destroyed. Many churches suffered heavy losses, with the exception "of those in the desert of St. Macarius and at Alexandria".[33]

The most severe dangers to the monasteries in the fourteenth century were not persecutions or internal disturbances, but the Black Death and a subsequent famine.

When Maqrîzî was writing, some time between 1419 and 1441, the Desert of Scetis had declined. He notes that previously one hundred monasteries stood in the Wâdî Habîb, of which only seven survived. The Monastery of al-Barâmûs, which he identified with the Monastery of Abû Mûsâ the Black, is mentioned as the seventy-sixth in his list of eighty-six monasteries. Maqrîzî thought that Maximus and Timotheus were the sons of a Greek emperor, educated by Anbâ Arsâniûs. After the death of his two sons, the emperor built the monastery and called it Barâmûs. He describes Abû Mûsâ the Black as a courageous robber who had slain a hundred people. Later he became a Christian and a monk and he wrote many books. He was one of those who passed the whole period of Lent without taking any food.[34]

Seventeenth- and Eighteenth-Century Travellers

The Monastery of al-Barâmûs, though comparatively insignificant in the early Middle Ages, supplied two monks who in the seventeenth century ascended the patriarchal throne: the hundredth patriarch, Anbâ Mattâûs III (1631-1646), and the 102nd patriarch Anbâ Mattâûs IV (1660-1675). The first European visitor in the seventeenth century to mention the Monastery of al-Barâmûs was the French consul, Fr. J. Coppin. He wrote about the monastery in 1638 and called it the "fourth monastery" of those in the desert of St. Macarius Bahr el Malamah, "the Sea of Reproach". The monks told him that when St. Macarius and his monks saw a ship with pirates approaching, they invoked the assistance of God, whereupon the waters of the gulf instantly receded, and everything that was there, including men, animals and the ship, was suddenly petrified.

Fr. Coppin concludes his chapter on the monasteries of the desert of St. Macarius by mentioning an additional monastery, that of Our Lady, which was very large, but slightly ruined.[35] The impression that one gains from Fr. Coppin's description is that by the beginning of the seventeenth century the Monastery of al-Barâmûs was one of the leading, if not the foremost monastery in the Wâdî 'n-Natrûn.[36]

Thévenot, writing in 1657, identifies it with "Dir el Saydet", that is to say, the Monastery of Our Lady. "It is very spacious, but a little ruinous. It hath a fair church and garden, but the water is brackish, and nevertheless, there are more monks in this monastery than in the other three because the revenue of it is greater, and they have some relicks also."[37]

When de Maillet visited Egypt in 1692 and passed by the Monastery of al-Barâmûs he heard the legend the monks had told Fr. Coppin. He wrote about the desert of St. Macarius or the Valley of Bahr bila Mâ', an Arabic term which means "sea without water". All he adds to the picture is that in this arid and desolate desert one finds two or three monasteries apart from the Monastery of St. Zachariah *(sic)*, which are inhabited by Coptic monks. "It is a small number of people that in our days inhabit these once famous monasteries."[38]

In 1710, Fr. du Bernat, S.J., proceeded from the Monastery of the Syrians to that of the Virgin of al-Barâmûs. He informs us that three or four stone throws from the monastery one could discover the sad remains of ten or twelve sacred buildings which were very close to each other, and among which one could still identify the Monastery of Moses the Black and the Church of St. Maximus and Domitius.[39]

The next visitor was Fr. Claude Sicard, S.J. in 1712. On 11 December, after the night office in the Monastery of the Syrians, Fr. Sicard departed for the Monastery of al-Barâmûs. The hegoumenos of the monastery, a young priest, received him. The place was occupied by twelve or fifteen monks, though some of them were laymen who had been admitted by order of the patriarch.[40]

In 1778, C.S. Sonnini, an officer in the French navy, left the village of Honeze for the Wâdî 'n-Natrûn. The first monastery he visited "is called by them Maximous, probably the Saint Maximus of the Catholic Legend."[41] Here Sonnini and his party were attacked by a group of Bedouins who robbed him of all belongings, even undressing him. After long debate and the heroic attitude of his servant, Husain,[42] his property was restored to him. Having overcome the danger of the Arabs, Sonnini and his party underwent a second embarrassment. "They (the monks) could have no doubt of our being Europeans. They pretended, however, not to believe it, and required that one of us should demonstrate to a father sent on purpose as an examiner, that we had not undergone any religious mutilation."[43]

Finally, he was permitted entry to the monastery, which he thought had been formerly inhabited by Greek monks who had been succeeded by Copts. The monastery, which he now identified as Zaidi al-Barâmûs (the Holy Virgin of al-Barâmûs), contained apart from the vaulted, low cells of the monks, a simple church without ornament other than a few ostrich eggs and some badly painted pictures of saints. The religious services were performed in Arabic and Coptic. "Want of occupation had made us devout, we seldom missed attending church." Of the reliquary, he quoted first the Arabs who "like true reprobates allege that the shrine contains only bones of camels and asses that have died in the desert. The monks, on the contrary, maintain that it is the repository of the bodies of seven saints, among whom they most particularly revere two, St. Maximus and St. Domadious." There were only three priests and some friars, but Coptic cultivators came from time to time to do penance... so when he visited there were twenty-three people in the monastery. "They eat in common in a refectory, and one of them reads during the meals." From Zaidi al-Barâmûs, Sonnini took with a compass the position of the building which could be seen from the top of the walls. After spending five days at Dair al-Barâmûs he proceeded to the Monastery of the Syrians.

He was followed by a French general. Count Antoine Andréossy, artillery officer and diplomat, had served as French ambassador in London, Vienna and Constantinople. He went on a military reconnaissance to the monasteries in the Wâdî 'n-Natrûn in January 1799. With military precision he measured the distances between the various monasteries: the distance between the Monastery of al-Barâmûs and that of the Syrians is 9,258 metres. In a general statement he observes that every monastery was enclosed by walls which are thirteen metres high and two and a half to three metres thick at their base.[44]

In 1799, only nine monks lived at the Monastery of al-Barâmûs, while the total number of monks in the Wâdî 'n-Natrûn had slightly increased from under forty in 1712 to fifty-nine.[45]

Nineteenth- and Twentieth-Century Travellers

In 1828, Lord Prudhoe visited the monasteries of the Wâdî 'n-Natrûn in search of Coptic manuscripts. He was shown the library at the Monastery of al-Barâmûs where he selected a number of manuscripts for purchase.[46]

In March 1837, the Honorable Robert Curzon left Cairo and travelled by boat to the village of at-Tarânah, the nearest place on the Nile to the monasteries. He went to Dair al-Barâmûs first: "This monastery consisted of a large stone wall, surrounding a square of about an acre in extent. A large square tower commanded the narrow entrance, which was closed by a low and narrow iron door. Within there was a good-sized church in tolerable preservation... two or three poor looking monks still tenanted the ruins of the abbey. They had hardly anything to offer us, and were glad to partake of some of the rice and other eatables which we had brought with us... we went into the square tower, where, in a large vaulted room with open unglazed windows, were forty or fifty Coptic manuscripts on cotton paper, lying on the floor, to which several of them adhered firmly, not having been moved for many years. I only found one leaf on vellum, which I brought away. The other manuscripts appeared to be all liturgies; most of them smelling of incense when I opened them, and well smeared with dirt and wax from the candles..."[47]

Dr. Tattam visited the Monastery of al-Barâmûs, in January 1839. He found one hundred Coptic and Arabic liturgies, and a large dictionary in both languages. "In the tower is an apartment, with a trap door in the floor, opening into a dark hole full of loose leaves of Arabic and Coptic liturgies. The superior of this monastery is a fine old man, exceedingly obliging, and would have sold the large selim, but dare not on account of the patriarch's having written in it a curse upon any one who should take it away. There was no person in the monastery who could write Coptic, or they would have copied it for Dr. Tattam, but they said that if he could obtain the Patriarch's consent, he should have the book itself. They also stated that some time since, a European who visited their monastery, had made such a strenuous attempt to obtain possession of it, that they were now almost afraid to show it to travellers."[48]

When Sir Gardner Wilkinson travelled to the Wâdî 'n-Natrûn in 1842, the Monastery of al-Barâmûs was inhabited by only seven monks.[49] That year a monk entered the monastery who some thirty years later was to become the 112th patriarch. Anbâ Kîrillus V had previously gone to the

Monastery of the Syrians, where he had stayed for only a few days. Then, at the age of twenty, he joined the Monastery of al-Barâmûs and after a month he became a monk. Only three other monks inhabited the monastery.[50] In 1844, he was called to become a parish priest in Cairo, but he soon returned to the monastery, where he was elected hegoumenos. During his time at the monastery the number of monks increased to thirty. He founded theological schools at Dair al-Barâmûs, Dair Anbâ Antûnîûs and Dair al-Muharraq, and he did much to further the study of the Coptic language.

Konstantin von Tischendorf visited the Monastery of al-Barâmûs at the end of his tour of the monasteries of the Wâdî 'n-Natrûn. When he called there he found twenty monks. "Here the cells were the blackest of all. The superior here had a peculiar custom; he sat beside me in the cell, and as often as a pause was made in the conversation, he interposed the formula of welcome, Salam, Salam, and repeated the pantomime of his hands. What I inquired for, and everywhere in vain, was manuscript accounts of the history of the monastery. But not a line of such a record was known. Thus they live carelessly from day to day. To such an existence, what is the past and what is the future?"[51]

On 23 November, 1875, Dr. Wilhelm Junkers stopped at the Monastery of al-Barâmûs where he was very politely received, though some of the questions of the monks appeared to him rather incoherent.[52]

One of the first travel guides to advise tourists to visit the monasteries of Wâdî 'n-Natrûn was Murray's *Handbook for Travellers in Lower and Upper Egypt* (1880). After dealing with the other three monasteries, Murray continues: "A ride of two hours from Deyr es Syrian brings us to Deyr Barâmûs, a large convent, for which an antiquity of sixteen hundred years is claimed. It boasts four churches, and one monk (in 1874), who was an Abyssinian."

Travelling from Bûlâq ad-Dakrûr via Kafr Dâûd, Fr. Michel Jullien, S.J., with priests Eugéne Nourrit, Joseph Noory and Jean Palamarie, arrived in 1881 at the monastery. Two monks, Abûnâ Girgis and Abûnâ Sulaimân had joined the group at Kafr Dâûd and led the way to the desert monasteries. The hegoumenos of the monastery, Abûnâ 'Abd al-Masîh, welcomed the missionaries and the traditional hospitality was extended to them.[53] The monastery was inhabited by twenty monks of whom four were priests. Fr. Jullien was shown around the monastery, and churches. In the Church of al-'Adhrâ he saw about a hundred books, most of them in Arabic and Coptic, the majority having been printed by Protestant agencies in London, New York or Beirut. Then they visited the refectory, which appeared to be the most ancient part of the monastery. He engaged in a religious conference and tried to persuade the Coptic monks to understand their "faulty schismatic doctrines". On their way from the Monastery of al-Barâmûs to that of the Syrians, they saw gazelles, the traces of desert wolves, and the footprints of an ostrich.[54] In 1883, Alfred J. Butler visited the Monastery of al-Barâmûs coming from the Monastery of Anbâ Bishoî. "Our guide and herald, deputed by the patriarch, had gone on some way before us: and when, on mounting the last ridge, we sighted the monastery, dark figures were faintly visible upon the distant parapets. As we neared, the monks descended, and stood grouped in clear relief outside, under the white walls of their fortress. When we were within two hundred yards of the gate, the monks advanced towards us with waving banners. They kissed our hands as we dismounted: then formed a procession in front of us, and advanced chanting psalms and beating cymbals and triangles, while the great bell of the convent clashed out a tumultuous welcome.[55] The service of welcome was conducted in the church dedicated to al-Barâmûs, a name of which the origin is uncertain. Unfortunately, a restoration not quite finished had stripped the church of every single feature of interest, and apparently changed even the old lines of the building... There is, however, a fine ancient church still remaining, though not undamaged by the whitewash, in which the monastery rejoices."[56] Attached to the Church of the Blessed Virgin Mary, Butler describes two chapels, dedicated to Mârî Girgis (St. George) and al-Amîr Tadrûs (St. Theodore the General). The former lies to the west of the main church, while the latter opens out of the middle of the north aisle which it adjoins. In the Chapel of the Archangel Michael, "lies a pile of loose leaves of manuscripts, which cover nearly half the floor of the chapel to a depth of about two feet: and here I thought at last was a real chance of undiscovered treasure. So I spent some hours in digging among the pile, in choking and blinding dust; armful after armful was taken up, searched, sifted, and rejected. Here and there a tiny fragment of early Syriac, Coptic, or even Greek on vellum, half a leaf of a Coptic and Ethiopic lexicon; several shreds of Coptic and Arabic lexicons; countless pages of medieval Coptic or Copto-Arabic liturgies: this was the only result of the most diligent search, and the quest ended in final disappointment. The monks were very good-natured, allowing me to take away my little pieces of worthless paper as memorials of my visit, but declining with courteous firmness to give or sell the whole collection of rubbish; for they required the leaves, they told me, to bind their new books, and all the paper in Cairo would not answer their purpose so well." After that, Butler conversed with the kindly old hegoumenos who was in special distress because the Lay Council in Cairo had threatened to sequestrate the revenues of the monastery and to administer the estates as a sort of ecclesiastical commission. Generally speaking, the monastery appeared to be cleaner than the others. It was inhabited by about twenty-five monks, the number that Huntington had found there two centuries before.

In 1892, Anbâ Kîrillus V, wishing to have the sole administration over the Coptic church, attempted to abolish the church council, the Maglis al-Millî, elected by members of the Coptic church, which had been authorized by *décret-loi* in 1883. The members of the Maglis al-Millî signed a petition requesting the government to intervene. The patriarch was exiled to Dair al-Barâmûs, and the bishop of Sanabû accepted to act as *locum tenens* in the absence of the patriarch. He engaged the services of the Maglis al-Millî, whereupon he was excommunicated by the patriarch. Upon the intervention of Butrus Ghâlî Pasha, a person of note in the Coptic church, the situation was resolved. The functions of the Maglis al-Millî were modified, and the bishops petitioned the khedive Abbas II, for the return of the patriarch. He returned on 9 January, 1893, after six months' exile.

During the last decade of the nineteenth century, the Monastery of al-Barâmûs was the scene of internal disturbance. Naoum, a Syrian monk, was ordained hegoumenos of the monastery, and later, on 17 October, 1897, bishop. Known as Anbâ Isîdûrûs, he was excommunicated by Anbâ Kîrillus V on 31 December, 1897 for insubordination. Isidore was an industrious scholar who published twenty-five books on Coptic theology, pastoral theology and history, though many of his volumes bear the marks of an apology which was not critical and which was full of prejudice.[57] In 1927, he published the Canons of Ibn al-'Assâl and Kîrillus III. At the beginning of 1941, he submitted a petition to Anbâ Yûânnis XIX, begging him to forgive him, and in March of that year, with the help of Abûnâ Dâûd al-Maqârî, he obtained absolution from the patriarch.

Another monk engaged in theological studies at the Monastery of al-Barâmûs was 'Abd al-Masîh ibn Girgis al-Mas'udî who, having entered Dair al-Muharraq, joined the Monastery of al-Barâmûs at a later date. 'Abd al-Masîh was the author of works on Coptic dogmatics and of a diatribe directed against the Protestants. He should not be confused with two other monks who were theological writers and who happen to bear the same name.[58]

In March 1904, Agnes Smith Lewis and Margaret Dunlop Gibson visited the Monastery of al-Barâmûs which they considered much cleaner and in better order than the other monasteries they had seen. They also gained the impression that it was visited much more frequently by foreigners, which made them believe that they may not have been the first women to visit this monastery.[59]

During the last few days of June 1905, the Kaufmann expedition arrived in the vicinity of the desert monasteries. The first monastery they reached was that of al-Barâmûs. "A few hundred yards in front of the monastery we made a brief halt in order to load our guns, a proceeding which resulted in a curious misunderstanding. The guards of the monastery had long spied us through a loop-hole in the battlements, and the proceedings with the guns aroused suspicion."[60] After J.C.E. Falls handed his card to the monks and surrendered his weapons, the party was hospitably received. They were informed that no stranger ever came to the monastery in summer. Apparently, the preliminaries before entering the monastery were dictated by prudence and the fact that a few weeks before, an Arab had shot a monk. "Of the thirty monks who inhabited the little town formed by a chaos of houses, cells, chapels, and corridors, some at least understand a little of another tongue besides Arabic, the chief priest or abbot, Anbâ Ghabriâl, knows Coptic pretty well, and was not a little proud when his knowledge of Greek and Coptic manuscripts was proved by the monks."

Durning their survey of the monastery they were taken to the remains of the once valuable library and, towards the evening, a bath was prepared.

The three-storied outer-wall supported by lofty pillars was apparently 170 paces long, and almost as broad. Falls visited the qasr with its many chambers and subterranean cells. Very little remained of the mass of fragments of manuscripts which Butler had seen in one of the adjoining chambers. The expedition was told about an anchorite who lived within the monastery walls. "A quietist in the stillness! A sage amid the unrest of the desert! A talented saint in the company of careless, thoughtless monks! An aspiring character and yet without ambition, a personality, a recluse, a noble man!"

In the Church of al-'Adhrâ, Falls saw the reliquary of the two saints, Maximus and Domitius, who he thought were the sons of Emperor Leontius. He mentions the valuable treasure of the monastery, an amphora containing a wine fifty years old, some of which was offered to the guests. In the same room was kept the Holy Myron (Chrism), concealed in a niche in the wall. After inspecting all points of interest, the members of the expedition departed from the monastery in the direction of Dair as-Suriân.

In 1909 and 1910, and again in 1910 and 1911, the Metropolitan Museum of Art Egyptian Expedition commissioned W.J. Palmer-Jones to spend several weeks in the monasteries of the Wâdî 'n-Natrûn to make plans of buildings and supplement the same by drawings and photographs.[61]

In 1912, Jean Brémond went on a pilgrimage to the monasteries of the Wâdî 'n-Natrûn. Coming from Alexandria, he got off the train at Tiyâ 'l-Barûd to change for Khatâtba. In the wâdî, he was the guest of Debourg, director general of the Egyptian Salt and Soda Company. Quoting figures from 1910, he informs us that the Wâdî 'n-Natrûn was inhabited by 763 people, of whom 61 were able to read and to write; 672 were Muslims, 64

Copts, 19 Catholics and 8 Protestants.[62]

Brémond visited al-Barâmûs first, and noticed the new episcopal residence, built by the Bishop of Alexandria, Mgr. Yûânnis. The style of this building resembled that of the new bourgeois homes of the Egyptians. Brémond wrongly concluded that the monastery belonged to the See of Alexandria, and that the bishop visited the monastery to enjoy the clean air of the desert. The monks showed Brémond around the monastery and he compared his observations with those of Fr. Sicard and Fr. Jullien. Brémond's booklet makes interesting reading though it is difficult to date his visit.

In October 1913, Johann Georg, visited the desert monasteries of the Wâdî 'n-Natrûn. The party, consisting of Marcus Simaika, the Reverend Dr. Karge and the duke, travelled by train from Cairo to Khatâtba. Here they changed for a special train of the Salt and Soda Company that took them to Bîr Hooker. The duke was seemingly impressed and moved by the ecclesiastical pomp with which the monks of al-Barâmûs welcomed him. He noticed some building and reconstruction activity. His view of the renovation of the main church is critical: "The haikal has been decorated in an ugly manner, purple and pink. It is inexplicable to me, how it is possible to create such a monstrosity." The duke refers to the library as a "mere collection of books". There were almost no manuscripts, and those which were there, were of little or no value. Apart from the main church, he visited the ancient church, which he thought contained some interesting things. He noticed the beautifully carved haikal doors and some capitals. The refectory, which he assigned to the seventh century, seemed more like a prison than a dining hall. Though he saw bread in the dining-hall, he did not taste it. Then he was shown a bell with the names of the four evangelists engraved in Gothic, which he identified as belonging to the end of the fifteenth century.[63]

In 1920, Hugh Evelyn White, H. Burton and W. Hauser went several times for many weeks to the Wâdî 'n-Natrûn monasteries to complete the work of the Metropolitan Museum of Art Egyptian Expedition begun by Palmer-Jones. They supplemented the collection with drawings and photographs of the monastery, and gathered the material that a few years later was published by Evelyn White.[64]

In 1923, Dr. William Hatch visited the Monastery of al-Barâmûs with his Arab servant 'Abduh. His impressions were favourable. It was the most prosperous and well-kept monastery of the Wâdî 'n-Natrûn group, and thirty monks were living there. The hegoumenos, Cyril, welcomed Hatch cordially and invited him to remain in the monastery for several days. The library was clean and well-arranged and he saw many Coptic and Arabic manuscripts, as well as a number of printed books. "There were no loose leaves lying about to be had for the asking, and I was obliged to leave al-Barâmûs with no souvenir of my visit except the memory of a pleasant day."[65]

Johann Georg's second visit took place fifteen years after his first venture into the Desert of Scetis. He was presented with an initial from a fifteenth-century document. The bell, which had caught his attention in 1912, was still there, and he decided it had once belonged to a Franciscan church.[66]

In the spring of 1930 and 1931, Prince 'Umar Tûssûn visited the Wâdî 'n-Natrûn with Professor Breccia and Dr. Puy-Haubert. He wanted to substantiate the wide studies of the history of the desert monasteries which he published in 1931 under the title *Etude sur le Wadi Natroun, ses moines et ses convents.* This work was the third of its kind, after Professor F. Larsow's historical treatment of the desert monasteries which prefaced the *Festal Letters of St. Athanasius* (1852), and Evelyn White's book. The prince's information is revealing. From the following statistical study it is obvious that the Monastery of al-Barâmûs was the wealthiest monastery in the desert of the Wâdî 'n-Natrûn, at least in terms of real estate. The property of the four monasteries in the Wâdî 'n-Natrûn according to the figures given to the prince by the patriarch was as follows:[67]

The Monastery of Abû Maqâr .... 145 feddans
The Monastery of Anbâ Bishoî .... 106 feddans
The Monastery of the Syrians .... 134 feddans
The Monastery of al-Barâmûs .... 244 feddans

In addition to the land owned by the respective monasteries, they all owned houses in towns and cities from which they collected the rent.

In 1931, Mary Rowlatt set out to visit the desert monasteries in the Wâdî 'n-Natrûn. In her delightful narrative, *A Family in Egypt,* she describes in detail the difficulties of the car journey that took her two days from Cairo, a distance that can be easily covered now within two hours. "We did the last bit on foot, as both cars had stuck, so we approached the first monastery in absolute silence. And the silence of the desert can be absolute; the only live things in view were a few swallows which circled round our heads, swooping forth and back again in great curiosity. On arrival we clanged the great bell in a whitewashed tower above us and waited. Eventually a young bearded monk opened a postern gate and welcomed us."

In its sessions from 1933-1935 the *Comité des Monuments de l'Art Arabe* commissioned its architect, Edmond Pauty, to visit the four monasteries in the Wâdî 'n-Natrûn, and to study them from an architectural and archaeological point of view. In the *Bulletin de la Société d'Archéologie Copte,* VII, Pauty briefly describes some of the architectural characteristics of the four monasteries, beginning with Dair Abû Maqâr which he considers to be in good condition. He observed that the cells and the common rooms had been recently restored. Following the description of the Monastery of St. Macarius are studies of Dair Anbâ Bishoî, Dair al-Barâmûs and Dair as-Surîân.

The role of the Monastery of al-Barâmûs from the seventeenth century onwards was insignificant. External violence, as mentioned by Sonnini, may have been one of the reasons for its decay. Only six of the 116 patriarchs came from the Monastery of al-Barâmûs.[68] By the end of the nineteenth century, however, partly due to the influence of Anbâ Kîrillus V, the situation had changed. The monastery advanced in material wealth and prosperity and the monks replaced some of the ancient buildings with new Levantine structures. One of these new Levantine, half French-looking houses is well described by H.V. Morton in *Through Lands of the Bible.* Morton, who visited the Monastery of al-Barâmûs in 1937, informs us that he was impressed not only by the strength of the wall "but also by the vast archway which formed so strange a contrast to the gate itself. The archway was made for giants, but the gate for dwarfs."[69] At the time of his visit the monastery was inhabited by thirty-five monks.

The Monastery Today

The monastery has four churches. The Church of the Holy Virgin (al-'Adhrâ) is so entangled in a maze of structures that it is difficult to see anything but its roof. The church was renovated and replastered in 1986. To the north of the nave near the western end is the Church of St. Theodore the General (al-Amîr Tâdrus), and in the west is the baptistry. Only two of the four monasteries, Dair Anbâ Bishoî and Dair al-Barâmûs, have baptistries. Added on to the west of the Church of al-'Adhrâ is the Chapel of St. George (Mârî Girgis). At the north wall of the Church of al-'Adhrâ is a new (1957) ivory inlaid feretory with glass windows which contains the bodies of St. Moses the Black and St. Isidore. A dedication plaque states that the feretory was a gift of Anbâ Banîâmîn, metropolitan of Manûfîah. The ancient feretory stands vacant on the south side of the church. The bodies of SS. Maximus and Domitius are said to be buried under the central haikal. Fr. Jullien was told that the remains of the two saints were buried under the floor of the left aisle. The Church of al-'Adhrâ has altogether three haikals which show elements of widely different periods, some as old as the ninth century, while other parts show Fatimid influence. The church is decorated with a number of icons representing Anbâ Antûnîûs and Anbâ Bûlâ; Abû Nofar (St. Onuphrius); SS. Maximus and Domitius; Anbâ Abullû, Anbâ Abîb and Anbâ Barsûm; Anbâ Kîrillus and the Holy Virgin.

The Chapel of St. Theodore the General (al-Amîr Tadrûs) is entered from the nave of the main church. Its interior is dark and it is no longer used for services. The haikal was once used as a store room for salt. The Chapel of St. George (Mârî Girgis) is entered from the west end of the north aisle. It is not used for services. As at Dair Anbâ Bishoî, the baptistry adjoins the north-east corner of the church. Recently (1957-58), a window was cut in the west wall of the baptistry to admit some light to the room.

At the time of Butler's visit to the monastery in 1883, the Church of St. John the Baptist was not quite completed. This church was built by Anbâ Kîrillus V. The south haikal used to shelter a neatly arranged and classified library. The style of the building is hybrid and the predominant colour is light blue. This church was renovated in January 1981.

The qasr has three storeys. The uppermost storey is occupied by the Church of St. Michael. The walls have evidently been replastered recently and the manuscripts Butler saw have all been taken away. The little room on the roof was once inhabited temporarily by Abûnâ Sarâbâmûn, who also lived as a solitary in a cave about thirty minutes distant from the monastery, which he visited at certain times such as Holy Week, when he used the cell in the qasr. He was very practical: when the machine-pump in the north-west corner of the garden broke down sometime in 1920, the only one capable of repairing it was Abûnâ Sarâbâmûn.

This abode seems to have attracted a number of solitaries. When A.F. Kersting visited the Wâdî 'n-Natrûn monasteries in or around 1949, his attention was caught by an Ethiopian solitary in the qasr, who had lived in solitude for twelve years. He had neither spoken to nor seen anybody during this period.

The walls around the monastery are ten to eleven metres high, and about two metres thick. One has a magnificent view from the top of the walls, both of the interior of the monastery and of the vastness of the desert.

The refectory, which is not used at present, is parallel to the main church. At the time of Sonnini's visit, meals were still eaten in the refectory, and the stone lectern with its roughly incised cross was also still in use. Next to the refectory stands an oil-press and a wine-press.

The guest house is a nineteenth-century Levantine villa which is comfortably furnished. A number of portraits decorate the reception hall: Anbâ Athânâsîûs, metropolitan of Banî Suîf; Anbâ Murqus, metropolitan of Abû Tîg; Anbâ Sâwîrûs, metropolitan of Minya; Anbâ Banîâmîn, metropolitan of Manûfîah; Anbâ Tûmâ, the late metropolitan of Tantâ; Anbâ Makârîûs, bishop of the Monastery of al-Barâmûs, and Abûnâ Bârnâba (Barnabas), at one time hegoumenos of the Monastery of al-Barâmûs.

The library, housed first in the qasr, and later in the south haikal of the Church of St. John the Baptist, has been transferred to a room on the first floor in the eastern part of the monastery. The library contains approximately three thousand volumes which are kept in several cabinets neatly arranged, according to subjects: ritual, theological, hagiographical, biblical, exegetical, medical, legal, mathematical, engineering, etc. The classification of the library was the work of the famous Abûnâ 'Abd al-Masîh ibn Salîb al-Barâmûsî who was known throughout the Wâdî' 'n-Natrûn for his great learning. It is said that, besides Arabic and Coptic, he knew Hebrew, Syriac, Greek and Latin, and had a reading knowledge of English and French. He died in 1940 at the age of seventy.

The high water tower was completed in 1959. Since the enthronement of Pope Shenûdah III in 1971 the monastery has undergone several internal renovations. Within the old walls, an additional row of monastic cells, storage rooms for provisions from the monastic dependency, and a pharmacy have been built. Inside the gate there is a kiosk selling souvenirs, devotional prints, medals and leather crosses. The new iconography in the chapels of St. George and St. Michael is the work of Abûnâ Kîrillus al-Barâmûsî, who follows the neo-Coptic style of Professor Ishaq Fanûs.

Outside the old walls, an area of two feddans is being cultivated. The impressive building to the left serves as residence and chapel of Bishop Arsânîûs (1982). The entrance to the new compound is marked by miniature copies of the two bell–towers of the monastery. The improvements include two guest houses for spiritual retreats (1981), six water pumps that provide sufficient water for the monastery and the new buildings, a sheepfold, a henhouse and two new generators. The macadamized road from the highway through the desert to the monastery was completed in 1985.

Under the leadership of Anbâ Arsânîûs, the bishop of the monastery, the number of monks has steadily increased. Twenty monks belonged to the monastery in 1960 and forty-six in 1970, while in 1986 there were eighty-three monks, of whom fifty live in the monastery, while thirty-three serve as parish priests in Egypt and overseas.[70] The amîn ad-dair is Qummus Abraam, the guest father Abûnâ 'Abd al-Masîh and the librarian Abûnâ Augustinus. Abûnâ Lûqâ and Abûnâ Ghobrîâl are in charge of the medical clinic.[71]

The Caves around Dair al–Barâmûs

Anchoritic life in the caves around the monastery experienced a twentieth-century revival through the extreme asceticism of the Ethiopian Abûnâ 'Abd al-Masîh al-Habashî, who for thirty-five years (1935-1970) inhabited a cave four and a half kilometres west of the monastery. He died in Jerusalem in 1973. He inspired Abûnâ Mînâ al-Muttawahad al-Baramûsî, the late Pope Kîrillus VI; Abûnâ Antûnîûs al-Surîânî, the present Pope Shenûdah III; Abûnâ Mattâ al-Maskîn and numerous other monks, who in the meantime serve as bishops and metropolitans.[72]

The limestone cave of the late Pope Kîrillus VI, known as the Rock of Sarabâmûn, about two and a half kilometres north-west of the monastery, has become a popular place of pilgrimage. The site is marked by twelve elevated wooden crosses. The interior of the spacious one-room cave is adorned with numerous icons and pictures of the wonder-working pope and his patron saint Abû Mînâ of Maryût. Various votive-offerings and an Arabic New Testament are found in the cave.

In the desert around the monastery are several caves inhabited by hermits. The distance of these caves from the monastery varies between five and ten kilometres. Some caves are situated in the Bahr el-Faregh.

6

DAIR
ABÛ MAQÂR

St. Macarius and the Foundation of the Monastery

The foundation of Dair Abû Maqâr (the Monastery of St. Macarius) is closely associated with the life of one of the greatest desert fathers of the Coptic church, St. Macarius the Great (Abû Maqâr). The story of his life is told in the *Vita Macarii* by Serapion, the fourth-century bishop of Thmuis, who claims to have been a disciple of St. Antony and a friend of St. Macarius. With St. Macarius the Great the real history of the monastic life in the Desert of Scetis commences. St. Macarius died only a short time before Palladius visited Scetis in 390.[1] He is believed to have been about ninety years old when he died, which would place his birth at about 300.

The saint of Scetis was the son of a village priest. His parents' property was confiscated, and St. Macarius was born into poverty. He learned the Scriptures and was ordained a reader. As was the custom, his parents decided he should marry, but St. Macarius avoided associating with his wife because of his high esteem for virginity. He earned a subsistence by going out with the caravans to the desert of Natrûn to fetch salt. On one occasion the caravan camped in the vicinity of the wâdî, which was to become his future abode. While he was asleep he had a vision, in which an angel promised that his followers would inhabit that land. On his return home, his wife was stricken with a fever, and died soon afterwards.

After distributing his possessions among the poor, St. Macarius settled as a solitary near a neighbouring village. A girl from this village accused St. Macarius of seducing her, whereupon the villagers hung sooty pots and pans around his neck and beat him, saying: "This monk has seduced our

72

daughter." The girl bore a child, but confessed then that another man was the father. St. Macarius' reputation was restored, and the people began to revere him for the way in which he had borne the false accusation so meekly. This experience led him to the inner Desert of Scetis, where, at that time, no ascetics had settled. He became the pioneer of the settlement which was to produce so many saints in the centuries that followed. His first settlement was in the vicinity of the present Monastery of al-Barâmûs. It was here that St. Macarius gave guidance and counsel to the two "Little Strangers" from overseas, Maximus and Domitius.

After the death of the Roman princes, St. Macarius was led by an angel to a rock south of the wâdî, and the angel said unto him: "Begin to make for thyself a dwelling at this place, and build a church, for certainly after a while, a number of people will inhabit this place." This church, with the cells around it, forms the nucleus of the present monastery. However, although a community of monks grew up around him, St. Macarius lived as an anchorite.

In 374 the emperor Valens[2] expelled the Orthodox from Alexandria and the rest of Egypt, and St. Macarius was banished to an island.[3] A few years later, he returned to the Desert of Scetis. Serapion relates that at the death of the saint, "the monks came from their cells and threw themselves upon his holy body ... and placed his holy body in a cave near the church which he had built." Though he had instructed his disciples to hide his body, "people from Chechouir, his country, came and gave to his disciple, John, the gold which he was forbidden to love, and he showed them the tomb of the saint. They took him to the town and built a church in his memory, where he remained buried for about 170 years, (probably 270 years) until the time of the domination of the Arabs. As to his disciple John, because of his love for wealth, he was attacked by elephantiasis after the death of our father Macarius."[4]

Macarius was succeeded by Paphnutius. Anbâ Bishoî, in his *Life of the Greek Saints Maximus and Domitius,* writes: "Abba Paphnutius, the disciple of Abba Macarius, became the father of Scetis after him..." Serapion regards Paphnutius as the greatest of Macarius's disciples. The monks called the hegoumenos of Dair Abû Maqâr the father of Scetis. Abba Paphnutius, born between 301 and 311, was a follower of St. Antony, and retired to the desert. He could expound the Old and the New Testaments without reading from them.

Anbâ Kîrillus, the twenty-fourth patriarch, lived in the monasteries in the desert of St. Macarius for five years, reading the books of the Old and New Testaments to Anbâ Tawfîlus (Theophilus) (385-412).[5]

The monastic communities of Scetis suffered severely from three attacks by hordes of Berbers in the first half of the fifth century. The third sack of the monasteries is associated with the martyrdom of the forty-nine monks of Abû Maqâr. The monks of the monastery, who consider themselves the custodians of the spirit of perseverance and of the relics of the forty-nine Martyrs, relate the following story which occurred in 444: One of the monks, Anbâ Yûânnis, invited the others to share the glories of martyrdom. Some of the fathers withdrew to the keep,[6] but others gladly submitted to the swords of the invading Berbers. A courier had been sent by the king[7] to ask the monks to pray for the presumptive heir. As the visitor witnessed the bloody massacre, he was overcome by a vision in which he saw angels taking the souls of the martyrs to heaven. Thereupon he decided to join the martyrs.

When the Berbers completed their devastations, they moved on to the Monastery of St. Bishoî where they washed the blood from their swords. Thus the water of the well was blessed by the blood of the martyrs, and people who drank from it were relieved from diseases and suffering. The monks who escaped the massacre took the martyrs and buried them in a cave near the monastery. Later the bodies were moved to the Church of St. Macarius.

Anbâ Daniâl was taken prisoner by the Berbers three times. Once he was ransomed. The second time he escaped. The third time he killed his captor. His administrative qualities led him to be elected hegoumenos of the Monastery of St. Macarius at a time when the emperor Justinian was attempting to impose the "Tome of Leo"[8] upon the monks of Scetis. Anbâ Daniâl resisted this, was driven from the monastery, and found refuge at Tambuk, a village in the Delta. After the death of Justinian in 565, the saint returned to his monastery.

The desert monks were easy prey for the Berbers, and the Monastery of St. Macarius, along with the other monasteries of Scetis, suffered a fourth attack around 570.[9] The monks scattered. Abûnâ Tawdrûs (Theodorus) fled to Terenuthis, Abûnâ Irenaeus to Gaza, and Abûnâ Mârkallûs (Marcellus) who had remained in Scetis was sold into slavery in the Pentapolis.

The Council of Chalcedon and the Story of St. Hilaria

To understand why the Church of Egypt separated from the rest of the Christian world, we must retrace some of the steps that led to this tragic schism. The decision of the Council of Chalcedon in 451 forced the Egyptian church to withdraw from the rest of Christendom. In 448 Eutyches (380-456), archimandrite of a monastery in the vicinity of

Constantinople, had been deposed by Flavian, the patriarch of Constantinople, because of his zealous adherence to the doctrines of Apollinarius. Eutyches denied that the manhood of Christ was consubstantial with ours, a view which went far towards rendering our redemption through Him impossible. He also maintained that there were "Two Natures before, but only One after the Union" in the Incarnate Christ. A council was called to meet at Ephesus in 449. Here Chrysaphius, the all-powerful eunuch of the palace of Theodosius II, was determined to put matters right with the help of his supporter Dioscorus, patriarch of Alexandria (444-454). Eutyches was temporarily reinstated and Flavian, Eusebius and Domnus, who were his chief opponents, were deposed. The proceedings of this assembly, however, were so disgraceful that the council has been nicknamed Latrocinium or "the robbers' council".[10] For the time being, however, the faith of Egypt prevailed. On the death of Emperor Theodosius II, his sister Pulcheria ascended to the imperial throne, and having executed Chrysaphius without legal trial, she gave her hand to Marcian (450-457) who displayed great zeal for the imperial cause.

In 451 another council was held at Chalcedon. From the very beginning Anbâ Disqûrus (Dioscorus) was treated as if he were on trial. The council's deliberations resulted in a condemnation of Eutyches and the patriarch Dioscorus was deposed, not for heresy, but because, though thrice summoned to appear at the council, he refused to attend. Later, Eutyches himself was excommunicated by the Egyptian church for his erroneous beliefs.

To what an extent the monks at Scetis were troubled by the theological debates across the sea is difficult to determine. The story of one of the "woman monks,"[11] Hilaria, the eldest daughter of Emperor Zeno (474-491), serves as a link between Chalcedon and the Monastery of Abû Maqâr. In 482 Zeno published his *Henoticon* or "Instrument of Union". Addressing the "monks and laity throughout Alexandria, Egypt, Libya and Pentapolis" he sought compromise.[12]

Profoundly influenced by the martyrdom of the forty-nine fathers of Scetis, St. Hilaria decided to enter the monastic life herself. Disguised as a courier she travelled to Alexandria, and from there to Scetis, where she was met by Anbâ Banfu (Pambo). She was admitted to the monastery, and was assigned to a cell. Because of feminine characteristics (she had no beard) she soon became known as Hilary the Eunuch. In the meantime, her younger sister fell ill, and her father determined that she should travel to Egypt to visit Hilary. When the princess and her company arrived in the desert, Hilary the Eunuch was called and her sister was miraculously cured. She returned to Constantinople, and Zeno became much interested in the work of the monks at Scetis. Zeno suffered from heart trouble, and could not undertake the long journey to Egypt, but asked if Hilary might be sent to him. Still disguised as a monk, Hilary went to Constantinople and was introduced to the emperor who asked why he had kissed the princess and shared his bed with her. St. Hilaria realized the serious predicament in which she was placed and disclosed her real identity to her father, requesting him to keep it secret. Out of gratitude for the healing of his younger daughter, the emperor issued an edict "in favour of the monks of Scetis, granting to them each year 3,000 ardebs of wheat for the sacrifice of his daughter and six hundred measures of oil".[13] Maqrîzî[14] reports that Zeno "brought every year to the convent of Bû Maqâr what was wanted of corn and oil for the maintenance of those who lived in it."[15]

In the *Synaxarium*, the Coptic church commemorates Anbâ Yûânnis, the twenty-ninth patriarch, who, much impressed by Zeno, accepted the *Henoticon*, and re-established communion with the See of Antioch. Zeno sent vessels of corn, wine and oil and many riches to satisfy the needs of the monks of Abû Maqâr.[16]

The Centre of Ecclesiastical Prestige

The Monastery of Abû Maqâr gained great importance during the middle of the sixth century, when it became the official residence of the Coptic patriarchs of Alexandria. Maqrîzî reports the events leading up to the emigration of the Copts to the Monastery of Abû Maqâr. The Copts were still in control of the Alexandrian See, when Justinian, dissatisfied with the situation, summoned one of his governors, Apollinarius, and his Melkite troops to Alexandria. When Apollinarius arrived at the church in Alexandria he changed his military uniform, and put on the robes of a patriarch and conducted a service. The people, armed with stones, compelled him to withdraw. Then he collected his forces and pressed the inhabitants of Alexandria to accept the decisions of the Council of Chalcedon. "O citizens of Alexandria, leave the teachings of the Jacobites, if not, I fear the emperor will kill you and confiscate your belongings and your wives." But the people were ready to stone him. He notified his troops, and two hundred thousand people were killed. Many people escaped to the monasteries of the Wâdî Habîb. The Melkites occupied the churches of the Copts, and the seat of the patriarch was moved to the Monastery of Abû Maqâr.[17] It is difficult to ascertain if the patriarchs lived at Dair Abû Maqâr continuously as early as the sixth century.

The rebuilt monasteries of Scetis were consecrated after the widespread devastations of the fourth Berber raid. The original Church of Abû Maqâr was abandoned, and a new church was built where the Church of Abû Maqâr now stands. A delegation of monks from Dair Abû Maqâr came on the day of the Nativity to Alexandria to request Patriarch Anbâ

Banîâmîn I (622-661) to consecrate their new church in the monastery. On his arrival, he was received by the young monks with palm branches in their hands, while the older monks "chanting like angels" carried smoking censers in their hands. During the rite of consecration the patriarch saw a vision of a seraph and of St. Macarius. Then he marked the sanctuary with the chrism, and he saw a vision of the hand of Christ upon the walls anointing the sanctuary. Following the consecration of the church, Anbâ Banîâmîn was bidden, in another vision, to draw up the canons for the monastery regulating the conduct of the priests and monks. These canons are as follows:[18]

1. No priest shall ascend to this sanctuary until he has put on his pallium first, before he carries the incense into the sanctuary.
2. No priest or deacon shall communicate therein until he has vested himself in the pallium.
3. No priest or deacon shall speak in the holy dome any idle words, nor sit therein to read a book. And he that shall break that canon shall be anathema.
4. If any priest or monk shall enter into this dome, unless he be appointed for the service of this sanctuary, let him be anathema.
5. If any of the priests belonging to this place bring a strange priest or an official into this dome and holy tabernacle, for the sake of human glory, let him be anathema.
6. If any man shall persist in entering this holy dome, the Lord Jesus Christ shall cast him out.
7. And if any man transgresses in order that he may have a lot in this holy place by means of money or bribe, then let him, and everyone who assists him to enter it for the sake of human glory, be degraded, especially if he be notorious for evil and pride.

In addition to the efforts of Anbâ Banîâmîn, John the Hegumen played a major role in the reconstruction of the monasteries in Scetis. John was born sometime between 585 and 605. After he became a monk, he was captured three times by the Berbers who took him prisoner and made him a slave. Thus he shared the experiences of Anbâ Danîâl, and Anbâ Samwîl of al-Qalamûn. About 641 he became the hegoumenos of Dair Abû Maqâr and was instrumental in the rebuilding of the monasteries. That he was a man of deep spirituality is testified by the historian who said that "he never communicated of the Holy Mysteries without seeing the Lord and Saviour in his vision, with our Lady the Virgin, and great secrets were made manifest to him."[19] When John the Hegumen died in 675, he left his impress upon a group of disciples. Anbâ Abrâm and Anbâ Girgis were probably the two best known and most influential of his followers.

Anbâ Abrâm was born around 608. His father was a wealthy man who had distinguished himself by his generosity towards the less fortunate. His mother, a God-fearing woman, had been carried away by the Persians. When Anbâ Abrâm was thirty-five, he decided to retire to the Desert of Scetis, where he joined John the Hegumen. One day he met Anbâ Girgis who had been a simple shepherd before he became a monk. This meeting established an intimate friendship between the two saints, who were regarded with the highest esteem. "They walked in the way of the great Antony, and brought it to perfection."[20] They settled in the Monastery of Abû Maqâr where they shared a cell. Their tomb still existed in the first half of the thirteenth century.

The Monastery of St. Macarius remained for centuries the most important institution of the Desert of Scetis, and the hegoumenos of the monastery was regarded as the "Father of Scetis".

Sometimes the internal history of al-Islâm was affected by the monasteries, as, for example, in the eighth century when it was claimed that the prayers of the monks of Dair Abû Maqâr had determined the fall of the Umayyad Dynasty. During the reign of Marwân II (the last of the Umayyad caliphs at Damascus, 744-750), the monks were severely persecuted. "They oppressed us even more cruelly, as they did to Ignatius, the saint and martyr, when they delivered him to the ten lions." But Marwân's career was seriously endangered at this time by the Abbasids, and the victory of the Abbasids over the Umayyads brought a temporary end to the difficulties of the monks.[21]

The Monastery of St. Macarius, like the other monasteries of Scetis, was sacked for the fifth time during the patriarchate of Anbâ Murqus III (799-819). But soon after the destruction, the monasteries were rebuilt by Ya'qûb, a priest of the Monastery of Abû Maqâr. He had escaped the destruction by the Arabs, and had departed to a monastery in Upper Egypt, "while awaiting the time when he might return to the Wâdî Habîb." After the death of Anbâ Murqus III, Anbâ Ya'qûb was elected to the patriarchate, and the work of restoration was begun. He sent messengers to all the fathers and to the cells saying: "If anyone needs anything for his cell, let him come and take it." The monks responded gladly and returned to the desert. While still a priest, he had begun to rebuild the sanctuary of St. Sinuthius (Shenûdah), which is to the south of the sanctuary of St. Macarius, and the monks began to assemble there, instead of in the ruined church.[22]

Anbâ Ya'qûb began work that was carried on during the reign of Anbâ Yûsâb (830-849) by the oeconomus Sinuthius. The middle of the ninth century was peaceful. The monasteries in all grew and increased in number, above all the monasteries of the Desert of Scetis, especially that of St. Macarius. Abûnâ Shenûdah "raised monuments in honour of St. Macarius, vineyards and gardens and cattle and mills and oil-presses and many useful things that cannot be numbered."

Life in the Desert of Scetis was attractive and a large number of monks entered the monasteries at that time. Those who went to the Wâdî Habîb were not only those of the Orthodox faith, "but also heretics, on account of the wonders that were manifested in that church."[23]

In addition to the ecclesiastical prestige that the monastery had enjoyed since the days of Justinian, another factor conferred fame on the institution, especially after the beginning of the ninth century. For not only did the monastery become the centre of patriarchal activities, it also became the patriarchal necropolis. When Anbâ Mîkhâîl II died in 851 the monks placed his body in the Church of Abû Maqâr.[24]

Anbâ Mîkhâîl, or Khâîl II, was succeeded by Anbâ Quzmân II, (851-858) of the Church of St. Macarius. His patriarchate began inauspiciously, for, on the feast of St. Menas, two men started a riot in the church, and one of them killed the other. Whereupon Anbâ Quzmân was imprisoned, and it was only later that he was permitted to live in the exclusively Christian city of Damîrah.

The fifty-fifth patriarch, Anbâ Shenûdah (859-880), who had served as oeconomus of the Monastery of St. Macarius, exercised his patriarchal office with great efficiency. "He built the church which is in the Monastery of Abû Maqâr and other churches,"[25] and on the day following the Nativity in 850, he was consecrated to the patriarchate. "...And they declared with one voice, swearing: There is none worthy of this degree, except the oeconomus of the Church of Abû Maqâr, and all of them said: Hagios, Hagios, Hagios."

Doctrinal controversies, however, again disturbed the peace of the Desert. In the second and third centuries a heresy arose which was termed Monarchianism. There were two kinds of this heresy, and the second kind, the Modalist or Sabellian heretics, were also termed Patripassians, as it was a corollary of the doctrine that the Father suffered as the Son. A similar doctrine was held by some of the bishops in Upper Egypt in the ninth century, for "they said with their tongue which deserves to be cut and to be cleft, that the nature of the divinity died. They were all inhabiting a village of a district in Upper Egypt called al-Balyana." The patriarch summoned these heretics to the Desert of Scetis. "Anbâ Shenûdah performed a good deed, in order that it might serve as a censure on the bishops and others and on everyone who errs from the faith, in that he caused the bishops of Upper Egypt to stand up in the midst of the congregation of the fathers, the saintly monks, in the Church of Abû Maqâr on the Sunday of the Holy Easter, and they made an obeisance to the congregation and asked them to pardon them for what Satan had done to them through temptation."[26]

By the beginning of the tenth century, monasticism in the Desert of Scetis may well have reached its height. Anbâ Ghabrîâl (910-923) came from the Monastery of Abû Maqâr. Tempted by a multitude of desires of the flesh, the older monks helped him overcome weaknesses. Having spent most of his life in the desert, he was buried like his predecessor in the Monastery of Abû Maqâr.[27]

After the death of Anbâ Quzmân III in 932, Anbâ Makarîûs I (932-952) ascended the patriarchal throne. He came from the township of Shubrâ, and entered the Monastery of St. Macarius.

Some Muslims had a high esteem for Patriarch Anbâ Afrâm (Ephraim, known as the Syrian merchant, 975-978) and the power of the prayers that were offered by the monks. During the reign of al-'Azîz "the Orthodox people" with their threefold *Kyrie eleison* apparently moved "part of the Muqattam hills between Cairo and Misr".[28] The last days of Anbâ Afrâm's reign were greatly troubled by Abû as-Surûr, a Copt of great influence who persisted in retaining a number of concubines, after having been admonished by the patriarch. He was excommunicated, and then took revenge by poisoning Anbâ Afrâm.

Anbâ Fîlûtâûs (979-1003) succeeded Anbâ Afrâm. During his reign, a certain Anbâ Bafnûtîûs lived at Dair Abû Maqâr for thirty-five years before he was consecrated bishop. During his episcopacy, which extended from 980 to 1006, he never changed his garments, except for the celebration of the Divine Liturgy.[29]

Anbâ Fîlûtâûs was followed by Anbâ Zakharîâ, the sixty-fourth patriarch. During his patriarchate Anbâ Mînâ, the bishop of Tânah, divided the revenues which he had collected into four parts and buried them in four different places. Anbâ Mînâ had a brother, Anbâ Makarîûs, who was bishop of Upper Minûf and secretary of the synod. When Anbâ Mînâ was about to die, he sent messengers to his brother to inform him about the hidden treasures. But Anbâ Makarîûs was slow in coming and Anbâ Mînâ wrote four messages specifying the four places where the money was hidden. When Anbâ Mînâ was in agony and "he cast one of the four pieces into his mouth and chewed it up... then he chewed up the second piece of paper and... likewise the third. As he was about to chew the fourth piece of paper, his brother, Anbâ Makarîûs arrived. Anbâ Mînâ brought out the piece of paper from his mouth and delivered it to his brother."[30] Anbâ Mînâ died, and Anbâ Makarîûs found the place where ten thousand dinars were hidden. He took the money and built with it a skene[31] in the name of Abba Macarius in Wâdî Habîb. This is the beautiful sanctuary to the south of the haikal of Benjamin.

The monastery supplied numerous ecclesiastical leaders, including Danîâl, who became Metropolitan of Ethiopia. The Monastery of Abû

Maqâr gained prominence, during the widespread persecutions of al-Hâkim (996-1021). Anbâ Zakharîâ, as well as most of the bishops, found refuge in the Desert of Scetis. At that time a Turkish amir obtained the head of St. Mark the Evangelist. On learning that the Christians would pay a large sum of money for it, he took the head to Cairo and sold it for three hundred dinars to one Buqairah al-Rashîdî who carried it to the patriarch at the Monastery of St. Macarius.[32]

Anbâ Zakharîâ (Zacharias), after facing the persecution of his church, imprisonment and torture; after being cast to the lions and saved by the grace of God, went to rest in peace. He was followed by Anbâ Shenûdah II (1032-1046) who had become a monk at the age of fourteen in the skene of Anbâ Makarîûs. He was a man of great learning.

Because of the many services rendered by the monastery during the persecution of al-Hâkim, special privileges were granted to the monks. One of those privileges was their right to participate in the nomination and election of the patriarch. Four distinct bodies took part in the election: the bishops, the clergy of Cairo (or Alexandria), the notables of Cairo (or Alexandria), and the superiors of the Wâdî Habîb. Many historical factors contributed to a close relationship between Dair Abû Maqâr and the patriarch.

The monks of the Monastery of Abû Maqâr observed the custom of keeping the consecrated elements from Palm Sunday until the Wednesday of Holy Week. When Anbâ Akhristûdulûs visited the monastery he abolished the practice, threatening to anathematize those who should do it afterwards.

Many miracles are reported during the patriarchate of Anbâ Akhristûdulûs. One of these occurred at the Monastery of Abû Maqâr, where the icon of Abû Mînâ in the skene of the Church of Abû Maqâr exuded blood.[33]

Some interesting statistics about the strength of the desert monasteries in the Wâdî Habîb are quoted by Qummus Armâniûs for the period of the patriarchate of Anbâ Akhristûdulûs (1047-1077). The Monastery of Abû Maqâr was still by far the most important monastery in the Desert of Scetis, claiming more than fifty per cent of the total number of monks.[34]

The Monastery of Abû Maqâr	400
The Monastery of Anbâ Bishoî	40
The Monastery of St. John the Short	150
The Monastery of St. John Kame	25
The Monastery of the Virgin of al-Barâmûs	60
The Monastery of al-Barâmûs	2
The Monastery of the Syrians	60
	737

The Monastery of Abû Maqâr served as a patriarchal residence on and off from the days of Justinian in the sixth century. One of the functions of the patriarch has always been the consecration of the Holy Chrism used at Chrismation in the rite of Holy Baptism and in the service for the Consecration of Churches. The rite of the Consecration of the Holy Chrism was regularly performed at the Monastery of St. Macarius, from the early Middle Ages at varying intervals.

However, the flourishing period of desert monasticism had passed. In 1088, Mawhûb, a deacon of Alexandria, journeyed to the Wâdî 'n-Natrûn. A number of Coptic notables were staying at the Monastery of St. Macarius, and he met "the deacon Abba Habîb Mîkhâîl of Damanhûr, Anbâ Kîrillus II, the sixty-seventh patriarch, and with him three bishops, Anbâ Ghabrîâl of al-Buhairah, Anbâ Ibrâhîm of Dibkwa, and Anbâ Khâîl of Nusa. Of the seven hundred monks, four hundred belonged to the Monastery of St. Macarius.[35] If this figure is compared with those from previous ages, the decline in the number of monks is very noticeable. In the middle of the sixth century, John of Petra lived in the Desert of Scetis, where he "counted" 3,500 fathers. In the ninth century, Epiphanius Hagiopolites visited the Monastery of St. Macarius, and he concluded that the monastery contained a thousand monks and a thousand cells. That some of these figures are exaggerated seems likely, when one reads of the seventy thousand monks who saluted 'Amr ibn al-Asî on his return from Alexandria, or the fifty thousand who greeted the two Macarii on their return from exile.

The monks at the Monastery of Abû Maqâr demanded a large supply of food and goods. Anbâ Kîrillus II dedicated "what he was wont to receive from certain sees to the Monastery of Saint Abba Macarius and they were: Damîrah, Abûsîr, Banâ, Damanhûr and al-Ihnâsîah."[36]

After the death of Anbâ Kîrillus II in 1092, Anbâ Mîkhâîl IV (1091-1102) was elected patriarch, and like his predecessors, proceeded to the Monastery of Abû Maqâr to be enthroned. His successor was Anbâ Makârîûs II (1103-1129) who had been a monk at St. Macarius' monastery before becoming patriarch. He was consecrated in Alexandria and his enthronement took place in the Church of al-Mu'allaqah in Old Cairo. Anbâ Makârîûs II was succeeded by Anbâ Ghabrîâl ibn Turaik (1131-1145), who had passed much of his life as a layman in government service. He was noted for his deep spirituality and honesty. It is said that Ghabrîâl, during his sixteen years' reign, consecrated no fewer than fifty-three bishops, and that he refused in every case to accept the presents offered. He issued many new canons and laws.

In this connection it might be interesting to mention that there is some evidence that by the middle of the twelfth century the Monastery of Abû

Maqâr had developed a "use"[37] and it is likely indeed that the other monasteries in Scetis followed this example by establishing their respective local "uses".

From the Twelfth to the Sixteenth Century

During the patriarchate of Anbâ Ghabrîâl II (1131-1145), a discontented monk named Halus, who was the steward of the revenue derived from the chrism, went to al-Hâfiz and blackmailed his fellow monks. Thereupon, he received from the government the authority to search the Monastery of Abû Maqâr for a treasure that was alleged to be hidden there. His search was a very costly affair, for, among other things, he burned the screen of the haikal of Benjamin. He kicked the screen with his feet in his scorn and pride, and as punishment God struck him in his foot with a malignant corrosive ulcer.

During this period, there is evidence of a temporary occupation by some Syrian monks, who may have come from the Syrian monastery. A graffito in the Church of St. Michael in the qasr of the monastery reads: "Remember, O Lord, thy servant the weak and sinful Elias, in name a monk and priest from the country of Marde, and the Syrian monk Habib, and ... in the holy dwellings of Anbâ Makârîûs and his ... these were in the year 1507 of Jarvani."[38] A further graffito testifies to the visit of a patriarch of Antioch, Mâr Ignatius.[39]

The successor of Anbâ Ghabrîâl was a monk of the Monastery of Abû Maqâr, known as Anbâ Mîkhâîl V, who had distinguished himself by his accurate observance of the monastic discipline, but who was so ignorant that he could neither read nor write Coptic or Arabic. After only three months of office, he was poisoned by one of the monks of the same monastery.

During the patriarchate of Anbâ Yûânnis VI (1189-1216) there was in the Monastery of St. Macarius a monk who apostatized, and gained a livelihood as a government secretary. Touched with remorse, he presented himself before Sultan al-Malik al-Kâmil I (1218-1238)[40] and asked to be allowed to re-embrace Christianity, adding that if this request were refused, he would gladly suffer martyrdom. The sultan released the monk, who returned to the monastery and gave himself up to penance.

After the death of Anbâ Yûânnis VI in 1216, the Alexandrian See remained vacant for eighteen years. During this period, in 1228, al-Malik al-Kâmil visited the Monastery of Abû Maqâr. The monks entertained him and his suite to the best of their ability, and he, in return, bestowed upon the monks large stores of provisions which consisted of 330 ardebs of corn, two hundred of meal, sixty of beans, and as many of peas. In addition, he granted several privileges to the monastery. He exempted the monks from paying tribute, and he removed the Muslim treasury officials who had been living in the monastery.[41] Interesting and significant for us is the monks' complaint that there was no patriarch. Eighty priests had been members of their monastery, but this number was reduced to a mere four. The monks' concern reveals that they expected the patriarch to be elected from their own monastery.

The patriarchate of Anbâ Kîrillus III (1235-1243), also known as Dâûd ibn Laqlaq, was important. The patriarch visited the monasteries in the Wâdî Habîb and then declared them to be "patriarchal", that is, he considered them exempt from the jurisdiction of the diocesan bishop, and placed them under direct control of the patriarchate. The reactions of the monks at Dair Abû Maqâr showed evidence of insubordination to the demands of the patriarch. In Holy Week of 1237, the monks staged a revolt against their spiritual leader which was put down by the redeeming and conciliatory influence of Yûsâb ibn al-Muhabrak, Bishop of Fuwah.

Some forty years after the visit of Sultan al-Malik al-Kâmil, the Bahri Mamluk Sultan, Baibars I (1260-1277) visited at-Tarânah, and afterwards the valley of the Wâdî Habîb where he stayed in the monasteries.[42]

During the patriarchate of Anbâ Butrus V (1340-1348), who succeeded Anbâ Baniâmîn, Egypt, like Europe, was visited by the Black Death, and whole families were exterminated. Maqrîzî declares that fifteen thousand died in Cairo on one day, and there is no doubt that the monasteries were severely affected. Anbâ Butrus died in 1340 and Anbâ Murqus IV was elected. A second plague ravaged Egypt in 1353, and people who had survived the former, fell victim to the latter. Maqrîzî writes: "The most famous of the monasteries is that of Abû Maqâr, and in front of it are the ruins of a great number of monasteries... It is told that fifteen hundred monks used to stay there, though now only a few of them remain. – There are altogther three Maccarii: the eldest one, to whom the monastery belongs, Abû Maqâr of Alexandria, and Abû Maqâr the bishop. Their decayed bones are in three wooden tubes, and the Christians of the monastery honour them. In it is also the letter which 'Amr ibn al-'Asî wrote to the monks of the Wâdî Habîb regarding the collection of the tax...[43]

One of the fifteenth-century travellers to visit the Monastery of St. Macarius was Josse van Ghistele, who spent from 1481 to 1484 in Egypt. "We lodged in a village called Alterana (at-Tarânah), because one of our servants told us that in the neighbourhood there was the fine Monastery of St. Macarius, which merited the trouble of being seen, and that the sultan himself held it in great esteem. We passed the night in this village, and we were so well received there by the lord who commanded there, that he gave us on the next day three of his Mamluks to conduct us to the monastery.

"After hiring donkeys and mules, we set out for the Monastery of St. Macarius, which was a day's journey from there in the middle of an immense desert, infested by leopards, boars, wolves and other dangerous animals. This monastery has the size of that of Bandeloo in the country of Waes, but it is less well built. There is shown in front of the church a place where St. Macarius was accustomed to preach to the people, after he had come out from Armenia, to come to do penance in this place. The body of the saint does not rest there, for it is recounted there, that he left this country, and that he passed through the West and died there. When the monks heard that we were pilgrims coming from Ghent, a city where St. Macarius is buried and where his body is held in great veneration, they rejoiced exceedingly, and they gave us an excellent reception. They showed us a certain privilege, which this monastery possessed for the ringing of the bells. It is a piece of fine cloth coated over with dough, clear and shining as a mirror.[44] The signature of Muhammad, which is placed on this piece is nothing else than the impress of his hands, which he had previously dipped into ink."[45]

Sixteenth- and Seventeenth-Century Travellers

The first sixteenth-century travellers to the Desert of Scetis were not much interested in the monastic life, and their remarks give us little or no information as to the state of the monasteries.

Leo Africanus (1491-1552) mentions the Monastery of St. Macarius only very briefly. "The third (the Monastery of St. Macarius) stands in the wilderness, to the west of Bulac. It is the monastery which in some histories is called Nitrie, and I think, because in that quarter the waters of Nilus being thickened by the heat of the sun in low places, are converted into salt and nitre."[46]

Not much more information is provided by Pierre Belon du Mans, who visited Egypt in 1537.[47] An anonymous Spanish Franciscan, visiting Egypt in 1553, merely points out that the Monastery of St. Macarius is a hundred miles from Cairo, and contains the body of the saint.[48]

As in the case of Pierre Belon du Mans, it is questionable whether le Sieur de Villamont, who was in Egypt in 1590, ever saw the desert of St. Macarius. He writes, however, that in the vicinity of it one finds the aquiline stones which are helpful for the delivery to women in labour.[49]

In the last decade of the sixteenth century, there was correspondence between Pope Clement VIII and Anbâ Ghabriâl VIII, Patriarch of

Alexandria. The pope sent his legate, Girolamo Vecchitti, to the patriarch in an endeavour to unite the Alexandrian See with the Latin church. In response to the papal mission, the patriarch commissioned two monks of the Monastery of Abû Maqâr and a deacon of Alexandria to return the courtesies. In January 1595, two monks, Abûnâ Yûsûf ibn Mikhâîl and Abûnâ 'Abd al-Masîh al-Makînî ibn Butrus, joined the Latin church.

To George Sandys, who visited Egypt in 1611, the desert of St. Macarius was merely interesting because of a certain plant "low, leafless, brown in colour, branched like coral, and closed at the top: this in time of labour of women, they set in water, in some corner of the room, which strangely displayeth, procuring easy deliveries."[50] This is the Rose of Jericho, *Anastatica Hierochuntia,* a plant which dries up, but when placed in water revives and becomes green.

Another passing reference to the Monastery of St. Macarius comes from Fr. Eugene Roger, who mentions that the Ethiopians recognized as their sovereign pastor the patriarch of the Copts, who resided in Egypt at the Monastery of St. Macarius. Furthermore, he states, that the patriarch had in Ethiopia a patriarchal vicar, who they called Eteche or Comos, who had under him several bishops who were dispersed throughout the province and who obeyed the patriarch of the Copts.[51]

The Monastery of St. Macarius has sheltered a considerable library since the Middle Ages. This is partly due to the grant that the emperor Zeno had bestowed upon the monastery. Furthermore, the transfer of the patriarchal residence from Alexandria to the monastery in the sixth century may well have been another determinant for the accumulation of books: Though many of the ancient manuscripts perished in the successive devastations of the monastery, by the tenth and eleventh centuries the library had been restored, and the growth of the collection continued until the Black Death depopulated the Desert of Scetis. The library remained intact until the seventeenth century, when European bibliophiles ventured to the Desert of Scetis to collect ancient manuscripts for continental collectors.

The first study and description of the monasteries and their libraries was presented to Nicholas Claude Fabri de Peiresc, the French archaeologist and scholar, by Fr. Cassien of Nantes. In the *Correspondence de Peiresc avec plusieurs missionnaires et religieux de l'ordre des Capucins, 1631-1637,* Fr. Apollinaire de Valence mentions that Fr. Cassien visited all four monasteries in the Wâdî 'n-Natrûn, but that he saw only three libraries, since the key for the fourth library could not be found. He took notes on the greatest part of the books he saw, among which he discovered a large Arabic volume, which was a commentary of St. John Chrysostomus on the Gospels. There were also homilies attributed to St. Simeon Stylites and books by St. Basil, St. Gregory the Theologian and others.[52]

In his desire to obtain as many volumes as possible, Peiresc, who became abbot of the Monastery of Guistres in 1618, used the services of many priests. Pietro Gassendi informs us that Peiresc "conceived very great hopes of obtaining out of the East both Coptic and other rare books, when about the very same time (1633) that very good man Aegidius Lochienses, a Capuchin, returned out of Egypt. For he, being received with great exultation by Peirescius, ... told him of rare books which were extant in divers convents and monasteries."[53]

Gilles de Loche (Lochiensis) saw eight thousand manuscripts in the monastery. Urged to follow up the clue given by Gilles de Loche, another Capuchin, Agathange de Vendome, wrote to Peiresc from Cairo in 1634, that he was on the point of securing a manuscript of the Psalms from the Monastery of St. Macarius. The most remarkable manuscript obtained by Fr. Agathangelus from the monastery was the *Codex Barberianus Orientalis,* which is a polyglot psalter written in five columns in Ethiopic, Syriac, Coptic, Arabic and Armenian. The manuscript was sent to Peiresc, but was captured on the way by pirates and taken to Tripoli, where it was bought back. Subsequently, it was lost again, but rediscovered in 1637 and bought for Cardinal F. Barberini by John Paul Lascarius.[54]

Collectors like Colbert and Coislin took away Syriac manuscripts from the neighbouring Dair as-Suriân, and may also have secured Coptic manuscripts from Dair Abû Maqâr.

In 1638, the French consul at Damietta, Fr. J. Coppin began his essay by praising St. Macarius, after whom the desert was named. At the time of his visit, only four monasteries were inhabited. Apparently well-acquainted with the way to the monasteries, he mentions the price of two piastres for the hire of a horse and four piastres for each "Cavalier" who accompanied the party, which, however, was to be paid in the presence of the Cachef. The first monastery he discovered, after leaving the village of Tarânah, was that of St. Macarius, where the body of the saint and those of many other saints are buried. In the keep of the monastery the monks kept provisions and the books which they valued so highly and with which they would not part on account of the "anathema" that would be pronounced upon them.[55]

The Monastery of Abû Maqâr was quite frequently visited by Frenchmen in the middle of the seventeenth century as is evident from the graffiti in the Chapel of St. Michael in the qasr. On the plaster of the north wall are scratched the names or initials of three seventeenth–century visitors: Claud Durand 1640, M.M. 1640, and ʿAnthoine Ba— 1644.

During this period the Monastery of St. Macarius, like the Monastery of St. Antony, served as a training-school for Franciscan missionaries. A letter sent on 18 April, 1639, by Fr. Antonius de Virgoletta to the *Propaganda* states that missionaries were to be sent either to the Monastery of St. Macarius or to the Monastery of St. Antony for the purpose of studying the Arabic language.[56]

In or around 1638, the Monastery of St. Macarius became a haven of refuge for Franciscus of Como. Franciscus, prefect of the mission, had been sent to Egypt to work with Marcus of Lucca for the union of the Copts with the Church of Rome. Pressure and persecution, however, led him to retreat to the Monastery of St. Macarius. In 1641, Franciscus became a teacher of Arabic in Jerusalem and later Custodian of the Terra Santa.

In 1649, le Sieur de la Boullaye le Gouz visited Egypt. He describes in his memoirs the natron which then was exported to Rouen, where it was used by Norman linen manufacturers for bleaching. Though le Gouz mentions the Monastery of Abû Maqâr, there is no evidence that he visited it.[57]

In 1657, Thévenot described the Monastery of St. Macarius: "This is a very ancient monastery, the walls are very high, but it is much decayed. There are many holy bodies in it, but only one of these approved of by the Church of Rome, to wit, that of St. Macharius, as also five or six altar tables of lovely marble. Within the precinct there is a kind of a big square tower, into which you enter by a drawbridge; and wherein there is a church, a well, and all that is necessary for the church, and the sorry sustenance of the monks, who sometimes retreat into it. For when they find themselves abused, and pursued by stranger Arabs, they betake themselves to this kind of stronghold, and pull up the drawbridge after them, keeping there whatever they have of value in the monastery, especially all their books which they so esteem, that no monk dares to sell, or put out of the way any of them, under the pain of anathema. This monastery is the greatest, but also the most ruinous, and especially the church that seems to have been very fair in times past. There is no garden belonging to it, and the water which the monks drink is somewhat brackish."[58]

The library of Dair Abû Maqâr was still the main attraction for the bibliophiles in Europe. A letter written on 30 October, 1646 to the French chancellor in Paris informs us of the great demand for the manuscripts of Dair Abû Maqâr. "My consorts, the merchants of Egypt who are at Paris have told me that Your Grandeur desired to have the works of St. Ufreme (Ephrem) and the manuscripts of Dair Abû Maqâr and others which will be found in Egypt."[59] And Galland writing in 1679: "Try to have the books which are at the Monastery of St. Macarius in Egypt and at Mount Sinai in the hands of the monks who are very poor."[60]

In 1670, Goujon ventured to the great desert, which was three or four days' journey from Cairo, and was sanctified by the penitence of the holy anchorites of the early church. The first monastery Goujon visited was Dair Abû Maqâr, where the monks showed him the relics which were kept in a sepulchre of stone with an iron grating. The second monastery, which impressed Goujon on account of its wealth, was dedicated to the Blessed Virgin Mary and was inhabited by twenty monks. From there, he went to the Monastery of St. George (Anbâ Bishoî) which had fallen into ruin, and which was inhabited by only a few monks.[61]

Around 1680, Fr. Marcus of Lucca visited Dair Abû Maqâr where he spent eight months trying to persuade the monks to join the Catholic church. But in spite of the persistent efforts by Fr. Marcus, the monks of Dair Abû Maqâr preserved their independence from the See of Rome.[62]

When Robert Huntington visited the monasteries in 1678 or 1679 he described the Monastery of St. Macarius as being the most ruinous of them all, and he found nothing worthy of mention in it except many manuscripts, such as a large volume of St. John Chrysostom in Coptic on parchment, a colossal tome on St. Matthew, lections of the church for the whole year in four volumes in Coptic and others.

Thirty years later, in 1707, the papal librarian Elias Assemani went on the order of Pope Clement XI to the Desert of Scetis, where he secured a significant series of Syriac manuscripts.

When Fr. du Bernat, S.J., visited the monasteries of the Wâdî 'n-Natrûn in 1710, the Monastery of Abû Maqâr was inhabited by only four monks. In the monastery he was shown the bodily remains of St. John the Short, though the monastery of the latter was completely ruined. He noticed the Tree of Obedience where once upon a time the Monastery of St. John the Short stood. Altogether, only twenty-three monks lived at that time in the four monasteries of the Desert of Scetis.[63]

Then, on 5 December, 1712, Fr. Claude Sicard, S.J., accompanied by the hegoumenos of the Monastery of St. Macarius, visited the four monasteries of the Wâdî 'n-Natrûn. His first stop was at the village of Atrîs where he found a hospice for the solitaries of the desert.[64] On 7 December he left Atrîs and reached the Monastery of St. Macarius just before sunset. He mentions the travels of Paula and Melania, and the five thousand monks that inhabited the holy places. Speaking about Dair Abû Maqâr he was obviously much interested in the tower with the Chapel of St. Michael and the library which contained three or four chests of ancient Arabic or Coptic manuscripts. At the time of his visit, the monastery was inhabited by the "prêtre religieux", a doorkeeper who was also a monk and two secular deacons. Apparently much impressed by the religious practices, he describes how these monks after their office retired to their cells, where they prostrated themselves at the feet of their superior. The monastery contained two churches, a small one which was dedicated to St. Macarius, and a second one, much larger, but half-ruined, which was dedicated to St. John. In the latter church he was shown a chapel dedicated to St. Apollinaria, the daughter of Anthemius, a consul during the reign of Arcadius. Furthermore, he was shown four small coffins which, the Copts say, contained the bodies of the three Macarii and St. John the Short.

Seven years after the visit of Elias Assemani, another member of the Assemani family visited the monastery as an agent of the Vatican library. This was Joseph Simon Assemani (1687-1768), a Maronite of Mount Lebanon. After his college training in Rome, he was sent to Egypt and Syria to search for valuable manuscripts. On his first mission to Egypt and Syria, he secured one hundred and fifty valuable documents. At the Monastery of Abû Maqâr "he acquired manuscripts of the highest quality written in the Coptic tongue,"[65] the collection that is now in the Vatican. In gratitude for his exploits, the pope conferred upon him the titular archbishopric of Tyre. On his visit to the Monastery of St. Macarius in 1715, Joseph Assemani was accompanied by Fr. Claude Sicard. Fr. Sicard sums up their journey: "Nous trouvâmes dans tous ces lieux un assez grand nombre de livres très rares." There is no doubt that after the exploitative visits of the papal librarian the monks began to re-examine their policy regarding manuscripts.

On 18 September, 1729, Fr. François Sevin wrote a letter to Maurepas in which he stressed the urgency to obtain manuscripts from the Monastery of St. Macarius. "Mr. Le Maire, the consul of Tripoli in Syria, did not encounter the same obstacles, I add here a memorandum, which his excellency received these last days and in which he speaks with great praise about the libraries of the Monastery of St. Macarius. I think, as Mr. Le Maire, that the consul of Cairo would easily succeed in getting the books in question from the hands of the monks, who are so little worthy to possess them. A consul, who is clever and skilful, is a more suitable person for these undertakings, than the most scholarly man in the world."[66]

The next visitor, le Sieur Granger, who was interested in seeing the library, was refused entry, and the monks' attitude convinced him that they were not willing to part with their books at any price.[67] Granger, who visited the Monastery of Abû Maqâr in 1730, found the monastery in ruins, the monks poor, ignorant and badly lodged.

Sonnini, who visited the monasteries of the Wâdî 'n-Natrûn in 1778, did not venture to the Monastery of Abû Maqâr because of the many unpleasant experiences he had had with marauding Bedouins who robbed and stripped him in front of the Monastery of al-Barâmûs. However, he mentions the Monastery of Abû Maqâr, and adds that the Arabs called these ruins in the environs of the monastery the "Castle of the Virgins", a strange name for a retreat inspired by an aversion to women.[68]

In 1779, Count d'Entraigues, the young nephew of M. de Saint Priest, the French ambassador to Constantinople, was sent to Egypt under the pretence of having him study the results of the mission of M. de Tett, who served as inspector general of the commercial ports of the Levant (Echelles du Levant). In actuality, this young man was encouraged to travel to Egypt so as to remove him from the temptations and the libidinous nights of Pera.

Accompanied by a dragoman, two janissaries, and a dozen Arabs, he set out to visit the monasteries in the desert of St. Macarius, one of the reasons being to atone for his sinful life. In the monasteries he was received by a group of feeble monks, who apparently showed signs of coarseness and fatigue on account of their prayers and fasting. The count then pretended to have discovered, without actually having obtained them, the most valuable manuscripts among which was a complete edition of Diodorus of Sicily, one manuscript of Polybius, and the vanished *Hypotyposes* of Clement of Alexandria. All of this of course, was a matter of pure imagination on the part of the young traveller, who, according to his own avowal, neither knew Greek nor was capable of deciphering any manuscript.[69]

Twenty years after Sonnini's visit in January 1799, the French general, Antoine F. Andréossy went on a reconnaissance of the Natrûn valley for Napoleon's army. Andréossy measured the various distances between the monasteries and established their exact geographical locations. At that time, the Monastery of Abû Maqâr was inhabited by twenty monks. Its water was quite salty but Andréossy mentions another well, some four hundred metres away from the monastery, the water of which was very good. The general mentions the disorder and the poverty of the monks which did not permit them to beautify the churches. He must have seen the library for he mentions the books, "manuscrits ascétiques" on parchment in the Coptic language with an Arabic translation on the margin. The monks were apparently very friendly with the neighbouring Arabs, in so far as the monks supplied the latter with food which they gave to them over the wall, for they never opened their gates to them.[70]

Nineteenth- and Twentieth-Century Travellers

In about 1818, a fragmentary Bohairic psalter was removed from the Monastery of St. Macarius and given by B. Drovetti to Peyron. It is now at Turin. Whether Drovetti personally visited the monastery or acquired the manuscript from some other person is not known.

In January 1839, Dr. Tattam visited the Monastery of St. Macarius, where he discovered about one hundred liturgies, and a beautiful copy of the Epistles in Coptic, which the monks, however, would not sell. There were also, as in the other monasteries visited by Tattam, a great number of loose leaves, from which he selected about one hundred, from two or three different vocabularies, and he was permitted to take these away.[71]

In 1843, Sir Gardner Wilkinson visited the monasteries of the Wâdî 'n-Natrûn. After having called on the monks of the Monastery of the Syrians, he visited the "Dayr Makarios", where he saw many manuscripts bound and in good condition, yet the whole ground in the tower of the monastery was strewed with the torn leaves and fragments of manuscripts "which having been copied, the monks considered of no further use." The monks, for the most part were exceedingly ignorant, and their whole knowledge and thoughts were much confined to very limited theological learning. While in the Monastery of the Syrians, Sir Gardner suffered from the assaults of some hundreds of bugs. The Monastery of Abû Maqâr, however, was free from this scourge, and of the other two monasteries (Dair al-Barâmûs and Dair Anbâ Bishoî) he could say nothing. At the time of his visit, the monastery was inhabited by twenty-two monks, and thus rated as the second strongest monastery in the Wâdî 'n-Natrûn.[72]

On 18 April, 1844, Konstantin von Tischendorf sailed from Bûlâq to at-Tarânah in order to visit the Coptic monasteries of the Libyan desert.[73] The first monastery to be visited was Dair Abû Maqâr, where he was hospitably received. "We found fifteen brethren in it, while Sicard saw here only two monks and two secular deacons. Their countenances were all sallow, and several of them of a sickly yellow, they almost all suffered in their eyes, and the superior was totally blind... The cloister fare is more than meagre. Meat is indulged in but on few days in the course of the year. The chief food consists of nothing but bread steeped in a concoction of a disagreeable flavour, consisting of lentils, onions, and linseed oil." Here Tischendorf observed the celebration of the Eucharist. "Two peculiarities struck me in the arrangement of the church. The one is the oven behind the sacristy, employed in baking the sour sacramental bread... The other peculiarity is a four-cornered stone basin in front of the church, which is used for a sacred bathing ceremonial." Tischendorf's main purpose in visiting the monastery was to search for manuscripts, and so he went to the tower, where he saw the manuscripts heaped indiscriminately together. Lying on the ground, or thrown into large baskets beneath masses of dust, he found innumerable fragments of old, torn and ruined manuscripts.

From the seventeenth century onwards, the outside world has penetrated the desert. The following note, however, suggests the reverse. When the Suez Canal was opened in November 1869 by Empress Eugénie, the celebrations were attended by Anbâ Dîmîtrîûs II, the 111th patriarch, who at one time was a monk, and later the hegoumenos of the Monastery of Abû Maqâr.

In 1873, Greville Chester went to the Monastery of Abû Maqâr to study some of its archaeology and architecture, though he was not permitted to enter the keep, because, shortly before, a man called Fortune Ame had robbed the monastery of its silver plate and all the valuable manuscripts.[74] One of the first travel guides to refer to the Monastery of St. Macarius was Murray's *Handbook for Travellers in Lower and Upper Egypt.* "This excursion does not present any great attraction to the general traveller, but those who care for Christian architecture and antiquities will find much of interest. It may be done in six days: First day, Cairo–Tirranah (at-Tarânah); second day, Tirranah–Dair Abû Maqâr; third day, Dair Abû Maqâr–Dair Surîân and Anbâ Bishoî; fourth day, Dair Surîân–Dair al-Barâmûs; fifth day, Dair al-Barâmûs–Tirranah; sixth day, Tirranah–Cairo. The usual route from the Nile to the valley of the Natrûn Lake is from Tirranah, or the start may be made from Banî Salâmah, another village a little higher up the Nile. Both places may be reached from Cairo by water or by rail. Camels or donkeys and a guard can be obtained in Tirranah for the journey of ten to twelve hours across the desert to Wâdî 'n-Natrûn. The headman of Tirranah is a Copt, from whom it is well to get an introduction to the Qummus of Dair Macarius. The journey across the desert is very monotonous, but at length, after crossing an elevation covered with shining black pebbles, the long lines of Dair Macarius come in sight. This convent is surrounded by a lofty wall with an entrance on one side so low that you are obliged to stoop down on entering.... As soon as the bell has announced the arrival of a stranger, proper inquiries and observations are made to ascertain that there is no danger in opening the door for his reception, and no Arabs are admitted, unless, by forming his escort, they have some one responsible for their conduct. Near Dair Macarius are the ruins of three other convents and about half a mile to the east are mounds of pottery that indicate the site of an ancient town, perhaps Sciathis."

In 1881, on their way from the Monastery of Anbâ Bishoî to that of Abû Maqâr, Frs. Jullien, Noory and Nourrit stopped at the Tree of Obedience, which, tradition has it was connected with the life and work of St. John the Short. According to Fr. Jullien, the tree is a *zizyphus spina-Christi,* the species that provided the thorns for the crown of Christ.[75] The priests stopped for a little while to say a prayer, and then continued their way to the Monastery of Abû Maqâr.[76] The priests visited the various churches and were shown the bodies of some sixteen patriarchs in the Chapel of St. Michael. As in the other monasteries, Fr. Jullien entered into religious discussions with the monks in an attempt to convince them to return to the Latin church.

Two years later, in 1883, Alfred J. Butler visited the desert monasteries of the Wâdî 'n-Natrûn. He had wanted to make the journey in the spring of

1881, but the Khedive ordered careful inquiries to be made by the authorities, and the result was a prohibition. It was reported that the Bedouins were in a restive and hostile mood owing to some recent fighting with Egyptian soldiers, and would be certain to rob and turn back any travellers they might encounter in the desert, though on the whole the chances were against their caring particularly for unnecessary murder. In the winter of 1883-4, Butler returned to Egypt, and this time the Khedive pronounced the route secure. "We were, however, recommended to wear the tarbush or fez, as the sight of western hats is somewhat irritating to the children of the wilderness. The Coptic patriarch furnished us with letters both to the priest at Tris (Atrîs) which, although a Muslim village, contains a small Coptic colony and two churches, and also to the superiors of the four monasteries in the desert." From Atrîs, Butler entered the desert, "stumbling on over loose sand mixed with rushes and Christ-thorn.... We hastened on, and found the monks waiting in a group outside the Dair to receive us: they kissed our hands with exclamations of thankfulness for our safe arrival, and led us through the narrow doorway within the fortress, where we were soon lodged in the guestchamber, and lay on rugs upon the floor to rest and wait for our tents and camels.... Next morning, the unwonted sound of a church bell roused us at five o'clock, and with the dawn we got a view of the monastery, which the darkness of the night before had rendered impossible." Butler points out the three churches, the refectory, the qasr and its chaples. The number of monks at Dair Abû Maqâr was twenty, of whom twelve were in priests' orders. They were allowed sometimes to visit the patriarch, and even to see friends living in Cairo, by special permission, but they had to return to live and to die in the desert.

On 16 March, 1896, the Honourable Arthur Silva White left the Pyramids of Giza on his march to the Oasis of Siwa. Following the ancient pilgrimage track, on the third day of his journey White reached the Monastery of Abû Maqâr. "On ringing the bell, a monk appeared at the top of the parapet, and inquired our purpose. This known, he retired, with a muttered phrase that sounded unlike a benediction; and shortly afterwards, the *kummus* or abbot arrived, appearing mysteriously round the angle of the wall, to interview us. After compliments, we were permitted to enter through the heavy ironbound door, the laborious opening of which recalled a scene in the Middle Ages. Over the cigarettes, the *kummus* was communicative. He asserted that Dehr Makar was the most ancient of the monasteries, and that its revenues were derived chiefly from land of which he was the owner; that there were thirty monks in seclusion, who worked during the day and prayed at night."[78]

On the first Sunday of December 1899, Professor Dr. Georg Steindorff, accompanied by the German consul in Alexandria, Curt

Freiherr von Grünau, arrived at the Monastery of Abû Maqâr on their way to Siwa. They examined the monastery very thoroughly, and their description of the buildings, the churches and the tower is enlightening.[79] The water for the monks came from a well located behind the Church of St. Macarius, and it was very good for drinking purposes. Steindorff suggests that this might be the well dug by St. Macarius. After visiting the churches which are all correctly identified, he went up to the qasr where he found the library in a wild and chaotic condition. He looked for valuable manuscripts, but could not find anything of great value. The only curiosity which he discovered was an old and torn French-Arabic elementary grammar. In 1899, the monastery was inhabited by twenty monks all of whom were fairly young. In the afternoon of the same day, Steindorff and his party departed from the monastery in a westerly direction to Maghârah and Siwa.

Following Butler and Steindorff, Gayet was one of the first scholars to be concerned with the archaeological and architectural features of the monasteries in the Wâdî 'n-Natrûn. In his excellent work, *L'Art Copte,* published in 1902 in Paris, the coptologist and architect presents many interesting illustrations, sketches and blue-prints.[80] About the same time, Joseph Strzygowski visited the Monastery of Abû Maqâr, where, among other things, he studied the wooden screens in the chapel of the first floor of the qasr.[81]

In March, 1904, Agnes Smith Lewis and her sister, Mrs. Margaret Dunlop Gibson, may well have been the first ladies to visit the Monastery of Abû Maqâr. They reached the Desert of Scetis on dromedaries which they had hired in Cairo. They entered Dair Abû Maqâr through a very low doorway. At the monastery they were introduced to an old monk who had spent forty-five years in the monastery. For the past six years, however, he had been a solitary, emerging from the wilderness only on Sundays to attend the church service in the monastery. Interested in manuscripts, the two ladies entered the keep, where they saw books as well as manuscripts kept in a very untidy manner in a three-shelved cupboard. Those which Agnes Smith Lewis saw were late Arabic texts, and apparently of no great value. At the end of the room she then discovered a table with a pile of manuscripts which had lost their bindings, among which were many loose leaves, but they too were all in Arabic. "I could very easily have placed some of the manuscripts under my travelling cloak without the slightest fear of detection, but my conscience would not allow me to do so."[82] Later, during their visit, the ladies approached the monks with a request to buy some of the manuscripts but they met with a refusal.

The Kaufmann Expedition visited the monasteries of the Wâdî 'n-Natrûn in 1905. Before proceeding to Dair Abû Maqâr, they visited the salt works which had been established by an Englishman named Hooker in 1890. The well, Bir Hooker, and the little colony of officials and workmen were named after him. In 1896 the management passed into Swiss hands, and four years later an English joint stock company took over the business which provided salt for the whole of Egypt. Among the possessions of the salt factory was the vehicle used by Empress Eugénie at the opening of the Suez Canal. Hooker had bought the carriage from the khedival stables in order to have some means of transporting distinguished visitors to the wâdî. Before reaching the Monastery of Abû Maqâr, Ewald Falls records that they hunted a gazelle to vary their daily menu. The monastery was inhabited by twenty-five monks, and it appeared to be the poorest monastery. The whole place showed signs of terrible decay. The gloomy principal church, with the exception of the decoration of the haikal and the reliquary with the bodies of the three Macarii, possessed nothing that they had not seen in finer and better condition in other monasteries. The names of foreign visitors adorned the nave, and the monks asked their guests to eternalize themselves with grafitti.[83] Behind the principal church of the monastery was the "Macarius well", which furnished good water. The water-wheel was fairly large, and instead of a pail, clay vessels brought up the clean water from a depth of more than ten metres. Close to the monastery, traces of hyenas and wolves led to ruins which the Arabs described as remains of the "Qasr al-Banât," or "Castle of the Virgins". A dozen or so lesser ruins could be found in a circumference of a few hours' ride, fallen to pieces and buried in sand.

In the winter seasons of 1909-1910 and 1910-1911, the Metropolitan Museum of Art Egyptian Expedition studied the monasteries of the Wâdî 'n-Natrûn. Palmer-Jones, W. Hauser and H. Burton were engaged in making drawings and sketches, and in taking photographs of the architecture of the churches and other buildings. Unfortunately, the work was suspended first by Palmer–Jones' departure from Egypt, and then by the First World War.[84]

The Monastery of Abû Maqâr was the last monastery in the Wâdî 'n-Natrûn that Johann Georg, Duke of Saxony, visited in 1912. Coming from Dair Anbâ Bishoî, his first impression of Dair Abû Maqâr was that of a desert fortress.[85] The duke strongly criticized the renovations which had obliterated some of the ancient valuable wall-paintings. From the Church of Abû Maqâr he obtained two icons which portrayed the heads of two apostles. In the Church of St. Iskhîrûn the wall-paintings had been destroyed, though some could still be identified. After that, the duke went to the Church of the Forty Martyrs[86] which was used for the principal services. He found the interior of the church interesting because of the pillars with their ancient capitals. The refectory was even darker than those of the other monasteries, and appeared to him more like a prison. The monks used it during the feasts. The Church of al-ʿAdhrâ in the keep attracted his attention. Also situated in the keep are the Chapel of St. Michael and two other chapels with wall-paintings from the twelfth century. In one of the chapels he discovered fragments of manuscripts from the thirteenth to fifteenth centuries. All the members of the party of visitors, which included Marcus Simaika, Dr. Karge and the duke, took some of the fragments, as if they were souvenirs. Finally, Johann Georg went to the monastery library where he discovered several Coptic manuscripts of the tenth and eleventh centuries on parchment. On the advice of Marcus Simaika he tore some of them from their covers and took them with him. From Dair Abû Maqâr they rode on their camels to a small railway station, where a special train waited to take them to Cairo. A few days later, the hegoumenoi of Dair as-Surîân, Dair Anbâ Bishoî and Dair al-Barâmûs, visited the duke at Shepheard's Hotel in Cairo.

During the First World War the Monastery of Abû Maqâr was visited by Dr. G.A. Auden who obtained some leaves of manuscripts, including one from the Difnâr.

In 1920-21, Hugh Evelyn White visited the monastery. His purpose was to study the literary material that was still there. "When, on Palm Sunday, 1920, I first visited the monastery to study its archaeology, one of the monks who was guiding me over the keep, led me into the inner of two communicating rooms which occupied the south-west angle of the second floor. Descending beneath the floor by a trap-door, he reappeared with his arms full of loose leaves of paper manuscripts in Coptic and Arabic which he tossed carelessly upon the floor. It was clearly imperative to search this waste-paper deposit; however, I concealed my eagerness until I should have made good my footing in the monastery. But as soon as I was on friendly terms with the monks, I asked and obtained the consent of the Amin ed Der to allow me to examine the secret chamber for myself. To this he and the other monks good-naturedly agreed. The "oubliette" proved to be about two and a half metres deep, and to occupy the whole interspace between the second-floor room and the dome of the first-floor room below. Here, mixed with the large broken baskets seen by Tischendorf, with rags, broken glass, wood fragments, and large stones, was a vast quantity of loose leaves, some in chaotic heaps, others half–buried in the thick bed of dust or soil with which the crown of the dome beneath was overlaid. Paper predominated, but here and there search revealed a leaf or a fragment of parchment. Working by candlelight, for there was no window or loophole, and in some haste, I collected all the parchment I could find and some paper leaves taken almost at random. These the monks most kindly permitted me to take away with me when I left the monastery.... Examination soon showed the importance of a number of the leaves, and systematic search through the whole contents of the 'oubliette' was consequently desirable."[87]

In April 1921, Evelyn White returned to the Monastery of Abû Maqâr to resume his work. The hegoumenos of the monastery, Abûnâ Maksîmûs authorized him to search for and take away to Cairo any loose leaves or fragments. "The monks, less complaisant than formerly, affected to regard the project as a piece of sacrilege and read over to me certain of the anathemas directed against any who should remove from the monastery the books in which they had once been inscribed. These warnings being of no avail, they implored me not to carry away the whole of their paper. They became so pathetic that in a weak moment I consented to take only a large section. On these terms the monks withdrew their opposition and left me to incur my own damnation unmolested. For five days, from Thursday in Holy Week, therefore, I worked in the oubliette, turning over and scrutinizing, handful by handful, the entire mass of paper, raking through the mass of dust, and selecting every fragment of Coptic which seemed in the least likely to be of value. The process, carried on in appalling conditions, was repeated thrice and resulted in the recovery of many more parchment leaves and fragments and some hundred paper leaves. On Easter Monday, I left the monastery and returned to Cairo. To illustrate the accidents which beset the working archaeologist, I may add that I was nearly arrested at the railway station of Khatâtba at the instant of the abbot of another monastery, who had hastily concluded that my spoils were snatched without his leave from his own convent." The manuscripts discovered by Evelyn White are now exhibited in the Coptic Museum in Old Cairo.

In the month of February 1923, Dr. J. Rendel Harris, Herbert G. Wood and Dr. William H.P. Hatch, who served as annual professor to the American School of Oriental Research in Jerusalem, went to the monasteries in the Wâdî 'n-Natrûn. "Since many important manuscripts had been discovered in these desert monasteries in times past," writes Hatch, "we hoped that we might perhaps have the good fortune to find some Christian work in Coptic or Syriac that had eluded former searchers. Such was the purpose of our journey, and in some measure our hopes were realized."[88] At the time of his visit, Hatch states that the once populous region was inhabited by only eighty-three monks in the four monasteries, of which fifteen inhabited Dair Abû Maqâr.

The party was hospitably received at the monastery. Hatch was shown the mummified bodies of twenty saints. He tried to take a photograph of the hegoumenos, but the latter protested vigorously, and he refrained from doing so. The party was chiefly interested in the library, and the monks were very willing to let them inspect it and showed them every courtesy. "I detected in a wooden box several paper leaves rudely bound together which seemed to me more interesting than the rest, and I quietly laid them to one side. When we were ready to leave the convent, I asked the prior if I might take them with me, and after some hesitation he allowed me to do so."

In 1925, M.A. Kammerer, Commissaire-Directeur de la Caisse de la Dette Publique, visited the Monastery of Abû Maqâr. On entering the monastery, he saw to the right a church with cupolas that reminded him of a mosque without a minaret. "The more one examines these Coptic churches, the more one discovers their resemblances to mosques."[89] Kammerer tried to explain this by stating that, after the Arab conquest, many of the churches were transformed into mosques, and that this type then became the predominant form of construction. Noticing the ruins within the monastery, our visitor ascribes the general decay to the fact that it is the most ancient of the monasteries in the Wâdî 'n-Natrûn.

In the late 1920s Marcus Simaika arranged for the cataloguing of the manuscripts in the monasteries of the Wâdî 'n-Natrûn, which was completed in March 1929.

In the spring of 1930, and again in 1931, Prince 'Umar Tûsûn accompanied by Dr. Puy-Haubert and Professor Breccia visited the four monasteries of the Wâdî 'n-Natrûn. The prince divided the history of the monastic movement into ten periods, tracing the increase and decrease of the number of monasteries in the Natrun Valley. Furthermore, he identified the sites of the abandoned monasteries and erected cement columns with copper plates, giving the names of the monasteries. Though the cement columns are still there, the copper plates have been stolen by the Bedouins. The following chart is a condensed resumé of 'Umar Tûsûn's study.[90] It indicates which monasteries were functioning during each of the ten periods.

1st period (565-605) Dair Abû Maqâr, Anbâ Bishoî, St. John the Short, al-Barâmûs.

2nd period (859-881) Dair Abû Maqâr, Anbâ Bishoî, St. John the Short, al-Barâmûs, The Virgin of al-Barâmûs, St. John Kame, Syrians.

3rd period (1017) Dair Abû Maqâr, Anbâ Bishoî, St. John the Short, al-Barâmûs, The Virgin of al-Barâmûs, St. John Kame, Syrians.

4th period (1209) Dair Abû Maqâr, Anbâ Bishoî, St. John the Short, al-Barâmûs, The Virgin of al-Barâmûs, St. John Kame, Syrians, Anbâ Arsânîûs.

5th period (1330) Dair Abû Maqâr, Anbâ Bishoî, St. John the Short, al-Barâmûs, The Virgin of al-Barâmûs, St. John Kame, Syrians.

6th period (1347)　Dair Abû Maqâr, Anbâ Bishoî, St. John the Short, al-Barâmûs, The Virgin of al-Barâmûs, St. John Kame, Syrians, Anbâ Nûb, Abyssinians, Armenians

7th period (1440)　Dair Abû Maqâr, Anbâ Bishoî, St. John the Short, al-Barâmûs, The Virgin of al-Barâmûs, St. John Kame, Syrians.

8th period (1482)　Dair Abû Maqâr, Anbâ Bishoî, St. John the Short, The Virgin of al-Barâmûs, St. John Kame, Syrians.

9th period (1672)　Dair Abû Maqâr, Anbâ Bishoî, St. John the Short, The Virgin of al-Barâmûs, Syrians.

10th period (1710)　Dair Abû Maqâr, Anbâ Bishoî, The Virgin of al-Barâmûs, Syrians.

When the famous traveller H.V. Morton visited Dair Abû Maqâr in 1937, he noticed "a gaunt-looking monk kneeling (on the roof of a cluster of cells) and making prostration after prostration". He was told by other monks that this particular monk had not spoken to anyone for seven years. "Isolated in an uninhabited corner of the monastery, he lives there, a hermit in the desert. He leaves his cell only to attend church and to collect a few scraps of the hard bread on which he lives. He is thirty years of age."[91]

The Monastery Today

The Monastery of Abû Maqâr is the most outstanding and interesting monastery in the Wâdî 'n-Natrûn. It has supplied more patriarchs than any other,[92] and it can boast of more places of worship than any other. The most significant building is the Church of Abû Maqâr. The present church is merely a remnant of a once beautiful and majestic building, of which large portions have been destroyed. The church has two haikals, to the south, the haikal of Anbâ Baniâmîn, to the north, the haikal of St. John the Baptist.[93] The eastern niche of the former haikal was, at one time, the seat of the patriarch. On the south side of the choir stands the feretory with the bodily remains of the three Macarii and St. John the Short. Recently, the church has been decorated with pictures of Abû Maqâr and the three Macarii. The northern haikal, which is dedicated to St. John the Baptist, is interesting because of its "inner choir", and a shrine built by Mîkhâîl Yûsûf and his brother Bishoî in 1930. The feretory contains the relics of Anbâ Mîkhâîl II (831-851); Anbâ Mîkhâîl III (881-907); Anbâ Ghabrîâl I (910-921); Anbâ Quzmân III (921-933); Anbâ Makarîûs (933-953); Anbâ Akhristûdulûs I (1047-1077); Anbâ Kîrillus II (1078-1092); Anbâ Yûannis V (1146-1166); Anbâ Murqus III (1174-1189); Anbâ Yûannis XV (1619-1629); and the son of Martinius, a minister in the reign of Theodosius the Younger.[94]

The Church of Abû Iskhîrûn honours St. Iskhîrûn of Qallîn, and possibly owes its dedication to its having served as a resting place for St. Iskhîrûn's relics while his church in the Monastery of Anbâ Bishoî was being built.[95] The church has three haikals, but only two altars. The church may well have been built in the fourteenth century. Butler, visiting the church in 1883, found posted on the wall by the haikal-screen a paper covered with finely written Arabic characters. When translated it proved to be a form of thanksgiving for an event which had taken place the previous year.

The Church of ash-Shiyûkh or the Church of the Forty-nine Martyrs was used for the Liturgy during the Fast of the Nativity and on the Feast of the Nativity.[96] During this period, the relics of the three Macarii and St. John the Short are transferred from the Church of Abû Maqâr and placed at the north wall of the choir. The church is adorned with five icons representing the three Macarii, Abû Maqâr, St. Mark, St. George, and the Blessed Virgin. The forty-nine Martyrs, and the "magistrianus" and his son are buried here. After the martyrdom of the forty-nine, "the monks feared for the bodies and took them from the place of martyrdom near to the Church of Abû Maqâr. They constructed for them a crypt on which they built a church during the reign of the Patriarch Theodosius... Their church is to-day in the monastery called by their name in Coptic Bihimsa Basit, that is forty-nine."[97]

The qasr of the Monastery of Abû Maqâr is by far the most interesting of its kind, because of its many chapels and churches. One enters the qasr by a narrow drawbridge which leads to the first storey of the building. The interior of the tower is divided into three floors. Of the ground floor Evelyn White gives the following description: "In its present state it is an unpleasantly impressive place. Nearly all the windows are blocked and the chambers are the haunt of countless bats, to whose long tenancy the deadly odour which infects the atmosphere is due. The heavy stillness, broken only by the soft fluttering and eerie squeaking of the bats, the grim massiveness of the blackened and unplastered masonry half seen in the dim and broken light, and the damp corruption of the air impress the unaccustomed visitor like some infernal charnel house. Yet it is evident that when the light and air found admittance, the ground floor was by no means an ignoble place."

On the first storey is the Chapel of al-'Adhrâ, a relatively new church with three haikals. The screen, which may be the work of a thirteenth–century artist, is the only thing of note.

On the second storey are three churches which are remarkable on account of their wall-paintings. The Church of Michael the Archangel is the northernmost, and ranks as a "proper church" in the patriarchal list of churches provided by Somers Clarke.[98] It has one haikal which has a beautiful screen. The south wall of the church is decorated with pictures[99] representing a whole gallery of warrior saints: St. Eusebius,[100] St. Basilides,[101] St. Justus,[102] St. Apoli,[103] and St. Theoclea.[104] On the north wall within the choir-screen is a painting of St. Michael, and a little further to the east a small figure, probably that of St. Hilaria.

At the time of Butler's visit, no less than sixteen patriarchs were kept here in plain deal boxes. Eight cases, each containing two bodies, were piled one upon another at the south side of the altar. They were not hermetically sealed, and one could clearly see the shrivelled forms of the patriarchs lying like mummies in their coffins. In 1920, the relics of the patriarchs were still kept in a large wooden feretory on the south wall of the sanctuary. However, they have since been transferred to the Church of St. John the Baptist.

In the nave of the church there are in all nine pillars with interesting capitals, some Doric, others Corinthian, with crosses carved among the foliage.

The Church of St. Antony, St. Paul and St. Pachomius is situated south of the Church of St. Michael on the second floor. On the north wall of the chapel are paintings of the three founders of Egyptian monasticism to whom the church is dedicated.

The Church of as-Suwâh or the Church of the Hermits or Wanderers in the desert is the southernmost of the three churches on the second floor.[105] The wall-paintings of the church represent nine figures of hermits. These are: Anbâ Samwîl,[106] Anbâ Yuhannis,[107] Anbâ Nofer,[108] Anbâ Abrâm,[109] Anbâ Girgis,[110] Anbâ Abullû,[111] Anbâ Abîb,[112] Anbâ Mîsaîl,[113] Anbâ Bîgîmî.[114]

The qasr can be dated by a Syriac graffito in the Church of St. Michael which informs us that the church was in use in 1196. The belfry overlooking the monastery walls has one bell. In earlier times there were two, but the larger one was removed by Muhammad 'Alî to be placed upon the Citadel in Cairo. The monks informed me that the bell broke during the transport and so never reached its destination.

The plantation to the east outside the original walls was begun in 1925 by Anbâ Abrâm who served as hegoumenos of the monastery and as bishop of Balyana. In 1954, a round water tower was built.

In 1960, the amîn ad-dair was Qummus Athânâsîûs. Only eight monks of the thirty-two belonging to the monastery resided in the desert. The others lived in the monastic dependency in Atrîs near Khatâtba.

In 1969 Anbâ Kîrillus VI ordered Abûnâ Mattâ al-Maskîn with his twelve monks to leave the desert of the Wâdî Rayân, fifty kilometres south of the Fayyûm, where for ten years they had lived in desert caves, and to settle at Dair Abû Maqâr. This was the beginning of a spiritual and architectural restoration of the monastery. At that time, only six elderly monks lived at the monastery and the historic buildings were on the point of collapse. Today more than a hundred monks, many of whom are university graduates in the fields of agriculture, pharmacology, medicine, education, engineering, veterinary medicine, etc., make up the monastic community.

One of the most urgent tasks was the restoration of the old and dilapidated buildings, many of which were pulled down and replaced by more than one hundred and fifty new cells, a refectory for the daily agape meal, a library, a spacious guest house, several reception rooms and visitors' quarters. The new buildings (which also include a bakery, barns and garages as well as storage and repair facilities) occupy an area of ten acres, six times that covered by the old monastery.

The restoration of the historic buildings has been supervised by the Department of Antiquities and by Dr. Peter Grossmann of the German Archaeological Institute. During the restoration of the large Church of St. Macarius in the autumn of 1978 the monks claim to have discovered the relics of St. John the Baptist and those of the ninth-century B.C. prophet Elisha. They were found in a crypt below the northern wall of the church. The relics were gathered and placed in a special reliquary before the sanctuary of St. John the Baptist in the Church of St. Macarius.[115]

A modern printing press, installed in 1978, produces the monthly magazine *St. Mark* and other publications in Arabic and foreign languages. The monastery's dispensary is staffed by several monks, two qualified physicians, an ophthalmologist, a dentist and several pharmacists. It serves the four hundred labourers, and visitors as well as the monks.

Since 1975 the monks, like those of the other monasteries, have reclaimed and cultivated large areas of desert. One kilometre to the north of the monastery large farm buildings have been set up to house cows, buffalos, sheep and poultry. Noteworthy is a new type of beet fodder, which the monks have cultivated for the first time in Egypt. In 1978 President Sadat donated two thousand feddans of desert land to the monastery, with two tractors and a new well, drilled to obtain sub-soil water.

The monastic life centres on the daily common meal or agape which is eaten in the refectory at the ninth hour when twelve psalms are said. Once a week, on Sunday morning between two and eight a.m. the Divine Liturgy is celebrated. It is followed by the agape. Other meals are taken by the monks in their cells, which all contain small kitchens.

The monastery sometimes receives a thousand visitors a day, many of whom are seeking to secure a blessing from the place, hallowed by the prayers of such great desert fathers as St. Macarius the Great, St. John the Short, St. Paphnutius, St. Isidore, St. Moses the Black and St. Pimen. The monastery maintains friendly links with several other monasteries including the Benedictine monastery at Chevetogne in Belgium, Solesmes Abbey and the Monastery of the Transfiguration in France, Dair al-Harf in Lebanon and the Convent of the Incarnation in England. Several monks from these monasteries have stayed for some time at Dair Abû Maqâr.[116]

7

DAIR
ANBÂ BISHOÎ

The Life of St. Bishoî

Like the majority of Coptic monasteries the foundation of the Monastery of Anbâ Bishoî is closely associated with the life of its patron saint. According to the monks of Dair Anbâ Bishoî, St. Bishoî was one of a family of many children. When an angel appeared and called him into the desert, he responded willingly and went to Scetis, where he joined Anbâ Yuhannis (St. John the Short), who had lived there alone for many years. But after a while, Anbâ Yuhannis recommended that St. Bishoî leave him and live by himself in a cave.

While observing the solitary life, St. Bishoî experienced several visions of Christ. On one occasion Christ passed by his cell, and St. Bishoî stooped down to wash his master's feet, after which he drank the water as a blessing. Another time, some monks who had heard about St. Bishoî's visions asked him to lead them to Christ. A few days later, after receiving a message from the Lord, St. Bishoî instructed the monks to proceed to a certain place in the desert, where Christ would await them. As they passed on their way, they saw an old man, feeble and worn out, asking to be taken along by the monks. But the monks, anxious to meet Christ, ignored the pleading of the old man. In the last of the group of monks was St. Bishoî. When he saw the old man, he took pity on him, and carried him along to his destination. When St. Bishoî met the monks at the place where they were to meet Christ, he straightened his back, and the stranger disappeared. Christ had sat at the roadside, waiting to be helped. In their haste to see Christ they had forgotten to be Christians.

Another story is related by the monks of Dair as-Suriân which explains the origin of the high tamarind tree in their monastery. St.

Ephraem had wandered to the Desert of Scetis in order to assure his salvation, for it had been revealed to him that St. Bishoî had found redemption through his solitary life in the Wâdî 'n-Natrûn. When St. Ephraem met St. Bishoî, they realized that they could not communicate with each other, for the visitor spoke only Syriac. God, however, intervened, and they understood each other. St. Ephraem, when visiting St. Bishoî, left his staff outside the cell of St. Bishoî where it took root and grew into a mighty tree. Today this tree is still to be seen in the Monastery of the Syrians.[1] A room which once housed a printing press has been built around this tree, and the monks meet every afternoon under the tree to say vespers.

Both St. Bishoî and St. John the Short escaped the first sack of the monastery in 407. The former found refuge in a mountain near the Fayyûm, where he met the anchorite Paul of Tammûwah with whom he established a great friendship.[2] St. John the Short went to the Monastery of St. Antony. Three months after Anbâ Bishoî arrived in the Fayyûm, he died. Anbâ Athânâsîûs, bishop of the Fayyûm, wanted to remove the bodily remains of the saint of Scetis to his city, but the ship in which the body was placed refused to sail. Then the anchorite Jeremiah was consulted, and he revealed to the bishop that this had happened because the two friends should not be separated. So, when Paul of Tammûwah died, both bodies were eventually taken to the Fayyûm where they were placed in a shrine at the Monastery of Anbâ Shenûdah.

The Sacks

The history of Dair Anbâ Bishoî follows more or less that of the other monasteries in Scetis. Like Dair Abû Maqâr, Dair al-Barâmûs, and Dair Yuhannis Colobus, Dair Anbâ Bishoî suffered five sacks by the Berbers. Maqrîzî concentrates on the fourth destruction of Dair Anbâ Bishoî which occurred during the patriarchate of Anbâ Andrûnîqûs (Andronicus) (616-623). Anbâ Andrûnîqûs was followed by Anbâ Banîamîn I (623-662), who "reconstructed the Monastery of Abû Bishoî and the Monastery of the Virgin of Abû Bishoî, both being located in the Wâdî Habîb".[3]

The fifth sack of Scetis, which occurred in 817, was as serious as the previous devastations, for the desert monasteries had been depopulated and their churches and cells burnt. The majority of the monks escaped to other monasteries. Yet fifteen to twenty years later, the Desert of Scetis had become again a haven for anchorites and monks. This was during the patriarchates of Anbâ Ya'qûb (819-830) and Anbâ Yûsâb (830-849). "When the time of the persecution had come to an end, they removed the body of St. Bishoî and that of St. Paul of Tammûwah to the Monastery of St. Bishoî in the Desert of Scetis. The body of the saint worked many wonders and miracles, and his body is preserved intact until now without any corruption. The saint stayed for twenty-seven years in the desert of Scetis... ten years in the Desert of Antinoë (south of the Fayyûm) and twenty years in the world before becoming a monk, his whole life was ninety-seven years."

The violent destructions of the monasteries from the fifth to the ninth century were due to the marauding nature of the Berbers. The most serious persecution of the Christians in the Middle Ages occurred during the patriarchate of Anbâ Zakharîâ (1004-1032) and the Fatimid caliphate of al-Hâkim bi-'Amr-illah (996-1021). This persecution was provoked by a discontented Christian. The caliph is said to have been excited against the Christians by a certain monk's ambition for high ecclesiastical office.[4] Abûnâ Yuhannis (John) had gone in person to the patriarch and requested that he be appointed to one of the vacant dioceses. But the council of bishops rejected the request, and the monk went to complain to the caliph. Thereupon the caliph issued letters to the patriarch advising him to grant the monk's request. At that time, the patriarch had gone to the monasteries in Scetis, where he remained for a period of nine years. He turned over the whole matter to his nephew, Anbâ Khâil, Bishop of Sakhâ, an adversary of John the monk. Determined that John should not be promoted, he hired a party of Arabs, who took him, stoned him, and threw him into a dry well. At the bottom of the pit John found a cave which saved him from the shower of stones his assailants rained on him, and eventually John escaped and related his experience to the patriarch. A little while later, when two dioceses had become vacant and had been filled, presumably by wealthier candidates, John could no longer postpone his revenge and sent a letter to the caliph.

The patriarch was immediately thrown into prison. But when he was cast to the lions, God protected him from them. Then, "Al-Hâkim ordered the lions to be starved again, and that, when their hunger became violent, a sheep should be slain and that the patriarch should be divested of his clothing, and that his body should be smeared with sheep's blood, and that the lions should be set loose upon him."[5] But as in the case of Daniel[6] the lions did not hurt the patriarch, and he regained his liberty.

The persecution of the Christian population this time was particularly severe. "In 1005 a general order was issued for the destruction of all Christian churches and the confiscation of their land and property. The Christians were offered the choice of becoming Muslims, or leaving the country, or else wearing a heavy cross as a mark of their degradation."[7] The monasteries in the Desert of Scetis had enjoyed an immunity which attracted many Christians, and with the patriarch "most of the Christians also used to enter the desert twice in the year, namely at the Feast of the Epiphany and the Feast of Easter. They used to long for the Eucharist, as a babe longs for the milk of its mother's breast." The only places of worship which remained unmolested were the desert monasteries. The end of al-Hâkim's life is mysterious. It is thought he was assassinated during one of his nocturnal expeditions to the Muqattam heights, but since his corpse was never discovered, his followers believed that he had been taken up into heaven, and would re-appear on the earth at some future time. Bar-Hebraeus, on the other hand, claims that he went into the Desert of Scetis, became a monk, and ended his life there, and that Christ appeared to him.[8]

The numerous stories about the saintly Bessus, a monk from the Monastery of St. John Kame, belong to this period. A story related by the deacon Abû Habîb Mikhâil ibn Badîr al-Damanhûrî tells of a quarrel between two monks from the Monastery of Anbâ Bishoî. They went to Bessus to be reconciled. One of them consented to a reconciliation but the other refused. After three days, the disobedient monk returned to Bessus, suffering from leprosy. A miracle, however, cured this once disobedient, but now penitent monk.

From the Eleventh to the Sixteenth Century

During the patriarchate of Anbâ Kîrillus II (1078-1092), Mawhûb, the deacon of Alexandria, visited the Desert of Scetis to make an inventory of its inhabitants. At that time, the Monastery of Anbâ Bishoî, with its forty monks, had only one tenth of the number of monks attached to the Monastery of Abû Maqâr.[9]

Towards the end of the thirteenth century, the Ethiopian saint, Takla Haymanot, visited Egypt and Palestine. In the *Ethiopian Synaxar* and in the *Life of Takla Haymanot* we read that the saint worshipped at all the holy places in Palestine and afterwards visited the monks in the Desert of Scetis. St. Takla Haymanot was rebuked by the patriarch of Alexandria for making frequent pilgrimages to Jerusalem, and told that he would be better occupied in founding a monastery, than in wandering through foreign countries.[10]

From the fourteenth to the sixteenth century new problems undermined the stability of the desert monasteries. Throughout this period, the Monastery of Abû Maqâr had remained in the foreground, because of its traditional association with the election and enthronement of patriarchs. Of the other monasteries, little is known. In 1330 Benjamin II (1327-1339) determined to visit the monasteries to restore the Monastery of Anbâ Bishoî. Ants had destroyed much of the woodwork and the buildings were now about to collapse. Having visited the other monasteries he set about the restoration. In memory of this restoration work the monks placed the patriarch's bodily remains in the Church of Anbâ Bishoî. In the south-west corner of the south aisle the feretory of Anbâ Banîamîn II still stands. Ten years after the visit of Anbâ Banîamîn II, Anbâ Butrus V (1340-1346) visited the monasteries, and stayed at Dair Abû Maqâr for the consecration of the chrism.

During the first half of the fourteenth century the great Arab geographer Ibn Fadl Allah al-'Umarî accompanied Sultan al-Malik an-Nâsir Muhammad ibn Qalawûn, on a journey to the valley of Natrûn. The following is his brief report: "The seven convents are situated in Lower Egypt. They are found in an isolated place amid the sand and salty marshes amidst of a thirsty and tiring plain because of its very dryness. Its inhabitants drink water from cisterns or wells and they live in extreme privation. The Christians look after their needs and present them with precious gifts. The Coptic writers and the officers of the sultan surround them with care in order to find a place of retreat in case of disgrace. I do not know the particular history of these convents nor do I know of verses composed in their honour to cite. But I have depended on hearsay about their fame and the spread of their renown."[11]

As has been observed elsewhere in this book, the Black Death, which occurred in the fourteenth century, was disastrous for the monasteries in the Desert of Scetis. The desert, which had at one time contained a hundred monasteries, had merely seven in 1442. Apart from the patriarchal Monastery of Abû Maqâr, Maqrîzî mentions the Monastery of Abû Yuhannis al-Qasîr which was supposed to have been built by Constantine. Previously many monks inhabited this monastery, "though now there are only three monks left". The Monastery of Anbâ Yuhannis Kame and the Monastery of St. Elias, which belonged to the Ethiopians, were both in ruins; worms had eaten up the woodwork, and they had collapsed. The Monasteries of Anbâ Nûb and of the Armenians had been destroyed. The Monastery of Anbâ Bishoî had survived because it was very large.[12] The seventh monastery mentioned in the list of Maqrîzî is that of al-Barâmûs.

Seventeenth- and Eighteenth-Century Travellers

The first of the French travellers to mention the Monastery of Anbâ Bishoî was Fr. J. Coppin. He writes in 1638, that the "Monastery of Ambacioche" was the "second convent", after that of St. Macarius.[13] The Monastery of Anbâ Bishoî is connected with that of Abû Maqâr by the "Way of the Angels". This is a path which the hermits used on Sundays to attend the celebration of the Divine Liturgy. Fr. Coppin also mentions a little dome which was part of the Church of St. John the Short, as well as a tree which was given the name of Shagarat at-Ta'ah or the Tree of Obedience. At this time, twenty monks lived in the monastery, and the church, a beautiful building, was consecrated in honour to the Blessed Virgin Mary.

Thévenot, who was in Egypt in 1657, gives an illuminating description of the Wâdî 'n-Natrûn monasteries and adds advice on how to get there. "One should also see the desert of St. Macharius, where there are four monasteries, of St. Macharius, the Syrians, Balsarion, and of our Lady".[14] He continues: "You must endeavour to agree as cheap as you can, and it must be made in presence of the Cachef, before you set out, for if you delay till you come back, they'll exact the more. The hire commonly for going out and coming is two piastres for each Horse or Camel... besides three or four piastres for every horseman that accompanies you." Thévenot mentions a village called Dris (Atrîs), where the monks had a house. He repeats Fr. Coppin's observation that the "Angels' Way" connects the Monastery of Abû Maqâr with the Monastery of Anbâ Bishoî, and the many ruined monasteries. "It is not good to follow that "Angels' Way" nor to be too curious in asking questions of the Arabs about it, for then they would conclude, that you were come to search for some treasure hid in it, which they fancy the Franks know of. Among these old buildings you see the ruins of a monastery, built in honour of St. John the Short and the dry rod, which being watered by that good hermit, was changed into a fair tree, which is to be seen at this day, as a monument of the merit of obedience. The Monastery of Anbâ Bishoî is the pleasantest of all the four, for it has a fair church, a lovely garden, and good water, with a big tower in it. There were a great many holy bodies therein, which on Palm Sunday 1656 were burnt by a spark that fell from a taper that had been left burning there; whereupon the monks being vexed that they had lost their saints, gave it out that they had been carried away by a French merchant, who came into those quarters to buy natron. But finding that the device would not take, though it would cost the merchant money, they raised some dead bodies and brought them into their church, publishing that they were the bodies of their saints, which had escaped out of the French ship, and were come back to their church."

In 1672, Fr. Johann Michael Wansleben planned his journey to the "desert de Saint Macaire".[15] Like his predecessors, Wansleben refers to the "Way of Angels". From an ancient Arabic manuscript Wansleben concludes that the desert had previously contained seven monasteries. Of these only two were important: the Monastery of the Syrians, and that of Anbâ Bishoî, which both had good water. Again, like Fr. Coppin and Thévenot, Wansleben referred to the Tree of Obedience, which the monks still call today Shagarat at-Ta'ah.

The next traveller was Robert Huntington, who served as chaplain to the Levant Company before he became bishop of Raphoe in Ireland. He found the Monastery of Anbâ Bishoî less ruinous than the other monasteries, and added that the refectory was furnished with stone seats and a table to accommodate from fifty to sixty persons.

In December 1712, Fr. Claude Sicard, after visiting the monks of the neighbouring Monastery of the Syrians, went to the Monastery of Anbâ Bishoî, where he found only four monks. His very brief description suggests that he visited the monastery merely in passing.[16]

The next visitor to mention the Monastery of Anbâ Bishoî was le Sieur Granger who called the monastery "Deir Labiat". Granger, who visited the Wâdî 'n-Natrûn in 1730, was not interested in architecture, archaeology nor monks, which explains his superficial references to the Coptic monasteries.[17]

In 1765, the historian and scholar al-Warthilanî al-Husain ibn Muhammad as-Saîd made a pilgrimage from Morocco to Mecca. In his book *Nuzhat al-Anzar fi Badl 'Ilm at-Târîkh wa 'l-Akhbar* he relates his experiences. "We then left as-Shammama in the direction of the Wâdî al-Ruhbân, which is the valley of the monks. It is a large and long valley where one finds castles or monasteries for Christian monks who have come from Egypt in order to give themselves up to the worship of God. In Egypt there are Christian communities which pay tribute to the sultan. The Wâdî al-Ruhbân is a large sandy valley where palm trees, plenty of water, and divers species of wild beasts as well as oxen, ostriches, gazelles, wild cows and game can be found. This valley was given to the monks because it offers refuge to the Christian monks who settle in groups in their respective monasteries and no stranger is admitted. They possess neither land nor herds. The Christian 'Dhimmî' of Egypt are in contact with them. They sent them their *ex-voti* and their charities which consist of food supplies and clothes."

Two years later, al-Warthilanî returned from his pilgrimage and passed by the monasteries of the Wâdî 'n-Natrûn again. "Then we left in the morning and continued our route until we arrived very near the qasr or monastery which offers shelter to the Christians, that is the monks. Having arrived at the door of the monastery, we saw them (the monks) appearing and they began to talk with us. They asked us for news from Egypt and its inhabitants. We told them of all that had happened to the inhabitants of Egypt and Salih Bey who was in Upper Egypt, and we informed them that a battle had taken place between them. Its result was the routing of the troops of Egypt who then left by boats. We stayed in the empty qasr which was situated at the very end of the monastery where we, the sons of Sidî Muhammad al-Hag, entered and where we spent a wonderful night."[18] Whether this hospitality was a matter of Christian charity or the result of an agreement reached beforehand, is difficult to ascertain. We do know that the monasteries of the Wâdî 'n-Natrûn were obliged to assist pilgrims to Mecca by providing for them food and drink, as is stated in the "Letter of Protection" which Muhammad ibn 'Abd al-Muttalib was supposed to have issued to the Copts.[19]

On 14 January, 1778, C.S. Sonnini "passed in front of one of these monasteries, called Anbâ Bishoî, which is but a few paces from that we had quitted (Dair as-Surîân), the monks were waiting for me at the gate; they importuned me to go in for a moment, and, in order to determine me, they said that they were in possession of the body of a saint, which was as fresh and florid as if still alive. They appeared very much offended at my resisting such an attraction, but the true cause of the discontent they expressed was the disappointment of the money which they expected to obtain from my visit."[20]

When General Antoine Andréossy visited the Monastery of Anbâ Bishoî, in January 1799, there were twelve monks. The French general describes a custom practised by the neighbouring Muslims: when a Muslim wants to build a pigeon-house, he sends a letter and a gift to the monks who, in return, give him a "billet mystique" which on being placed in the pigeon-house ensures its prosperity.[21]

Seventeenth–, Eighteenth– and Nineteenth–Century Cartographers

From the seventeenth century onwards, cartographers made use of the geographical material supplied to them by travellers, whether scientists or priests. The monasteries of the Wâdî 'n-Natrûn are found on almost all maps of Egypt after the middle of the seventeenth century. The *Nova Aegypti Tabula* identifies the Wâdî 'n-Natrûn with S. Antonii Desertum, and places the Monasterium S. Macarii on the Mediterranean coast in the vicinity of Alexandria.[22] Not much more exactness is provided by Michalet's *Les Déserts d'Egypte, de Thébaide d'Arabie, de Syrie & etc., où sont exactement marquez les Lieux habitez par les Sainctes Pères des Deserts.* This map, which claims to give the proper positions of the caves and sites of the desert fathers, though beautifully executed, does not merit any serious attention from a geographical point of view. A map drawn by the pious artist Michalet in 1693 is of no help for the study of Coptic monasticism. Schenk's *Aegypti Recentior descriptio: Aegyptis & Jurcis, Elchibith: Arabibus, Mesre & Misri: Hebrais, Mitsraim* of ca. 1700 also places S. Antonii in S. Macarii Desertum (Wâdî 'n-Natrûn).

One of the first maps to give fairly correct positions for all four Wâdî 'n-Natrûn monasteries is Lotter's *Le cours entier du grand et fameux Nil appellé la Rivière de l'Egypte dans l'Ecriture Sainte avec la Basse et la Haute Egypte.* This map also mentions the small villages of Quafredaoud, Teranie and Etris (Atrîs). Richard Pococke who visited Egypt around 1737, provided important cartographical information which appears on Covens et Mortier's map *Carte de l'Egypte et le cours du Nil.* The four Wâdî 'n-

Natrûn monasteries are given a relatively accurate position. The Monastery of al-Barâmûs appears under the name Monasterium S. Paesii.[23] A few years later, in 1753, Robert de Vaugondy published his *Carte de l'Egypte Ancienne et Moderne,* largely based upon the information provided by Pococke's map. On this map, the Monastery of al-Barâmûs is called the Monastery of S. Paes (of the Holy Son), and the Monastery of Anbâ Bishoî is omitted. Almost identical as regards positions and names of the monasteries is Bonne's *Carte de l'Egypte Ancienne et Moderne* published by Lattré in 1762.

The most famous cartographers of the eighteenth century were Guillaume Delisle and J.B. Bourguignon d'Anville, who acquired a wealth of information for their compilations of maps. In 1765 B. d'Anville (1697-1782) published a map entitled *Egypt called in the Country of Missir.* Three monasteries of the Wâdî 'n-Natrûn are mentioned, but their positions are badly confused; the shrine of Sitt Dimîânah is called Gemiana, but the two villages of Terane and Etris (Atrîs) are correctly placed. Samuel Dunn's *Ancient and Modern Egypt* (1786) again borrows heavily from Vaugondy and Bonne, at least as far as the naming and the position of the monasteries are concerned. The Monastery of al-Barâmûs is called S. Paes, and the Monastery of Anbâ Bishoî is omitted. The monasteries of St. Antony and St. Paul are in their proper positions. Almost identical to Dunn's map is that of Delineato. His *l'Egitto Antico e Moderno* appeared in 1798, and it lists three of the Wâdî 'n-Natrûn monasteries: S. Paes, Monastero dai Siriaci and S. Macario; while John Wallis' *A Map of the Mouths of the Nile* omits all the Wâdî 'n-Natrûn monasteries, and merely mentions St. Geminian's.

One of the first German maps to give the position of the four Wâdî 'n-Natrûn monasteries is F.L. Güssefeld's *Charte von Aegypten* (1800), printed by J.B. Homann. Unfortunately, Güssefeld's map confuses the position of the two Red Sea monasteries, and St. Paul's monastery appears north of St. Antony's, an error which was copied later by W.M. Leake in his *Map of Egypt* (1818). Enouy's map compiled from draughts of the Scientific Institute in Cairo in 1800 mentions the Lake of Natron, but not the monasteries. The shrine of Sitt Dimîânâh is again called Gemiane.

L.S. de la Rochette's *Lower Egypt and the adjacent Desert with a part of Palestine* (1802) is interesting. He not only gives the positions of the monasteries, but also the route which Sonnini took in January 1778, when he went from Abûkîr to Dair al-Barâmûs. He also marks the annual route of the Natron camel caravans, which was followed by Browne in 1792, and by Andréossy in 1799. Furthermore, he indicates the route followed by pilgrims coming from Barqa and travelling via Dair al-Barâmûs to Tarânah. On this map, the Monastery of Abû Maqâr is called "Amba Monguar". John Cary's *A new Map of Egypt* (1805) gives the same detailed information as that of de la Rochette. Lapie's *Carte Historique, Physique et Positique de l'Egypte* also provides the reader with the routes leading from Tarânah to the Couvent d'el-Baramous and from Mit Salameh to the Couvent de S. Macaire. The second Arrowsmith map of Egypt appeared in 1832. It shows the caravan routes from "Baramous Greek Convent" to Tarânah, and the routes from "Amba Bicoi" and the "Conv. of St. Macarius" to Mit Salameh. Arrowsmith also gives the route of Pacho's visit to Dair Anbâ Bishoî in 1825. Monastery ruins are indicated in the "Wady Moileh", no doubt those of Dair Anbâ Samwîl.

Nineteenth- and Twentieth-Century Travellers

In 1820, a large army of 1,300 men commanded by Husain Bey Shamishara passed by the monasteries of the Wâdî 'n-Natrûn. Muhammad 'Ali, who had invaded the Sûdân, felt the need to protect his western flank and thus commissioned this large force to cross the desert via the Wâdî 'n-Natrûn and the Oasis of Gara and to occupy the Oasis of Siwa.[24]

On 25 November, 1820, Heinrich Freiherr von Minutoli left the camp of the Jovaisi and passed the monasteries of the Wâdî 'n-Natrûn. He referred to the monasteries as "Labiat, Ou Serian and Aboumakar". Though he had intended to visit the monasteries, he gave up his plan, when he was informed that the inhabitants were rather rough and without any "Geisteskultur".[25]

In 1835 and 1841, Russegger, an Austrian scholar of natural history and science, visited Egypt as part of a tour through Europe, Asia and Africa. Of the four monasteries in the Wâdî 'n-Natrûn he mentions only two, that called "Labiat" which is to be identified with the Monastery of Anbâ Bishoî, and that of "U Serian", which is Dair as-Suriân.[26]

In 1837, after Lord Curzon had left the Monastery of al-Barâmûs, he established his headquarters in the Monastery of the Syrians. From here he visited the Monastery of Anbâ Bishoî and that of "Abou Magar". Both monasteries were inhabited only by three or four monks who conducted the services in their respective churches.[27]

In January 1839, Dr. Tattam and his step-daughter, Miss Platt, visited the Monastery of Anbâ Bishoî. Dr. Tattam examined the monastery's books, "which were about a hundred and fifty in number, and all Arabic and Coptic liturgies, with the exception of one fine copy of the Four Gospels in Coptic, and an old imperfect copy of the Book of Genesis. On the ground floor (of the qasr) was a large vaulted apartment, very lofty, with arches at each end, perfectly dark, and so strewn with loose leaves of old liturgies, that scarcely a portion of the floor was visible. And here we were all fully occupied in making diligent search with each a lighted taper, and a stick to turn up old fragments. In some parts, the manuscripts lay a quarter of a yard deep, and the amazing quantity of dust was almost choking, accompanied by a damp and fetid smell, nearly as bad as in the tombs of the kings.... We were afterwards conducted to the top of the monastery, which is flat-roofed, by a broad flight of stone steps, unenclosed, and between the outer wall and the tower."[28]

In 1844, the German scholar, Konstantin von Tischendorf, visited the monks of Anbâ Bishoî. He found only four monks: "The superior was an old man of a hundred and twenty years of age, who sits all day long upon a cross bench, and sings aloud both day and night. To this old man heaven hangs down its holy lamps so low into the narrow valley of the earth, that his eyes, already closed to the world, see God only, and his lips do nothing but pray. I visited him in his cell the instant I heard his unceasing prayer. Upon my departure from the monastery, he came forth, supported by his staff, and appeared to me to speak with perfect intelligence. A benediction from these aged lips deeply affected me."[29]

When another German traveller, Dr. Wilhelm Junkers, knocked at the doors of Dair Anbâ Bishoî in November 1875, he was not allowed to enter. He heard later that a stranger had stolen manuscripts from the library which caused the seven monks of the monastery to be frightened of European visitors.[30]

In 1881, after leaving the Monastery of the Syrians, Frs. Jullien, Nourrit and Noory and Mr. Palamarie visited the Monastery of Anbâ Bishoî, then the largest of the four monasteries in the Wâdî 'n-Natrûn. It also had the best water. According to Fr. Jullien, the monastery was started by two brothers, Isaiah and Paese, sons of a wealthy merchant. Isaiah's body is still preserved in the church that bears his name. As at the Monastery of al-Barâmûs, the visitors engaged in doctrinal conversations with the desert monks, and Fr. Jullien records that the acceptance of the doctrine of the two natures of Christ was no problem, whereas the doctrine of the supremacy of the pope provoked horror.[31]

Two years later Alfred Butler, coming from the Monastery of Abû Maqâr, visited the Monastery of Anbâ Bishoî. "We had heard that Anbâ Bishoî contained the best well of water of all the four monasteries, and we resolved therefore to make it our headquarters for the remainder of our visit, a decision which we had no cause to repent. We found our arrival was not expected: the iron-plated postern was closed, and we had to ring some time at the bell, which is hung on the convent wall and sounded by a cord swinging loose below."[32] "The principal church, which bears the name of Anbâ Bishoî, is an extremely fine building, the main features of which are of the basilican order, and the two satellite chapels or churches which open out from the choir. That at the north side is dedicated to al-'Adhrâ, and contains the bones of Anbâ Bishoî in a reliquary, the other on the south side is larger, and is covered with a most magnificent dome: the altar, which is dedicated to Abiskhairon,[33] has for its slab a shallow marble tray of oblong form. A narrow passage north of the altar leads to the baptistry, which lies adjoining the chapel of the east: it contains a plain round font of the usual type. The qasr contains little of interest except a series of lofty vaulted chambers, which judging from the fragments of Coptic and Arabic volumes scattered about the floor, once served as the convent library."

On his return from the Oasis of Siwa in April 1896, Arthur Silva White made a slight detour, in order to visit the monasteries of the Syrians and that of Anbâ Bishoî. "There are twenty monks at Suriânî and fourteen at Bishoî. The former is the most interesting of the three monasteries I visited in the Natrun Valley and certainly looked the most prosperous. It was here that the so-called Syrian library was discovered. Both monasteries have good gardens and wells nearly a hundred feet deep, from which a copious supply of water is drawn up by oxen working a *sakkia*. The monks of Dehr Suriani were more sociable and entertaining than the others. They returned my visit and appeared to be delighted with their reception in my tent."[34]

When Ewald Falls departed from the Monastery of the Syrians in the summer of 1905, he went to the Monastery of Anbâ Bishoî and tasted the water. "The pump which brings forth the precious liquid is in the third of the courtyards, and furnishes enough water for a tropical garden with many culinary vegetables, of which the monks are very proud. Notwithstanding this favourable condition, in comparison with the Macarius monastery it seemed to me to be most behindhand."[35]

The buildings of Anbâ Bishoî underwent so much restoration at the beginning of the last century, that it is difficult to trace out the old kernel. There is scarcely anything left of the old library. It was located in the qasr, and it must have been rich in illuminated books. Falls noticed the "warning" that is added to a great number of books. The following text appeared at the end of a Synaxarium: "This book is an eternal inheritance for everlasting preservation in the church of the great and perfect St. Anbâ Bishoî in his monastery, which is situated in the desert of Shihat, in al-Asket in Wâdî Habîb, the balance of the heart. No one has the right to remove the same from the inheritance of the said monastery out of any frivolous ground, and anyone who acts contrary to this and does remove it, shares the lot and fate of Diocletian the unbeliever, Herod the apostate, Simeon the magician, and Judas the traitor; on the obedient, to the contrary, will there fall for ever and aye the blessing and reward of God; Amen! Amen! Amen!" Furthermore, Falls records the story of the "waterless river" which was told him by the monks òf Dair Anbâ Bishoî. "Hermits had settled near the hill of the 'eagle's stone' on the bank of the stream, they were constantly attacked by river pirates, until, through the hermits' prayers the water sank and then vanished forever."

In 1910, Walter Tyndale proposed to visit the Coptic monasteries in the Wâdî 'n-Natrûn. He made the acquaintance of Palmer-Jones in Cairo. Palmer-Jones was "an enthusiastic architect who had measured up some of the early Coptic monasteries, and had also reconstructed on paper dynastic buildings of which little but the plan is at present traceable."[36] Travelling by train along the edge of the Libyan desert, Tyndale and Palmer-Jones eventually arrived at a station called al-Khatâtba, where they were met by the agent of the Salt and Soda Company. Twice a week, a steam-train went from al-Khatâtba to the rest-house in the valley. After a night in the Wâdî 'n-Natrûn rest-house, Palmer-Jones and Tyndale went to visit Dair Anbâ Bishoî, which they thought looked more like a medieval fortress than a retreat for monks. The gateway was large and imposing; but the door itself was small and sufficiently recessed to be defended through the loopholes in the projecting jambs. "We were received by the prior in a bare and once whitewashed room, with a wooden bench round the walls. After the usual salutations, he ordered coffee, and even produced cigarettes; but argue as long as we liked, he would not give us permission to sketch in the convent. The permission my friend had got, from the patriarch in Cairo, mentioned the other convents, and not the one we were in; we should be allowed to see the church, but no sketching was to be done." Palmer-Jones had worked in this monastery during the winter of 1909-10 and had not thought it necessary to get authorization to make a few sketches.

When Johann Georg, Duke of Saxony, visited the monasteries of the Wâdî 'n-Natrûn for the first time in 1912, he stopped for only a little while at the Monastery of Anbâ Bishoî. He was on his way from Dair as-Suriân to Dair Abû Maqâr. The monks received the duke with all ecclesiastical protocol. He mentions the major church of the monastery which was rather new, and criticizes the fact that the haikal doors had been recently painted in a "horrible and ugly manner."[37] He went up to the keep, but was little moved by the Chapel of St. Michael on the top floor.

In 1920, Hugh Evelyn White spent six weeks alone in the Wâdî 'n-Natrûn taking the necessary notes to complete the work of the Metropolitan Museum of Art Egyptian Expedition which had been started by Palmer-Jones in 1909. In November and December 1920, H. Burton, W. Hauser and Evelyn White went again to the monasteries for the purpose of supplementing the collection of photographs and architectural drawings.

Three years later, in 1923, Dr. William Hatch of the Episcopal Theological Seminary in Cambridge, Mass., visited the Monastery of Anbâ

Bishoî and was conducted by the hegoumenos to an upper room, where there were fragments of paper manuscripts lying on the floor in great profusion. "I rummaged at will among the debris and picked up several leaves containing parts of Matthew, Luke, Acts, and James, as well as some liturgical fragments. All these were willingly given to me for the asking."[38] At the time of his visit the monastery was occupied by twenty-two monks.

Twice, in 1930 and 1931, Prince 'Umar Tûssûn, Professor Breccia and Dr. Puy-Haubert visited the Monasteries of the Wâdî 'n-Natrûn. The statistical information provided by the prince gives the various sizes of the four monasteries in 1930. Their surface areas were as follows:[39]

The Monastery of Abû Maqâr ...... 1 Feddan 21 Karat 6 Sahm
The Monastery of Anbâ Bishoî ...... 2 Feddan 16 Karat 14 Sahm
The Monastery of the Syrians ...... 1 Feddan 16 Karat
The Monastery of al-Barâmûs ...... 2 Feddan 13 Karat

On the pillars of an ancient church on the first floor of the qasr of Dair Anbâ Bishoî are numerous graffiti. Apart from an inscription "L. A. Elsworth August 25th 1909" we discover a note which commemorates the visit of a patriarch. On Easter Sunday 1934, the patriarch of Antioch, Anbâ Ighnâtîûs, visited the monastery and from there went to Dair as-Surîân. Apparently at that time, it rained very heavily in the Wâdî 'n-Natrûn.

In preparation for her volume *Das Christlich-Koptische Aegypten einst und heute,* Dr. Maria Cramer visited Dair Anbâ Bishoî and Dair as-Surîân on 18 March, 1956. Dr. Cramer was shown the beautiful *scriptura illuminata* of the master calligrapher Anbâ Makârîûs III, the 114th patriarch (1942-45), who came from the Monastery of Anbâ Bishoî.

The monasteries of the Wâdî 'n-Natrûn, especially the Monastery of the Syrians and the Monastery of Anbâ Bishoî, have repeatedly attracted the interest of foreign diplomats. Thus we find that Christian D. Holten-Eggert, ambassador of the Kingdom of Denmark, visited the monasteries of Wâdî 'n-Natrûn over twelve times between 1956 and 1958.

The Wâdî 'n-Natrûn has attracted biologists, geologists and gamehunters for many centuries. Scientists, like Granger, went to the Desert of Scetis in search of biological specimens. In the nineteenth and twentieth centuries, these expeditions became more numerous, and every aspect of life in the Wâdî 'n-Natrûn has been studied.[40] Many scientists have visited the monasteries and enjoyed the hospitality of the monks. Sportsmen used to go from Cairo and Alexandria to the Wâdî 'n-Natrûn in search of game. Meinertzhagen informs us that the last wild pig was shot in the Desert of Scetis in 1892.

The Monastery Today

The visitor to the Monastery of Anbâ Bishoî will find five churches or chapels. The Church of Anbâ Bishoî, which is the main church; the Church of Abû Iskhîrûn; the Church of al-'Adhrâ; the Church of Mârî Girgis; and the Church of St. Michael on the roof of the qasr.

The Church of Anbâ Bishoî has three haikals. It belongs to the most ancient part of the monastery, and dates from the ninth century. Set in the floor, at the western end of the church is the lakan, a marble basin which is used in the Maundy Thursday Rite for the footwashing. In the south-west corner of the nave there stands the feretory of Anbâ Baniâmîn II which is adorned with icons of the three Macarii, St. Thomas and the Crucifixion. The church, which has undergone several restorations, was newly redecorated in 1957. In the north-east corner of the choir stands a feretory containing the bodily remains of Anbâ Bishoî and his companion Paul of Tammûwah. Furthermore, the monks claim the body of St. Ephraem the Syrian.

The Church of Abû Iskhîrûn is reached from the south side of the choir of the main church.[41] To the north of the haikal is the baptistry. To the north-east of the main church is the Chapel of the Holy Virgin. This chapel is used by the monks during the winter months for the Divine Liturgy. The Church of Mârî Girgis, which at one time was used as a storage place for palm fibre, is not used now for services. The ancient refectory is connected with the western end of the church of Anbâ Bishoî.

The twelfth-century qasr is entered at first storey level by means of a drawbridge which rests on the roof of the gatehouse. On the second storey of the qasr is the Church of St. Michael. The icons on the iconostasis, which date from the eighteenth century, have been restored. They show the twelve apostles vested in pontifical vestments. In no other monastery is the Church of St. Michael so isolated as in the Monastery of Anbâ Bishoî. It is probable that at one time the qasr had an additional floor, like those of the other monasteries.

At one time, the library was housed in the qasr. A small room in the monastery-yard now contains the remains of the library, and the books are stored in two cabinets with six shelves each. There are approximately five hundred volumes.

Despite the renaissance of the Monastery of St. Macarius under the leadership of Bishop Mikhâîl of Asyût and Abûnâ Mattâ al-Maskîn, the Monastery of St. Bishoî has emerged as the principal monastery in the Wâdî 'n-Natrûn. In the Middle Ages the spiritual leadership of the Coptic church came from the Monastery of St. Macarius (from the seventh to the thirteenth century twenty-five of the thirty-six patriarchs had been monks at Dair Abû Maqâr). Of the bishops currently serving in Egypt and abroad, Dair as-Suriân and Dair Anbâ Bishoî have supplied seventeen and fifteen respectively.

Dair Anbâ Bishoî won additional fame when Pope Shenûdah III spent some forty months (between September 1981 and January 1985) of enforced exile in a cell in the extensive plantations of the monastery. During this time the pope ordained about a hundred young men as monks. Since his release the stream of visitors to the monastery has steadily increased. Women, in particular, repair to the relics of St. Bishoî, which are believed to be incorruptible.

Since 1981 the Monastery of St. Bishoî has served as the papal desert cell, to which Pope Shenûdah III withdraws whenever possible. Several new buildings south of the historic monastery have been established. These accommodate approximately one hundred cells, conference facilities for ecumenical and local seminars and administrative centers, garages, repair shops, etc. The "papal pond" in this area is filled with trout, which the pope enjoys feeding.

The churches, the keep, the reception and guestrooms have been either rebuilt or refurbished. Noteworthy is the haikal-screen in the Church of Anbâ Bishoî with the paintings of the Apostles and the desert fathers by Ishaq Fanûs. On the second floor of the keep three new chapels have been installed and the Church of St. Michael, on the roof of the keep, has been completely renovated. Here modern iconography has been executed by the nuns of the Convent of St. Dimiana, Bilqâs. A kiosk selling souvenirs, crosses, devotional literature, etc. is situated outside the old wall on the way to the plantations.

Under the energetic leadership of Anbâ Sarabamûn and Qummus Sidraq al-Bishoî the number of monks at Dair Anbâ Bishoî has increased from twelve monks in 1960 to one hundred and twenty monks in 1986, of whom about thirty serve Coptic churches in Egypt and overseas.

8
DAIR AS-SURÎÂN

St. John Kame

For many centuries the name of St. John Kame has been closely associated with Dair as-Surîân (the Monastery of the Syrians). There are even some people who claim, mistakenly, that he was its founder. It is more than likely that after the destruction of the Monastery of St. John Kame, between 1330 and 1442 or even later, the monks of that monastery migrated to the Syrian monastery, transferring at the same time a commemoration tablet[1] and the relics of their patron saint.[2] This would explain the presence of two national groups in the Syrian monastery at the beginning of the fifteenth century.

St. John Kame was a native of Jebromounonson in the district of Sais in the western Delta. He was forced into marriage at an early age, but he persuaded his bride to permit him to live the life of a monk. Moved by a vision, he entered the Desert of Scetis where he became a disciple of Anbâ Teroti who inhabited a cell in the vicinity of Dair Abû Maqâr. After some time an angel directed him to go to the cell of St. John the Short, and here he shut himself up in a cave. "Now it befell, in the holy night of the Lord's Day, the while he stood performing his Synaxis, that the Holy Theotokos Mary came in unto him in great and unspeakable glory and a multitude of angels accompanied her. He fell upon his face from fear, but the Theotokos raised him and said unto him: 'Peace be unto thee, John, beloved of my Son Jesus, and of his Good Father and of the Holy Spirit. Be of good courage and steadfast and become a mighty man, having great endurance, fighting against the evil hostile spirits, that contend with thee. And lo, I am with thee until thou shall overcome them all and their evil, and fulfill the will of my Son... and there shall be unto thee multitudes of children and they shall build a church in thy community and shall call it by my name... the angels shall visit thy monastery and shall watch over thy children... And she gave unto him three gold *solidi* having upon them the sign of the Cross and said unto him: 'Take these and put them in the purse of the ministry and the blessing of my Son shall be in it forever.' When she had said this unto him, she wished him peace and filled him with strength and she was hidden from him in great glory."[3]

Before long the virtues of St. John Kame had attracted some three hundred disciples who gathered around him and built "a great ocean of dwellings and high towers and walls firmly established." For the community of this monastery, St. John Kame drew up canons and regulations.

Before the saint died he left the Desert of Scetis, following the instructions of an angel to go south to Upper Egypt.[4] The influence of St. John Kame is evident from his disciples, among whom were: "our father Shenouti... and my father Papa Mark, his successor after him, and my father Coluthus, and my father the deacon George, and my father Antony, and my father George, of whom is borne witness that they were worthy of the grace of the Holy Spirit."

The memorial tablet says that he died on the 24th Kihak at the first hour of the night in the year 575 A.M. (A.D. 859).

The Gaianite Heresy

The Monastery of the Syrians was founded in the sixth century. It came into existence as a result of the Gaianite heresy, which spread in the patriarchate of Anbâ Tîmûthâûs III (517-535). The emperor Justinian was using all available methods to impose the Chalcedonian decrees upon the non-Chalcedonians. In 518 Anbâ Sâwîrûs, Patriarch of Antioch, and Anbâ Yûliânûs, Bishop of Halicarnassus, were driven from their sees and took refuge in Egypt. Here, these two men developed divergent views on the nature of the body of Christ, as to whether or not it was corruptible. Julian, and subsequently Gaianus, held the view that Christ's body was incorruptible. The followers of this view became known as the Aphthartodocetae, or less properly, the Phantasiastae. Being a strict follower of Eutyches,[5] Julian argued that to deny the doctrine of the incorruptibility of the body of Christ was to admit the position which the Greek and Latin Churches had taken up at the Council of Chalcedon in 451. Severus argued that the corruptibility of the body of Christ was an essential doctrine, for he felt that otherwise, the truth of Christ's Passion would be denied. Severus' followers became known as the Corrupticolae or Phthartolatrae, that is the worshippers of the corruptible.

These theological discussions had an important effect upon the monks of the Desert of Scetis. Julian issued a statement, the *Tomarion*, "with an evil purpose... in which he expressed his approval of the faith of Eutyches, the unbeliever... he sent this book about Egypt to the monks of the desert. And they received it, and fell into the snare except seven persons, whose hearts were enlightened, and so they would not accept it, for they heard a voice saying: 'This is the impure *Tomarion*.' Then those who had fallen into the error of Julian rose up against them, and killed two of them. So the rest were scattered, and began to celebrate the liturgy in their cells in the Monastery of St. Macarius and in other monasteries. And this was the cause of their separation."[6]

That churches and "towers" (monasteries) were built at this time is attested by the *History of the Patriarchs*. Dorotheus, who took care of the affairs of the aged monks, and who had rejected the Julian heresy, approached Aristomachus, the governor of Egypt, begging him to authorize the building of churches and towers. The governor granted the request and the Orthodox monks were able to return to the desert, where they lived in their own monasteries.

The Monastery of the Syrians seems to have originated as a duplicate monastery to Dair Anbâ Bishoî. It was known as the "Theotokos", or Mother of God, monastery. The monks attached great significance to the Incarnation.[7] The teachings of the Gaianites or Aphthartodocetae were considered by their opponents as a kind of Docetist heresy, which, denying the doctrine of the Incarnation, consequently lowered the status of the Holy Virgin. To emphasize their Orthodoxy, they retained the name of the patron saint and added to it the title of the Theotokos.

The Beginnings of the Monastery

The first Syrian monks arrived in the Desert of Scetis at the beginning of the ninth century. Matthew and Abraham of Tekrit (the ancient metropolis of the Syrian Jacobites) settled in the western desert about the time of the fifth sack of the desert monasteries. A note in a Syriac manuscript of the middle of the ninth century contains the first reference to the Syrian monastery: "Let each who reads pray for Isaac and Daniel and Shalmun, chaste monks of Mâr Junah of the Syrians, that is in Maris, who gave this book, with nine others, to the Monastery of the Mother of God of the Syrians which is in the desert of Egypt... They entered this monastery in the days of the holy, blessed patriarch Mâr Cosmas of Alexandria (851-859) and Mâr John of Antioch (846-873) and in the presence of the honoured old man, the monk Bar 'Idai, head of the monastery."[8] The first hegoumenos of the Syrian monastery was possibly Bar 'Idai. He made

Abraham and Matthew responsible for the institution which they had restored after the fifth sack of Scetis had left it in ruins.

A great deal of our knowledge of the monasteries of the Desert of Scetis comes to us not as is to be expected from Coptic, but from Syriac sources. For alongside the foundation of the Monastery of the Syrians, came the establishment of a library. There is reason to believe that the Syrians at that time were well versed in art and literature.[9] This was reflected in monastic life, as is evident from the art treasures and the earliest collections of manuscripts made by Matthew and Abraham.

The Tekrit-Syrians, who had a colony in Fustât, donated to the purchase of the otherwise abandoned monastery. A Syrian named Marutha, the son of Habîb, bought the monastery for the use of his devout countrymen. This transaction took place at the beginning of the eighth century. However, Butler says that Dair as-Surîân owes its foundation to the Persian wars when much of Syrian life and learning was removed to Egypt. This would place the date of the purchase in the seventh century.[10]

Before this, in the fourth century, Syrian monks lived in an older Syrian monastery in the Desert of Scetis. The *Synaxarium* mentions two martyrs, Eunapius and Andrew of Lydda, who apparently lived in some kind of Syrian monastery[11] and internal sources reveal that a Syrian community existed in Scetis in 576. With the presence of Syrian monks in the Western desert, Marutha's purchase of a home for his compatriots becomes very comprehensible.

The Growth of the Monastery

In the tenth century, the Monastery of the Syrians gained in prominence. Incised in the haikal-screen of the Church of the Holy Virgin is a reference in the Syriac language to a hegoumenos, Moses of Nisibis, who had the doors constructed during the patriarchate of Mâr Cosmas III of Alexandria (920-932) and Mâr Basil of Antioch (932-935). Moses of Nisibis was a remarkable man. Among other things he is credited with valuable additions to the monastic library. In 927 he went to Baghdad, as a representative of the desert monasteries, to obtain tax exemption for the monasteries from the Abbasid Caliph al-Muktadir bi'llah (908-932). On his travels, he secured many valuable volumes which greatly enriched the library collection.

Following the patriarchate of Anbâ Mînâ II (956-974), a Syrian merchant named Abrâm ibn Zar'ah ascended the patriarchal throne. He was a pious and charitable man who, among other things, abolished simony, which the patriarchs used to practice.[12] It happened, "that when he was a layman, he went to the Monastery of Abba Macarius in the Wâdî Habîb to pray there." During the reign of Anbâ Fîlûtâûs (979-1004), the Syrian monastery was associated with the Coptic patriarch. A synodical letter, written in 987 by Fîlûtâûs to Athanasius VI of Antioch shows that the monastery was under the patronage and the protection of the Copts.

By the eleventh century, according to Mawhûb's census of 1088[13] the Syrian monastery rated as the third largest community in the Wâdî Habîb. With its sixty monks, it was as large as Dair Anbâ Bishoî and Dair al-Barâmûs together.[14]

The Western desert become even more international towards the end of the eleventh century when the Armenian Catholicos St. Vahram, known as Gregory II, decided to retreat into solitude and to consecrate himself to a life of prayer. Having adopted the rule of St. Antony, he was inspired to live on the top of the mountains. He abandoned the patriarchate to George, his chancellor. When the Armenian king heard of this, he attempted to stop the Catholicos from executing his plans.[15] The king failed and in 1074, St. Vahram went from Constantinople to Rome, and from there to Egypt in order to visit the desert, where the ancient fathers lived. There he established his patriarchal throne, and was welcomed with high honours by the Egyptian king.[16] He was followed by a large group of Armenians who arrived and joined him. There were thirty thousand Armenians in Egypt. Before St. Vahram's visit an Armenian monk known as al-Manakis had entered the Desert of Scetis and associated himself with the saintly monk Bessus.

Little is known about the history of the Syrian monastery in the thirteenth and fourteenth centuries. A scribal note of the middle of the thirteenth century leads White to believe that "at this time (1254) the number of monks at the Syrian monastery must have been comparatively large". Refugees fleeing before the western advance of the Mongols, may have found refuge in the Wâdî Habîb, and thus the monasteries may have experienced a short time of prosperity.

Decline and Revival

A hundred years later the Desert of Scetis was struck by the Black Death. A note in a Syriac manuscript informs us that John, a visitor to the Monastery of the Syrians, found in it but a single monk. "I, John, a desert monk from the Convent of the house of Mar Simeon of Kartamin, read in this book of stories of the Saints... I, John, entered this monastery in the year 1724 of the Greeks (1413). I only found one single monk in this monastery, Rabban Moses of Husn Kifa: God pardon him."[17]

Maqrîzî merely states that "a monastery opposite the Monastery of Bû Bishaî belonged to the Jacobites; for three hundred years, however, it has been in the possession of Syrian monks and at this time it is in their hands. The district in which these monasteries are situated is known by the name of 'Lake of the Monasteries'."[18] By this time, the monastery seems to have regained some of its importance.

By the end of the fifteenth century, the fifty-ninth Antiochene patriarch, Ignatius XI (1484-1493), visited the monastery. Certain benefits and privileges were bestowed and a second visit from the patriarch strengthened the bonds between the See of Antioch and the monks of the Wâdî Habîb. It is natural to connect his visits with the revival which took place at this period. The hegoumenos of the monastery at this time (1484) was Qummus Kîrîâqûs.

In the second half of the fifteenth century, several Syrian monks engaged in outstanding literary activities. Dâûd ibn Butrus was the author of thirty-eight homilies, Habîb of Takrit wrote twenty homilies dealing with the ascetic life, and Garir of Takrit wrote a historical treatise about the names of the church fathers. The monastery had recovered from the plague and gained new strength. The restoration was to be long-lasting, as is evident from a scribal note in a manuscript[19] written in the Monastery of the Syrians in 1516. This relates that at the time of the hegoumenship of Cyric of Mount Lebanon, there were altogether forty-eight monks, of whom twenty-five were Egyptian. This is the earliest evidence of the return of Egyptians to the Monastery of the Syrians. The ninety-fifth patriarch, Anbâ Ghabrîâl VII, (1526-1569) had been a monk at Dair as-Surîân before he ascended the patriarchal throne. During his patriarchate, the monastery was so strong that it could dispatch fifty per cent of its monks to the two monasteries in the Thebaid. In 1484, Dair Anbâ Antûnîûs and Dair Anbâ Bûlâ were destroyed by the Bedouins. With the help of twenty monks of the Dair as-Surîân, Dair Anbâ Antûnîûs was rebuilt while ten monks from the Syrian monastery were commissioned to assist in the reconstruction of Dair Anbâ Bûlâ.

In 1584, Qummus John was the hegoumenos of the monastery. Forty years later, in 1624, Qummus 'Abd al-Masîh al-Ambirî made extensive improvements to the churches and the guest house of the monastery. Among other things, he renewed the icons, and added substantially to the library collection. Later he was consecrated to the Abunate of Ethiopia, where he was known as Anbâ Akhristûdulûs (Christodoulos). The last days of his life, however, he spent in the Desert of Scetis, and he was buried in the Church of the Forty Martyrs of Sebaste.

Slowly the Syrian influence decreased. During the hegoumenship of Qummus 'Abd al-Masîh, a Syrian monk, Thomas of Mardin, made the following statement: "I, the servant, entered the Monastery of the Virgin in the Desert of Scetis, and I saw therein writings without number arranged without order, and I began in love, and dusted them and counted them. They came to 403 books. Also I arranged them in the tower of the fortress..."[20]

Seventeenth- and Eighteenth-Century Travellers

The Lutheran missionary to Ethiopia, Peter Heyling of Lübeck (1607-1656), visited the Monastery of St. Macarius in 1633. In his zeal to convert the monks to the Lutheran doctrine he joined the monastery after having been circumcised and rebaptised. He engaged in theological disputes with the Capuchin missionaries and Coptic monks, but after three months he was arrested by Arab mercenaries in the service of the Capuchin fathers. He left for Cairo, where he was introduced to the Syrian archbishop, who advised him to go to the Syrian monastery, which still obtained its supplies from Cairo rather than from Atrîs. In 1634 he entered Dair as-Surîân. Heyling was the last visitor to mention the partial occupation of Dair as-Surîân by Syrian monks.[21]

In 1638 the French consul at Damietta, Fr. Coppin, gave a brief account of the Syrian monastery, having visited the monastery at least once, probably in search of manuscripts. He says that the monastery was dedicated to St. George and located in the vicinity of the Monastery of Ambabioche (Anbâ Bishoî). It was apparently sparsely inhabited and in great disorder. He noticed two churches in the monastery, one being for the Syrians or Jacobites who came to visit the desert, while many relics were kept in both churches. Fr. Coppin goes on to refer to the story of the Tree of St. Ephraem.[22]

In 1657, Thévenot visited the Syrian monastery, which stood "a quarter of a league distant from Ambabichoye, it is but small, but very pleasant, has good water, and is the best in order of all. There you see two fair Churches, one for the Syrians and another for the Copts, in which are many Relicks. In this last is the staff of St. Ephraem, who being come to visit another Hermite, and having left his staff at the Door, whilst he was in discourse with the other whom he came to see, his staff took root and blossomed, and is now a lovely great Tree, and the only in Egypt of its kind."[23]

Wansleben reiterates what Thévenot says. He, too, speaks of the two churches in the monastery and mentions the "arbre miraculeusement cru du baton de St. Ephraem."[24] One cannot help but be reminded of the Glastonbury thorn, a kind of Levantine hawthorn, which though sacrilegiously cut down by Oliver Cromwell's soldiers, regrew, and flowers at Christmas as well as in spring. As the story goes, this tree sprang from the staff of St. Joseph of Arimathea, who is said to have come to England with the Holy Grail and built the first church at Glastonbury.

Six years after Wansleben's account, Robert Huntington, chaplain to the Levant Company, visited the Syrian monastery, but remarked on nothing there save a Syrian Old Testament in the library, and the Tree of St. Ephraem, which he considers, "is clear proof that the monastery once belonged to the Syrians." In a letter from Dublin, about the Porphyry Pillar (Pompey's Pillar in Alexandria), Dr. Huntington refers to the Monastery of the Syrians. "In the chief monastery of the four now remaining dedicated to the Blessed Virgin, the two stones which secure their entrance are of the like, if not the very same substance, which I more particularly observed upon the account of their ingenious contrivance."[25] These two mill-stones can still be observed by the visitor in front of the north gate of the monastery.

News of the monastery's extensive library had travelled across the seas to European bibliophiles. In 1700, Pope Clement XI (1700-1721), a generous patron of art and literature, commissioned Gabriel Eva, the hegoumenos of the Monastery of St. Maura, Mount Lebanon, to see Patriarch Anbâ Yûânnis XVI to ascertain his sentiments towards the Roman church. On his way, Gabriel Eva visited the important monasteries of Egypt, and on his return to Rome informed the pope about the library treasures which he had seen. In 1707, Elias Assemani was sent to Egypt, where he secured forty volumes from the Monastery of the Syrians for the Vatican library.[26]

A more extensive account has been provided by Father Claude Sicard.[27] He visited the monasteries in December 1712, and was impressed by the Monastery of the Syrians. "It is the best of the four... it has a very pleasant garden with a number of trees of various species, tamarinds, dates, and a large tamarind tree which grew out of the staff planted by St. Ephraem." The hegoumenos of the monastery received him with "grandes démonstrations d'amitiés", and after prayers in the Church of the Holy Virgin he participated in the refectory meal which consisted of lentil soup and bread. He reports that: "The monks spend their days in psalmody and manual work, and only rarely leave the monastery because of fear of wandering Arabs."

In 1715, another Vatican librarian, J.S. Assemani, a relative of Elias, visited the Monastery of the Syrians in company with Fr. Claude Sicard. They called first at the Monastery of Abû Maqâr, where they were most successful in their mission to obtain ancient books. At the Monastery of the Syrians they also discovered some excellent Syriac manuscripts, though Fr. Sicard does not mention which volumes they were given.

Fifteen years after J.S. Assemani's visit, Tourtechot de Granger went to Dair as-Suriân. But—as at the Monastery of St. Macarius—he was refused admittance to the library, nor could he purchase any of the manuscripts.[28] A natural historian, Granger was interested in the geological structure of the Wâdî, and gives an account of how St. Ephraem caused the waters to recede by prayer.

The history of the Syrian monastery mentions two hegoumenoi of the monastery, Qummus Manqâriûs (1773) and Qummus Kelâda an-Nasekh (1774). Until 1774, the hegoumenos of the Syrian monastery used to reside in Tarânah near Manûfiyah. From then on, however, the hegoumenoi lived in Atrîs, from where they organised the supplies for the monastery.

On 13 January, 1778, Sonnini visited the "Monastery of Saide Sourian." He writes that it was formerly in the possession of the Syrians, who have been succeeded by the Copts.[29] "The ancient Syrian church is still standing, and it is tolerably handsome and decorated with sculpture and paintings in fresco. Upon one of the pillars are cut the names of several European travellers, Baron and Granger.... The place of retreat, or little fort, was as well constructed as that of Saide el Baramous, and the monks appeared to be less filthy, and not so grossly ferocious. Their superior was a man turned of thirty, absolutely without a beard, and not having a single hair on any part of his body. These monks also have a little garden, which is more extensive and better cultivated than that belonging to the other convent." In one of the courts, Sonnini noticed an immense tamarind tree, which the Copts consider to be the effect of some miraculous vegetation. Then follows the story of St. Ephraem.

When W.G. Browne visited the Monastery of the Syrians in 1792, it was quite impossible for him to obtain any manuscripts, either in the Monastery of Anbâ Bishoî or in the Monastery of the Syrians. He writes: "During my stay near the lakes, I visited two of the Coptic convents, that called the Syrian, and that of St. George (sic), where I could observe no traces of any European traveller... these convents contain each of them several religious, who retain all the simplicity of the primitive ages. I inquired for manuscripts and saw in one of the convents several books in the Coptic, Syriac and Arabic language. The superior told me that they had near eight hundred books, but positively refused to part with any of them, nor could I see any more."[30]

A few years after the visit of W.G. Browne, Count Andréossy visited the Monastery of the Syrians. The books were on parchment and cotton paper, and he actually removed some of them. He measured the miraculous tree of St. Ephraem: it was six and a half metres high and the circumference was three metres. He identified the tree as a *Tamarindus Indica* of which the Syrian monks (sic) believed that they were the sole possessors.

Andréossy obviously confused the story of St. Ephraem with that of the Tree of Obedience.[31] At the time of his visit, eighteen monks inhabited the monastery.

Nineteenth– and Twentieth–Century Travellers

The first Englishman to bring to light any of the treasures of the Syrian monastery was the Duke of Northumberland, who, in 1828, accompanied by Linant-Bey, undertook a journey across the Egyptian desert to the lonely Wâdî 'n-Natrûn, for the express purpose of endeavouring to procure a copy of a Coptic and Arabic dictionary, which he had understood was to be found there.[32]

In his description of Wâdî 'n-Natrûn, Baron Taylor (or, by his real name, Fr. Laorty-Hadji),[33] who visited Egypt in 1828 and 1830, provides much the same information as General Andréossy. Impressed by the hospitality of the monks, he describes how they share their food, their bread and their dates with the Bedouins. His special attention, however, was directed to the miraculous tree.

In 1837, Lord Curzon visited the Syrian monastery where he was hospitably received by the hegoumenos and fourteen or fifteen Coptic monks.[34] He purchased several Coptic manuscripts which were lying on the floor in one of the niches of the tower. One of these was a superb manuscript of the Gospels, two others were doing duty as coverings to a couple of large open pots or jars which had contained preserves, long since evaporated. On the floor, Curzon found a fine Coptic and Arabic dictionary. After his purchases, the blind hegoumenos declared that there were no other books in the monastery. Curzon, however, being very persistent because he had been told by a French gentleman in Cairo that there were ancient manuscripts in the monks' oil cellar, used all means available to him to obtain them.

He produced a bottle of rosoglio and, aware of its potency, he began to persuade the hegoumenos. "Next to the golden key, which masters so many locks, there is no better opener of the heart than a sufficiency of strong drink... I have always found it to be invincible; and now we sat sipping our cups of the sweet pink rosoglio... and the face of the blind abbot waxed bland and confiding... I had, by the by, a great advantage over the good abbot, as I could see the workings of his features and he could not see mine, or note my eagerness about the oil-cellar..." At last, Lord Curzon persuaded the hegoumenos to permit him to descend the narrow staircase to the oil cellar, where he discovered a narrow low door, and after pushing it open, he entered into a small vaulted room which was filled to the depth of half a metre or more with the loose leaves of Syriac manuscripts. In addition, he discovered to the great surprise of the monks, a mysterious box which to his disappointment contained only one book. After this, as many Coptic and Syriac manuscripts as possible were stowed away in one side of a great pair of saddle bags.

More significant was Curzon's discovery of an Ethiopian community in the south-east corner of the monastery. The Ethiopians occupied a room that was eight metres long, six metres wide, and three and a half metres high, roof of which was formed of the trunks of palm trees, across which reeds were laid. The interior of the walls was plastered white with lime and the windows were unglazed. Curzon noticed, among other things, an extensive library. The books were enclosed in a case, fastened with leather thongs, and to this case was attached a strap for carrying the volume over the shoulders. All the Ethiopian monks could read fluently out of their own books which was more than the Copts could do. He was informed that the monastery in which they had lived in the Desert of Scetis had fallen into decay, and that they now lived at Dair as-Suriân. They were occasionally recruited by pilgrims who passed by on their way from Ethiopia to Jerusalem. An Ethiopian community had existed in the Wâdî 'n-Natrûn towards the close of the twelfth century. Maqrîzî mentions the Ethiopian Monastery of the Holy Elias. When it was destroyed the Ethiopians went to the fine Monastery of the Virgin of St. John the Short which was situated near the Monastery of St. John the Short.[35]

The next bibliophile to visit the Syrian monastery was the Reverend Henry Tattam, archdeacon of Bedford, who came, early in 1839, in search of Coptic manuscripts. When he arrived, "pipes and coffee" were brought to him, after which the priests conducted him to their churches, and showed him the books they used. They wanted to know why he was visiting them. He said cautiously that he wished to see their books. They told him they had no more than what he had seen in the church, whereupon he told them plainly that he knew they had. They laughed and, after a short conference, said that he should see them. The bell soon rang for prayers, and he accompanied them to their service, and then returned to his tent, where some of the monks visited him in the evening, and brought him a present of bread. The following day, immediately after breakfast, Dr. Tattam went into the monastery to examine the manuscripts, and endeavour to buy some of them. The priests conducted him to the tower, and then into a dark vault, where he found a great quantity of very old and valuable Syriac manuscripts. He selected six quarto (or small folio) volumes. He was next shown a room in the tower, where he found a number of Coptic and Arabic manuscripts, principally liturgies, with a beautiful copy of the Coptic Gospels. He then asked to see the rest: the priests looked surprised, to find that he knew there were others, and at first seemed disposed to deny that they had any more, but at length they produced the key of the apartment where their other books were kept, and admitted him. After looking them over, he went to the Superior's room, where all the priests were assembled, about fifteen or sixteen in number. One of them brought a Coptic and Arabic selim which he wished to purchase, but they informed him that they could not part with it as it was forbidden to be taken away by an interdiction at the end, but they consented to make him a copy of it. He paid for two of the Syriac manuscripts he had placed in the Superior's room, for the priests could not be persuaded to part with more."[36]

In February 1839, Tattam revisited the monasteries and secured a large sack full of splendid Syriac manuscripts on vellum. In 1843 the British Museum delegated Tattam to secure the remainder of the collection. "Tattam not unreasonably left the negotiations for the purchase to the sheikh of a village on the borders of the desert and to his own dragoman, but with unspeakable foolishness left the delivery and the removal of the books to the pair. The natural result followed. Tattam secured a large part (but only a part) of the collection for which he paid, the monks held back the remainder, and the sheikh and the dragoman, we may be sure, took their share of the purchase money." Three hundred and fourteen manuscripts arrived at the British Museum in 1843.

In 1843, Sir Gardner Wilkinson went via Tarânah to the Wâdî 'n-Natrûn, where he visited the Monastery of the Syrians. He noticed that "some of the monasteries at the Natron Lakes have a collection of books composed of Arabic, Coptic and Syriac manuscripts. Many of them are copies of older manuscripts which had been injured by time and accident... Mr. Tattam, on his visit to these monasteries a few years ago, brought away upwards of fifty volumes. Among them was a treatise of Eusebius, not previously known, and on his return in 1843, he obtained four times that number of manuscripts, all indeed that were not used by the monks." Sir Gardner stayed at the Monastery of Abû Maqâr and at that of the Syrians. Of the latter he says: "Every civility is shown to the stranger during his stay which I experienced at Dair Surian... the room allotted was well lighted, but I recommend to visitors to remove the mats before they take up their abode there, otherwise they are not likely to pass a comfortable night, under the assaults of some hundreds of bugs, and they will run a risk of carrying away many score in the baggage, which may continue to torment them and people the houses of their future hosts." At the time of Sir Gardner's visit, the Monastery of the Syrians was the biggest, having thirty or forty monks living within its walls.[37]

When, in 1844, von Tischendorf visited the Monastery of the Syrians, he was shown the tree of St. Ephraem. The purpose of his visit was to search for manuscripts, but all he found were some Syriac, together with a couple of Ethiopic fragments. The majority of the manuscripts were liturgical, though some of them were biblical.[38] "The excessive suspicion of the monks, however, renders it extremely difficult to induce them to produce their manuscripts, in spite of the extreme penury which surrounds them. For my own part, I made a most lucky discovery of a multitude of Coptic parchment sheets of the sixth and seventh century, already half destroyed, and completely buried beneath a mass of dust. These were given to me without hesitation." The monastery was inhabited by over forty monks, and it appeared the handsomest and richest of all. "Hence it was they, that, least of all, thanked me for what I supposed a considerable present, which according to my custom I left with them at my departure... they are too much accustomed to the visits and to the gold of the English."

A year after von Tischendorf's visit a certain Auguste Pacho approached Dr. W. Cureton, Canon of Westminister and an orientalist. Early in 1845, Pacho, a native of Alexandria and nephew of Jean-Raimond Pacho, whose posthumous publication of his travels in Africa had won him a considerable reputation,[39] visited London. He hoped to obtain some confidential employment, for which his knowledge of oriental manners rendered him admirably qualified. He was introduced to Dr. Cureton by a letter from Reinaud, President de l'Académie des Inscriptions et Belles Lettres of the Institute of France. Pacho told Cureton that a large proportion of the Syriac library that Tattam had paid for was still in the hands of the monks. Cureton asked him to go to Egypt and fetch the books and to bring back every piece of Syriac he saw.[40]

It was not easy for Pacho to purchase the manuscripts. The monks were afraid to part with their treasure, for on the day they had delivered the books to Tattam's agent, and received payment, they were deprived of the tenure of a tract of land on the borders of the Nile. They considered this a punishment from heaven.

Pacho stayed with the monks for six weeks, and so won their confidence that they ventured to show him the remainder of the library and even offered to negotiate the sale of some volumes. Pacho withheld the remaining part of the total sum to be paid, making sure that no manuscript had been concealed or retained by the monks. When he found that no more books were produced, he concluded that he had indeed, obtained the whole of the remaining part of the library.

Before he delivered the remainder of the money he asked the monks to sign a document, in which they affirmed that they had sold to him all their Syriac manuscripts, and that, if any should be discovered in their monastery, or elsewhere in their possession, these were to become at once Pacho's property. Further, to be still more secure, he required the hegoumenos to publish a sentence of excommunication against any one of the monks who should have kept any part of this Syriac collection. One of the monks, who had concealed a part of a book, was terrified by this denunciation, and sent it to him afterwards. The British Museum obtained more than 170 items. But when in 1851, Pacho offered an additional ten manuscripts to the trustees of the museum, the suspicion was justified that he had betrayed the authorities in London. That Pacho did not clear out the monastery is evident from the fact that fragments of Syriac manuscripts were found there in 1921. Furthermore, we know now that Pacho sold several manuscripts to the Imperial Public Library in St. Petersburg in 1852.

In February 1852, Heinrich Brugsch journeyed to Egypt at the order of King Friedrich Wilhelm IV of Prussia to make scientific explorations. Arriving at the Monastery of the Syrians, he was heartily welcomed by the monks who were much relieved at seeing European visitors rather than Bedouins.[41] Brugsch observes that the monks prayed three times a day, before sunrise, at noon and in the evening. Though the water was rather salty and bad, Brugsch and his colleagues were greatly impressed by the hospitality that the monks showed to them. After visiting the church and the refectory, he went to the library where his every movement was carefully watched by the monks. "We expected to see an orderly library with books arranged on shelves, but what a chaotic disorder. About forty volumes, mostly Arabic and Coptic manuscripts, were lying around, torn out pages from books covered the dirty floor, the covers of the books either rotten or eaten up by worms. And some of these manuscripts could easily date back four to five centuries. To buy them from the monks, however, was impossible indeed. For certain Englishmen had recently bought several hundred manuscripts for very little money from the library of Dair al-Barâmûs which they sold for much more money." Brugsch was told that every manuscript in the monastery contained a warning that it was not to be sold to any stranger under the threat of losing eternal salvation.

The first Protestant missionaries to Egypt were five Germans who were sent by the Church Missionary Society in 1825. Restrained from direct work among the Muslims, they turned their efforts chiefly to the Copts. They met with no opposition from the Coptic patriarch and found a free opening for the sale and distribution of the Bible and Christian tracts. They were even allowed to preach in Coptic churches and monasteries.[42]

The first American missionary to go to the monasteries of the Wâdî 'n-Natrûn was the Reverend Gulian Lansing of the United Presbyterian Church, who visited the Monastery of the Syrians in 1862. In the Monastery of Abû Maqâr he met Abûnâ Makârî whom Dr. Lansing met at Dair Sitt Dimîânah a year later. Abûnâ Makârî accompanied the American on a desert walk from the Monastery of Abû Maqâr to the Monastery of the Syrians. "Then, he was glad to walk with me six hours over the desert to the other convent for a few piastres... I found him in our long walk a very attentive and interested listener to the doctrines of Protestantism."[43]

Anglican missionaries also showed considerable interest in the Coptic monasteries. In 1887, the Reverend R. Raikes Bromage, parish priest of Christ Church, Frome, accompanied by John Sidley, Abûnâ Butrus, and Surîâl Effendî Saîd, visited the four monasteries in the Wâdî 'n-Natrûn. The patriarch had written numerous introductory letters which enabled the party to be graciously received at all monasteries. Bromage was permitted to celebrate the Divine Mysteries according to the Anglican rite in the main church of Dair al-Barâmûs. This incident is important because it was the first non-Latin Western communion service to be celebrated in a Coptic monastery.

The Syrian monastery attracted pilgrims and visitors throughout the nineteenth century, though many of them were either Egyptians or people working with the Salt and Soda Company at Bîr Hooker. The numerous graffiti on the walls of the choir of the Church of the Holy Virgin testify to the frequent visitors. An inscription written in 1801 commemorates the visit of a certain Faragallah Atabawî (?). 'Asaâd Nasr and Macarius Antonius who were in the monastery in 1828 inscribed their names on the south side of the choir and added the usual petition for the blessings of God. An employee of the Salt and Soda Company, one Costandi, came to the monastery in 1861.

In 1873, Greville J. Chester visited the monastery and wrote his "Notes on the Coptic Dayrs of the Wady Natroun". A careful student of ancient architecture, Chester writes about three churches in the monastery: "'Adhra Mariam, Abou Hennes and Baramooti Syriani and 'Adhra Bis Syriani, while three others lay in ruins". In the Church of Abû Hennis, Chester saw an epiphany tank as well as relics of saints and a pulpit with ancient icons. Here, Chester also saw an ancient Arab chandelier which was similar in form to the glass lamps from the Mosque of Sultan Hassan.[44]

The first guide to list the monasteries of the Wâdî 'n-Natrûn is Murray's *Handbook for Travellers to Lower and Upper Egypt*. After describing the main features of the Monastery of Abû Maqâr, Murray continues: "Three hours from Dair Abu Makar is Dair Suriani, the most beautiful convent of all. It was built by one Hennes whose tree is still seen about a couple of miles to the southward near the ruins of two other convents. It is supposed to resemble Noah's ark in form, though in no other respects; for here the admission of women is strictly prohibited. This convent contains three churches, one of them, Adra Bi Suriani, has a beautifully carved screen door inlaid with wood and ivory, and an iconostasis also inlaid with ivory; in a chapel is a curious double picture on a panel with two saints on one side, and a crowned female head, perhaps Empress Helena, on the other."[45]

In the winter of 1883-84, Alfred J. Butler, fellow of Brasenose College, Oxford, visited the Monastery of the Syrians. He observes: "No one whose imagination has been kindled by the romantic story of Curzon's visit to the monks of the Natrûn valley, would resist a feeling of keen excitement as he neared the walls of Dair as-Surîânî, where Curzon discovered that horde of ancient literary treasure which alone would make his name famous. The excitement is not lessened if the traveller carries, as the present writer carried, about his waist a heavy belt of gold, wherewith he hopes to retrieve some fragment of treasure still remaining: and even if the sense of adventure were wanting, one could not resist a novel feeling of fascination in surveying the singular beauty of the convent. For as the eye follows it, half-climbing the gentle slope of a desert hill, half-resting on the broad flat summit, its lines are extremely graceful... Traces of Syriac literature remain there even to this day, but there are no Syrian inmates now, nor are there either books or monks of Abyssinian origin, such as Curzon discovered.

"The monks, as usual, received us with great kindness, and were eager to show us over the monastery. They pointed out to us the ancient and venerable tamarind, a rare but not unknown tree in Egypt, which is said to have grown from a walking stick thrust in the ground by St. Ephrem, and they told us the legend, just as their predecessors have told it to travellers for generations before them."[46]

Isambert's travel guide, published in 1890, is the second to describe the monasteries of the Wâdî 'n-Natrûn. He advises travellers to visit the Monastery of the Syrians which he considers the most important of the group, being inhabited by thirty or forty monks.[47]

The next guide to refer to the monasteries of the Desert of Scetis is Baedeker's in 1892. Travellers, coming from the Oasis of Siwa, are advised to stop and visit the Natrûn monasteries, of which the Monastery of the Syrians is the most outstanding. It was built by a saint named Honnes or Johannes the Dwarf, and is at present occupied by thirty to forty monks. This monastery contains an Ethiopian college, an observation which Baedeker no doubt culled from the account of Lord Curzon. Those who are interested in discovering ancient manuscripts are warned by Baedeker "that there is little chance of finding any more valuable manuscripts here, as all, except those required for the religious services, have been transferred to the library of the Coptic patriarch in Cairo."[48] He adds that a visit to the Monastery of Anbâ Bishoî and al-Barâmûs scarcely repays the trouble and is not to be recommended.

Joseph Strzygowski in 1900 was the first scholar of Coptic architecture to study the now famous stucco ornaments in the Church of the Holy Virgin.[49] It was he who drew attention to the relationship between the stucco-work of the church and that of the Mosque of Ibn Tûlûn in Cairo. A year later, the coptologist A. Gayet published his book *L'Art Copte* with an extensive study on the architectural features of the Monastery of the Syrians, adding to his valuable description sketches and drawings of the churches and their interior.[50]

The first women to visit the Monastery of the Syrians may well have been Dr. Agnes Smith Lewis and her sister, Mrs. Margaret Dunlop Gibson. In 1904, travelling by camel from Cairo, the two ladies had first called on the monks of Dair Abû Maqâr. From there, they rode to the Syrian monastery which impressed them as being by far the prettiest of the monasteries.[51] They were conducted to a small room in the qasr, where they found two little cupboards full of books, and a stone reservoir, partly beneath the level of the floor, containing a collection of loose leaves. Mrs. Gibson noticed two very fine Coptic manuscripts of the New Testament dated respectively 1220 and 1256. While being conducted around by the monks, they were told about a hermit who for twelve years had lived far away in a cave. Recently, he had returned to the monastery and was now living alone in a cell, receiving daily provisions of bread and water from the other monks. Dr. Lewis photographed fragments of the *Mythological Acts of the Apostles*. The preface to her book tells how, by accepting help from the Egyptian Salt and Natron Company at Bîr Hooker, she was able to pitch her tent outside the monastery gate and how the monks made available to her a dark room to change film plates.

In 1905, Ewald Falls, a member of the German Kaufmann Expedition to the Libyan Desert, visited the Monastery of the Syrians. In the Church of the Holy Virgin, Falls noticed two bronze hoops hanging from the ceiling by chains. These ancient chandeliers seemed similar to those in the basilica of St. Peter in Rome. He describes in minute detail the beautiful woodwork of the haikal doors, and seemed to be much impressed by the treasures of the monastery in general. He remarks on the losses the monasteries suffered through the thefts of foreigners as well as the destruction due to ignorant monks, who permitted pieces of the tarsia work to be broken off and carried away as souvenirs.[52]

In 1895, Qummus Hannâ Isnawî was followed by Qummus Mâksîmus Salîb as hegoumenos of the monastery. The records of the monastery inform us that during the hegoumenship of Maksîmûs (1895-1939) many improvements were carried out, especially with regard to the walls. The well and the waterwheel were repaired, and the sum of L.E. 10,800 was spent on general repairs and improvements.

In 1909-10, the Syrian monastery was visited by members of the Metropolitan Museum of Art Egyptian Expedition. W.J. Palmer-Jones, W. Hauser and H. Burton spent several weeks making plans of the main structures, which they supplemented with drawings, sketches and photographs.

In the following year, 1910-11, Palmer-Jones revisited the monastery accompanied by the artist Walter Tyndale. They went from the Monastery of Anbâ Bishoî to that of the Syrians. "A spreading sycamore-tree, with a goat and one or two sheep lying in its shade, gave the place a less dead-alive look than had its neighbour." Palmer-Jones and Tyndale had lunch in the company of a hen and a brood of chicks who seemed to appreciate the samples of their food. "The church was very interesting, and a more important structure than the previous one, but so dimly lighted, that we had to wait till our eyes got used to the gloom before we could distinguish anything... I started a drawing of an interesting subject, one which might have consoled me for my disappointment in the other convent, had I been able to see more clearly what I was about." Only nine monks inhabited the monastery at the time of their visit.[53]

In 1912, Samuel Flury, following the excavations at Samarra, studied the stucco ornaments in the Church of the Holy Virgin at Dair as-Surîân, and concluded that the stucco-work must have been done after the construction of the Mosque of Ibn Tûlûn.[54] Flury points out the relationship between the Islamic artwork at Samarra and that at Dair as-Surîân, but maintains that Cairene workmen created the ornaments about the beginning of the tenth century.

In his first *Streifzüge* through the churches and monasteries of Egypt in 1912, Johann Georg, Duke of Saxony, visited the Monastery of the Syrians.[55] He was ceremonially welcomed by the hegoumenos and monks, and attended Divine Liturgy in the Church of the Holy Virgin. In the keep the duke noticed a pile of manuscripts strewn about in a disorderly manner but otherwise the Syrian monastery apparently exceeded his expectations.

During the First World War members of the British army went to the monastery, staying nearby for a few days. Graffiti in the Church of the Holy Virgin show that soldiers entered the monastery in the latter part of March, 1916.

In the spring of 1920, Hugh Evelyn White spent several weeks in the various monasteries of the Wâdî 'n-Natrûn completing the work begun by Palmer-Jones. The result of the work of Evelyn White, Hauser and Burton is published in the three volume masterpiece about the Wâdî 'n-Natrûn monasteries.

In February 1923, Dr. William H.P. Hatch departed from the Monastery of Abû Maqâr, and following the "Way of the Angels" arrived at the Dair as-Suriân. The monks showed him the famous tamarind tree. He also saw the mummies of two former hegoumenoi of the monastery, one Syrian, and the other Coptic. There were sixteen monks at the monastery when Dr. Hatch and his party visited it.[56]

In 1927, some fifteen years after his first visit to Dair as-Suriân, Johann Georg paid a second visit to the monastery. He mentions that the monastery had never been destroyed, and for this reason it still looked as if it belonged to the first millenium. The hegoumenoi of the monastery had always been known as great magicians, who owned a picture representing many soldiers. When the Bedouins were ready to attack the monastery, this picture was taken to the gate, and at the sight of this picture, the assailants ran away. Johann Georg was shown the Church of Anbâ Bishoî and he comments on an interesting altar belonging to the era of the foundation of the monastery. Before his departure, the monks presented him with a basket of fragments of manuscripts. He discovered among the fragments documents belonging to the twelfth and thirteenth centuries.[57]

In 1928, K.A.C. Creswell, a scholar of Islamic architecture, went to the Monastery of the Syrians to study the stucco ornaments in the Church of the Holy Virgin. Creswell attributes these to the beginning of the tenth century. He explains the Tulunide character of the ornaments by referring to the journey of the hegoumenos to Baghdad which took place about 914. On his return, the hegoumenos ordered the church to be decorated with those stucco ornaments which can still be seen.

In the same year, Herbert Ricke went to the Monastery of the Syrians to photograph and to study the stucco ornaments which he published in his volume *Aegypten*. The architectural-archaeological work was continued in the Monastery of the Syrians by the Commité de Conservation des Monuments de l'Art Arabe, and Ugo Monneret de Villard published in 1928 his study on the churches of the monastery. His principal attention was devoted to the ancient Church of the Holy Virgin, and he comes to the conclusion that the decorative cycles of the church, the stucco ornaments, the doors of the sanctuary and the choir and the wall-paintings should be attributed to the period of Moses of Nisibis, the first half of the tenth century.

In 1930 and 1931, Prince 'Umar Tûsûn accompanied by Dr. Puy-Haubert and Professor Breccia visited the Monastery of the Syrians. The Prince gives the number of monks who inhabited the Syrian monastery

from the middle of the seventeenth century to the twentieth century. The
following table is taken from his study:

1667	14 monks	1719	10 monks	1767	11 monks
1780	20 monks	1835	40 monks	1847	46 monks
1852	56 monks	1897	40 monks	1906	18 monks
1924	58 monks	1931	49 monks		

The Monastery Today

In the middle of the twentieth century the Monastery of the Syrians was the
best known and most frequently visited monastery in the Wâdî 'n-Natrûn.
This was due partly to its situation. At the same time it was the most
progressive monastery. The visitors' books of the monastery bear witness to
the large number of visitors from many countries who have ventured to the
desert of the Wâdî 'n-Natrûn. A historic visit took place in January 1959
when the Patriarch of Antioch, Anbâ Ighnâtiûs Ya'qûb III, came to the
Monastery of the Syrians, where he was shown around the churches.

The monks observe five seasons of fasting, during which visitors are
not permitted to enter the monastery: forty-three days before the Feast of
the Nativity of Our Lord, three days commemorating Jonah in the Whale,
fifty-five days before Lent,[58] the Fast of the Holy Apostles which extends
from Pentecost until 12 July, and fifteen days in commemoration of the
Assumption of the Blessed Virgin Mary, from 7-22 August. Wednesdays
and Fridays are fast days throughout the year, except during Paschaltide,
the fifty days from Easter to Pentecost. Apart from total abstinence from
meat, fish and dairy products during the fasts, the quantity of food taken
and the length of the period between eating depends entirely on the monk
himself.

The shape of the monastery has given rise to a strange interpretation
by the monks. The proportion of its length to its breadth is roughly that of
a ship, and this has led to the tradition that the monastery was built on the
model of Noah's Ark.

The principal church of the monastery is that of the Holy Virgin.
Because of its artistic treasures, this church has repeatedly attracted the
attention of archaeologists and architects. It belongs to the most ancient
constructions of the monastery, and is probably tenth century. A Syriac
note states that "in the days of Prior Saliba they wished to renew the vault
that is over the door of the church, and when they had dug, they found a
tablet written in Syriac and Egyptian: Marutha and Habîb, Tekritans,
notables deceased, they who bought this monastery for the Syrians for
twelve thousand dinars—we beg you brethren who find this memorial to
pray for them." Though this memorial is no longer there, the construction

mentioned may well be related to the present north entrance of the church. A date around 980 is reasonable for the building of the church. The eastern part of the church has three haikals, to the west of these is the choir and still further west the main nave which is flanked by two lateral aisles.

In the nave, almost in the middle, is the basin for the Maundy Thursday rite of foot-washing. At the eastern end of the north aisle stands the feretory of St. John Kame. From the western end of the north aisle one passes through a narrow passage to the cell of Anbâ Bishoî, a small square structure with an altar built against the east wall. The cell is roofed by a vaulted ceiling into which a hook has been driven. The monks say that Anbâ Bishoî used to pray in this cell day and night, his hair being tied to the hook to prevent him from falling asleep or sinking down. I have heard that a tunnel is supposed to lead from the cell to the Monastery of Anbâ Bishoî, though there is no archaeological verification for this.

The church's most outstanding attractions are the choir and the sanctuary doors of the church with their magnificent ivory inlaid ornaments. While the choir door has only six rows of panels, the sanctuary door has seven. The first row has six figures. The two central panels show Christ and the Holy Virgin Mary, the second and fifth panels show the Egyptian and the Syrian patriarchs, St. Mark the Evangelist and St. Ignatius, Bishop of Antioch, while the two outer panels show the two great patriarchs, Anbâ Dîsqûrus of Alexandria (444-454), and Anbâ Sâwîrûs I of Antioch (512-518). The balance between the Egyptian and Syrian ecclesiastical dignitaries represents the allegiance of the Syrian monks to the two patriarchates.

The second row of panels shows a repeated pattern of circles so interlaced as to form crosses. The third row has in each of the six fields six linked circles which are arranged in pairs, each circle containing a cross. The fourth row, though somewhat damaged, has in each panel a cross enclosed by a four-leafed shamrock with a trefoil at the junction of each leaf. Each panel in the fifth row has six swastikas enclosed by circles. The sixth row is a dark grille on a white ground based on linked circles. The seventh row has a pattern of a plain cross in a double-stepped framing, the design of the cross thus filling the whole panel. The date of this workmanship is tenth century. A Syriac inscription on the doors states that they were made in the reign of Anbâ Ghabrîâl I, the 57th Patriarch of Alexandria (910-921), and of Anbâ Yuhannis IV, the 25th Patriarch of Antioch (902-922).

The semi-domes of the choir have two wall-paintings. The southern semi-dome has the Annunciation and the Nativity of our Lord, the northern semi-dome the Falling-Asleep (Dormition) of the Holy Virgin. These paintings are the work of Syrian artists as the Syriac inscriptions testify. A recently discovered Coptic fresco under the former painting of the Ascension of Christ in the western semi-dome shows a unique theme: the Annunciation and the Old Testament prophecies of the perpetual virginity of the Theotokos. The prophets represented are Daniel (2:34, 45), Ezekiel (44:2), Isaiah (7:14), and Moses (Ex 3:2). In the centre is the text of Luke 1:28.

The main haikal of the church has the above-mentioned stucco ornaments. The altar is covered with a slab of black stone which was probably imported by the Syrians at the time of the building of the church. This church is used for the celebration of the Divine Liturgy during the summer months, while during the winter months services are held in the cave-church.

The Church of the Lady Mary (Sitt Miriam), or the cave-church, is situated in the northern part of the monastery. The church has three haikals and a nave with a marble lakan. When this church is in use, the relics of St. John Kame are removed from the Church of the Holy Virgin and are placed on the north side of the doorway of this church.

The Church of the Forty Martyrs of Sebaste is situated north of the Church of the Holy Virgin adjoining the east of the porch. In this church Anbâ Akhristûdulûs (Christodoulos), Abûnâ of Ethiopia in the beginning of the seventeenth century, was buried. Apart from this, the church is of little interest.

The qasr of the monastery stands to the west of the northern gate and comprises a basement and three upper floors. The second storey is of little historical interest while the third contains the Church of St. Michael. The church is used twice a year on the feasts of the Archangel. An icon of St. Michael decorates the north wall of the church. At one time the remains of the monastery library were kept "in a small vaulted room, in two modern cupboards, in which books of all ages and sizes are packed in a mass and a rubbish bin to which loose or torn pages are consigned." All books have since been removed to the library. The qasr has been greatly improved by replastering the walls on the inside as well as on the outside. Though at one time the qasr was inhabited by numerous solitaries, at present only one monk lives there from time to time, exchanging this abode for his cave, northwest of the monastery. He inhabits the first room to the east on the second storey.

The water tower, which was built in the eastern part of the monastery in 1955-6, provides running water.

Until the middle of the twentieth century the Monastery of the Syrians had only one gate in the western part of the north wall. In the early 1970s the southern part of the east wall was broken through and a gate with an imposing staircase leads to the monastery plantation inaugurated by Abûnâ Isîdûrûs in 1945.

The new building to the east of the Church of the Holy Virgin includes monastic cells, the library, a collection of historical and liturgical objects and a reception room. The three thousand volumes include several hundred manuscripts in Coptic, Arabic, Syriac and Ge'ez. They were catalogued by the late Yassa 'Abd al-Masîh, librarian of the Coptic Museum. One of the oldest manuscripts is a twelfth-century Coptic Gospel of St. John. Noteworthy is the tenth-century ebony reliquary which contained the relics of St. Severus of Antioch (sixth century); St. Dioscorus (fifth century); St. Cyriacus and his mother Julietta (fourth century); St. Theodore the Oriental (fourth century); the Forty Martyrs of Sebaste (fourth century); St. James the Sawn-Asunder (fourth century); St. Mary Magdalene and the desert fathers, St. John the Short and St. Moses the Black. The most valuable object is the twelfth-century marble tray with Greek and Nubian texts. Presumably, this tray belonged to the Ethiopian Monastery of St. Elias in the Wâdî 'n-Natrûn. Several Ethiopian objects (bookrests, hand-crosses, etc.) testify to their residence here in the nineteenth century.

Desert reclamation projects, now carried out by all monasteries, were actually inaugurated by Anbâ Tawfîlus at Dair as-Suriân in the 1950s and '60s, when this monastery was still prominent. Many of the senior bishops of the Coptic church, including Pope Shenûdah III, served as monks at Dair as-Suriân. Moreover, the retreat house in the orchard was the first facility of this kind for visitors and church groups, where ecumenical seminars were conducted. The twentieth-century monastic revival received its original impetus during the patriarchate of Anbâ Kîrillus VI at the Monastery of the Syrians. At present, the monastery under the leadership of Anbâ Tawfîlus and Qummus Tadros as-Suriânî has sixty monks of whom more than twenty serve churches in Egypt and overseas.

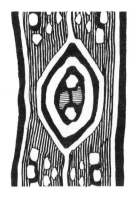

9
DAIR
ANBÂ SAMWÎL

Early Monasticism in the Fayyûm

The Monastery of St. Samuel (Dair Anbâ Samwîl) at al-Qalamûn belongs, historically speaking, to the Fayyûm monastery group. The Fayyûm is a large oasis about eighty-five kilometres south-west of Cairo and has a long Christian tradition. Of the early medieval monasteries of the Fayyûm, the Monastery of St. Samuel is the only one inhabited today.

The desert around the Fayyûm oasis, and especially the mountain of al-Qalamûn, was inhabited by anchorites as early as the end of the third century. The rise of Coptic monasticism in its primitive anchoritic type may have occurred more or less simultaneously in the various regions of Egypt. The fourth-century story of Panine and Panaw supports this. These two young men, dissatisfied with conditions at home, decided to enter the desert life so that they might grow in holiness. On their way, "they were met by the Archangel Michael, in clerical disguise, who guided them to the three saints, Timothy, Theophilus, and Christodorus of the mountain of al-Qalamûn in the Fayyûm".[1] St. Athanasius mentions that St. Antony visited the Fayyûm (then known as Arsinoë) and found the canal full of crocodiles.[2]

A significant reference comes from the pen of Anbâ Kîrillus who, in the fifth century, wrote to Calosiris II, Bishop of the Fayyûm, instructing him to read a letter to the monks of al-Qalamûn regarding the anthropomorphic heresy. It seems, therefore, that monasticism, both in its anchoritic and coenobitic form, began in the Fayyûm about the same time as it did in the Eastern desert and in the Wâdî 'n-Natrûn. All three localities were remote and offered every possibility for the solitary life.

The earliest monastery in the Fayyûm region was that of Naqlûn, situated about fifteen kilometres south of Madînat al-Fayyûm, the capital of the oasis. The history of the older Naqlûn monastery is interwoven with that of the monastery at al-Qalamûn. Both Abû Sâlih[3] and Maqrîzî[4] list the Monastery of Naqlûn first in their accounts of the Fayyûm. The close connection, perhaps even the friendly rivalry between the al-Qalamûn and Naqlûn monasteries, may have led eventually to the downfall of Naqlûn and the rise of al-Qalamûn.[5]

From the Seventh to the Seventeenth Century

St. Samuel (Anbâ Samwîl) was born in 598 in Pelkip and joined the ascetic life at a very early age. At the age of twelve he was ordained sub-deacon. Against the will of his father he entered the monastery at al-Qalamûn, was ordained deacon at eighteen and became a monk a few years later. He went to the Wâdî 'n-Natrûn, where under the care of Anbâ Agâthûn he learned the angelic life. During his lifetime Coptic Christians underwent several severe persecutions by the Persians and the Byzantine authorities. Several times, St. Samuel took refuge in the Monastery of al-Qalamûn. His theological activities, especially his keen opposition to the decrees of Chalcedon, called forth violent opposition from Cyrus, who tried to impose the decrees of Chalcedon upon the monks.

St. Samuel was imprisoned and beaten, and after severe questioning, was about to be publicly flogged when the civic authorities saved his life. After this, he took refuge in a certain church, where he was seized and carried away by the Berbers. He escaped, but was recaptured by his enemies who tried to force him to worship the sun, which he refused. Later on, he was tied to a young girl, and the two were left to guard the camels. But St. Samuel preserved his virginity. Set at liberty in return for the miraculous healing of his captor's wife, he returned to the al-Qalamûn valley, where he ended his days in peace. The hermit of al-Qalamûn lived fifty-seven years in his monastery and "his powers of spiritual and administrative leadership earned for him a place among the monastic stars of the first magnitude."

The relics of St. Samuel were discovered by Anbâ Ishaq. They were hidden under the alabaster altar of the ancient Church of Anbâ Misâîl, where they lay in the trunk of a palm tree. They were removed and placed in caskets which were covered with an embroidered cloth. Many miracles are associated with the relics of the saint, not only in connection with the monks, but also with the Bedouins and fellahin. As one of the monks said: "Anbâ Samwîl was the result of the prayers and supplications of his parents who had been childless for many years, so he is regarded by many people as the patron saint of fecundity, a specialist in removing the reproach of barren women." The name "Samuel" is common among the fellahin in and around Maghâgha.

St. Samuel was neither the father of the Fayyûm monasteries, nor the founder of any particular institution, but the rebuilder of an old settlement that had been deserted during the Persian persecution of Cyrus[6] between 631 and 641.[7] St. Samuel's talent was for organization. By the end of the persecutions, he had gathered a monastic community of forty-one monks, fourteen of whom had come from the neighbouring monastery of Naqlûn, and by the time of his death the number had increased to 120.

In the latter part of the eighth century, Anbâ Misâîl entered the monastery at the early age of twelve. This was when Anbâ Ishaq was the hegoumenos of Dair Anbâ Samwîl. At that time, there was a severe famine, and soldiers attacked the monastery, where the monks had been hoarding grain. The object of the government was to confiscate and distribute the supplies. As the soldiers approached the monastery, a rival band of warriors appeared and prevented the government forces from entering. The leader of this group was Anbâ Misâîl, who had enlisted the help of a number of anchorites living in the desert of al-Qalamûn. Anbâ Ishaq, in gratitude for the deliverance by Anbâ Misâîl, built a church in his honour.

The monastery flourished until the middle of the ninth century. In 842 the calligrapher Zacharias of the Monastery of St. Samuel wrote certain Synaxary lections for the Monastery of St. Michael in the Desert.[8] During the patriarchate of Anbâ Shenûdah (859-860) the Arabs devastated the monastery. "Among all the places which they pillaged was the Monastery of al-Qalamûn in the Fayyûm... They burnt the fortresses, and pillaged the provinces, and killed a multitude of the saintly monks who were in the monasteries, and they violated a multitude of the virgin nuns, and killed some of them with the sword."[9]

An Ethiopian story tells of a miracle which occurred at the Monastery of St. Samuel. "In this monastery was a beautiful church dedicated to the Holy Virgin, on the west wall of which was a large, wonder-working icon of the Virgin. There lived in the monastery a holy man who had fixed in his heart the salutation of the Angel Gabriel unto our Holy Lady, and he neither rested by day nor by night from reciting salutations. In the morning when the sun was rising, he ate a few herbs and beans, and everyone who spoke with him thought him to be mad. He ate nothing from that time until the same hour of the next morning. Furthermore, this monk did not receive the Holy Mysteries, except on three days in each year, Christmas, Epiphany and Easter. When the other monks saw him eating each day in the morning before the prayer of the third hour of the day, and knew nothing about his fasting, they imagined that he ate at the ordinary times of the day, and that he did not keep the ordinances of the monks. Then, on the day of the

Festival of the Nativity of the Holy Virgin, the hegoumenos of the monastery, Abba Isaac, told the other monks to seize him and to bring him to the church and to keep guard over him. At his earnest request, however, the monks who carried him with rude violence, took him to the icon of the Holy Virgin, and he prostrated himself in adoration before her. Now when the Blessed Lady knew of the sincerity of her monk, and the contempt with which the other monks had treated him, she put into his heart the good thought that she would reveal herself to the other monks. Then the monk again addressed the Holy Virgin, asking her to deliver him from the monks, and after having cast his skull cap into the church, he offered his prayers. The wall in the church was rent asunder, and he passed outside quickly through the opening. When he had gone out, the wall closed again, except for a small opening that was large enough for a man to put his hand into. Now the other monks recognized the righteousness of this monk. The bishop and the archbishop hearing about it, asked to get the skull cap of the monk so that they might obtain a blessing therefrom, but the monks refused to send it to them. So the monks placed the skull cap in the store chest of the church. Later, the bishop removed the skull cap and went to the wall that had been rent asunder and he obtained a blessing from the opening that was left. Several times the bishop attempted to remove the skull cap, though each time in vain. Miraculously the skull cap returned to its place in the church."[10]

The story is pure fabrication, but it is difficult to assign a date to it, although Ethiopian monks inhabited the Egyptian monasteries from the early Middle Ages onwards. During the patriarchate of Anbâ Mikhâîl (1092-1102), the Bishop of Cairo, Anbâ Sanhût, fell into disgrace. Anbâ Sanhût, a saintly man and one-time deacon in Dair Anbâ Bishoî, demanded the return of some written promises and documents from the patriarch which the patriarch later denied having written. Realizing that he was in danger of being caught by the bishop, the patriarch threatened him with excommunication. When Anbâ Sanhût learned of this, he retreated to the Monastery of al-Qalamûn, and the See of Cairo remained abandoned until the people of Cairo persuaded the patriarch to rehabilitate their spiritual leader.[11]

Abû Sâlih (1173-1208) refers to the walls, the abundant gardens, twelve churches, four large towers, and a high outlook from which approaching visitors could be seen and thus prepared for. "The sentinel strikes the wooden gong in different manners, according to the rank of the visitors, so that monks may know, when they hear it, who it is that is approaching."[12] The monastery was inhabited by 130 monks at this time.

The monastery was one of the more important ecclesiastical institutions in Egypt. The famous Arab encyclopaedist, Yaqût ar-Rumî

(1179-1229), mentions it in the geographical dictionary which he completed in 1224: "Dair al-Kalamoun in the land of Egypt and in the land of the Fayyûm is famous to the people and well-known."[13] During this period the monastery was at its height. In the beginning of the fifteenth century a monk of the Monastery of al-Qalamûn was elected to the patriarchate. He was Anbâ Ghabrîâl V (1409-1428). To this day, he is the only monk to have ascended the patriarchal chair from the Monastery of St. Samuel.[14]

Maqrîzî gives a less glowing account of the monastery. He mentions the gardens and the walls surrounding the monastery, but where Abû Sâlih saw four towers he saw only two. "This monastery is situated in the plain of al-Qalamûn, from where the traveller can reach the Fayyûm... The monastery has been given the name of St. Samuel who lived in the era between Jesus and Mohammad, and who died on the 8th of Kihak. There are many palms within the monastery that produce the Odschwe fruit; here also is the Lebach tree which is found only in this vicinity... This monastery has two qasrs built of stone, both being large, high and white. There is also a spring within and a spring outside the monastery. The valley contains many ancient places of prayer. Outside the monastery is a salt work, the salt of which is sold by the monastery. The income of this takes care of the whole region."[15]

In his book *Mémoires Géographiques et Historiques sur l'Egypte* (1811), Quatremère refers to the Monastery of al-Qalamûn de l'Arsinoite, situated in the nome of Arsinoë. Quatremère then merely quotes Maqrîzî.[16]

Nineteenth- and Twentieth-Century Travellers

It is difficult to determine exactly when the monastery was abandoned. Ahmad Fakhry suggests that it remained uninhabited for three hundred years.[17] Thus it was probably deserted at the beginning of the seventeenth century. Certainly when Giovanni B. Belzoni passed through the region of the "Wadi el Moueleh" in 1819 the monastery was uninhabited. "In this place I found a very large Christian church and convent. Some of the paintings on the wall are very finely preserved, particularly the figures of the twelve apostles on the top of the niche, over an altar; the gold is still to be seen in several parts."[18]

When Frederic Cailliaud crossed the desert of the "Wadi Moeyl" in 1819, he noticed a wall and some other structures, which he thought were of Roman origin. He also found sweet water.[19] Though probably ruined and damaged, it is interesting to note the extent of the ancient buildings that could still be identified at the beginning of the nineteenth century.

Wilkinson, travelling in 1832 from the "Fyoom to the little Oasis", mentions, that "the first halt is at a valley called Wadee Raian or Ryan, abounding with palm trees and water... about fifteen miles to the south-east of the Wadee Ryan is the valley of Moileh (the name Moileh seems to indicate a spot of bad water) with a ruined convent or monastery, and a spring of salt water. It may be visited on the way to Wadee Ryan, by making a small detour, and is curious as a Christian ruin. It contains two churches, one of stone, the other of brick, and is surrounded by a strong wall, with a tower of defence on the north side. In the churches are several Coptic and Arabic inscriptions, and figures of the apostles and saints, and the cornice that runs around a niche in the stone church is richly carved, though in bad taste. The total dimensions of the convent are eighty-nine paces by sixty-five."[20]

Almost half a century later, in 1886, Georg August Schweinfurth[21] travelled to the depression of the Fayyûm, and visited the still uninhabited monastery. He noticed the potsherds that were scattered around the building, and mentions two Corinthian capitals. In addition, he measured the ruins which apparently covered an area of fifty-five by sixty-seven metres. In the same year, Cope Whitehouse noticed ruins of ancient buildings in the Wadi Muellah and a fair amount of coarse vegetation near them.[22]

Beadnell, writing in *The Topography and Geology of the Fayum Province of Egypt* in 1899, gives the first report of a recent revival of the monastery. "Close to the north-end of the valley, and about thirty-three kilometres from al-Qâyât, lie the ruins known as Dair el Galamoun bil Muela. At the time of our visit a new square stone building was in course of erection and five or six persons were inhabiting the place. There are several small palms scattered about to the south of the monastery and an excellent running spring of clear water five hundred paces to the south-west. A new well is being sunk within the premises."[23]

Smolenski visited the monastery in 1908 and speaks of limestone and marble columns, of beautiful capitals and the remains of walls, all of which are reminders of a more glorious past.[24] The feretory of St. Samuel must still have been hidden away somewhere, for Smolenski did not see the relics, and his report that they were still in the monastery was based solely upon the testimony of his servant.

In the 1928 edition of Baedeker's *Aegypten und der Sudan,* the author refers to the "Der Amba Samuil", though he does not give any additional information about the monastery. Johann Georg, Duke of Saxony, intended to visit the monastery in 1928, but was prevented from carrying out his plan because of the unwillingness of his guides. But two years later he travelled to the monastery via the Fayyûm. On reaching the al-Qalamûn mountains, he had to leave his car behind and walk the last few miles. The monks informed him that a hegoumenos and twenty monks who had been excommunicated by the patriarch had established the monastery in 1897. After five years, the patriarch pardoned them and most of the monks returned to Dair al-Barâmûs, their original monastery. In 1930, the monastery was inhabited by seven monks under the leadership of Abûnâ Ishaq. Two monks were stationed in Maghâgha. Johann Georg felt that these monks were the poorest he had encountered. Apparently, he had difficulty taking photographs. "The hegoumenos considered it to be sinful to be photographed."[25]

In 1932, H. Munier visited the monastery and wrote a short history. He refers to the crypt which looked more like a casemate or store-room than a place of worship, and says that its walls were void of any inscriptions or paintings.

Ahmad Fakhry visited the monastery in 1942 and 1944, and he found four monks living there. A photograph of the four monks appears among the plates. At that time, the head of the monastic community was "an Abyssinian Gommos Raphael." Also in the photograph was Abûnâ Tawdrûs who had spent fourteen years in the monastery. Abûnâ Athânâsîûs and Abûnâ Mikhâîl were newcomers, who had not been at the monastery in 1942.

About fifteen years before his election as the 116th patriarch in 1959, Anbâ Kîrillus VI was hegoumenos of the Monastery of al-Qalamûn. Abûnâ Mînâ al-Muttawahad, as he was known, used to visit the monastery monthly, when he stayed in his Church of Abû Mînâ on the outskirts of Old Cairo.

In the middle of September 1955, Fr. Gabriele Giamberardini travelled with six other visitors from Maghâgha to the Monastery of Anbâ Samwîl. Their arrival was announced by the doorkeeper. Then they were welcomed by a blind old monk singing psalms, which provided an atmosphere of festivity and rejoicing. The monks assembled and formed a procession, and the guests were conducted to the guest-room in the first storey of the keep, where a luncheon of local bread, beans and onions was served. After lunch, they visited the churches and the archaeological sites. They were offered numerous personal invitations to the monks' cells. In the course of their visit, Fr. Gabriele met thirteen monks. Abûnâ Murqus was in charge of the monastery, since Qummus Mînâ, the hegoumenos, was absent. Abûnâ Rafâil al-Habashî was proud to mention to the visitors that he had spent thirty-three years in the mountains of al-Qalamûn, while Abûnâ Dimiân declared: "A year ago I was still in the Monastery of Anbâ Bûlâ where I organized and directed a campaign against Patriarch Anbâ Yûsâb II, which was successful. To-day he is at Dair al-Muharraq." Abûnâ Bûlûs, who was over a hundred years old, made an effort to come out of his cell to greet them.

Fr. Gabriele was informed by the monks that the monastery had been reinhabited in the last years of the nineteenth century by a group of monks who had left the Monastery of al-Barâmûs. Under the protection of Anbâ Kîrillus V and Anbâ Abrâm of the Fayyûm, the monks were enabled to re-establish themselves in the once abandoned monastery.[26]

I was told that after many years of desolation, the monastery was reinhabited in 1896 by Abûnâ Ishaq al-Barâmûsî and ten other monks who had come from the Wâdî 'n-Natrûn monasteries. In 1882, Abûnâ Ishaq al-Barâmûsî had entered the Monastery of al-Barâmûs. Dissatisfied with certain matters concerning the ascetic discipline in the Wâdî 'n-Natrûn, he gathered around himself several monks with whom he went to the mountain of al-Qalamûn, where he and his disciples reinhabited the ruined Monastery of St. Samuel. The first thing Abûnâ Ishaq did was to build a new qasr upon the foundations of the old one. Furthermore, he built a church and a school in al-Zawara, a village in the Nile valley. Abûnâ Ishaq was well known as an excellent preacher and administrator, serving the needs of his monastery as well as those of the fellahin living in and around al-Zawara. Many miracles are associated with the ministry of Abûnâ Ishaq.

In 1911, Abûnâ Ibrâhîm as-Samwîlî, who came from the Fayyûm, joined the monastery. He was sixteen. After the death of Abûnâ Ishaq in 1936, Abûnâ Ibrâhîm became the sub-hegoumenos of the monastery.

The remains of the ancient monastery described by Abû Sâlih are still partly visible. The monastery must have covered an area of about twelve feddans which was enclosed by a thick wall, the foundations of which are still recognisable, north of the present monastery. North-west of the monastery, the old wall appears to have had a width of eight metres, and was probably once one of the keeps which Abû Sâlih and Maqrîzî mention. The two furnaces outside the monastery walls to the south were used for the manufacture of bricks and other articles. On the north-west side of the monastery the foundations of several cells can still be identified, though most of the territory is covered with debris.

When I visited the monastery I was interested to see fifty-one silver coins from Fatimid and Ayyubid periods, which Abûnâ Mattâ al-Maskîn had found outside the west wall. This money may well have belonged to the monks, who had earned it by selling hand-woven baskets. In the past palm trees surrounded the monastery, and were used for the construction of the catacomb church of St. Samuel. Apparently the monks used to spend one third of their earnings on the poor outside the monastery, one third on the needs inside the monastery walls and one third on themselves.

The Monastic Renaissance

The Monastery of St. Samuel has benefited significantly from the recent monastic renaissance. The number of monks has increased and buildings have been extended. The three churches have been renovated and adorned with a wealth of neo-Coptic iconography.

The Church of the Holy Virgin with its nine domes was designed in 1958 by the monks who lived there under the leadership of Abûnâ Mattâ al-Maskîn. Two quarries, about one kilometre north· of the monastery, supplied the stones for the building. The church replaced the medieval building, referred to by Abû Sâlih. The relics of St. Samuel and St. Apollo are kept in the church.

The neo-Coptic iconography executed by Yusuf Girgis in 1984 represents the following themes: the enthroned Virgin and Child; St. Michael; the Annunciation; the Nativity; the Baptism; the Resurrection; the Ascension; St. George; St. Iskhiron; St. Menas; Noah and the ark; Daniel in the lions' den; the Three Youths in the furnace; the Ascension of Elijah; St. Makarius and cherubim; St. Macarius with SS. Maximus and Domitius; St. John the Little and the Tree of Obedience; St. Bishoi Christophorus; Patriarch Ghabrîâl V (1409-1427) of Qalamûn; Patriarch Timothy II (457-477); St. Stephanus the Anchorite; St. Galeon the Anchorite; St. Anthony and St. Paul the Theban; St. Apollo and St. Justus of Qalamûn.

In the Church of St. Misâîl on the first floor of the keep are kept the relics of St. Bisada and St. Domadius. In December 1976 the body of St. Bisada is said to have issued blood. This church with one haikal was built by Anbâ Ishâq in 1905. Also in this church, modern neo-Coptic iconography adorns the walls with the following themes: the Twelve Apostles with St. Samuel and St. Misâîl; the Seven Hermits (St. Paul the Theban; St. Bidjimi; St. Onuphrius; St. Timotheus; St. Misâîl; St. Galeon and St. Stephanus); St. Samuel and the angel guiding him to Qalamûn; St. John the Hegoumenos with St. Abraham and St. George the Hermit; St. Stephen the protomartyr and St. Peter the last martyr; St. Athanasius and St. Dioscorus; St. Shenudah and St. Pachomius; St. Bishoi and St. Paul of Tammuâh; St. Bisada and St. Domadius; St. Misâîl and cherubim.

The catacomb church is an underground sanctuary supposedly belonging to the fourth century. Though this date is improbable, there is no question that the church belongs to the oldest part of the monastery. The church, situated in the qasr, is dark and has a vaulted ceiling. It is about three metres in length (east-west) and six metres in width (north-south). The stone haikal-screen shows marks which indicate that six icons once decorated the church. Two steps lead up to the haikal at the east end of which there stands a marble column, one and a quarter metres high. This marble column, as well as those in front of the east gate, may well have belonged to the ancient Church of Anbâ Misâîl. It is very likely that the column in the catacomb church was transferred there by Abûnâ Ishaq at the beginning of the twentieth century.

When the monks returned at the end of the nineteenth century, the catacomb church served as living quarters. This was probably the best preserved section of the monastery.

This church, dedicated to St. Samuel, has been decorated with wall-paintings by Raghib Kamel. They show St. Samuel with his disciples St. Yustus and St. Apollo; St. Anthony; St. Bishoi and St. Macarius; St. John the Baptist; St. George and the Holy Virgin and Child.

The leadership of the monastery is in the hands of Anbâ Mînâ and the amîn ad-dair is al-Qummus Basilius as-Samwîlî. In 1985 fifteen monks and six novices inhabited the monastery. Two rows of new cells have been built and a new gate with two towers in the western wall provides access to the monastery. The walls have been repaired and considerably extended. About a hundred feddans of desert land have been added to the monastery complex. The chicken-farm has more than five thousand chickens. The farm also includes twelve cows, two hundred rabbits, a pigeon cote, geese and ducks. The landmark of the monastery, visible from afar, is the new water-tower, which is thirty-five metres tall.

To reach the monastery, one proceeds from Maghâghâ in a north-westerly direction to al-'Idwa, crossing the Bahr Yussuf Canal, and from there to the Desert Reclamation Project at Village 5, where the Monastery of St. Samuel maintains a rest-station. From there, a desert track leads to Dair Anbâ Samwîl. The monastery has a dependency at Maghâghâ.

The Cave of St. Samuel

Before the first monastery was established in al-Qalamûn, the monks lived in caves. These caves are to be found around the natural elevation in the Wâdî Mowâlih and the Bahr Bilâ Mâ.

Abû Sâlih mentions a cave "outside the monastery in which lives a monk who is named Muhna, and he never quits it by day or by night. He fasts during the whole week. The monks go to him to receive his blessings. Around his cave there are many fruitful palm trees. The wild beasts used to come together to him and not one of them hurt him, but they grew so tame that he was able to feed them out of his hand. The devils also appeared to him, and stood opposite to him, face to face, but could not reach him. This monk Muhna made at the beginning of his monastic life, before he shut himself up in a cave on the mountain, a church. It is said that the father Anbâ Samwîl used to worship on the mountain at a place called Rayân, opposite to the monastery."

The most important cave in this area is the cave of St. Samuel, about five kilometres east of the monastery in the mountain of al-Qalamûn.

On my visit to the monastery we travelled by donkey to the foot of the mountain and then, leaving the donkey behind, climbed the steep sandy ascent. The cave is situated at an altitude of a hundred metres, some fifteen metres below the mountain top. The entrance faces west, and the cave extends some thirty metres into the rock. At the end of the passage is a reservoir, which according to the monks is filled by falling rain. The cave is plain and without decoration, except for a few Arabic graffiti. Abûnâ Mînâ said: "Unfortunately, it is impossible for us to place an altar or icons here, because the cave is frequently used by the Bedouins. To them it is a place of shelter." The skull of a donkey and some hay verified his comment. Looking at the cave from the small balcony in front of the entrance, one notices two layers of plaster on the walls as well as on the floor. One layer is white, the other layer a pinkish colour, suggesting that the cave must have been inhabited by monks for a long period.

St. Samuel apparently lived here during the last years of his life, visiting the monastery at intervals. It is probable that the cave was more easily accessible then than it is now. At the end of the nineteenth century, Abûnâ Yuhannis is reported to have lived here. Abûnâ Ishaq himself only stayed in the cave for a short time. The monks say that the cave has always been inhabited by anchorites, and it is quite possible that again in the twentieth century some young monk will take up the life of cave asceticism, and follow the examples of his illustrious predecessors.

10
DAIR AL-MUHARRAQ

The Holy Family in Egypt

The history of the foundation of the Monastery of the Blessed Virgin Mary (Dair al-Muharraq) is closely interwoven with the tradition of the journey of the Holy Family to Egypt. In the Gospel of St. Matthew[1] we read that, "when they (the wise men) were departed, behold, the angel of the Lord appeared to Joseph in a dream, saying, Arise, and take the young child and his mother, and flee into Egypt, and be thou there until I bring thee word: for Herod will seek the young child to destroy him. When he arose, he took the young child and his mother by night, and departed into Egypt: And was there until the death of Herod: that it might be fulfilled which was spoken of the Lord by the prophet, saying, 'Out of Egypt have I called my son'."[2]

On leaving Palestine, the Holy Family, together with Salome, the midwife, travelled in a south-westerly direction until they reached the fertile area of the Nile valley.[3] They went via Tell al-Bastah, Bilbais, Samanûd, al-Matariyah, and Babylon to the site, where the suburb of Ma'adî has been built. Here they embarked on a boat and sailed to Upper Egypt until they reached the village of Qusqâm.[4] Near Qusqâm, Joseph built a small house of bricks and covered it with palm-leaves. The Holy Family stayed there for three years, six months and ten days. This is the site of the Dair al-Muharraq. Herod died and the Angel of God appeared to Joseph and commanded him to: "Arise, take the child and his Mother, and depart into Israel."

Then the Holy Virgin besought Christ to grant honour and esteem to this house, which gave shelter to them in their exile, and Christ blessed the house and said: "Let the benediction of My good Father remain in this house forever. This house which you see, O my holy mother, will have in it a sanctuary dedicated to God, and people will offer sacrifices and ex-votos in it to the Lord, and those who will offer them will be the faithful of the Orthodox faith till the day of my second coming... And those who will come to this house with faith and worship, I will forgive all their sins, if they intend not to revert to them, and I will count them among the saints. If any of those who are in distress, trouble or loss come to this holy place and worship and pray in it, and demand congruous things, I will grant their requests and all their demands... O Mary, this house in which we are will contain holy monks on whom no ruler of this world shall be able to inflict any injury, because it became a refuge to us. And any barren woman who beseeches me with a pure heart and remembers this house, I will give her sons. All the people who come to this place with ex-votos and offerings for your holy name, I will inscribe my name on their offerings...."

After his resurrection, Christ gathered his apostles at Qusqâm in order to divide the nations of the world among his disciples. He consecrated the house, and St. Gabriel and St. Michael carried the vessel containing the water which he sprinkled on the church. The Holy Virgin, the twelve apostles, St. Mary Magdalene and Salome were present at the consecration. After the consecration, vestments were found along with the ritual used by the church. When everything was ready, Christ ordered St. Peter to celebrate the Divine Liturgy, and then the Holy Spirit came down. At that moment a large bird flew down from heaven, carrying wines and delicacies. It alighted in the centre of the church and everybody took from it. This house became known as the first church in the world, the Church of the Holy Virgin in Dair al-Muharraq.[5]

Two possible explanations have been made as to the origin of the name of this monastery. Some say that because the monastery is situated a distance from water, the land around it was called "al-maharraq" (burnt up), while others explain the name by referring to the grass which grew around the monastery and which could only be removed by burning (harîq).

The Founder of Coenobitic Monasticism

Historically, Dair al-Muharraq belongs to the group of monasteries established by Anbâ Bakhûm (St. Pachomius) or his immediate successors. Its situation as well as the type of monastic life suggests a Pachomian origin.

Anbâ Bakhûm, who is commemorated by the Coptic church on 14th Bashons, was born in the latter part of the third century in the nome of Sne. The courageous witness of the martyrs of the Diocletian persecution influenced Bakhûm's conversion to Christianity. Every Christian was compelled to perform military service and Anbâ Bakhûm was conscripted into the Roman army. After his conversion he took refuge with a hermit named Anbâ Balamûn of Dendera. Anbâ Balamûn was a leader of a group of ascetics and Anbâ Bakhûm shared his cell until he left the band of ascetics to found a community of his own at Tabennese.

Anbâ Bakhûm established several monasteries in Upper Egypt, all of which had something of a military character. The monks were grouped together according to the trade they practised, and daily manual work was obligatory for all who were healthy and young. A superior was responsible for each house, and the hegoumenos had charge over the monastery. The novices were assigned to elders who were responsible for their spiritual growth. The divine office, which consisted of Vespers and Nocturns, was compulsory for all monks, and here we find the beginnings of an orderly devotional life. A life of prayer was allied to physical work. The monks worked with the peasants in the field, and most of the novices were probably drawn from the peasantry.

Anbâ Bakhûm was a contemporary of St. Athanasius, the twentieth patriarch of Alexandria, who died in 373. St. Athanasius visited Anbâ Bakhûm in Tabennese before the latter died. St. Athanasius was restored to his see by the emperor Constantius in 349, and Anbâ Bakhûm died around this time.

The most important disciples of Anbâ Bakhûm were Anbâ Tawdrûs of Tabennese and Anbâ Ursiasiûs. Anbâ Tawdrûs was the son of Christian parents. When he was fourteen he joined Anbâ Bakhûm's institution at Tabennese. He was a favourite disciple of the first organiser of Christian monasticism: at the age of thirty he was appointed hegoumenos of Tabennese, and Anbâ Bakhûm intended him to be his successor. It was the custom, however, for the candidates for higher offices to refuse the proposed office. Anbâ Tawdrûs neglected to do so, and Anbâ Bakhûm appointed Anbâ Butrûniûs instead. But he died shortly after his nomination, and Anbâ Ursiasiûs was entrusted with the leadership of the Pachomian establishments. Before long he was faced with serious administrative difficulties. Later Anbâ Ursiasiûs appointed Anbâ Tawdrûs, who ruled the Pachomian monasteries for eighteen years, adding new communities and restoring harmony among the monks. He died in 368. Having been Anbâ Bakhûm's most intimate friend, he was able to develop the life of the communities on his teacher's lines. After Anbâ Tawdrûs' death, Anbâ Ursiasiûs resumed control of the monasteries and continued quietly and efficiently the work of Anbâ Tawdrûs.

On 20th Kihak, the *Coptic Synaxarium* commemorates the martyrdom of Anbâ Hâlyâs (Elias), Bishop of the Dair al-Muharraq, who confessed his Christian faith for which he was beheaded by Arian the Governor. His relics were hidden until the end of the persecutions, when they were taken to the church in the Dair al-Muharraq.[6]

Several Hundred Years of Silence

At the end of the fourth century, the twenty-third patriarch of Alexandria, Anbâ Tawfîlus (384-412), wanted to build a large and beautiful church to commemorate the Holy Family's residence on the site of the monastery, but the Holy Virgin appeared to him in a dream and said: "The Holy Trinity desires that this part of the monastery should remain as it is, in order that people, in centuries to come, may see the humility which made us choose this poor abode. Therefore, make no alterations or improvements in it"

Copts who live near Dair al-Muharraq refer to the place as the "Second Jerusalem" or the "Second Mount of Olives". The Holy Family's visit to the area has endowed it with great spiritual importance.

There is some evidence that the traditions were the product of the twelfth or thirteenth century since the locality of Qusqâm (al-Qûsia) does not appear in any traditions before this. The place became famous through a homily of Theophilus of Alexandria. As Monneret de Villard points out, the existence of an Arabic version of the tradition does not necessarily prove an ancient date, for we know of no Greek or Coptic version prior to the Arabic one. It is perhaps possible that a local legend, or legends were created to attract pilgrims and to use their offerings and gifts for a special building program.

De Villard suggests that the reconstruction of the Church of the Holy Virgin at Dair al-Muharraq, connected with certain miracles occurring at the same time, was the cause of the legend. Alternatively the legends arose around the pre-existing sanctuary and thus supplied the financial means for the rebuilding of the church. Since there is some architectural evidence to place the rebuilding of the church in the twelfth century, it would be logical to assume a similar date for the original stories of the Holy Family's travels.[7]

Almost nothing is known about the history of this monastery. Johann Georg, who visited it in 1927, was much disappointed because he had no opportunity to indulge in his hobby of collecting ancient Coptic treasures. Qummus Quzmân Bishaî al-Muharraqî explained to me: "Our monastery has suffered not only from raids and sacks, but we have had our share of internal difficulties. Our forefathers were killed, and our records and books were burnt. Those books that survived the flames were carried away. We are poor as to our history and our tradition."

Only four patriarchs have come from Dair al-Muharraq: Anbâ Ghabrîâl IV, the 86th patriarch (1370-1378); Anbâ Mattâ I, the 87th patriarch (1378-1408); Anbâ Mattâûs II, the 90th patriarch (1452-1465); and Anbâ Yûânnis XII, the 93rd patriarch (1480-1483).

The *Ethiopian Synaxarium* provides some details about the life of Anbâ Mattâ I (1378-1408). He had been a monk at the Red Sea Monastery of St. Antony before going to Dair al-Muharraq. It was from the latter, however, that he was elected to be patriarch of Alexandria. From the Monastery of St. Antony "he departed to Dabra Kueskuam, and he dwelt there, and he fought so strenuously that, at length, when he gazed upwards he could see our Lord Jesus Christ sitting on the right hand of his Father; and when he looked downwards he saw Him in the abysses in great glory. When Anbâ Gabrîâl IV died, they (the bishops and priests) appointed Abba Mattâ to succeed him as archbishop against his will, and when he refused they set guards over him, and the following day all the bishops told him that they had seen a vision and that he was suitable for the office of archbishop. When Abba Mattâ heard this, he knew that they would not let him go, and he took a razor secretly and drew it across his tongue and cut it off. And that night our Lady Mary came to him, and anointed his tongue with oil, and healed it, and it became as it was before he cut it. And they took him to the city of Alexandria, and when they enthroned him... a voice was heard from heaven saying, 'He is worthy, He is worthy,' "[8] We read elsewhere that Anbâ Mattâ was much concerned with the raising of the moral and spiritual standards of the monks at Dair al-Muharraq and Dair Anbâ Antûnîûs. He was seriously engaged in some reform, though apparently his efforts were in vain.[9]

Both Abû Sâlih in the beginning of the thirteenth century and Maqrîzî in the middle of the fifteenth century mention the monastery briefly. Both testify to the pilgrimages to Dair al-Muharraq. Abû Salih states: "Pilgrimages have been made by many multitudes from all districts to this church from ancient times, because it has been celebrated on account of signs and wonders and the healing of various diseases."[10] Maqrîzî lists Dair al-Muharraq as the forty-second monastery and speaks of the great feast, known as the palm feast and Pentecost, which attracts a large crowd of people.[11]

Dair al-Muharraq, or a church in the immediate vicinity of this monastery, was inhabited by Ethiopian monks between the fourteenth and sixteenth centuries. During this period Ethiopian communities were established along the pilgrimage route from Ethiopia to Jerusalem, and Qusqâm near Dair al-Muharraq is specifically mentioned.[12] Brother Nicholas, travelling from Ethiopia to Cairo in 1470, refers to the cities of "Mesia, Asue and Manfelout," and describes going through Egypt to the Monastery of the Coptic Christians in ten days.[13]

Fr. Francesco Suriano writing in 1484 states: "Above Cairo, two days' journey on the Nile to the south, there is a Christian country and homeland called Manfluth, where there is a monastery of the Jacobites. In that monastery there is a chapel where the Blessed Virgin dwelt with her son and Joseph all the time they were in exile in Egypt... In which place many and divers diseases are cured up to the present day, according to what men worthy of faith told me in Cairo."[14]

In 1673, Johann Michael Wansleben travelled up the Nile, visiting the province of Manfalût and fifty-one other villages, thirty of which were situated in the vicinity of the river. There he counted twenty-one churches or monasteries. He mentions twelve more monasteries close to the Nile. These include the Monastery of the al-Muharraq, and that of the Ethiopians, close to which was the Monastery of the Archangel Gabriel which is in Buh.[15] The connection between the monastery and the Ethiopians has always been intimate. The Ethiopians call it the Monastery of Qusqâm and Emperor Iyasu II (1730-55) built a church in Gondar which is called the Church of Kueskam. A legend relates that Queen Mentwab visited Dair al-Muharraq and took some dust from the monastery which she placed under the altar of the Church of Kueskam in Gondar.

In the beginning of the nineteenth century, E. Jomard wrote that Dair al-Muharraq was inhabited by twenty monks and two hundred other people. This is the only reference to this monastery in his monumental study of Egypt, *Description de l'Egypte*.[16] That the monastery had considerably decreased in influence is also attested by 'Abd al-Masîh al-Mas'udî. In 1857, during the days of Qummus 'Abd al-Malak al-Hurî, Qummus 'Abd al-Masîh al-Mas'udî al-Kabîr ibn Girgis left Dair al-Muharraq with a group of monks for the Monastery of al-Barâmûs.[17]

Dair al-Muharraq escaped Catholic missionary efforts but from the middle of the nineteenth century Protestant missionaries visited the monastery. By 1865, the missionary work of the United Presbyterian Church of America at Asyût had been so well established that the missionaries could turn their attention to the monks of Dair al-Muharraq. The history of the mission says that "through the diffusion of religious knowledge from the Scriptures and other books, distributed and read, many came about the mission at Asyût, and a great movement among the monks in Dair al-Muharraq occurred, in which several of the monks proposed leaving the monastery and going to Asyût to study theology."[18]

The second exodus of monks from Dair al-Muharraq to the Monastery of al-Barâmûs occurred in 1871, when Qummus Bûlus al-Gildawî ibn Ghobrîâl left the monastery with a group of young monks and students. Qummus Bûlus had been hegoumenos, but he was relieved of his post because he distributed too much of the property to the poor.

In 1873, G. Rohlfs set out on an expedition to the Farâfrah and Siwa oases. The first place he visited was Dair al-Muharraq, where the expedition was ceremoniously welcomed and taken into the monastery in procession. The bells of the churches rang, speeches were made, and the guests were shown through the churches of the monastery. Before their departure, the monks offered them lamb, turkey, eggs, butter and honey.[19]

In 1883, Fr. Jullien, S.J., visited the Dair al-Muharraq which, at that time, was one of only seven inhabited Coptic monasteries in Egypt. Fr. Jullien compares the monastery with the other monasteries and comes to the conclusion that it was the wealthiest and largest.

Though the cells of the monastery could house three hundred monks, there were only eighty monks, of whom sixty were in priest's orders. The walls enclosed four hundred hectares of good land, and the monks were primarily engaged in cultivating this. The hegoumenos who received Fr. Jullien and his company begged them to stay in one of his apartments. He told them that Dair al-Muharraq was the most northern monastery of those established by Anbâ Bakhûm, and that it marked the northern border of the series of monasteries. For this reason it was called "Mukharrar" (the border) which was later corrupted into Muharraq.[20]

In 1888, Wilbour referred very briefly to "Dair al-Maharag." "In this Dair, the sore-eyed boy who was my donkey boy's boy, told me, live five hundred Christians, who have two thousand acres and more."[21]

In 1907, Hafiz Naguib,[22] known also as the "Honest Thief", entered the monastic life, though he was never baptized. Coming from Cairo, using the Christian name of Ghali Girgis, he went via Kafr Dâûd to Dair Abû Maqâr. He left after a short time because the water was so salty. At Dair Anbâ Bishoî he was made a monk, and was known as Abûnâ Ghobrîâl Ibrahîm. Hafiz wrote a poem in memory of his friend, Mustafa Kamil (1874-1908), leader of the Nationalist Party. The poem, which was discovered by Qummus Butrus, the hegoumenos of the monastery, was published, and the "monk" was strongly criticized by the patriarch for taking an interest in a political leader. Qummus Butrus advised his "monk" to enter Dair al-Muharraq. Again under the name of Ghali Girgis, Hafiz went back to Dair al-Muharraq where he was given the name of Abûnâ Fîluthâûs al-Muharraqî. Because of his superior learning he was appointed teacher in history, arithmetic and reading and writing. Among other things, Hafiz is remembered for his impressive lecture: *The Fundamentals of the Christian Religion and the Philosophy of the French Revolution,* which he delivered at the monastery on the occasion of the visit of Mustafa Bey

Helmî. After a while, Hafiz became well known in the monastery and its vicinity because of his piety, learning, and his so-called miraculous powers. But his relationship with his former friend, Qummus Sidârûs, deteriorated as time went on, and Hafiz left the monastery. On his way to Cairo, he was kidnapped by monks, but escaped. In Cairo, he met Anbâ Bakhûm, the bishop of Dair al-Muharraq, who advised him to go to the Antonian dependency at Bûsh, where Hafiz was much impressed by the more liberal attitudes of Anbâ Murqus. But his days in Bûsh were numbered. He was sent back to Cairo where he was introduced to Anbâ Kîrillus V, the patriarch. After this experience Hafiz went to Minya where he took off his monastic habit. Hafiz Naguib is one of the most interesting people to have lived in Egypt. His description of the monastic life as found in his autobiography shows a considerable insight into the situation of Coptic monasticism at the beginning of the twentieth century.

Some Outstanding Monks

"Wherever there is much sunshine, there is also much shade." The recent history of the monks of this monastery well illustrates this saying. No monastery has suffered during the last fifty years so much from internal disturbances and dissension as Dair al-Muharraq. There were uprisings of the monks against their hegoumenos in 1936, 1937, 1939, 1947, and 1959. During the 1960s a number of unfortunate incidents led to the violent deaths of several monks.

At the same time, the monastery has brought forth a number of great spiritual leaders, who have left a lasting impact upon the church.

One of the outstanding leaders of the church in the nineteenth century was Anbâ Yuhannis, the bishop of Manûfîyah. The following story is told about him: Muhammad 'Alî Pasha (1805-1848) had a daughter named Zuhra who, at one time, was extremely sick, possessed by an evil spirit. The doctors were unable to do anything for her, and it was suggested that no one could help the daughter except the Coptic patriarch. After being approached by Muhammad 'Alî, Pope Butrus VII (1809-1852) remembered Anbâ Yuhannis, who had been given the power by the Holy Spirit to cure the sick. So the patriarch asked the bishop to go to Muhammad 'Alî's palace and to pray over his daughter. The bishop at first refused, but the patriarch insisted, assuring him of his prayerful assistance. So the bishop went to Muhammad 'Alî's palace and prayed over the daughter, and in consequence the evil spirit left her and she recovered. When Muhammad 'Alî turned to the bishop and said, "What are you in need of for your troubles?", the bishop replied, "I am not in need of anything." But Muhammad 'Alî insisted on repaying the bishop for his trouble. The bishop said, "If you are really willing to give me what I ask, I beg of you that we may build our churches, as we please, and I beg of you that you treat our

Christian sons equally in all positions of government and public life." It is said that Muhammad 'Alî showed tolerance towards non-Muslims, and that, in spite of the prejudices of the people, he raised Christians to the rank of bey, which was unheard of amongst his predecessors.

Another saint highly venerated by the monks is Anbâ Mîkhâîl al-Buhairî (1847-1923). His numerous miracles have attracted the attention of many pilgrims, and an icon of him adorns the Church of the Holy Virgin. On 23 February 1991 the body of Anbâ Mikhâîl was placed on a feretory which now stands in the northern aisle of the Church of St. George. Some relics of the saint were transferred to the Dair al-'Azab in the Fayyûm, the Church of St. George in Ishnîn an-Nasâra, and the Dair Abû Mînâ at Maryût.

The most popular modern Coptic saint is Anbâ Abrâm (1829-1914), Bishop of the Fayyûm. Born in Dalga near Mallawî, he joined Dair al-Muharraq at the age of seventeen and received the monastic name of Bulûs Ghôbriâl. Bishop Yaqûb of Minya ordained him to the priesthood. During the patriarchate of Anbâ Demetrîûs II he served for five years as oeconomus of Dair al-Muharraq, until several greedy monks revolted against him. Anbâ Abrâm left Dair al-Muharraq for Dair al-Barâmûs. In 1881 he was consecrated bishop of the Fayyûm. He memorized the Holy Scriptures in the same way as the Muslims memorize the Qurân. He laid stress on Christians' responsibility to show charity to their neighbours and urged his fellow monks to continue and to grow in the ascetic life. His popular appeal, however, was due to the many miracles which he performed. He healed the sick irrespective of their economic status, and cast out devils where he met them.

The following story is told by Ahmad Yunis of Timsahiya, al-Qûsîa province. His parents had been married for many years, but they were without children. One day they went to Anbâ Abrâm in the Fayyûm to consult him about their misfortune. Having prayed, Anbâ Abrâm promised the couple a boy within a year's time, and he asked that he should be called "Ahmad". After a year, a boy was born and they called him "Ahmad". To this day, Ahmad Yunis considers himself the son of Anbâ Abrâm. Another story tells how one day, three Muslims decided to see Anbâ Abrâm. Knowing of his generosity, they wondered how they could profit from it. They decided that two of them should visit him and tell him that their friend had died, and that they needed money to bury him. Anbâ Abrâm gave them the money. When the two returned to their friend, they found that he had died. Whereupon they returned the money to Anbâ Abrâm confessing their sins. But he merely said: "It is the will of God."

When Anbâ Abrâm died in June 1914 the Coptic church lost one of its most dynamic personalities.

The Buildings of the Monastery

Dair al-Muharraq can be conveniently divided into two main sections, the outer and the inner court. A large wall with an irregular outline, resembling roughly the shape of a trapezoid, encloses the monastery buildings. The dimensions of the monastery are two hundred and seventy-five metres by one hundred and fifty-five metres. The ancient structures of the monastery situated in the western part have attracted the interest of both architects and historians. Here we find the Church of the Holy Virgin, the qasr and a small tower.

As mentioned before, the Church of the Holy Virgin claims to be the oldest in the world. Abû Sâlih states that the Church of the Holy Virgin was the first church to be built in Egypt. The monks informed me that the church was built immediately after St. Mark's arrival in Egypt, somewhere around 60A.D. The present church seems to have been built in the twelfth or thirteenth century. It is quite likely that an older building was altered or rebuilt. Monneret de Villard states that the monastery underwent a general restoration in the twelfth century, and it is possible that the Church of the Holy Virgin was included in this programme.[23]

Of special interest is the sigma-shaped altar-slab bearing the date of 11 December, 747. This stone was originally designed as an altar-slab, but it was later used as a funerary stele. Then, probably around the thirteenth century, it reverted to its original use as altar-slab in the Church of the Holy Virgin.

The church is situated a metre below the level of the inner court. According to tradition "the haikal was built on the ·site of the cave once inhabited by the Holy Family." Today, the church is used daily for the celebration of the Divine Liturgy. Since its renovation in 1935 by Qummus Tâdrûs 'As'ad, electric light has been installed and many prints, examples of contemporary Christian art, are attached to the beautiful wooden haikal-screen.

The wonder-working icon of the Holy Virgin and Child, popularly attributed to St. Luke the Evangelist, adorns the south wall of the choir. The icon is nineteenth-century and is the work of the Greek painter Eustathius or Astasi-ar-Rûmî. On the north wall of the choir is an icon of Qummus Mikhâil al-Buhairî (1847-1923). This icon was painted by one of the monks during the hegoumenship of Qummus Tâdrûs As'ad (1932).

Above the Church of the Holy Virgin there used to be the Church of SS. Peter and Paul.[24] This church was taken down in the latter part of the nineteenth century, when the new Church of St. George was built. Part of the haikal-screen of the old church can still be seen in the Church of the Holy Virgin.

The Church of St. Michael is situated on the second storey of the qasr, which the monks call the "acropolis". Abû Sâlih comments: "Adjacent to the church is a large and ancient keep which had fallen into decay but which was renewed and restored to its original condition by the Shaîkh Abû Zakharî ibn Bû Nasr, the administrator of Ashmunain in the caliphate of Hâfiz."[25] This places the reconstruction of the qasr between the years 1130-1149. We know that al-Hâfiz[26] was tolerant towards Christians, that he used to visit the monasteries, and that he had friendly relations with the patriarch. The original qasr, which dated from the eighth century, was rebuilt in the twelfth century. The purpose of the qasr, of course, was to provide shelter for the monks during an attack. The church is said to have been built by Anbâ Ghabrîâl VII (1526-1569). It is used three times a year on the Feasts of the Archangel, 8 November, 6 June and 6 July.

From the terrace-roof of the qasr one has a fine view over the monastery, the churches of the Holy Virgin and St. George, and the large necropolis which extends to the west of the monastery. The two small tombs on the roof were used for the burial of casualties when the monastery was attacked. A narrow extension of the terrace served as a latrine in times of attack. A slot in the floor served as a drain. A well, now closed, provided sufficient water for the besieged. The entrance to the qasr[27] is by means of a drawbridge which connects the first floor of the building with a smaller tower.

The largest church is that of St. George, built in 1888 by Qummus Salîb. The building incorporates modern Byzantine features. The altar and the haikal-screen are built of marble. The top of the marble screen is decorated with icons of the Twelve Apostles. Below those icons there are ten others representing from the south to the north: the Holy Virgin; Anbâ Bakhûm; St. George; St. John Chrysostom; St. Michael; the Holy Virgin; St. Gabriel; St. Basil the Great; the baptism of Jesus; St. Mark the Evangelist. Beneath the marble altar are the tombs of four monks who have contributed much to the glory of the monastery: the hegoumenos who built the church, Qummus Salîb, (died in 1905); Qummus Bakhûm I, the builder of the "Pachomian Castle" and the walls (died in 1928); Anbâ Mîkhâîl al-Buhairî who died in 1923 at the age of seventy six, and Anbâ Sâwîrûs (Severus), bishop of Dairût and Sanabû (died in 1927). South of the sanctuary is the baptistry.

The new Church of the Holy Virgin in the outer court was consecrated in 1964. This church has three haikals dedicated to St. Takla Haymanot (north); the Holy Virgin (centre) and St. George (south). The walls are richly adorned with paintings representing the desert fathers, the Byzantine doctors of the church and biblical events. Because of the historical relationship of this monastery with the Ethiopian church, St. Takla Haymanot, the national saint of Ethiopia, is especially venerated. The outer west wall has two niches with paintings showing Qummus Mikhâîl al-Buhairî (north) and Anbâ Abrâm of the Fayyûm (south). Above the entrance to the church there is a painting of the Flight of the Holy Family to Dair al-Muharraq.

The dome is adorned with a painting of the Pantocrator, while the four pendentives show portraits of the Four Evangelists. On the west wall of the church are two shrines, that of the Holy Virgin (north) and that of St. George (south). The baptistry, south of the nave, has two baptismal fonts and is adorned with a painting of the baptism of Christ.

Social and Educational Services

Dair al-Muharraq is a unique monastic institution, located on the edge of the desert, yet still within the fertile Nile valley. In many ways it resembles a large estate administered by the Church. The wealth of the monastery is evident in the splendour of its modern buildings, the most notable being the "Pachomian Castle."[28] This building reveals all the elegance of the nineteenth-century Levantine culture. Apart from six bedrooms for guests with baths and running water, the "Castle" has conference-rooms, sitting-rooms and a large dining-room, all of them comfortably furnished. The old library is housed on the ground floor, the episcopal suite is in the second storey. The "Castle" stands in an idyllic orange-orchard which was planted in 1912.

The Theological Seminary founded by Qummus Bakhûm I in 1905 is situated in the outer court. The buildings were completed in 1937. The seminary's director is Qummus Banîâmîn. In 1986 there were about a hundred students. The course of study extends over a period of five years and includes the following subjects: Theology; Old and New Testament in Arabic and Coptic; Old and New Testament exegesis; dogmatic theology; psalmody; and Coptic, Arabic and English. After completion of the seminary course, the monks are awarded a diploma in Theology.

The monastery also maintains a primary school nearby.

Every year, from 21 June to 28 June, a hundred thousand pilgrims journey to the monastery for the feast of the Consecration of the Church of the Blessed Virgin Mary. A fair with booths, games, side-shows, stores and other amusements and entertainments is set up outside the monastery walls. Buses, camels and donkeys transport the pilgrims to the monastery. It is difficult to describe the atmosphere of rejoicing and mourning, laughter and tears which is part of the pilgrimage. Pilgrims come to the monastery either to visit the tombs of their ancestors who are buried in the large necropolis outside the monastery, or simply for a holiday.

At the time of the pilgrimage, the gates of the inner court of the monastery are locked, while the pilgrims establish themselves in the outer court and in the fields outside the walls. An unfortunate and tragic incident occurred at the time of the annual pilgrimage in the summer of 1988. When a fire broke out among the pilgrims camping in the outer court of the monastery some twenty-six children, six women, and fifteen men were killed on account of the panic that ensued.

In order to accommodate some of the pilgrims two new guest houses for more than a hundred people have been constructed. During the feast in 1987 more than three thousand children were baptised.

Fifty monks live in the monastery, another ten serve churches in the Sudan, Jerusalem, Abû Tîg and Tanta. The head of the monastery is Anbâ Sawîrûs.

11
DAIR
ABÛ MÎNÂ

The Life of Abû Mînâ

St. Menas (Abû Mînâ),[1] who is commemorated by the Latin and Greek churches on 11 November, and by the Egyptian church on 15th Hatûr, was an Egyptian officer in the Roman army at the time of the emperor Diocletian.[2] His mother, Euphemia, and his father, Eudoxius, who was prefect of Phrygia in Asia Minor, provided St. Menas with a good Christian education. At the age of fifteen, after the death of his parents. St. Menas gave all his possessions to the poor intending to devote his life to the service of God. His father's successor in the prefecture, however, was much interested in the young man, and he compelled him to join the regiment of the Rutiliaces, which was stationed at Cotiaeum in Asia Minor. A law was passed saying: "Diocletian and Maximian proclaim in every land that everyone carry out the service of the gods," whereupon St. Menas fled into the desert, where he had a vision which inspired him to martyrdom.

On the occasion of games and a festival at Cotiaeum in Asia Minor, St. Menas stepped into the arena, and, in a loud voice confessed his faith in Jesus Christ. The governor Pyrrhus was compelled to carry out the imperial decrees, and St. Menas was imprisoned. Several times, St. Menas was given the chance to recant, but every time, the saint testified to his faith. All the horrors and tortures of the imperial Roman *quaestiones* could not persuade him to deny his faith. The only wish which St. Menas expressed was to be buried in his native land of Egypt. Finally, in 296, St. Menas won the martyrs' crown. Some time afterwards a troop of soldiers was ordered from Phrygia to the Cyrenaica, and the officer in their command was a Christian by the name of Athanasius. Desirous to fulfil St. Menas' last wish,

Athanasius took the saint's body to Egypt. At the first stopping place in Mareotis, after a successful battle had been waged, the camel carrying the body refused to advance any further, and thus, St. Menas was buried in the Western desert, near Lake Mareotis.

People soon began to visit his tomb. A lame boy who saw a shining light over the tomb was healed. A poor shepherd, whose sick lamb rolled on the ground and was later miraculously healed, attributed the cure to the therapeutic effects of the water of the well of St. Menas. News of the cures spread rapidly. The only daughter of St. Constantine the Great, who suffered from leprosy, was healed, and men and women suffering from diverse diseases were cured at the tomb of St. Menas.

St. Menas has been well-known throughout the centuries and in numerous countries for his many miracles, and many shrines and churches were built in his honour in Europe as well as in the Orient. A collection of reports of seventeen miracles of St. Menas, attributed to Anbâ Tawfîlus, patriarch of Alexandria, has been made available by the translations of Drescher. In addition to these, a few isolated miracles have been reported, many of which are no doubt derived from the common stock of folklore. It might be interesting to cite here a few modern miracle stories of St. Menas.

"Many years ago, on a spot in the cultivation in Upper Egypt where a church dedicated to Mârî Mînâ al-'Agayebî now stands, there was a square plot of halfa-grass. This site was claimed by the Muslims as the burial-place of a sheikh. There was a very poor man who lived in the town adjoining these fields and who acted as *farrâsh* at the sugar factory in the same town. One night while he was sleeping he felt someone give him a kick. This naturally aroused him, and he saw standing beside him a man whose face and form were of great beauty, and who was clothed in white garments. This man told the poor *farrâsh* that he was Mârî Mînâ al-'Agayebî, that he wished him to build a church, and that he would himself indicate the spot on which he wished it to be erected... Mârî Mînâ then led the *farrâsh* to the patch of halfa-grass in the fields and told him to dig the whole plot which he had measured out to a depth of two and half metres. Furthermore, the saint told him, that he would find a large quantity of bricks, enough for the building of the the church, while to the east he would find piles of white lime to be used in the construction of the building... The saint told the *farrâsh* that he was to start at once to build the church, and that if he disobeyed the orders he would be killed. Then Mârî Mînâ vanished. The *farrâsh* set to work and found everything as the saint had told him. The church still stands on this spot, but the old *farrâsh* who built it has, of course, been dead for a long time, and since his day the building has been enlarged by one of the Coptic bishops".[3]

Dr. T.D. Mosconas, librarian of the Greek Orthodox Patriarchate, refers to a story of a horseman who appeared in Mareotis a few days before the great battle of 'Alamain (October 1942), urging the allied soldiers in Egypt to fight shoulder to shoulder, alleged to be St. Menas, and in the *Egyptian Gazette* of 10 November 1942, we read, "St. Menas is now hailed by the Greeks in Egypt as the saviour of Alexandria from the onslaught of the Axis troops... It was a case of St. Menas v. Rommel, with the first round won by the Egyptian saint... The saint's festival was therefore celebrated with due solemnity, and at the Cathedral of St. Saba, Alexandria, H. B. Patriarch Christopher II was present at the Doxology. Many devout Greeks are already speaking of subscribing to the erection of a church to St. Menas to be situated somewhere near the site of the old monastery."[4]

The Shrine of Abû Mînâ

There were many martyrs' shrines in Egypt, but their popularity was generally localized. The only two martyrs' shrines which had an international reputation were those of SS. Cyrus and John at Abûkir and of St. Menas at Maryût, and the latter was undoubtedly the more celebrated. According to tradition, in the reign of St. Constantine (306-337), a small oratory was built over the tomb of the saint. "They hung a lamp in its midst... which remained burning, without ever going out, day and night. And all who took away some of the oil of the lamp to distant lands received healing; so that a great concourse gathered there as well as countless multitudes from every land coming thither at all times unceasingly."

During the patriarchate of St. Athanasius, (328-373), so the legend goes, a church was built over the tomb of the saint, and bishops, priests and laity rejoiced in the consecration of the first Church of Abû Mînâ. The fame of the signs and wonders which appeared in that church through the intercession of St. Menas, the martyr, was widely broadcast. Soon the church became too small to accommodate all the pilgrims who came from many parts of the ancient world.

During the fifth century the great basilica, erroneously confused with the Basilica of Arcadius, was constructed. This was the largest church in Egypt. To protect the site, Emperor Zeno erected a city and stationed a garrison of soldiers nearby.

An Ethiopic manuscript tells of Zeno's visit to the Shrine of St. Menas, and the subsequent occupation of the sacred site by twelve thousand soldiers to defend it against marauding Bedouins.[5] Furthermore, the emperor ordered that food for the people at the Shrine of St. Menas should be supplied by the inhabitants of Mareotis, and that pilgrims visiting the shrine were to pay a certain sum of money for the food which they obtained there. "And again in the time of Anastasius the king (491-518), pious zeal inspired the heart of the praetorian prefect since he too heard of wonders and miracles wrought by the holy Apa Mena. And furthermore he saw the hardships suffered by the many multitudes coming to the shrine. For, when they left the lake and entered upon the desert there, they found no lodging or water till they reached the holy shrine. And the prefect built hospices by the lake and rest-houses for the multitudes. And he had the market-place established among them in order that the multitudes might find and buy all their needs. He had spacious depositories constructed where the multitudes could leave their clothes and baggage and everything which they brought to the shrine."

We do not know how many priests and monks were attached to the Church of St. Menas, though Kaufmann says that several hundred priests, and thousands of shopkeepers, workmen, etc., inhabited the desert of Mareotis in the fifth and sixth centuries.[6]

The St. Menas Baths (discovered by the Kaufmann Expedition in 1907) contain evidence that large numbers of pilgrims went to the Shrine of St. Menas to be healed by the waters,[7] as people now go to Lourdes. Menas ampullae, embossed with the effigy of the saint together with inscriptions, containing the sacred water, were on sale and found their way into almost every part of the ancient world. In the Church of St. Menas, Kaufmann discovered an ancient Greek graffito by a pilgrim from Smyrna: "Take the lovely water of Menas and pain disappears".

About 570, the anonymous pilgrim of Piacenza visited the sacred site. "Descending through Egypt, we came to the city of Athlibis, and walked as far as the tomb of the blessed St. Menas, who works many miracles."[8]

When the Copts suffered persecution at the hands of Cyrus, Anbâ Banîâmîn I left the city of Alexandria through the western gate and walked to the town of Mareotis, and from there to al-Mûna, an oasis situated at the intersection of the ways from Alexandria to the Wâdî 'n-Natrûn and from Tarânah to Barqa. The patriarch worshipped at the great Church of St. Menas, and after a short rest, went on to the mountain, called Barnug.[9]

Apparently, the Shrine of St. Menas survived the attacks of the Bedouins, who successively destroyed the monasteries in the Desert of Scetis. It also seems to have escaped from the invading Persians, who came to Egypt at the beginning of the seventh century and destroyed so many of the churches and monasteries.

In his description of the Shrine of SS. Cyrus and John at Abûkir, St. Sophronius refers to the Shrine of St. Menas the Martyr and the abode chapel in front of the shrine, which were the pride of all Libya, "the country inhabited and protected by the saint both before his martyrdom for Christ and afterwards. And in truth the place deserves yet greater fame and glory; for through it Mareotis and the whole of Libya stand to this day, and above all, the great illustrious and Christ-loving city of Alexandria."[10]

By the beginning of the seventh century the Shrine of St. Menas had passed into the hands of the Melkites, and the Melkite patriarch of Alexandria, St. John the Almoner, visited the shrine. In *Une vie inédite de St. Jean l'Aumonier* we read that he (St. John the Almoner) was not only distinguished by the generosity of his intention for exchanging and buying back captives, but also by the frugality of his manner of life. He voluntarily supported cheap and modest things and a humble household. Once, taking a goblet of wine in the largest temple of the great martyr, Menas, while praising its perfume and good quality, he asked the steward from where it was taken and for how much it was bought, and on learning from him that it had been brought from Palestine, and that the wine was bought at high price, he could not bring himself to drink it, but answered, "the humble John will not drink excellent muscat wine, and especially at such a price–serve me rather with that of Mareotis of which both the taste is poor and the price (value) is set low."[11]

Abû Sâlih refers to the Monastery of the Martyr Menas, the owner of the three crowns, which came down to him from heaven. He was a native of Nakyûs, and is buried in the Church of Maryût, which was restored in 725 in the caliphate of Hishâm ibn Marwân, when al-Walîd ibn Rufa'ah was Wâlî, at the expense of all the Christians who lived in that quarter.

During the patriarchate of Anbâ Mîkhâîl (744-768) the question of the jurisdiction over the Church of St. Menas arose. Both Copts and Melkites requested a decision from the government. This was at the time of Marwân II (last of the Ummayad caliphs, d. 750), who had allowed the Christians to rebuild many of their churches. "But the friends of Theophylact the Chalcedonian, who was called Cosmas, said to him (Marwân): 'Verily there are many churches of ours in Egypt, of which the Theodosians, that is to say the Copts, took possession, when the government of the Romans was overthrown; and now we have no church there. We beg the prince to write for us to Egypt, and send by us letters commending that the Church of St. Menas at Maryût be handed over to us, so that we may communicate there.' " Cosmas took letters to 'Abd al-Malik, which directed him to settle the dispute between the Copts and the Melkites, requesting that the truth concerning the founders of the church be ascertained, and that the church be handed over to them. Upon receipt of the letter, the two patriarchs (Cosmas and Mîkhâîl) were summoned to appear before 'Abd al-Malik. They engaged in theological discourses and "the Orthodox (i.e. the Copts) with their arguments from the Holy Scriptures prevailed over the Chalcedonians, so that 'Abd al-Malik marvelled." Then the Chalcedonians went secretly to the government authorities, offering bribes, that they might favour them in their claims. The patriarch, Anbâ Mîkhâîl, assembled his bishops and wrote a letter, giving account of the foundation of the Church of St. Menas, and of the troubles and banishments endured by the fathers at the hands of the Chalcedonians. An excerpt of the letter is reproduced in the *History of Patriarchs:* "Mîkhâîl, by the Grace of God, bishop of the city of Alexandria and of the Theodosian people, to the governors, with regards to the church of the glorious Saint Menas at Maryût. At that time reigned the faithful and pious princes, Arcadius and Honorius, in the days of the holy Father, the patriarch Theophilus. He began to build the Church of St. John the Baptist, and when he had finished it, he built the Church of St. Menas at Maryût, and another church named after Theodosius, son of Arcadius, the prince, who helped him to build the churches. When Theophilus was dead, all his successors added to the church, little by little, until the days of the patriarch Timothy; so that it was he who completed it. After that time there came a diabolical prince, named Marcian; for it was he who divided the church through his corrupt creed, and banished the glorious father, the patriarch Dioscorus, who fought for the right faith of his fathers... And to this day we continue to dispute with the followers of that new creed."[12] The judge, finding that all the patriarch's words were true, decided in favour of the Copts.

The Patriarch Murqus (799-819) accepted two penitent heretical church leaders in the fold of the Orthodox faith and subsequently consecrated them bishops in the Church of St. Menas at Maryût, when all the Orthodox people were assembled to celebrate the festival of the martyr.

The next important reference falls in the patriarchate of Anbâ Ya'qûb (819-830). "Famine and plunder began to reappear at Alexandria; and the patriarch could not find that which he was wont to give to the churches, for nothing was left to him. And the visits of the faithful from all parts to the Church of the Martyr of St. Menas at Maryût were interrupted; and with them the patriarch used to trade. The cause of all this was the war and fighting that took place between the Egyptians and the Madlajites and Spaniards; and the scene of these disturbances was at Alexandria." The amir began to act harshly towards the father, demanding taxes which he could not pay.[13]

During the patriarchate of Anbâ Yûsâb (830-849), the churches and buildings of Abû Mînâ suffered considerable damage. In 836, al-Mu'tasim decided to build the Gausaq al-Khâqânî in Samarra with the most precious marble and stones available.[14] He sent men to Egypt with orders that the columns and marble should be taken from churches. "He who came to search for these things was a malignant heretic of the Nestorian sect, named Lazarus. So when he arrived in Misr, the people of his foul sect gathered together to meet him; and they were the Chalcedonian heretics dwelling in Alexandria. They led him out to the church of the martyr, St. Menas, at Maryût, in their great jealousy against it, and then they said to him: 'None of the churches is like this one, for all that thou hast come to seek thou wilt find therein.' So that Nestorian hastily arose, by the advice of the informers, and entered the church of the martyr, S. Menas. And when he looked at the building and its ornaments, and saw the beauty of the columns and coloured marbles which it contained, he marvelled and was amazed, and said: 'This is what the prince needs. This is here, and I knew nothing of it!' Therefore our father, the patriarch, hearing that this wicked person did not hold back his hand through the evil and malice that was in his heart, and learning what the heretics had found, said to him: 'Behold, all the churches under my jurisdiction are before thee. Do with them as the prince commands thee. But this church alone I desire thee that thou injure not. And whatever thou shalt ask of me I will deliver to thee.'

"Yet the heretic would not listen to the patriarch's words nor to his request, but answered him face to face with unseemly language, and then set to work and robbed the church of its coloured marbles and its unequalled pavement, which was composed of all colours and had no match, nor was its value known. And when the marble arrived at the city of Alexandria, that it might be forwarded to the court, the father was greatly grieved for the church and said: 'I know that thou art able, O holy Martyr, to exact just punishment for the wrong done to thee by this heretic, who has not respected thy house, although it is a consolation for all the faithful.' And he did not cease to mourn thus night and day for the calamity that had befallen this holy church. And he took care to restore it quietly. For he sent for surface decoration from Misr and Alexandria, and began to repair with all beautiful ornament the places where the pavements had been stripped, until no one who looked at them could perceive that anything was gone from them."[15]

In the middle of the ninth century, during the patriarchate of Anbâ Quzmân, a tragic incident occurred on one of the pilgrimages to the Shrine of Abû Mînâ. "When the feast of the martyr St. Menas drew near, the faithful people came together for the feast to present their offerings and their prayers in that church, which is the delight of all the Orthodox. There came together there people in whom were devils, and one of them leaped upon and attacked another one similar to him, and they did not cease strangling one another until one of the two died. When the amîr, the wâli of Alexandria, whose name was Ahmad ibn Dînâr, heard of this affair, he commanded that the father Cosmas should be seized, and he took him and tortured him until he had received from him all the contributions, which had been paid to him (the patriarch) on the day of the feast that year, and he left him none of them."[16]

It was customary for the patriarchs of the eighth and ninth centuries to go to the desert of Maryût on the feast of St. Menas, in order to celebrate the Divine Liturgy at the shrine. Anbâ Shenûdah went to the Shrine of St. Menas on 15th Hatûr. "While he was journeying on the way and we were following him, and before our arrival at the church, there gathered around us a great multitude of the faithful people, since they did not find water to drink. The reason for this was that the heaven had not rained for three years, and the wells and the cisterns had become dry. The patriarch, seeing the multitudes of pilgrims, celebrated the Divine Liturgy and besought the Lord that he should be mindful of his weakened and thirsty people. And when Anbâ Shenûdah had lifted up his hands to accomplish the prayer of sleep, a great thunderstorm broke from heaven and rain descended, filling the cistern and the wells." During the patriarchate of Anbâ Shenûdah the Shrine of Abû Mînâ was pillaged and destroyed by the Bedouins, who were led by a certain man from the Madalgah of Alexandria. "No one was able to fight against them. They were greater murderers than any people, and they could not be withstood. They took possession of the lands and of all the property of the church of the martyr Abû Mînâ at Maryût." The Bedouins did not cease pillaging the monasteries and shrines, and the Church of St. Menas at Maryût, which was the delight of all the Orthodox people in Egypt, became a desert.[17]

A fictitious description of the ruined city comes to us from a travel account given by al-Bakrî,[18] who wrote about the sacred site of St. Menas around the year 1086. "I left Terenouti, a Coptic episcopal city in the southwest part of the Nile Delta and followed the road to Barqa, and so reached Mînâ, which is composed of the forsaken cities in the midst of the sand desert, the buildings of which are still standing. The Arabs hide themselves in them in order to waylay travellers. Splendid well-built palaces, encircled by strong walls, are to be seen. They are generally surrounded by vaulted colonades, some of which serve the monks for dwellings. There are a few springs of fresh water, but they are rare. Thence you come to the Church of St. Menas, an immense building adorned with statues and paintings of great beauty, where lamps burn continually day and night. At the end of the building is a large marble tomb with two marble camels, and above them a man who places a foot on each of the camels, and one of his hands is open, the other closed. This statue, which is of marble, is said to represent St. Menas. In the same church are portraits of John, Zachariah, and Jesus on the inner side of a large marble column at the right of the entrance. In front of the figures is a door which is kept closed. The statue of the Virgin Mary is also to be seen covered with two curtains, and statues of all the prophets. On the exterior of the building there are figures which represent all kinds of animals and men of all callings. Among others may be distinguished a slave-dealer with a purse in his hand. In the centre of the church is an erection in the form of a cupola, under which are eight figures, if I am rightly informed, representing angels. By the side of the church is a mosque, the mihrab of which is on the south, where the Muslims come to pray. All the ground round the building is planted with fruit trees and carob-trees, from the soft sweet fruit of which syrup is prepared. Many vineyards are also to be seen, the grapes and vine of which are transported to Egypt. The town of Fustât sends every year a thousand dinârs for the maintenance of this church."

The Church of St. Menas was apparently still standing as late as the twelfth century, but the pilgrim city around it was in ruins, and the Bedouins were using the ruins as lurking places to lie in wait to plunder travellers. Incidentally, they seem to have been engaged in the same practice several hundred years later, when Muhammad 'Ali destroyed some of the few remaining buildings in the desert.

Abû Sâlih informs us that at the time of his writing, the shrine still existed, and that it still contained the relics of the saint. By the middle of the fourteenth century, the relics had been moved to the Church of St. Menas in Cairo. During this period the Shrine at Maryût finally succumbed to the hostile circumstances that had long been sapping its life: religious persecution and the general decline of the Coptic church; depopulation of the Maryût district; Bedouin incursions. According to the fourteenth and fifteenth Miracles in the Arabic series in *Kitâb târîkh hâyât al-shahîd al-'azîm mâr Mîna al-'adjâyibî*, attempts were made to steal the body of St. Menas from his church in Cairo under the patriarchs Peter V and Mark IV. The same book contains a *mîmar* describing the translation of the remains to Cairo under Patriarch Benjamin II (1327-1339).

The Discovery of the Shrine

Almost one thousand years of silence cover the remains of this once glorious Christian metropolis. The first European traveller to visit Karm Abûm,[19] or Abû Mînâ was J.R. Pacho, who passed Burma[20] on his way from Abûsir to Qasr al-Qatâgî,[21] in 1825. The next traveller to pass by the ancient ruins was Dr. W. Junkers, who mentions "Medinet el Kafirin" (City of the Pagans).[22]

In 1904, Admiral Blomfield published an article "St. Menas of Alexandria" in which he explains the use of the discovered terra cotta ampullae or flasks of Abû Mînâ, which according to him were formerly used as containers of the holy oil of St. Menas.[23]

A year later, in July 1905, the German Kaufmann expedition, after searching in the desert of the Auladali, discovered Karm Abû Mînâ.[24] A little Bedouin boy had offered to the explorers an *antica*, which was nothing less than a fine pilgrim's ampulla with the portrait of St. Menas, the camel and a Greek inscription. For two years, the Kaufmann expedition excavated the ruins of Karm Abû Mînâ. Among the important sites which were discovered was the Church of St. Menas, built over the tomb of the saint, and the Baths.

In the middle of the fifth century when the Church of St. Menas became too small for the many pilgrims who were attracted to this holy shrine, the great basilica was built. In the sixth century a monumental baptistry was added to the western part of the church. Its ruins are between twelve and fourteen metres high. The baptistry was a central building, square on the outside, and octagonal within, reminiscent of similar architectural work at Ravenna and in ancient Byzantium.

Kaufmann's second archaeological report begins: "If in regard to its traditional sources and to those furnished by the excavations, the great baptistry of the city of Menas is unique in its kind in the land of the Nile, it may be said of the monasteries, that the early Christian world has not known their like. Together with the sanctuaries, the buildings covered a space of more than forty thousand square metres." A large monastery or monasteries were attached to the Shrine of St. Menas, and the monks took care of the multitudes of pilgrims and sick people who came to the shrine to be healed. In 1906-07, the Kaufmann expedition excavated a great portion of the monastery, cells, halls and refectories, store-chambers and other rooms of the most varied purposes. All these discoveries point to an unusually large monastic establishment in the desert of Maryût.

Between the monasteries and the Bath of St. Menas stood the hospices for pilgrims (xenodochia).

At the end of the systematic excavations in the summer of 1907, the Kaufmann expedition discovered the famous Baths of St. Menas, which rounded off the picture of the sacred site as an ancient pilgrim city. By the side of a pilgrim's pool, with a surface of a hundred and fifty square metres and a large deep cistern built of freestone, the Baths of St. Menas were bounded by a region under which the imperial citadel of Zeno is to be sought. Here, another basilica, twenty metres long and ten metres wide, was discovered.[25]

In the following decades only occasional research efforts at the site were undertaken, first by the Graeco-Roman Museum in Alexandria (1915-1919), then by the German archaeologists F.W. Deichmann and A. von Gerkan (1934) and the British archaeologist J.B. Ward Perkins (1942) and the Coptic Museum in Cairo (1951-52). Since 1961, the German Archaeological Institute in Cairo has regularly worked on the site of Abû Mînâ each year for periods of several months. Originally the Coptic Museum worked with the German Archaeological Institute, but after 1964 excavations were carried out in connection with the Franz-Dölger Institute in Bonn. Since 1974 the German Archaeological Institute has assumed full responsibility for the excavations.[26]

Chronology of the Principal Sites

The southern part of the pre-Christian settlement served as a large pilgrimage centre. On the north side were the hostels, to the south the churches. The church complex within the centre consisted of three connected individual buildings, the great basilica (fifth century), the martyr-church (sixth century) erected above the crypt, and the Shrine of St. Menas (late fourth century) and the baptistry (sixth century). Pilgrims visited the double bath (fifth century) and the bath in the northern part of the site (sixth century). Outside the walls stood the north basilica (fifth or sixth century), which may have served as an episcopal residence during festivities. The east church (sixth century), uncovered in 1969, may have served as laura for hermits.

The New Monastery

One of Anbâ Kîrillus VI's first projects, after his enthronement in the spring of 1959, was the rebuilding of the Monastery of St. Menas (Dair Abû Mînâ) on the ancient site in the desert of Maryût. The Department of Antiquities had granted fifteen feddans to the Coptic patriarchate.

Early in the morning, on Friday, 27 November, 1959, two convoys of cars, one starting from Cairo, the other from Alexandria, made their way to the ruins of the Shrine of St. Menas. At 8 a.m., the convoy coming from Cairo reached the site of the ruins. An hour later, the convoy from Alexandria, including the cars with Anbâ Kîrillus; Anbâ Yuhannis, bishop of Gizeh; Abûnâ Mitîâs, private secretary to the patriarch; and Dr. Mûnir Shûkrî, president of the Mârî Mînâ Society, arrived at the government rest house of Abû Mînâ. An altar was set up over the tomb of the saint, and the Pope assisted by Anbâ Yuhannis, Abûnâ Mâkârî and Abûnâ Mitîâs celebrated the Divine Liturgy. Afterwards the patriarch drove to the site allocated by the Department of Antiquites for the building of the new Monastery of St. Menas. Then, at noon, the Pope laid the foundation stone of the monastery. After more than a millenium, the sacred site of St. Menas will again be inhabited by monks of Abû Mînâ. The following is the text on the foundation stone:

> The Monastery of Abû Mînâ Thaumaturgus, Its Foundation Stone was laid by the blessed hand of His Holiness, the Glorious Pope Anbâ Kîrillus VI, Pope of Alexandria and Patriarch of the See of Mark, and this was on the blessed Friday, the 27th of November, 1959, 17th of Hatûr, 1676 A.M.

Under the leadership of Abûnâ Mitîâs as-Surîânî; Abûnâ Angelus al-Muharraqî; and Abûnâ Angelus as-Surîânî, several cells and the Chapel of St. Samuel were built. These were dedicated and consecrated by Anbâ Kîrillus VI on 15 November, 1961. At the same time the pope laid the foundation stone for the Cathedral of St. Menas, though the construction under the supervision of Abûnâ Mînâ Apa Mînâ did not begin until 1969. On 15 February, 1962, the relics of St. Menas, which had been kept in the Church of St. Menas in Cairo, Fum al-Khalîg, were split up. Some remained at Fum al-Khalîg, some in the Church of St. Menas in Old Cairo and the rest were translated to the Monastery of St. Menas at Maryût, where they are kept in the Chapel of St. Samuel. The first public Easter service at the Monastery in Maryût was celebrated by Anbâ Kîrillus VI in 1963.

In 1962 work began on the construction of the Church of the Holy Virgin, the former rest house. This church was consecrated by the pope in 1965. At the same time, Anbâ Kîrillus VI submitted to Abûnâ Mînâ Apa Mînâ his will to be buried in Maryût. A year after his death on 9 March, 1971, Pope Shenûdah III transferred the bodily remains of his predecessor to Maryût, where they lie in the crypt of the new Basilica of St. Menas. On the feast of St. Menas 1976, Pope Shenudah III celebrated the first Divine Liturgy in the new cathedral. The monumental building with two large belltowers has seven altars. On the first floor above the narthex is the new extensive library, cared for by Abûnâ Achillides Apa Mînâ. The new monastery, surrounded by a wall, includes a row of cells, guest quarters, storage and kitchen facilities. The land of the monastery amounts to a hundred feddans. Under the leadership of Anbâ Mînâ Apa Mînâ (consecrated on 25 May, 1980) forty-five monks live at the monastery.

12

UPPER
EGYPTIAN
MONASTICISM

Upper Egyptian monasticism differed from monasticism in the Western desert in several ways. The Nile valley, with its ancient pharaonic monuments and tombs, offered other opportunites for the ascetic life. Anchorites occupied the tombs and tomb-chapels of their pre-Christian ancestors, while monastic communities evolved from small coenobitic settlements into powerful and wealthy landowners, led by energetic abbots, like Shenute of Atripe. Pachomius (fourth century), the organizer of Upper Egyptian monasticism, instituted the coenobitic life, that was to have a lasting impact upon the monastic movement in the East and the West. He insisted that the monks do manual work, thus creating self-supporting communities.

The geographical and numerical extent of Upper Egyptian monasticism at a given time is difficult to determine. Hundreds of monasteries existed in the Nile valley, some large, some small. In the fifth century in Oxyrhynchos (Bahnasa), there were twelve churches, ten thousand monks and twelve thousand nuns. Monastic centres stretched from Crocodilopolis (Fayyûm) on both sides of the Nile around Hieraconpolis (Minya) to Hermopolis (Ashmunain) Beyond Lycopolis (Asyût) and Panopolis (Akhmîm) hermitages and monasteries were cut into the soft limestone of the mountains on either side of the valley. Monks lived around the "Knee of the Nile" at Abydos, Chenoboskion (Kasr as-Sayâd), and Dendera. A chain of monasteries was established on the west bank between Naqada and Qamûla. The numerous tombs and temples on both sides of the banks of the Nile at Thebes (Luxor) were crowded with hermits and coenobites. On the west bank, at Hermonthis (Armant) and at Latopolis (Esna), monasteries and hermitages served hundreds of monks and nuns. The same pertains to the regions west of Apollinopolis Magna (Edfu) and Syene (Aswân).

The importance of Upper Egyptian monasticism, until recently only of interest to historians and archaeologists, has been called to our attention on account of the present monastic renaissance and the reoccupation of some of the formerly abandoned monasteries. Relatively little is known of the history of these sites. Most of the monasteries were devasted in the ninth century during the patriarchate of Shenute I (859-880). Maqrîzî listed fifty-nine Upper Egyptian monasteries. Of these, only eleven were inhabited, five of them by only one or two monks. Thirteen monasteries were still visited for the annual festivals. At least twelve monasteries were either deserted or completely destroyed. He merely mentions the names and locations of the remaining monasteries. Until the middle of the twentieth century, two active monasteries existed in Upper Egypt, the Monastery of St. Samuel at al-Qalamûn and the Monastery of the Holy Virgin (Dair al-Muharraq) at al-Qusıa. Due to the vigorous leadership of Pope Shenûdah III, the Upper Egyptian monasteries are now experiencing a revival.

Dair Durunka (Asyût)

The ancient cave-monastery and Church of the Holy Virgin about ten kilometres south of Asyût on the slopes of Istable Antar (stable of Antar) were recently repeopled with monks. The antiquity of the site is well established. Maqrîzî mentions that the Christians living there were learned in religion, expounding the Coptic language. They possessed many monasteries outside the city (Udrunka), but most of these have since been destroyed.

Through the efforts of Bishop Mikhâîl of Asyût, who at the same time serves as bishop of Dair Abû Maqâr, the monastery has been rebuilt to accommodate the large numbers of pilgrims who come between 7 and 22 August to commemorate the visit of the Holy Family to Asyût on their flight to Egypt. The new Church of the Holy Virgin was built in 1955. The former church and the buildings constructed in the caves and used by the monks are still visible. The site has been occupied by seven monks. who were initiated into monasticism by Bishop Mikhâîl. The amîn ad-dair is Abûnâ Ishai'a al-Maqârî.

Dair Anbâ Shenûdah (Sohâg)

Somers Clarke wrote: "This monastery is the noblest church of which we have any remains in Egypt, the chief monument of the Christians". The Monastery of St. Shenute or the White Monastery (ad-Dair al-Abiad), five kilometres west of Sohâg, was founded by St. Bigoul, the maternal uncle of

St. Shenute. In 385 Shenute became abbot of this monastery, following the rules laid down by St. Pachomius. In 431, Shenute attended the Third Ecumenical Council of Ephesus, where he opposed the christological and mariological teachings of Nestorius, the patriarch of Constantinople. Shenute was a zealous defender of the orthodox faith and a monastic reformer, who was prepared to employ physical force when dealing with disobedient monks. The successors of St. Shenute (d.449) were St. Beza (Wissa) and Zenobius. In the eleventh and twelfth centuries, the monastery served the Armenian community in Egypt. Bahran, vizier during the caliphate of al-Hâfiz, joined the monastery. According to Abû Sâlih, the relics of St. Bartholomew and St. Simon the Canaanite were kept in this monastery. Major restorations of the site were carried out in the thirteenth, nineteenth and twentieth centuries.

The monastery was visited by J.M. Wansleben (1672) and R.Pococke (1737), who ascribed the foundation of the monastery to St. Helena. Denon saw the monastery the day after the Mamelukes destroyed it in 1798. Robert Curzon (1838) visited the monastery and A.Butler (1884) restated the observations of other travellers. Fergusson (1893) published a plan of the monastery. However, the most significant studies were done by W. de Bock (1901), C.R. Peers (1904), W.M.F. Petrie (1907), Somers Clarke (1912) and Monneret de Villard (1925). A thorough architectural study of the buildings was carried out in the autumn of 1962 by the Technical Institute of Darmstadt. The purpose was to prepare models of the buildings for its possible renovation and reconstruction.

Only the Church of St. Shenute has survived. It shows striking resemblances to the structure of ancient Egyptian temples. Undoubtedly, the monastic buildings extended over a large area beyond the present site. One enters the enclosure through a gate in the south wall. The church occupies the major part of the interior. Noteworthy are the semi-domes with paintings of the Dormition of the Virgin (north), the Pantocrator (centre) and the Easter-Cross with two women and two angels (south).

The Monastery of St. Shenute is now occupied by Abûnâ Basilius al-Bishoî and three novices.

Dair Anbâ Tûmâ ('Arab Bani Wasil)

The Monastery of St.Thomas the Hermit (Anbâ Tûmâ), rebuilt in the eighteenth century, is situated at 'Arab Bani Wasil near Sâqulta al-'Arab on the edge of the desert. Noteworthy are the ciborium paintings of the enthroned Christ and the coronation of the Holy Virgin in the central haikal (eighteenth century). St. Thomas lived during the Diocletian persecutions. He was consecrated bishop of Mar'ash and attended the First

Ecumenical Council of Nicea in 325. The monastery is now inhabited by Abûnâ Abrâm as-Samwilî. Since 1985 many miracles are reported to have taken place at this monastery.

Dair al-Malâk Mikhâîl (al-Hawawish)

This is the northernmost monastery on the mountain ridge east of the village of al-Hawawish. The church has three haikals which are dedicated to St. George (north), the Archangel Michael (centre) and the Holy Virgin (south). Special services are held in this church on the feasts of St. Michael on 19 June and 21 November. The monastery is inhabited by Abûnâ Quzmân al-Bishoî.

Dair al-'Adhrâ (al-Hawawish)

Dair al-'Adhrâ (the Monastery of the Holy Virgin), east of al-Hawawish, is the southernmost monastery built upon the ridge that separates the fertile land east of Akhmîm from the desert. All of these small monasteries were rebuilt in the eighteenth and nineteenth centuries on the foundations of former monasteries or churches. The Church of the Holy Virgin in the eastern part of the monastery has five haikals, which commemorate St. Anthony, St. Paul the Theban, St. George, the Holy Virgin and St. Michael. Noteworthy are the coloured bricks decorating choir, nave and narthex. The monastery is served by Abûnâ Diusqurus al-Bishoî. The regular Sunday services are transmitted by loudspeaker. Special services are held on 12 December, the feast of the Presentation of the Holy Virgin; 29 January, the feast of the Falling-Asleep of the Holy Virgin; 28 June, the feast of the first church of the Holy Virgin at Philippi; and on 22 August, the feast of the Assumption.

Dair Anbâ Bakhûm (Minshât al-'Ammârî)

Dair Anbâ Bakhûm (the Monastery of St. Pachomius) lies nine kilometres east of Luxor in the village of Minshât al-'Ammârî. It has an inner and outer court. The Church of St. Pachomius has five haikals which are dedicated from north to south to St. Victor, St. George, St. Pachomius, the Holy Virgin and St. Michael. In the southern part of the church are three tombs of the Bishops Matthaus and Mikhâîl and an unknown priest, as well as the baptistry. The church is lit by small holes in the domes. The wooden ciborium above the central haikal belongs to the eighteenth century.

The monastery serves as residence for the amîn ad-dair of the Monastery of St. George at al-Riziqât. Since 1978 Qummus Bakhûm al-

Riziqî and three monks occupy the monastery. It is officially recognized by the Holy Synod of the Coptic church.

Dair al-Malâk Mikhâîl (Qamûlâ)

Dair al-Malâk Mikhâîl (the Monastery of the Archangel Michael) is the southernmost monastery of the group between Naqâda and Qamûlâ, situated on the west bank of the Nile approximately twelve kilometres north of Thebes. It is enclosed by crude brick walls, and the domes of the churches rise like inverted cups above it. Many Christian tombs are situated to the south and east of the monastery. According to Abû Sâlih, this monastery was also known as The Monastery of the Well, because of its excellent water. It once contained a keep, and it was surrounded by high walls. The relics of St. Pisentius are said to have reposed in this monastery. The entrance is through a gate in the eastern wall. The two churches are now sadly dilapidated and the monastery is occupied by Abûnâ Bûlâ al-Muharraqî.

Dair Mârî Girgis (al-Riziqât)

Dair Mârî Girgis (the Monastery of St. George) is situated on the edge of the desert at al-Riziqât, west of Dimuqrat and south-west of Armant. It is within the diocese of Bishop Ammonius of Luxor. The large Church of St. George with its twenty-one domes has six haikals which are dedicated from north to south to St. Matthew the Potter of Esna; St. Anthony; the Holy Virgin; St. George; St. Michael; and St. Ammonius and the Martyrs of Esna. The wonderworking icon of St. George is attached to the southern wall of the nave. The baptistry, which contains a large and a small baptismal font, is in the north-west corner of the narthex. Icons of the Annunciation and the Nativity of Christ by Filib Riad of Esna (1972) adorn the west wall of the gynaekion.

This monastery, which has served for many centuries as a pilgrimage site, was reoccupied by monks in 1976. The local administration is in the hands of Abûnâ Maqâr al-Riziqî. In 1986, fifteen monks inhabited the monastery, which is officially recognized by the Holy Synod of the Coptic church.

The place is well known throughout Upper Egypt for its annual mûlid from 10-16 November. This commemorates the consecration of the Church of St. George. Large numbers of pilgrims, Muslims and Christians gather for this feast in and around the monastery.

Dair al-Fakhûrî (Nag' al-Zineiqa)

Dair al-Fakhûrî (the Monastery of St. Matthew the Potter) is situated seven kilometres west of Asfûn, two kilometres beyond Nag' al-Zineiqa, on the edge of the desert. The monastery's prominent keep can be seen from a distance. The Church of St. Matthew has three haikals which are dedicated to St. Michael (north); St. Matthew the Potter (centre), and the Holy Virgin (south). The haikals are adorned with paintings of saints and angels (twelfth century), although these have been largely destroyed. On the right-hand side of the inner court there are six tombs, said to be those of bishops. According to the *History of the Patriarchs* Matthew was a fisherman, who built the monastery in the days of Alexander II (704-729), and many monks joined the monastery. In the tenth century the monastery was destroyed by Bedouins, but it was rebuilt shortly afterwards. Maqrîzî writes: "At Asfûn there was a large monastery, and Asfûn was one of the finest towns of Egypt and the monks there were famous for their learning and intelligence. With Asfûn also the monastery was destroyed."

Dair al-Fakhûrî was reoccupied by Abûnâ Murqus al-Fakhûrî, a widower, who withdrew to the abandoned site in 1975. At present three other monks reside at the monastery. The amîn ad-dair is Abûnâ Iqladîûs al-Bishoî. On 7th Kîhak (16 December), the monks commemorate the founder of the monastery, St. Matthew the Potter, who later served as abbot of the monastery in Aswân.

Dair Anbâ Bakhûm (Edfu)

Dair Anbâ Bakhûm (the Monastery of St. Pachomius) is situated on the edge of the desert five kilometres west of Edfu. Nothing is known about its history. The abandoned monastery, rebuilt by Bishop Hâdra, was reoccupied in 1975. The consecration took place in 1980. The Church of St. Pachomius has four haikals dedicated to St. Pachomius; the Holy Virgin; St. George and St. Michael. Twenty-three new cells and fifteen rooms for guests have since been constructed. The monastery is inhabited by thirteen monks and five novices. The amîn ad-dair is Qummus Tadros al-Bakhûmî; the xenodochos is Abûnâ Bafnutîûs al-Bakhûmî. The monastery belongs to the diocese of Anbâ Hâdra of Aswân. The mûlid is held on 14th Bashons (22 May), and is attended by many pilgrims.

13

MONASTICISM
IN THE FAYYÛM

Our knowledge of the historical development of the monastic life in and around the oasis of the Fayyûm is rather limited, especially if we compare it with the rich history of such prominent monastic centers as Nitria, Cellia, Scetis, or the Eastern Desert. By the middle of the third century, Christianity was well established in the oasis. Eusebius mentions a third-century Bishop Nepos of the Fayyûm, who was known for his millenial interpretation of the Bible. During the Diocletian persecutions, Christians in the Fayyûm suffered as much as others in Egypt. Two couples are commemorated for their martyrdom in the Fayyûm, Theophilus and Patricia[1] and Bartholomew and his wife.[2]

From the Monastery of Naqlûn we know of Abba Kaw, a monk of the cell near Bimai,[3] who settled in the desert south of the Fayyûm. He defied the orders to worship the idols and was taken to Bahnasa and finally executed with eight hundred Christians at Antinoë.[4] Another desert father of this region was Abba Stephen Falâsî.[5] In the course of his anchoritic life St. Antony the Great visited the Fayyûm where he confirmed many monks.[6] By the beginning of the fourth century, monasticism in the Fayyûm was as much developed as in the other centers.

Dair al-Malâk Ghobrîâl (Naqlûn)

The Dair al-Malâk Ghobrîâl is situated thirteen kilometres south of Medinet al-Fayyûm, and can be reached by following the road to Banî Suîf up to the Dair al-'Azab. At the end of the village turn right and drive parallel to the Bahr al-Gharaq as far as the bridge (six kilometres). Cross the bridge and follow the water-pipeline for another four kilometres through the desert. The monastery is situated on an elevation and can be seen from a distance.

The foundation of the Monastery of the Archangel Gabriel at Naqlûn is intimately connected with the legendary story of Aur, the illegitimate son of the queen's daughter and Abrashit the magician.[7] The Angel Gabriel appears as the guardian of Aur and leads him to the desert of Naqlûn where he builds a church in honour of the angel. This is replaced by a larger church of baked bricks and consecrated by Abba Isaac, Bishop of the Fayyûm. Also, Aur receives ordination and after the death of Abba Isaac succeeds him as bishop. However, he returns to Naqlûn and builds monastic cells and houses for pilgrims.[8] The consecration of the Church of St. Gabriel at Naqlûn is commemorated by the Coptic and Ethiopic churches.[9] According to B.T.A. Evetts, Bishop Aur of Naqlûn lived at the beginning of the fourth century.[10]

Archaeological evidence points to a Christian settlement at Naqlûn at the beginning of the fourth century. The inscription of a stela in the Church of St. Gabriel is dated and gives the 25th of Barmûdah, eighth indiction. This could be either 304-305 or 319.[11] From the fourth to the sixth century, the Monastery of Naqlûn was the leading monastery in the Fayyûm. With the emergence of the Monastery at al-Qalamûn, the Monastery of Naqlûn was pushed gradually into the background. On the approach of Cyrus the Persian, St. Samuel of Qalamûn persuaded the inhabitants of Naqlûn, where he had lived for almost four years, to flee to the mountains. After his release from captivity he set about the establishment of his monastery at al-Qalamûn, and two years later the group consisted of forty-one monks, fourteen of whom had come from the Monastery of Naqlûn. Thus from the middle of the seventh century onwards, the Monastery of al-Qalamûn began to surpass the Monastery of Naqlûn in importance.[12] An eleventh-century reference to this monastery mentions a deacon Macrobius who seems to have been left alone at Naqlûn.[13]

Abû Sâlih mentions two churches: the Church of St. Michael, "in which there is a pillar of marble that sweats as if water were flowing from it" and adjacent to the monastery a "church named after the Angel Gabriel, enclosed by a wall, which was erected before the church was begun." Both Abû Sâlih and (two centuries later) al-Maqrîzî associate the monastery at Naqlûn with Jacob (the son of Isaac, who enjoyed the shade and worshipped there) and with the sacrifices offered in the days of Joseph, who was said to have superintended the building of the Fayyûm and the Hajar al-Lahûn.[14] From the thirteenth to the fifteenth century the monastery contained the relics of Abba Kaw.[15] By the middle of the fifteenth century, however, the importance of the monastery had declined. Al-Maqrîzî omits any reference to the Church of St. Michael and merely speaks of the Monastery of al-Khashaba or the monastery of the Angel Gabriel, which stands under a hollow in the mountain.

When Johann Michael Wansleben visited the Fayyûm in August 1672 he found the Monastery of Naqlûn almost completely ruined, though its two churches still seem to have been standing. The Church of St. Gabriel he describes as being very beautiful, all painted within with pictures of stories from the Holy Scriptures, and having the nave supported by slender columns.[16] At the beginning of this century, probably during the episcopacy of Anbâ Abrâm of the Fayyûm,[17] the church was rebuilt. The remains of the wall-paintings were covered with a coat of paint, and the wooden roof was restored. In the winter of 1927-28 Johann Georg, Duke of Saxony, visited the site and provided the first account after the rebuilding of the church. He remarks: "Noteworthy are the capitals in the nave and in the haikals, which give the appearance of being Corinthian. The lectern, which may date to the twelfth century, is especially beautiful. Of interest also is the wooden ceiling."

Today the Church of St. Gabriel serves as parish church for the region of Qalamshâh, south of Medinet al-Fayyûm. Two monks, Abûnâ Joel al-Bishoî and Abûnâ 'Abd al-Masîh al-Bûlî reside in the once abandoned monastery. At the time of the annual mûlids large numbers of pilgrims from the Fayyûm and Banî Suîf assemble at the monastery and occupy the numerous dwelling places built for this purpose.[18]

The Church of St. Gabriel has three haikals, which are dedicated to the Archangel, St. George, and the Holy Virgin. Apart from the Corinthian capitals in the nave noted by Georg, other Corinthian capitals have been built into the walls, undoubtedly once part of the former churches of St. Michael and St. Gabriel. The mandatum tank is sunk in the floor in the south-western part of the nave. The icons of the church should be attributed to the eighteenth and nineteenth centuries. Of special interest is a nineteenth-century Jerusalem proskynitarion. The mediaeval wall-paintings on the west wall of the narthex show the Holy Virgin and Child flanked by two archangels and a saint (St. Pisoshi?).

In July and August 1991 twelve skeletons (eleven adults and one child) were discovered some hundred and fifty meters south-west of the monastery. These skeletons are exhibited in three showcases in the southern and northern aisles of the sanctuary. South of the church is a kiosk selling devotional pictures, literature, etc. The water for this monastery is drawn from the canal of al-Manhi, and it lies below the Monastery of Sidmant.

The Laura of Naqlûn

The legendary story of Aur contains a prophecy in which St. Gabriel addresses him saying: "This mountain shall prosper, and shall become as crowded as a dovecote by reason of the immense multitudes of people who shall come to visit it from all countries of the earth, and their prayers shall mount up to God." Archaeological evidence points to a laura of a significant number of caves south-east of the monastery. These caves, mentioned by Wansleben, are situated on the western slope and in the wâdîs of the north-western section of the Naqlûn range of hills. Most of them are just below the summit of the ridge. The openings of the majority of them face west, though some openings face south. On the western slope alone I counted fourteen caves. The caves can be divided into one-room and two-room caves. The walls are coated with a layer of plaster. Noteworthy are the niches for the storage of manuscripts, etc. Many of the caves are filled with sand.

Dair al-Hammâm

The Dair al-Hammâm or the Monastery of the Holy Virgin is situated in the desert on the edge of the Nile Valley near the village of al-Lahûn and the brick pyramid of Sesostris II. The distance from al-Lahûn to the monastery is about eight kilometers. According to tradition the monastery was founded by St. Isaac, a disciple of St. Antony the Great.[19] Born in Bawît, he entered the monastic life in the Dair al-Malâk Ghobrîâl. Later Pope Butrus II (373-78) sent him to this region where he gathered disciples from the Fayyûm. In the thirteenth century the monastery was surrounded by a triple wall. The Church of the Holy Virgin was spacious and beautifully designed; there was also a small church named after St. Isaac the martyr,[20] much visited in the Middle Ages.[21] The monastery used to belong to the diocese of the Fayyûm, but in 1985 it was placed directly under the authority of Pope Shenûdah III. On 9 May 1987 Abûnâ Palladius Anbâ Bishoî was commissioned to renovate the church and the monastery. Noteworthy are the constructions made by mud wasps on the outer wall. These insects appear annually from 10 January to 10 March. While the new Church of the Holy Virgin is under construction services are conducted in a small chapel. A kiosk offers souvenirs, pictures, and devotional literature for the visitors from the nearby villages and Banî Suîf.

Dair Mârî Girgis

The Dair Mârî Girgis (St. George) is situated about twenty-five kilometres south of Medinet al-Fayyûm at Sidmant al-Gebel on the banks of the Bahr Yusuf. In the thirteenth century the monastery was a center of learning. In 1260 Butrus as-Sidmanti, a Coptic theologian of distinction, inhabited the monastery. In the fifteenth century it was deserted. The monastic life at Sidmant al-Gebel was reestablished in the first half of this century by two monks from the Dair Anbâ Antûnîûs: Abûnâ Buqtur (d. 1937) and Abûnâ Mitîâs (d. 1947). The tombs of these monks are in the north-west corner of the Church of St. George. The monastery belongs to the diocese of Banî Suîf and al-Bahnasa. It is served by one monk. Thousands of pilgrims attend the annual Mûlid at the Dair Mârî Girgis, which is held a week prior to the Feast of the Ascension.

14

THE SOCIOLOGY OF COPTIC MONASTICISM

Motives for Becoming a Monk

People often ask why some men join the community of a desert monastery, or even retire into a cave to live. There are numerous reasons which may have caused a monk to retire from the world. In most cases, more than one reason may have been responsible for this decision.

Religious Experience

A religious experience is one of the most frequent reasons for determining the future of a man's life. This experience may come about in the form of a vision, a dream, or an inspiration which results from contemplation or ecstacy. The case of St. Macarius the Great offers a good example. One night, when he was in the Wâdî 'n-Natrûn, as camel driver, an angel showed him a vision of the inner valley and promised to him that it would be a place of dwelling for his followers. Soon after this experience, St. Macarius distributed his goods among the poor and embarked upon the ascetic life.

Sense of Guilt

A profound sense of guilt has led many people to a life of asceticism in the hope that by good works, such as renunciation, prayer, meditation and fasting they may atone in this world for their sins. St. Moses the Robber, an Ethiopian, had been a slave. His master had dismissed him for insubordination. He then became a robber, perhaps even a murderer, until he heard of the great ascetes of the Wâdî 'n-Natrûn. He met both St. Isidore and St. Macarius, and subsequently became one of the first monks in the Desert of Scetis.

The Teaching of the Gospel

St. Antony the Great was moved to his decision on hearing the teaching of the Holy Scripture. When one day he heard the text: "If thou will be perfect, go and sell all that thou hast and give to the poor" (*Matthew* 19:21), he sold all that he had, and retired to a cave. A large number of candidates are recruited for the monasteries by monks working in town and country churches. The biblical teaching in the Coptic churches lays great stress on the ascetic demands of Christ and His Apostles. Furthermore, the great esteem which the Copts have for the gospel strengthens its ethical and ascetic precepts.

Example

For those who are members of the churches of apostolic foundation, the monastic and ascetic life is considered to be spiritually and morally superior to that lived in the world. The monks, frequently referred to in the past as Angels of God, are regarded, therefore, with great respect. To follow their example is thought by many to be a surer way to eternal salvation than by remaining in this world. Individual monks who have radiated a deep spirituality have attracted others to follow them. A good example is the influence that Pope Shenûdah III and Abûnâ Mattâ al-Mâskîn have upon a number of young university graduates.

Identification with the Church

For those who take their faith seriously, to enter a monastery is proof of sincerity. The total identification of the person with the church, as it takes place in the monastery, has a special significance where the church represents the faith of a religious minority. It is not surprising, therefore, to find businessmen, lawyers, and other professionals among the desert fathers.

Ambition

Since the Canon Law of the Coptic church requires that the patriarch and the bishops be chosen from among the monks, there may be cases where a man embraces the monastic life out of a desire for leadership. Such men, therefore, regard the monastic life as a means rather than as an end.

Protest

The purist is dissatisfied with what he considers the worldliness of the Church, and in order to save his soul, he either withdraws to the monastery to live a life of religious certitude, or he will see to it that his withdrawal is interpreted as a kind of protest against this worldliness.

Economic and Adjustment Problems

In some instances economic difficulties as well as a desire to escape from the responsibilities of life have led men to become monks or ascetes. There are always people who fail to find satisfaction and fulfilment in the course of ordinary life. Their behaviour and their attitudes may be regarded as not fitting into the general environment, whilst, on the other hand, they are quite socially acceptable within the monastic community. Therefore, we see that it is not right to evaluate one social pattern by the standards and categories of another social pattern.

Roles in Coptic Monasticism

Apart from the positions which certain monks are assigned within the framework of Coptic monasticism, some monks assume roles which are neither official nor assigned. These roles derive from an individual's talent, interest or vocation, rather than position. A monk may "enact" a role, but he can never "occupy" a role. The term "role" is here used to mean a set of modes of behaviour which are thought of as constituting a definite unit. Thus, some monks, apart from their roles as members of a monastic community, enact the role of prophet, shepherd, priest, scholar, etc. These roles do not necessarily imply intrinsic superiority or inferiority from the point of view of monasticism. It means, however, that some monks possess qualities and gifts, which others may lack.

The Originator

The founders of the great centres of asceticism in the Wâdî 'n-Natrûn, the Wâdî 'Arabah, the desert of Qalamûn, and elsewhere, belong to this category. These men were more than teachers or prophets. They became founders of large Christian communities by the influence which their personalities and activities exercised upon their followers. Saints like Antony the Great, Macarius the Great, Pachomius, John the Short and Bishoî belong to this group. They were saints who have left an indelible impression upon the life of the Church and monasticism. Characteristic of their mission is the close association of their message with their personality and their way of life. The idea of vocation, which all these saints shared, implied a consciousness of its mandatory character. Though Christian asceticism did not begin with either St. Antony or St. Macarius, they were the originators and the builders of a way of life to be followed. Of the contributions that the Egyptian church made to Christendom, monasticism was the most genuine and powerful one.

The Reformer

In times of threatening decay or disintegration leaders arise who are difficult to classify in the traditional historical schemes. They are not on a level with the founders: their creative religious power does not match that of the originator. However, when abuses crept into the practice of the Christian faith, there were always reformers who by their wise judgment and counsel corrected such abuses and restored the faith to its inherent purity.

The classic example of such a reformer in Coptic monasticism is Anbâ Shenûdah (St. Shenute I, born about 333 near Akhmîm). Apart from his contribution as an original writer to Coptic ecclesiastical literature, Anbâ Shenûdah was a reformer against abuses which had arisen among the Christians in Egypt. For a period of fifteen years he served as hegoumenos of Dair Anbâ Shenûdah, where he corrected and punished insubordinate monks by severe beatings, and we hear that on one occasion at least one monk died from the severity of this discipline.

The middle Ages produced numerous outstanding reformers. The canons of four of them form part of the Canon Law of the Coptic church. Anbâ Akhristûdulûs (1048), sixty-sixth patriarch of Alexandria, wrote thirty-one canons to correct abuses which had arisen in the church. The same is true of the thirty-four canons of Anbâ Kîrillus II, sixty-seventh patriarch of Alexandria (1086). The laity was admonished to lead a more virtuous life in obedience to the laws and practices of the Church.

The specific contributions of the reformer vary. They differ in creative power and breadth of vision, in scope and persuasiveness. Some of these reformers display zeal for the due observance of rites and ceremonies, others excel as intellectual and moral guides. Some of these influential figures lived retired and secluded lives, radiating, as it were, a power which generated changes and transformations in the religious community of their time.

Over the centuries, many long established practices have been restated and corrected and it is impossible to list all the monks, bishops and patriarchs who have concerned themselves with the work of correction. Butrus Mitfah al-Antûnî (d.1875) was concerned with reforming the practice of monastic fasting, that is, shortening the long and frequent fasts. As a reviver of an ancient school of monasticism, Anbâ Kîrillus VI belongs to the illustrious company of the reformers. The coenobitic form of ascetic life as promulgated by St. Pachomius in the fourth century was reintroduced through the spiritual and administrative charisma of Pope Shenûdah III. This coenobitic-ascetic way of life has also found its expression at Dair Abu Maqâr, under the leadership of Abûnâ Mattâ al-Maskîn.

The Priest

The authority of the priest derives from his ordination to the priesthood whereby he is empowered to celebrate the Divine Liturgy, to administer the sacraments of baptism and penance, and to perform certain other specific acts, such as the blessing of animate and inanimate objects, the expounding of the Holy Scriptures and the precepts of the Church, etc. This authority is, strictly speaking, delegated to him from the bishop who, in early times, was the sole administrator of the sacraments and the approved interpreter of Holy Scriptures and tradition. The priesthood is, therefore, an official order which sets apart the recipient. To this order some monks gladly accede, whilst others refrain from receiving it, fearing that they may lose their *prophetic charisma*. A classic example of this fear of receiving Holy Orders is given by Palladius: "They say concerning Abba Apos, who afterwards became bishop of Oxyrhynchos, that, when he was a monk, he laboured with great toil in the ascetic life, and that he was moved every hour by Divine Grace, but that after he became bishop, though he wished to perform the same labours, he was not able to do so. And he cast himself before God, and made supplication unto Him, saying: 'Peradventure, O my Lord, it is because of the bishopric that thou hast removed Thy grace from me'..."

Many of the finest and most spiritual monks in the monasteries in the twentieth century are not ordained to the priesthood, either because they feel themselves unworthy to stand before the altar and to celebrate the Holy Mysteries, or out of fear of losing their gifts through receiving this order.

On the other hand, there are monks to whom the priesthood is the most essential part in their spiritual life and the most natural application of their monastic ideal. The life of Peter the Presbyter illustrates how a monk, after much reluctance on his part, was ordained to the priesthood, after which he performed the morning and evening offering of incense and celebrated the Divine Liturgy every day.

There are several monks who are, in the true sense of the word, priests, not only because of their priestly orders, but also on account of their natural propensity to the priestly office. For many years Abûnâ Timûtâûs as-Suriânî served the church in the Izbawiya, Cairo, and it is said of him that he could not live without his prayers and celebrations at the altar. The same can also be said of Anbâ Kîrillus VI, who celebrated the Divine Liturgy daily for thirty years, and to whom the priestly function was an integral part of his spiritual life.

The Prophet

Coptic monasticism is characterized by its asceticism, mysticism and sacerdotalism. Few people will admit that the prophetic office is also found among the desert fathers. Palladius bears witness to this. On a certain day he happened to meet Paphnutius who was "such a gentle man that his meekness overcame the gift of prophecy which was found with him; now the former (his meekness) was voluntary, and the latter (his gift of prophecy) was an act of Divine Grace." The prophetic charisma implies immediate communion with God, and the intensity of it may even be more significant than its continuance. The prophet is conscious of being the instrument, the mouthpiece of the Divine Will, though the Coptic prophet, in addition to this, is always aware of the fact that he is at the same time, a "slave", a "servant", or a "miserable creature". This point is important to remember, when one evaluates some of the radical remarks of a man such as Abûnâ 'Abd al-Masîh al-Habashî, a solitary who lived in a cave in the vicinity of the Monastery of al-Barâmûs, and is a prophet according to his own way of thinking. His sharp criticism of the institutionalism of the church results from a conviction that the spiritual life is of necessity opposed to the institutionalized life, that the world is evil and doomed to destruction, and that any contact with the world is harmful to the spirituality one may have acquired.

The prophetic character of the anchorites may occasionally be so anti-ecclesiastical, that the prophet no longer avails himself of the ministry and the sacraments of the Church. He achieves communion with God without the ecclesiastical means of grace, thus he cuts off himself from the fellowship of the living Church.

By nature, the desert prophet is isolated and the radius of his message is limited to his disciples. He does not address himself to the nation in the sense of the classical Old Testament prophets. He is more passive, and thus might fall rather into the category of the "seer". Though certain of his mission, he, nevertheless, stresses his humility, an attitude comparable to that of St. John the Baptist who said: "...even He Who comes after me, the thong of whose sandals I am not worthy to untie" (*John* 1:27).

The Scholar

It has been said that the so-called anti-intellectualism of Coptic monasticism may be due to the non-intellectual activity of its founder, a view which is supported by St. Athanasius who is quoted as saying that St. Antony did not take to schooling. Once a philosopher who came to see St. Antony said to him: "Father, how do you hold up, deprived as you are of the solace of books?" But St. Antony replied: "My book, philosopher, is Nature, and thus I can read God's language at will."

The scholar has vision, insight and a creative ability, and places his thoughts at the disposal of others. His primary concern is an intellectual endeavour to discover truth. Coptic monasticism has always been more contemplative and passive in character than Western monasticism. At the same time, however, it has not lacked the scholastic impulse. Indeed, the ancient Egyptian church has provided many illustrious and well-educated scholars. Palladius writes: "By the side of Chronius, there used to dwell a certain man who was called James the Lame, and he was an exceedingly learned man. Also Paphnute, who possessed the gift of knowledge to such a degree that he knew how to expound the books of the Old Testament and New Testament without reading from them." Anbâ Shenûdah may be regarded as the most eminent of the ancient Coptic scholars. He made the dialect of his own district of Atripe the recognized literary medium of Egypt for the following four centuries. His writings (letters, homilies and rules) made a profound impression upon the life of the monasteries and the Coptic church.

Every age produced its scholars, and in the seventh century, monks such as John of Nikiu and Menas of Pschati engaged in the scholastic pursuit. One of the famous nineteenth-century scholars was Abûnâ 'Abd al-Masîh ibn Girgis al-Barâmûsî, who provided for the Egyptian church a text of dogmatic theology. He engaged in apologetic writings and was known as a famous theologian. His nephew, Abûnâ 'Abd al-Masîh ibn Salîb al-Mas'udî al-Barâmûsî was equally important. He was well versed in Coptic, Syriac, Ethiopic, Greek and English, and served for many years as librarian of the libraries of the four monasteries in the Wâdî 'n-Natrûn.

The Scribe

The criterion of the scholar is an independent zeal for research, a concern for the discovery of truth in his particular field of study. The criterion of the scribe, a more passive being, is his concern to preserve the works of the past and to make them available to future generations. His role is essential to an institution which holds fast to tradition, and sees its ideal type in the past.

The forerunner of the scribe in Coptic monasticism was the "memorizer." His role was to memorize the sayings and the traditions of the desert fathers, so that they could be handed down to future generations of monks.

The scribes used a variety of styles of writing for the copying out of manuscripts. There is, for example, the cursive style in which letters are ligatured, which resembles modern handwriting. This was used mainly for private correspondence and contracts. The "uncial" or more rigid style, with separately spaced letters, was used for texts which were intended for public reading, and had to be clear and easily legible (the printed text of today). Finally, the ornate calligraphic book-script with finely proportioned letters was used for the Holy Scriptures.

Every generation had its scribes. Among the famous scribes of the sixth century was Ephraem, who lived at Dair Anbâ Shenûdah at Atripe, and copied out the rules and precepts of Anbâ Shenûdah. He placed some of these copies in jars and sent them to the Monastery of Abû Masis. When the supplies of vegetables ran short in that monastery, the monks opened the jars, expecting to find preserves but instead, they found the copies of the rules of Anbâ Shenûdah which they apparently read with much edification.

Sometimes, the scribe was also an illuminator who decorated the sacred texts with coloured ornamentation, the purpose of which was, at least at the beginning, to direct the reader's attention to the titles of the books. Coptic sacred texts often show elaborate designs and arrangements of spirals, buds, twigs, leaves, flowers, birds, fishes and food-baskets. A famous calligrapher and illuminator of the ninth century, Abûnâ Zakharia as-Samwîlî, copied out several Synaxary lections for the Monastery of St. Michael in the desert. One of the most illustrious calligraphers and illuminators of the present century was Anbâ Makarîûs III, the 114th patriarch of Alexandria. A copy of several hundred calligraphic designs of crosses and Coptic letters is kept in the library of Dair Anbâ Bishoî.

The printing press, however, has largely replaced the scribe. Yet, even now there are monks engaged in the copying out of the sacred texts used for divine worship. Abûnâ Shenûdah al-Barâmûsî has copied out numerous sacred texts for his monastery and Dair as-Suriân. Among his recent work is a commentary on Romans by St. Chrysostom and parts of the Difnâr.

The Shepherd

The shepherd of the monastery may be the bishop, a hieromonk or a simple monk. He is characterized by his concern for and understanding of his fellow monks. He is the human channel through which the grace and love of God flows, he is the mediator, the "natural" confessor of the monks. He is a sympathetic listener who understands the problems and the temptations which confront the desert fathers. Every monastery has monks who are appointed as father confessors; the shepherd, however, is neither appointed nor assigned his role. The history of Coptic monasticism mentions numerous monks who are remembered because of the pastoral care and guidance which they gave to their contemporaries.

One of the first shepherds of the monks in the Desert of Scetis was Paphnute Cephalas, who succeeded Isidore, as hegoumenos of Scetis. He is said to have travelled into the inner desert, searching for the hermits who lived in remote parts, who were unknown to people generally. There he met St. Timothy and St. Onuphrius.

St. John the Hegumen became a monk in the Desert of Scetis at the beginning of the seventh century. He was captured three times by the raiding Berbers. About 641, he became hegoumenos of Dair Abû Maqâr, where he left his impress on a group of disciples, of whom the best known were Abraham and George. Another outstanding shepherd of the desert was St. John Kame, who gathered around him three hundred disciples. He built a monastery and a church which formed a new foundation in the Desert of Scetis. His profound guiding influence was manifested in the lives of some of his disciples such as Shenûdah, Murqus, Colluthus, George the Deacon, George the Presbyter and others, who were trained under him.

The Ascete

Though Egyptian monasticism and asceticism are usually regarded as synonymous, this assumption is not always correct, at least at the present time, since not all monks are necessarily ascetes in the strict sense of the term. Again, we must be careful not to confuse asceticism with mysticism. The distinction is clearly pointed out by a monk of the Eastern church who states: "Between the ascetic life, that is, the life in which God's action predominates, there is the same difference as between rowing a boat and sailing it; the oar is the ascetic effort, the sail is the mystical passivity which is unfurled to catch the divine wind." This means, that the ascetic life is a life of "acquired" virtues, depending upon fasting, patient endurance, vigils, abstinence, weeping and mourning, voluntary poverty, humility, love and hospitality.

It is difficult to define an exact ascetic pattern among the monks of Egypt. All of them, however, held that the gratification of the senses was sinful, and that the desires of the flesh were to be subdued by fasting, abstinence, vigils, prayer and contemplation.

Asceticism in Coptic monasticism is expressed in two forms: the solitary or anchoritic and the communal or coenobitic type. Historically speaking, the solitary life preceded the coenobitic life. It is only when the spontaneous and radical ascetic expression as found in the third century, when hermits became institutionalized and regulated, that the need arose for organization, that is for monastic rule and discipline.

Though the great hermits of the Wâdî 'n-Natrûn and the Wâdî 'Arabah began their ascetic life as solitaries, they made their followers enter the coenobium first in order to be trained in the practice of asceticism. St. Antony forbade the young and inexperienced to enter the desert without passing through a period of probation. Thus, in order to live the solitary life, the monk had to prove his worthiness first in the communal life, and only after a period of probation was he permitted to undertake the solitary life.

The Solitary

From the third to the present century, certain monks have felt that the ascetic ideal can be attained only by living the solitary life, that is, dwelling in caves of the most simple and primitive character, in some instances, mere holes hewn out in the rock and provided with some rough masonry.

According to Pope Shenûdah III, who lived the life of a solitary for many years, there are five stages or grades through which the solitary must pass before he reaches the stage of absolute isolation from the world. They are as follows:

1. As a member of a coenobitic community.
2. As a beginner in the solitary life within the monastery itself. The beginner observes complete silence, performing his work quietly, while remaining in his cell. He thereby develops a feeling of alienation from the community, so that he becomes "a stranger" among his brethren.
3. Persevering in this solitude for several weeks. At this stage, the monk still lives in the monastery, but leaves his cell only once a week on Sunday to attend the celebration of the Divine Liturgy.
4. The fourth stage is his transference from the monastery to the cave, so as to be removed from all people.
5. The final stage is that of the itinerant anchorite, who lives in caves, unknown to anyone save God.

Should, by chance, a solitary pay a temporary visit to his fellow monks or for some other reason be forced to leave his cave, he must on his return go through the above mentioned stages of preparation again before be can resume his solitary life.

In the summer of 1959, Abûnâ Antûniûs, the present Pope Shenûdah III, was summoned by Pope Kîrillus VI to leave his cave and to reside in the patriarchate in Cairo. After two months, however, he felt the need to return to the cave life. Accordingly, he went first to the monastery, where he shared in the monastic life. Then he stayed for a time in a cell in the monastery plantation, where he prepared to resume his life in the cave.

The Coenobitic Monk

Even in the early days of Egyptian monasticism, some solitaries formed communities, which became known as *coenobia,* which were governed by a coenobiarch. The Antonian *coenobia* had only a simple organization without hard and fast rules or regulations. The death of the respective organizer or first coenobiarch marked a decisive stage in the process of organization. The example of the coenobiarch, who in his lifetime had received obedience and respect from his disciples, soon became the pattern and ideal to be followed. Coenobitic communities rapidly sprang up throughout Egypt, and some of them followed the individualistic character of the Antonian rule, whilst others adhered to the regulated monasticism of the Pachomian rule.

The twentieth century has witnessed, to some extent, a rediscovery of the coenobitic ideal. At Dair Abû Maqâr, the monks share in communal meals, a practice once observed in all monasteries, but abandoned several centuries ago. They possess no personal property, not even their garments. In the case of temporary absence from the monastery, they leave the keys of their cells with a fellow monk. However, although the monks stress the virtues of communal life, the group is still characterized by a high degree of individualism.

The Disclaimer

The disclaimer is a saintly monk, who does not wish to be known as such, and consequently gives a false impression of himself. There is a story told about Abba Arsenius, who being afraid of being overcome at night by the devil, asked two of his friends, Abba Alexander and Abba Zôîla, to keep watch over him. However, instead of watching, his disciples fell asleep, whilst Abba Arsenius pretending to be asleep, kept vigil and fought the devil.

The disclaimer may pose as insane, and he may say things which no one would expect a monk to say, merely to cover up his real spiritual life. This is exemplified in the following story of Abûnâ Q.: it was a Friday, and some of the monks were engaged in a manual task. As this was somewhat difficult, one of the monks said to Abûnâ Q. "You can help us, you are a strong man." "Indeed, I am," replied Abûnâ Q., "seeing that I have just eaten half a dozen eggs." (In reality, Abûnâ Q. observes the fast regulations very strictly.) Another monk asked Abûnâ Q. about a quotation from Holy Scriptures. Abûnâ Q. replied, "I don't know, all I read is the Readers' Digest." (Abûnâ Q. is known for his encyclopaedic knowledge of the Holy Scriptures.)

The Charismaticus

The charismaticus has the gifts of grace (charismata). These spiritual gifts may include the power to heal, to restore to health, to exorcise evil spirits, etc. In many instances, the charismaticus is considered by the people to be also a thaumaturgus, a wonder-worker, who is able to perform miracles on account of his profound spirituality.

The Coptic church has produced many thaumaturgi throughout the centuries. The most famous of the early thaumaturgi was Menas, the soldier. Then there was Matthew the Potter, hegoumenos of a monastery in the mountain of Aswân, who wrought many miracles and in many encounters contested successfully with the devils of the desert. Pimen of Minya suffered much during the Diocletian persecution. On the death of Diocletian, he entered a monastery in the vicinity of al-Ashmunain, where he became famous for his power to heal the sick. Once a Roman princess came to him to be healed. He received her without special deference, and refused the gifts which she offered for her recovery. Peter the Presbyter, an ascete, was another famous healer. He also possessed the charisma to reconcile those at variance with each other. Badasius, a monk in one of the Pachomian monasteries, was held in great esteem for the many miracles of healing which he performed.

Every century has produced thaumaturgi who healed the sick irrespective of their religious tenets. Anbâ Sarabamûn, bishop of Manûfiyah, healed Zuhra, the daughter of Muhammad 'Alî, and Anbâ Ishaq of the Fayyûm healed Hassan the "one-eyed" of Maghagha. Many of the Coptic thaumaturgi have been famous because of the power of their prayers, especially with regard to rendering barren women pregnant, or causing them to bear male offspring.

Naturally, as in all professions, there have been.charlatans, but those may be easily recognized, for the true charismaticus does not accept remuneration for his services under any consideration.

Indeed, the true charismaticus is humble. His charisma is the result of contemplation and a constant awareness of the Divine Presence. Anbâ Kîrillus VI was a thaumaturge who was blessed with charismata for many years.

EPILOGUE

We have now reached the end of our study of Coptic monasticism, and in it we have traced the long and distinguished history of the Coptic church. At one time, the total number of monks in Egypt may well have surpassed half a million. This is partly substantiated by the reports of contemporaries. Rufinus (372) claims to have known of ten thousand monks in the Fayyûm alone, whilst Palladius (387) speaks of five thousand in the Wâdî 'n-Natrûn. The establishment of Anbâ Bakhûm in Tabennese comprised three thousand, whilst that of Anbâ Abûlû in Bawît, near Asyût, numbered five thousand at the beginning of the seventh century. John of Petra (550) speaks of 3,500 fathers in the Desert of Scetis, and St. Jerome judged the number of monks in Egypt to be fifty thousand, whilst Cassian gives an estimate of five thousand. In Nikiu, in Lower Egypt, at the beginning of the seventh century, there were seven hundred hermits distributed all over the district, without counting other religious communities, and under Anbâ Shenûdah at the White Monastery, there were 2,200 monks, a number which undoubtedly increased. At Oxyrhynchos, ten thousand monks are reported to have lived, of whom five thousand stayed in the city, whilst the others resided in the suburbs.

Nothing is gained by comparing these figures, or even by trying to prove their historical veracity. One thing is certain, and that is, that Coptic monasticism was a force in Egypt.

Apart from the number of the monks there is another point which is worth noticing. This is the ecumenical character of Coptic monasticism. St. Jerome informs us of a large number of Latins, who could be found in the monasteries of the Thebaid, and we are informed in the *Vita Pachomii* that at Pabau, there was a special house for Greek, Roman and other foreign Christians. In the twelfth century, at least five different national communities were represented in the Wâdî 'n-Natrûn: Egyptian, Armenian, Syrian, Ethiopian, and Nubian. Furthermore, there is evidence for believing that the national groups enjoyed an intimate relationship, that is, that they came together for convocations on the great festivals in commemoration of the saints of Scetis.

This international and ecumenical background is important, especially in our days, when Christianity in particular, and religion in general, is confronted by a world of materialism, for only by concerted effort and working in an eirenic spirit can the Church overcome the world.

The growing interest and concern of Christians from all parts of the world in the Coptic church can be seen in the increasing number of visitors to the monasteries and the increasing amount of literature dealing with the subject of Coptic monasticism. This may certainly prove to be a blessing, since thereby the virtues of desert monasticism can find a means to radiate into the world. For the desert spells quietness and peace, in which the presence of God can be felt more easily than in the noisy and turbulent world.

The reader of this study of past and present monasticism will most probably ask, what of the future of Coptic monasticism? If in the fifth and sixth centuries the strength of monasticism in Egypt was a matter of quantity, its strength in the twentieth lies in quality, and from this point of view, there appears to be sufficient evidence to state that for the present and for the immediate future Coptic monasticism has a sounder and more stable basis than it ever had before. The future of Coptic monasticism as well as that of the Church is fully assured by Jesus' promise: "Lo, I am with you always, even unto the consummation of the ages."

NOTES

Chapter 1: St. Antony the Ascete

(1) Clarus, L., *Das Leben des Heiligen Antonius von Athanasius dem Grossen*, 1857. Ellershaw, H., *The Life of St. Anthony in Select Writings and Letters of Athanasius*. (Nicene & Post Nicene Fathers, II, 4.) Lavaud, R., *Antoine le Grand, Père des Moines*, 1913. McLaughlin, Dom J.B., *St. Anthony the Hermit by St. Athanasius*, 1924. Mertel, H., *Des Heiligen Athanasius Leben des Heiligen Antonius*, 1917. Meyer R.T., *St. Athanasius, The Life of St. Anthony*, 1950. Queffelec, H., *Saint Anthony of the Desert*, 1954.

(2) St. Antony was born in 251 in Coma, now Qimân al-'Arûs, some 75 km. south of Cairo.

(3) *Matthew*, 19:21.

Chapter 2: Dair Anbâ Antûnîûs

(1) Evetts, B.T.A., *Abû Sâlih*, 161.

(2) The *Tau*, St. Antony's T-shaped stick, is still employed by the old monks to lighten the physical strain of standing during their long services.

(3) From a personal letter by Mrs. Winifred Holmes.

(4) Arius (ca. 250-366) a learned theologian and successful preacher in Alexandria. Because of his subordinationist teaching about the Person of Christ he was excommunicated by Alexander. His teaching was condemned, largely through the influence of St. Athanasius, at the Ecumenical Council of Nicaea in 325 A.D.

(5) HPCC, *P.O.*, I, 414.

(6) Flavius Julius Constantius (317-361) was the son of Constantine the Great and was a strong supporter of the anti-Athanasian party.

(7) *Ethiop. Synax.*, Tekemt 20, Budge I, 175.

(8) The Council of Chalcedon in 451 affirmed the definition of Nicaea (325) and of Constantinople (381). It therefore excluded the views of those who confused the divine and human natures of Christ in one. It affirmed the position of the existence of one person in two natures, which are united unconfusedly, unchangeably, indivisibly and inseparably.

(9) Butler, *The Arab Conquest*, 68.

(10) Neale, *A History of the Holy Eastern Church*, II, 57.

(11) Leroy, *Moines et Monastères du Proche Orient*, 48.

(12) *Ethiopian Synax.*, *P.O.*, IX, 418 f.

(13) Wüstenfeld, *Maqrizi*, 59.

(14) HPCC, *P.O.*, V, 101.

(15) Synax., *P.O.*, III, 258 f.

(16) *HPEC*, II, II, 119.

(17) Especially during the patriarchate of Christodoulus (1047-1077 A.D.).

(18) Malan, *Maqrizi*, 94.

(19) Evetts, B.T.A., *Abû Sâlih*, 20-43.

(20) Crum, *Catalogue*, 138.

(21) Renaudotius, *HPAJ*, 563.

(22) Evetts, B.T.A., *op. cit.*, 160

(23) Piankoff, *Peintures*, 163.

(24) Evelyn White, *Monasteries*, II, 389.

(25) *Ethiop. Synax.*, Hamle II, Budge IV, 1107.

(26) Marino Sanuto, *Secrets for True Crusaders*, 60-61.

(27) Ludolf von Suchem, *Description of the Holy Land*, 80.

(28) Niccolo di Poggibonsi, "Oltramare" in Golubovich, *Biblioteca Bio-Bibliografica della Terra Santa*, V. (1346-1400). cap. 194.

(29) *Ethiop. Synax.*, Ter 5, Budge II, 453.

(30) *Le Saint Voyage de Jérusalem par le Baron d'Anglure en 1395*, 167 f.

(31) Ghillebert, *Oeuvres de Ghillebert de Lannoy*, 69.

(32) Röhricht, Meisner, "Die Pilgerfahrt des letzten Grafen Philipp von Katzenellenbogen", *Zeitschr. dtsch. Altertum* 1882, NF 14, 348-71.

(33) Rabino, *Le Monastère de Sainte-Catherine*, 67. For the coat of arms p. 71, No. 46. This graffito, as it was placed on the west wall of the church, is almost completely destroyed. The coat of arms shows three linden-leaves arranged around a circle. A better coat of arms of the same pilgrim is preserved on the north wall of the church.

(34) Pero Tafur, *Travels and Adventures 1435-1439*, 59.

(35) Wüstenfeld, *op. cit.*, 87-88.

(36) Felix Fabri, *The Book of Wanderings*, II, 573.

(37) Hofmann, G., "Kopten und Aethiopier auf dem Konziel von Florenz." *Orient. Christ. Per. 8* (1942), 11-24.

(38) Wansleben, *Nouvelle Relation*, 301.

(39) Schefer, *Le Voyage d'outremer de Jean Thénaud et la relation de l'ambassade de Dominico Trevisan auprès Soudan d'Egypte*, 81.

(40) Brown, *History of Africa*, III, 1022.

(41) Monks of Dair as-Suriân, *Sirat al-Anbâ Yuhannis Kame...*, 53.

(42) Belon du Mans. *Les observations de plusieurs singularitéz et choses mémorables...* 129.

(43) Alvarez. *Verdadeira Informacao das Terras de Preste Joao, etc.*, in Cerulli, *Etiopi in Palestina*, I, 399.

(44) Cerulli, *op. cit.*, II, 419.

(45) Also on the wooden screens of the Church of St. Mark in the garden of the monastery.

(46) Jullien, *Voyage dans le desert de la Basse-Thébaide aux couvents de St. Antoine et de St. Paul*, 42.

(47) Coppin, *Relation des Voyages*, 307.

(48) Coppin, *op. cit.*, 275.

(49) Golubovich, *Biblioteca Bio-Bibliografica della Terra Santa...*, III, *Etiopia francescana* I, 187.

(50) *Ibid., Etiopia francescana*, I, 92, 217n.

(51) Ignazio da Seggiano, *Documenti inediti sull' apostolato Minori Cappuccini nel Vicino Oriente,* (1623-1683), 142.

(52) Rabbath, *Documents inédits pour servir à l'histoire du Christianisme en Orient,* I, 510. This was done in spite of the prohibition of the Sacra Congregatio de Propaganda Fide, which prohibited the *communicatio in sacris eum dissentibus* on March 21, 1627. Non debere Missionarios divina celebrare in ecclesiis, in quibus simul haeretici sua profana et sacrilega exercitia habent. Ut tamen catholicis fiat satis, super altaribus portatilibus in privatis domibus positis, sacrum peragendum esse (De Vries, "Das Problem der Communicatio in sacris cum dissentibus").

(53) Monceaux et Laisné, "Mission de M.M. de Monceaux et Laisné, voyages de vaillant en Orient (1667-1675)." Omont, *Missions Archéologiques Françaises...,* I, 35.

(54) Wansleben says about the water: "They drink it, it is not very wholesome, chiefly for those who are not accustomed to it; for the Nitre which infects it, causeth Bladders to rise under the skin, and torments such as drink of it with itching, as I have found by experience."

(55) Wansleben, *op. cit.,* 302 f.

(56) De Maillet, *Description de l'Egypte,* 319-324.

(57) Omont, *Missions Archéologiques Françaises en Orient aux XVII et XVIII siècles,* I, 283.

(58) Omont, *op. cit.,* II, 1208. (MS.)

(59) Paul Lucas, *Voyage du Sieur Paul Lucas fait en 1714 par ordre de Louis XIV,* III, 149.

(60) Pococke, *A Description of the East,* 128.

(61) Sicard, *Description de l'Egypte,* III, 280.

(62) Graf, *Gesch. d. christl. arab. Lit.,* IV, 138.

(63) Granger, *Relation du Voyage fait en Egypte, en l'année 1730,* 97-121.

(64) Pococke, *op. cit.,* 128.

(65) Savary, *Lettres sur l'Egypte,* II, 57.

(66) Forbin, *Travels in Egypt in 1817-18,* 31.

(67) Piankoff, *Russian Travellers,* 62.

(68) Platt, *Journal of a Tour through Egypt,* II, 93. A selim is a mediaeval Coptic-Arabic vocabulary.

(69) Wilkinson, *Modern Egypt and Thebes,* II, 381.

(70) Piankoff, *op. cit.,* 63.

(71) The Living Bodiless Creatures are mentioned in *Is.* 6:1-3, *Ezek.* 1:4-8, *Apocalypse* 4:2-8.

(72) Piankoff, *op. cit.,* 65.

(73) Massaia, *I mei 35 anni di missione nell' Alta Etiopia,* II, 21 f.

(74) Chester, "Notes on the Coptic Dayrs of the Wadi Natroun and on the Dayr Antonios in the Eastern desert," 105 f.

(75) Jullien, *Vogage,* 70.

(76) Schweinfurth, *Auf Unbetretenen Wegen,* 173.

(77) Cogordan, *Relations du voyage fait au couvent de St. Antoine...,* 72.

(78) Lewis, "Hidden Egypt", 746.

(79) Johann Georg, *Neue Streifzüge durch die Kirchen and Klöster Aegyptens,* 32-43.

(80) Horner, *The Coptic Version of the New Testament in the Northern Dialect,* I, lxv.

(81) Piankoff, *Whittemore,* 19 f.

(82) Chaine, "Le couvent de St. Antoine," 246 f.

(83) Morton, *Through Lands of the Bible,* 340.

(84) Giamberardini, *St. Antonio Abate Astro del Deserto,* 31.

(85) Tunnel: length, 11 m., height, 1.50 m., width, 0.60 m. Cave: length, 7 m., height, 2.50 m., width, 2.00 m.

(86) A study of a sample of water from the spring of St. Antony has revealed that the chloride concentration is 386 ppm., and the total electrolytes (Na Cl) 1158 ppm. The total electrolytes of the spring of St. Paul's monastery are 1228 ppm. The chloride concentration of the water from the Monastery of the Syrians shows 243 ppm. and that of Dair Anbâ Bishoî 121 ppm. while the total electrolytes of the Syrian monastery's water are 848 ppm., and that of Anbâ Bishoî 462 ppm.

(87) Palladius, *The Paradise or Garden of the Holy Fathers,* I, 173-174.

(88) Fontaine, "Le Monachisme Copte et la Montagne de Saint Antoine," 20.

Chapter 3: Dair Anbâ Bûlâ

(1) In Coptic texts his name is invariably Paule which in Arabic becomes Bûlâ.

(2) St. Athanasius also wrote a biography of St. Paul which unfortunately is no longer extant. It is quoted in the abridged form in the *Synaxarium.*

(3) Hardy, *Christian Egypt: Church and People,* 37.

(4) Palladius' *Paradise of the Holy Fathers* was written in 420 A.D. at the request of Lausus, a high ranking officer at the court of Theodosius II. For this reason the work of Palladius has been frequently referred to as the Lausiac History.

(5) Johann Georg speaks of a "hölzernen Sarg" or "Holzkasten", a wooden box. Johann Georg, *op. cit.,* 22.

(6) This refers to the persecutions of Decius (201-251) and Valerian (253-260).

(7) According to St. Jerome, Anbâ Bûlâ was 16 years of age when his parents died.

(8) Butcher, *The Story of the Church of Egypt,* I, 327, f.

(9) Antoninus Martyr, *Of the Holy Places Visited,* 34.

(10) Graf, *Gesch. d. christl. arab Lit.* II, 327 n.

(11) Evetts, B.T.A., *Abû Sâlih,* 167.

(12) Evelyn White, *The Monasteries of the Wâdî 'n-Natrûn,* II, 390.

(13) D'Anglure, *Le Saint Voyage de Jérusalem par le Baron d'Anglure en 1395,* 174.

(14) Ghillebert, *Oeuvres de Ghillebert de Lannoy,* 70.

(15) Kammerer, *La Mer Rouge, l'Abyssinie et l'Arabie,* I, 27.

(16) "Numur" in Arabic means leopards, panthers, tigers.

(17) Wüstenfeld, *Maqrizi's Geschichte der Copten,* 88-89.

(18) Monks of Dair as-Suriân, *Sîrat al-Anbâ Yuhannis Kamâ...,* 53.

(19) Coppin, *Relation des Voyages faites dans la Turquie, la Thébaide, et la Barbarie,* 313.

(20) Golubovich, *Biblioteca Bio-Bibliografica della Terra Santa... III., Etiopia Francescana,* I, 187.

(21) De Maillet, *Description de l'Egypte,* 321.
(22) Fedden, *A Study of the Monastery of St. Antony,* 43.
(23) Pococke, *A Description of the East,* 128.
(24) Habashî, "Al-Adyurah ash-Sharqîah wa'd-Dair al Muharraq," 51.
(25) Sicard, *Lettres Edifiantes et Curieuses,* III, 300.
(26) Granger, *Relation du Voyage fait en Egypte,* 115.
(27) Pococke, *A Description of the East,* 128.
(28) One verst = 1.067 m.
(29) Piankoff, *Russian Travellers,* 62.
(30) Platt, *Journal of a Tour through Egypt,* II, 97-98.
(31) Keimer, "Les Prosternations pénitentiaires des Moines du Couvent de St. Paul dans le désert de l'Est," 21.
(32) Piankoff, *Russian Travellers,* 65.
(33) Schweinfurth, *Auf Unbetretenen Wegen,* 198.
(34) Jullien, *Voyage,* 56 f.
(35) Lewis, "Hidden Egypt", 746.
(36) Somigli, T., *Il P. Fortunato Vignozzi da Seano,* 84.
(37) Fowler, *Christian Egypt: Past, Present and Future,* 199.
(38) Johann Georg, *Neueste Streifzüge,* 20 f.
(39) For a comprehensive study of the flora in the monasteries, *cf.* Taeckholm. "Report on the Botanical Excursion of the Desert Institute to the Red Sea Coast and the two Qalâlahs in Spring 1956," *Bulletin de l'Institut du Désert d'Egypte,* VI, 2, July 1956.

Chapter 4: The Valley of the Wâdî 'n-Natrûn

(1) 2000-1785 B.C.
(2) Porter, *Topographical Bibliography of Ancient Egyptian Hieroglyphic Texts,* VII, 317.
(3) The founder of the 12th Dynasty was Amenemhet (ca. 2000-1970 B.C.). When he reorganized Egypt he started a policy for defending his western frontier, and built a fortress at the Wâdî 'n-Natrûn for this purpose.
(4) Synax., *Patr. Orient.,* XVI, 409.
(5) Evelyn White, *The Monasteries of the Wâdî 'n-Natrûn,* II, 17-42.
(6) Palladius, *The Paradise or Garden of the Holy Fathers...* I, 120.
(7) Strabo, Book XVII, i, 23.
(8) Palladius, *op. cit.,* I, 99.
(9) Palladius, *op. cit.,* I, 225.

Chapter 5: Dair al-Barâmûs

(1) Barâmûs from the Coptic Parômaios = belonging to the Romans.
(2) Amélineau, *Histoire des Monastères de la Basse-Egypte,' vies des Paul, Antoine, Maxime et Domèce, Jean le Nain,* 48 ff., 262 f.
(3) Valentinian I, Roman Emperor of the West from 364-375.

(4) Palladius, *The Paradise or Garden of the Holy Fathers...* I, 240-242. In this connection it is interesting to note that the monks of Scetis knew of two Roman princes, Arcadius and Honorius, sons of the Roman emperor Theodosius who were taught by Anbâ Arsânîûs Arsenius is believed to have come to Scetis in 394. Could it be possible that some confusion with this story accounts for the royal element in the tradition of the "Little Strangers"? For by the 15th century, Anbâ Arsânîûs is reported to have been the teacher of Maximus and Domitius, and not of Arcadius and Honorius.

(5) Palladius, *op. cit.,* I, 113, 240, 271, 273.

(6) Amélineau, *op. cit.,* 315.

(7) By the end of the fourth century, four fairly independent communities existed in the Desert of Scetis. The community of the Romans (Barâmûs), the community of St. Macarius, the community of St. John the Short, and the community of St. Bishoî.

(8) *The Blessed Man Ammonius* could repeat the books of the Old Testament and New Testament by heart, and he also used to read the books by Origen. Palladius, *op. cit.,* I, 105.

(9) The most influential leader of the Origenist party was the monk Isidorus. Palladius, *op. cit.,* I, 89. Bishop Theophilus of Alexandria addressed the monks of the Western Desert: "If you really admit that God's countenance is such as ours, anathematize Origen's books, for some have drawn arguments from them in contrariety to our opinion." Socrates, *The Ecclesiastical History,* 311.

(10) Amélineau, *op. cit.,* 133-137.

(11) We see here the classical prototype of "withdrawal" and "return" reenacted in the history of the monastic societies of Scetis. Toynbee, *A Study of History,* 217 f.

(12) Dair al-Barâmûs, Dair Abû Maqâr, Dair Anbâ Bishoî, and Dair Yuhannis Colobus.

(13) Philostorgius, *The Ecclesiastical History,* 511.

(14) Palladius, *op. cit.,* I, 215.

(15) Synax., *P.O., XVIII,* 591 f.

(16) As in the case of the monasteries, barbarians (though of Teutonic origin) besieged Rome in 410.

(17) HPCC, *P.O.,* I, 473.

(18) *Ibid.*

(19) HPCC, *P.O.,* I, 506.

(20) Malan, *Magrizi,* 76.

(21) HPCC, *P.O.,* X, 436 f.

(22) Wüstenfeld, *Maqrizi,* 58.

(23) HPCC, *P.O.,* X, 508.

(24) *HPEC,* II, I, 52 f.

(25) *HPEC,* II, I, 60.; II,III, 315.

(26) Canons of Christodoulus, *Muséon,* XLV, 71-84.

(27) *HPEC,* II, III, 246, 286.

(28) Lane-Poole, *History,* 143.

(29) *HPEC,* II, III, 241.

(30) Larsow, *Die Festbriefe des Hlg. Athanasius,* 7.

(31) Wüstenfeld, *op. cit.,* 91.

(32) *Eth. Syn.*, P.O. VIII, 312 f.

(33) Neale, *A History of the Holy Eastern Churches*, II, 323.

(34) Wüstenfeld, *op. cit.*, 109 f.

(35) This referred to the Monastery of the Virgin of Barâmûs.

(36) Coppin, *Relation des Voyages faits dans la Turquie, la ‹Thébaide, et la Barbarie*, 345.

(37) Thévenot, The Travels of Monsieur de Thévenot into the Levant, I, 244.

(38) De Maillet, *Description de l'Egypte*, 296.

(39) Du Bernat, *Nouveaux Memoires Des Missions...* II, 68.

(40) Sicard, *Lettres Edifiantes et Curieuses*, III, 189 f.

(41) Sonnini, *Travels in Upper and Lower Egypt*, 340.

(42) According to the monks this very Husain was the "most formidable of the Bedouins, the most determined of the robbers... who ten years before, in 1768, had breached into the great wall and pillaged and sacked the monastery".

(43) Probably to see whether they were circumcised or not. The apparent interest in this operation attributed to Coptic ‘ monks is also substantiated by Ludovico di Varthema, who visited Egypt in 1503. *Cf.* Ludovico di Varthema, *Travels, etc.*, 285.

(44) Andréossy, *"Mémoire sur la vallée des lacs de Natrun,"* 298 f.

(45) In 1712: al-Barâmûs: 12-15 monks, Suriân: 12-15 monks, Bishoî: 4 monks, Abû Maqâr: 4 monks.

(46) *Quarterly Review*, LXXVII, 51.

(47) Curzon, *Visits to the Monasteries in the Levant*, 82-4.

(48) Platt, *Journal of a Tour through Egypt*, I, 386.

(49) Wilkinson, *Modern Egypt and Thebes*, 1, 386.

(50) *The History of the Patriarchs*, III, IV, and Addition, *MS.* 219 in the Coptic Museum, 270.

(51) Tischendorf, *Travels in the East*, 53.

(52) Junkers, *Reisen in Africa, 1875-86*, I, 37.

(53) Jullien, *L'Egypte. Souvenirs Bibliques et Chrétiens*, 38 f.

(54) As to the existence of ostriches in the Wâdî 'n-Natrûn, the monks claim to have discovered several old nests. At one time the ostrich was quite common in the Wâdî 'n-Natrûn. In 1816, J.L. Burckhardt saw ostriches in the desert between Cairo and Suez. Prince Halim Pasha relates that he saw destroyed nests of ostriches at a distance of a day's journey from Cairo. Pococke (1743) noticed the bird in the district south-west of Alexandria, and Minutoli observed "groups of 10 to 15 ostriches" on his way from Alexandria to Siwah. *Cf.* Finsch, O., *Baron Carl Claus von der Decken's Reisen in Ost Afrika*, IV, 598.

(55) Butler, *The Ancient Coptic Churches of Egypt*, I, 327.

(56) Butler identifies Maximus and Domitius as sons of the Greek Emperor Leo according to a 14th cent. *MS.* (Bib. Or. 258. fol. 16).

(57) Graf, *Gesch. d. christl. arab. Lit.* IV, 115, 116, 145-8.

(58) 'Abd al-Masîh ibn 'Abd al-Malek al-Mas'udî al-Muharraqî and 'Abd al-Masîh ibn Salîb al-Mas'udî al-Barâmûsî.

(59) Lewis, "Hidden Egypt," 757.

(60) Falls, *Three Years in the Libyan Desert*, 74 f.

(61) Jones, "The Coptic Monasteries of the Wâdî 'n-Natrûn", *Metr. Mus. Bull.*, 6, 7.

(62) Brémond, *Pèlerinage au Ouadi Natroun,* 14 ff.

(63) Johann Georg, *Streifzüge,* 29.

(64) Evelyn White, *The Monasteries of the Wâdi 'n-Natrûn,* II, III.

(65) Hatch, "A Visit to the Coptic Convents in Nitria," 100.

(66) Johann Georg, *Neue Streifzüge,* 44.

(67) Toussoun, *Etude sur le Wadi Natroun,* 50.

(68) Anbâ Akhristûdulûs (1047-1078), Anbâ Yûânnis XIV (1571-1586), Anbâ Mattâûs IV (1660-1675), Anbâ Kîrillus V (1874-1927), Anbâ Yûânnis XIX (1928-1942), Anbâ Kîrillus VI (1959-1971).

(69) Morton, *Through Lands of the Bible,* 234.

(70) Qummus Mikhâîl at Kröffelbach, Germany; Abûnâ Rufail in Hamburg, Germany; Qummus Arsânîûs in Holland; Qummus Yuhanna in Vienna, Austria; Qummus Filibus in Rome, Italy; Qummus Palladius in Stockholm, Sweden.

(71) Four monks are physicians.

(72) For my visit with Abûnâ 'Abd al-Masîh al-Habashî, cf. Meinardus, O. *Monks and Monasteries of the Egyptian Deserts.* Cairo, AUC Press, 1961, 153 f.

Chapter 6: Dair Abû Maqâr

(1) Palladius was born in 364 in Galatia and became an ascete in 384. In 388 he visited Alexandria and subsequently stayed for several years with Dorotheus in the desert. He visited the Desert of Scetis around 390. In 400, he met with St. Jerome in Bethlehem. St. John Chrysostomus consecrated him as bishop of Helenopolis. He died in 431.

(2) Valens (364-378), East Roman Emperor was baptized by Eudoxus, the Arian Bishop of Constantinople.

(3) Socrates, *Ecclesiastical History,* 241-2: Sozomen, *Ecclesiastical History,* 271.

(4) Synax., *P.O.,* XVI, 258 f.

(5) HPCC, *P.O.,* I, 428 f.

(6) This tradition is the first record that gives evidence of the existence of the keep or qasr in the Wâdî 'n-Natrûn.

(7) Theodosius II (408-450), son of Arcadius was Emperor of the East.

(8) The *Tome of Leo* is the letter sent by Pope Leo I to Flavian, patriarch of Constantinople, on 13 June, 449. In it, St. Leo expounds the Christological doctrine of the Latin Church, according to which Jesus Christ is One Person in Whom are Two Natures, the Divine and the Human, permanently united though unconfused and unmixed. Each of these exercises its own particular faculties, but within the unity of the Person. This was given formal authority by the Council of Chalcedon (451) as the classical statement of the Catholic doctrine of the Incarnation: 'Peter has spoken through Leo.'

(9) HPCC, *P.O.,* I, 473 f.

(10) The *History of the Patriarchs* mentions Dioscorus I only in a few lines. He endured severe persecution for the Orthodox Faith at the hands of Marcian and his wife, and they banished him from his see through the partial action of the Council of Chalcedon, and their subserviency to the will of the prince and his wife. But at that time the creeds were separated, and the sees were torn asunder.

(11) The story of Hilaria is undoubtedly apocryphal. We find similarities to this story in the traditions of Pelagia who also assumed male attire and travelled to Jerusalem, and of Marina who for forty years lived in a monastery. Only after her death was the secret of her sex discovered. Other well known examples are Eugenia, the daughter of Philip, prefect of Alexandria under Commodus. As a monk, Eugenia edified all and became hegoumenos of a monastery. Apollinaria was the daughter of the Emperor Anthemius. After visiting Palestine, she came to Alexandria, where she procured an Egyptian monastic habit and departed for Scetis. There she lived alone in the desert for some time and then attached herself to St. Macarius. Other woman-monks were Euphrosyne, Theodora and Anastasia. The practice of the so-called woman-monks was strongly condemned by the canons of the Council of Gangra in the 4th century, where we read: "If a woman, under pretence of asceticism shall change her apparel and, instead of a woman's accustomed clothing, shall put on that of a man, let her be anathema." Schaff, *A Select Library of Nicene and Post-Nicene Fathers,* Second Series XIV, 87 f.

(12) The *Henoticon* was put forward in 482 to secure the union between non-Chalcedonians and Chalcedonians. It condemned both Nestorius and Eutyches by its assertion that the Orthodox Faith was epitomized in the Nicene-Constantinopolitan Creed together with the Twelve Anathematisms of St. Cyril of Alexandria. It omitted all reference as to the number of the "Natures" of Christ, and really made important concessions to the Egyptians. It was widely accepted in the East, but never countenanced in the West.

(13) Malan, *Maqrizi,* 60; HPCC, *P.O.* I, 449.

(14) Synax., *P.O.* XI, 636.

(15) Maqrîzî (1364-1442) served as deputy qâdî in Cairo, as teacher of tradition at the Mu'aiyadiyab madrasah and later in the al-Ashrafiyah and al-Ikbaliyah madrasah in Damascus.

(16) Synax., *P.O.* XVI, 354.

(17) Wüstenfeld, *Maqrizi,* 44.

(18) HPCC, *P.O.* I, 513 f.

(19) HPCC, *P.O.* V, 82.

(20) HPCC, *P.O.* V, 182 f.

(21) Marwân II was finally defeated at Busir, in the district of al-Ashmunain in Upper Egypt. Here the last Damascus caliph of the Umayyad dynasty fell fighting in 750 A.D.

(22) HPCC, *P.O.* X, 453 f., 538 f.

(23) HPCC, *P.O.* X, 538.

(24) Synax., *P.O.* XVI, 324.

(25) *HPEC,* II, I, 19.

(26) *HPEC,* II, I, 31.

(27) *HPEC,* II, II, 118.

(28) Evetts, B.T.A., *Abû Sâlih,* 118.

(29) Synax., *P.O.* XVI, 373.

The disregard for the body, its cleanliness and care, was due to a dualistic philosophy which considered the body as an aspect of matter, and therefore essentially bad. St. Antony never bathed his body in water, nor did he as much as wash his feet or even allow himself to put them in water without necessity, and St. Ammon, who never saw himself naked, justified his attitude by saying: "It does not become a monk to see his own person exposed," and the Blessed Evagrius said: "From the time that I entered the desert I have never washed, and I have never eaten any vegetable, or any fruit, or any grapes." St. Jerome felt, that cleanliness of the body was a pollution of the soul, and said "who is once washed in the Blood of Christ, need not wash again."

(30) *HPEC*, II, II, 178.

(31) A skene is the dome of a church, but the term may also be used for the space beneath the dome, also used for the place of the singers and readers in front of the sanctuary.

(32) *HPEC*, II, II, 201.

(33) *HPEC*, II, III, 302.

(34) Omar Tousson, *Etude sur le Wadi Natroun*, 27.

(35) *HPEC*, II, II, 241.

(36) *HPEC*, II, III, 331.

(37) A "use" is a local modification of the standard rite.

(38) This date corresponds to 1196.

(39) This patriarch was with great probability Anbâ Ignatius XI (1484-1493) who visited the monasteries of the Wâdî 'n-Natrûn.

(40) Al-Malik al-Kâmil, after the death of al-Adil, was left with the difficult task of clearing Egypt of the Crusaders who had landed near Damietta. It was in 1211 during the siege of Damietta that St. Francis of Assisi approached and challenged the Sultan to become a Christian.

(41) There was a widespread practice of appointing Muslims as supervi-sors or guardians of Christian shrines. From 1244 until the present day the doors of the Church of the Resurrection in Jerusalem are guarded by two Muslim families. one of whom keeps the key, while the other has the right of opening the doors.

(42) Quatremère, *Histoire des Sultans Mamlouks de l'Egypte*, I, 246.

(43) Wüstenfeld, *Maqrizi*, 110.

(44) The Monastery of St. Catherine possesses also a firman which claims to have been issued by Muhammad and written by 'Alî. All religious groups have cooperated in the manufacture of false documents, which were supposed to have been issued by the Prophet.

(45) Saint-Génois, *Les Voyageurs Belges en XIII-XVII siècle* 169-170.

(46) Brown, *The History and Description of Africa*, III, 1022.

(47) Belon du Mans, *Les Observations de plusieurs singularité*, 96.

(48) Luke, *A Spanish Franciscan's Narrative*, 61.

(49) Villamont, *Les Voyages*, III, xiii, 587.

(50) Sandys, *Travells*, 85.

(51) Roger, *La Terre Sainte ou Description topographique très particulière des Saints Lieux, et de la Terre de Promission*, 398.

(52) Gravit, "Peiresc et les études coptes en France au XVIII siècles," 14.

(53) Simaika, *Catalogue of the Coptic and Arabic Manuscripts in the Coptic Museum*, xxxi.

(54) Burmester, "Comptes Rendus", *Bull. Soc. Arch. Copte*, XIII, 206. In 1638, Agathangelus of Vendôme and Cassianus of Nantes went to Ethiopia. Agathangelus, who knew Arabic, had visited several Coptic monasteries and converted or believed he had converted one of the monks of the Monastery of St. Antony, Abûnâ Murqus, who in 1635, was sent by the Coptic Patriarch as Abûnâ to

Ethiopia. It was he who denounced the Capuchins and thus was the cause of their execution. They were hanged at Gondar by the cords of their Franciscan habits. For four nights miraculous lights were reported to be seen above their bodies, and the terrified king ordered them to be buried. Their beatification began in 1665, but was interrupted for two hundred years, until it was taken up again in 1887 by Cardinal Massaia. Finally, on 7 January, 1905, the two martyrs were declared blessed by Pope Pius X.

(55) Coppin, *Relation des Voyages faits dans la Turquie, la Thébaide, et la Barbarie*, 343. The practice of adding anathemas to sacred texts goes back at least to the 13th century. We read in a Gospel text of 1229, which was purchased by the priest Gabriel for the Church of the Angel Michael from the Monastery of St. Antony, that it should "not be sold or pledged or carried off from it to any other. And whoever takes it with the design of covetousness the Lord Jesus Christ shall give him no portion with Christ, either in this time or in the time to come. And Christ shàll cause the Angel Michael to be charged with the punishment of him in this world and the next. Amen."

(56) Golubovich, *Biblioteca Bio-Bibliografica della Terra Santa...*, III, *Etiopia Francescana*, I, 92.

(57) Le Gouz de la Boullaye, *Les Voyages et Observations*, 384.

(58) Thévenot, *The Travels of Monsieur de Thévenot into the Levant*, I, 242.

(59) Mazarin et Séguir, "Mission du P. Athanase à Constantinople, en Chypre et au Mont-Athos," Omont, *Missions Archéologiques Françaises en Orient aux XVII et XVIII siècles*, I, 11.

(60) Galland, "Mémoire des observations que l'on peut faire.dans les voyages de Levant, remis à M. Galland, lors de son voyage, par M. Colbert," Omont, *op. cit.*, I, 207.

(61) Goujon, *Histoire et Voyage de la Terre Sainte*, 320.

(62) Orbis Seraphieus. *De Missionibus fratrum Minorum*, II, iii, IV, 252.

(63) Du Bernat, *Nouveaux Mémoires des Missions de la Compagnie de Jésus dans le Levant*, II, 33, f.

(64) Sicard, *Lettres Edifiantes et Curieuses*, II, 175 f.

(65) Simaika, *op. cit.*, xxii.

(66) Omont, *op. cit.*, I, 500.

(67) Granger, *Relation du Voyage fait en Egypt*, 1.79.

(68) Sonnini, *Travels in Upper and Lower Egypt*, 309.

(69) Auriant, *Revue Blue*, May 17, 1930, quoted by Carré, *Voyageurs et Ecrivains Français*, 106.

(70) Andréossy in *Description de l'Egypte*, I, 298.

(71) Platt, *Journal of a Tour through Egypt*, I, 284.

(72) Wilkinson, *Modern Egypt and Thebes*, I, 389. As-Surîân: 30-40 monks, Abû Maqâr: 22 monks, Anbâ Bishoî: 13 monks, al-Barâmûs: 7 monks. *Ibid.*, 387.

(73) Tischendorf, *Travels in the East*, 45.

(74) Chester, "Notes on the Coptic Dayrs of the Wady Natroun..." 106.

(75) For a discussion on the identity of the tree, *cf.* Fleury, Rohault de, *Les instruments de la Passion*, Paris, 1870.

(76) Jullien, *L'Egypte, Souvenirs Bibliques et Chrétiens*, 50.

(77) Butler, *The Ancient Coptic Churches of Egypt*, II, 290.

(78) White, *From Sphinx to Oracle*, 28.

(79) Steindorff, *Durch die Libysche Wüste zur Amonoase*, 23.

(80) Gayet, *L'Art Copte*, 168-172.

(81) Strzygowski, *Koptische Kunst*, 148.

(82) Lewis, "Hidden Egypt", 754.

(83) Falls, *Three Years in the Libyan Desert*, 98 f.

(84) Jones, "The Monasteries of the Wadi Natrun." *Metr. Mus. Bull.* 6 and 7.

(85) Johann Georg, *Streifzüge*, 37.

(86) Johann Georg no doubt meant the Church of the 49 Martyrs.

(87) Evelyn White, *The Monasteries of the Wâdî 'n-Natrûn*, I, XII.

(88) Hatch, "A visit to the Coptic Convents in Nitria," 93.

(89) Kammerer, "Les Monastères," 134.

(90) Toussoun, *Etude sur le Wadi Natrun*, 51-58.

(91) Morton, *Through Lands of the Bible*, 248.

(92) Twenty-nine patriarchs came from the Monastery of St. Macarius.

(93) Until the middle of the 14th century, the Church of St. John the Baptist was known as the Church of St. Mark. The haikal of St. Mark certainly adjoined the sanctuary of Benjamin immediately to the north, for the narratives of the Consecration of the Chrism in the *Book of Chrism* (1305, 1330, 1340) describe in detail the solemn procession in which all the important parts of the Great Church were visited. The haikal of the Church of St. Mark was probably built to accommodate the head of St. Mark during the brief period of its deposit in the monastery. When the chrism ceased to be consecrated in the monastery, and the intimate connection with the throne of St. Mark came to an end, there was no longer any need for a haikal of St. Mark.

(94) Emperor Theodosius II (401-450) succeeded his father Arcadius as Emperor of the East in 408. It was during his reign that the Forty-nine Martyrs witnessed for their faith and suffered martyrdom.

(95) Burmester, "The Date of the Translation of Saint Iskhîrûn," *Le Muséon*, (1937), 53-60.

(96) Forty-three days before the Feast of the Nativity.

(97) Synax., *P.O.* XI, 702.

(98) Clarke, *Christian Antiquities*, 202.

(99) Ancient Syriac and Armenian graffiti superimposed upon the wall-paintings are barely visible. We find numerous Syriac graffiti on the north-western pillar of the church. These graffiti appear side-ways on the pillar, thus suggesting that they may have been written before or during the construction of the church.

(100) St. Eusebius (23rd Amshîr) was the son of Basilides. As a member of the Roman army, he was sent to Egypt. He witnessed for Christ in front of the Governor Maurianos and suffered torture. Upon the demand of the Emperor Diocletian, Eusebius was finally beheaded.

(101) St. Basilides (11th Tût) is one of the most distinguished of martyrs under the reign of Diocletian. Basilides was tortured and put to death by Masouros, the Governor of the Pentapolis.

(102) St. Justus (10th Amshîr) was the son of the Emperor Numerian and Patricia who was the sister of Basilides. Shocked by Diocletian's anti-Christian attitudes, he joined his cousin Eusebius in protest. He was sent to Antinoë where he was executed.

(103) St. Apoli (1st Mesore), the son of Justus Stratelates, belonged to the

Basilides family. He was sent to Alexandria and from there to Bubastis. He was cast into a dungeon and then beheaded.

(104) St. Theoclea (11th Bashans) was the wife of Justus and thus belongs to the Basilides family. Her suffering for her faith caused the conversion of her fellow-prisoners. She suffered martyrdom during the Diocletian persecution.

(105) The following note is attached to the nave-screen of the church: "In this Church of the Hermits who are fifty-eight Saints, (there are) on the north wall nine pictures. On the east, the picture of Anbâ Samwîl, who is known as the head of the Dair al-Qalamûn; on its west, Anbâ Yûânnis, Qummus Shabrâhât. Among the Hermits, the Forty-nine Elders are not painted here. And Abû-Nûfâr (Onuphrius) the Hermit, and the hair of his beard (is) long (and) covers his body. And west of them, Anbâ Abrâm at the railing (balustrade), and his picture is damaged by rain (from) a hole (in) the ceiling, and Anbâ Gâûgâ (George). And Anbâ Abullû and Anbâ Abîb and Anbâ Mikhâîl the Hermit and Anbâ Bîgîmî at the side of the west wall: and they painted them here (in) the year 1233 of the Martyrs, and they consecrated them with their Church—Remember me, O my God, I (am) Thy servant, the wretched Qummus 'Abd al-Masîh Salîb al-Barâmûsî, and by his (sic) prayers, O Lord vouchsafe to us forgiveness of our sins, and have mercy upon us according to Thy great mercy. To Thee (be) the glory. Year 1632. O Master, I beseech Thee with all my bowels and my mind (or heart) that Thou give to me a share with those who have received a good portion in this Mountain and these holy places, and that Thou grant to me strength to the extent that Thy providence has permitted my existence in this life, that I may visit (them) every year, and that my visit may be in accordance with Thy heavenly glory. Its writer is Bâsîlîûs, Metropolitan of the See of Abû Tîg. Its composition was on the 7th of Babah, 1616, and its scribe was the wretched one, Your son, the Qummus 'Abd al-Masîh Salîb."

(106) St. Samuel (8th Kihak) was born at Tkello in 597. He entered the Monastery of al-Qalamûn at the age of 18. He became a monk in Scetis as a disciple of Anbâ Agathûn. At the time of the Persian conquest, Samuel returned to al-Qalamûn.

(107) St. John the Hegumen (30th Kihak) was born in the 6th century. He became a monk in the desert of Scetis, and was captured several times by the Berbers. About 641, he became hegoumenos of the Monastery of St. Macarius. He died about 673.

(108) St. Onuphrius (16th Hatûr) was a contemporary of St. Paphnute Cephalas who lived in the 4th century. He was a hermit who lived in the inner desert.

(109) St. Abraham (9th Tubah) lived in the 7th century and gained fame as a disciple of John the Hegumen.

(110) St. George (18th Bashans), at one time a shepherd, became a monk. As a friend of Anbâ Abrâm the two hermits settled at the Monastery of St. Macarius.

(111) St. Apollo (25th Babeh) and his friend Anbâ Abîb joined a monastery in which they lived a life of strict asceticism. Later in his life, he was given the responsibility of supervision of several monasteries. He was a contemporary of Abû Maqâr the Egyptian.

(112) St. Abîb (25th Babeh) was the friend of Anbâ Abullû.

(113) St. Mîsaîl (13th Kihak) was admitted to the Monastery of al-Qalamûn. He is remembered for his courageous stand against the government forces which

wanted to occupy the Monastery of al-Qalamûn.

(114) St. Bigimi (11th Kihak), as the result of a vision, entered the inner desert, where he led a highly ascetic life, offering 4,800 prayers every day, and fasting for a stretch of 80 days.

(115) Meinardus, O., "The Relics of St. John the Baptist and the Prophet Elisha. An Examination of the Claims of their recent Invention in Egypt", *Ostkirchl. Studien*, 29, 1980, 118-142.

(116) See "Welcome to: The Monastery of St. Macarius", Monastery of St. Macarius, 1983.

Chapter 7: Dair Anbâ Bishoî

(1) The story is probably mere fiction, due to the Syrian monks who from comparatively early times settled in this desert, and who may have considered such a story the best means of establishing their right to be there.

(2) We hear of many famous friendships formed between ascetes: Banina the priest and Naou the deacon; Apip and Apollo, who together entered a monastery and suffered martyrdom; Dioscorus and Aesculapius, ascetes in the desert of Akhmîm; George and Abraham of Dair Abû Maqâr; Menas and Michael of the Monastery of St. Antony (these two friends later went to the Dair Abû Maqâr, where they became disciples of George and Abraham). Mercurius and Ephraem were monks in the Thebaid and were martyred. Ptolemy and Zacharias of Sakha became monks in the Monastery of St. Colobos. Paul and Timath, who dwelt in the Desert of Scetis.

(3) Wüstenfeld, *Maqrizi*, 48.

(4) *HPEC* II, II, 181 f., 207 f.

(5) *HPEC* II, II, 193.

(6) Daniel 6:22.

(7) Wüstenfeld, *op. cit.*, 63 f.

(8) Budge, *Bar Hebraeus*, I, 189.

(9) "In the aforesaid desert there were at that time about 700 monks of whom there were 400 in the Monastery of Abba Macarius, 165 in the Monastery of Abba Yohannes, 25 in the Monastery of Abba Kame, 20 in the Monastery of Baramus, 40 in the Monastery of Abba Pshoi, 60 in the Monastery of the Syrians, and two monks in the Cave of Abba Moses—a Syrian and a Copt—besides the anchorities who we did not see and did not know." *HPEC* II, II, 242.

(10) *Ethiop. Synax.*, 14 Nahassé, Budge IV, 1245. According to Budge, whose date is hopelessly out, Takla Haymanot visited Jerusalem between 735 and 766 A.D. when he was 69 or 70 years of age. Budge, *The Life of Takla Haymanot*, I, LII, LXI.

(11) Ibn Fadl 'Allah al-'Umari, *Masâlik al-Absar fi Mamalîk al-Amsar*, I, 374.

(12) Wüstenfeld, *Maqrizi*, 111.

(13) Coppin, *Relation des Voyages faits dans la Turquie, la Thébaide et la Barbarie*, 344.

(14) Thévenot, *The Travels of Monsieur de Thévenot into the Levant*, I, 242.

(15) Wansleben, *Nouvelle Relation en forme de Journal, d'un voyage fait en Egypte en 1672*, 213-229.

(16) Sicard, *Lettres Edifiantes et Curieuses...* III, 178.

(17) Granger, *Relation du Voyage fait en Egypte, en l'année 1730,* 179.

(18) Al-Warthilanî, *Nuzhat al-Anzar,* 243, 244, 606, quoted by Toussoun, *Etude sur le Wadi Natroun,* 45-46.

(19) A copy of this document is in the Münchener Staatsbibliothek, Cod. arab. 210.

(20) Sonnini, *Travels in Upper and Lower Egypt,* 368.

(21) Andréossy in *Description de l'Egypte,* I, 292.

(22) This may be a production by Willem Janscon Blaue (1571-1638).

(23) For this name I suggest that it may be a latinized form (plural) of "pais" and refers to Maximus and Domitius of al-Barâmûs.

(24) Belgrave, *Siwa, the Oasis of Jupiter Ammon,* 102.

(25) Minutoli, *Reise zum Tempel des Jupiter Ammon in der Lybischen Wüste,* 195.

(26) Russegger, *Reisen in Europa, Asien und Africa,* I, 189.

(27) Curzon, *Visits to the Monasteries in the Levant,* 84.

(28) Platt, *Journal of a Tour through Egypt,* I, 279.

(29) Tischendorf, *Travels in the East,* 53.

(30) Junkers, *Reisen in Afrika 1875-1886,* I, 44.

(31) Jullien, *L'Egypte, Souvenirs Bibliques et Chrétiens,* 46.

(32) Butler, *The Ancient Coptic Churches of Egypt,* II, 309.

(33) Abû Iskhîrûn.

(34) White, *From Sphinx to Oracle,* 266.

(35) Falls, *Three Years in the Libyan Desert,* 92.

(36) Tyndale, *An Artist in Egypt,* 90.

(37) Johann Georg, *Streifzüge,* 36-37.

(38) Hatch, "A Visit to the Coptic Convents in Nitria", 99.

(39) Toussoun, *Etude sur le Wadi Natroun,* 49.

(40) For a study of the geology of the Wâdî 'n-Natrûn, *cf.* Blankenhorn, *Geologie Aegyptens. Führer durch die geologische Vergangenheit Aegyptens von der Steinkohlperiode bis zur Jetztzeit.* The salt distribution in the Wâdî 'n-Natrûn was investigated by Stocker, *Der Wasserhaushalt ägyptischer Wüsten-und Salzpflanzen,* 122-126. Rothshild and Henley, visiting the Wâdî 'n-Natrûn in 1903, observed a few gazelles. Hares were fairly common, and judging by their tracks, a species of jackal occurred, known by the natives as "dib". Wild boars, which even until the 1950s were fairly numerous, are now entirely extinct. De Winton, "List of Mammals etc.", 281, Hoogstraal of NAMRU 3 (1959), lists the following mammals in the Wâdî 'n-Natrûn: Lesser rat-tailed bat, Tomb-bat, Horseshoe bat, Long-eared bat, Libyan long-eared hedgehog, Charming gerbil, Henley's Pygmy gerbil, Anderson's Egyptian lesser gerbil, Pallid gerbil, Lesser Egyptian gerboa, Cairo spring mouse, Rothshild's hare, Egyptian fattail sand rat, Egyptian fox, Sand fox, Fennec, House rat, Egyptian bandicoat rat, Slender-horned gazelle. See also Hoogstraal, *New Mammal Records from the Western Desert of Egypt,* 10-11. Meinertzhagen, *Nicoll's Birds of Egypt,* I, II, lists the following birds in Wâdî 'n-Natrûn: Brown-necked raven, Short-toed lark, Bar-tailed desert lark, Crested lark, Desert horned lark, Bi-fasciated lark, Blueheaded wagtail, Clamorous red warbler, Rufous warbler, Graceful warbler, Fan-tailed warbler, Little owl, Little bittern, Marbled teal, Little grebe, Stone-curlew, Cream-coloured courser, Little ringed

plover, Kentish plover, Kittlitz' plover,Spurwinged plover, Black-winged stilt, Avocet, Water rail, Moorhen.

(41) Abû Iskhîrûn of Kalen was one of the soldiers of Arianus, the governor of Antinoë, who suffered severely under the persecutions of Emperor Diocletian.

Chapter 8: Dair as-Surîân

(1) This marble stele with a Coptic text commemorating St. John Kame is affixed to the west wall of the choir of the Church of the Holy Virgin in the Monastery of the Syrians.

(2) When Anbâ Banîâmîn II visited the monasteries of the Desert of Scetis in 1330, the tour of inspection included a visit to the Monastery of St. John Kame. Maqrîzî informs us that the Monastery of St. John Kame and the Monastery of St. Elias which belonged to the Ethiopians were destroyed by a worm that caused them to collapse. Wüstenfeld, *Maqrizi*, 111.

(3) Abba John Kame *P.O.*, XIV, 344 f.

(4) The departure may be identified with the flight from Scetis on account of the fifth raid of the Berbers in 817.

(5) Eutyches (*ca.* 378-454) was archimandrite of a large monastery in Constantinople. He denied that the manhood of Christ was consubstantial with ours, and maintained, that were two natures before, but only one after the Union in the Incarnate Christ.

(6) HPCC, *P.O.* I, 454.

(7) The devotion to the Blessed Virgin Mary is very marked with 32 feasts in her honour and an officium known as the Theotokia. The Theotokia corresponds to the Parvum Officium B. V. Mariae of the Latin Church, but unlike that office, does not reproduce the canonical hours, though it varies for the different days of the week. Like the Parvum Officium it is appended to the office of the day and it is most generally used during the month of Kihak (Dec. 10—Jan. 9), when it serves as devotion preparatory to the Feast of the Nativity.

(8) Wright, *Cat. Syr. MSS.*, in Brit. Museum, No. DCCLXXXI, 766.

(9) Butler, *The Arab Conquest of Egypt*, 93 f.

(10) *Ibid.*

(11) Synax., *P.O.* I, 293

(12) *HPEC*, II, II, 135.

(13) *HPEC*, II,II, 242.

(14) *HPEC*, II, II, 241.

(15) Dulaurier, *Chronique du Mathieu d'Edessa*, XCIX, 160.

(16) The Fatimid Caliph Mustansir bi'llah.

(17) Wright, *Cat. Syr. MSS.*, in Brit. Museum, No. MXXXII, 1199.

(18) Wüstenfeld, *Maqrizi*, 111.

(19) Zotenberg, *Cat. MSS. Syr.* Bibliothèque Nationale, Paris, No. 74, 44 f.

(20) Wright, *Cat. Syr. MSS.*, in Brit. Museum, No. CCCLXXIV.

(21) Meinardus, "Peter Heyling", *OkSt*, 14, 1965, 306 f., 18, 1969, 16 f.

(22) Coppin, *Relation des Voyages faits dans la Turquie, la Thébaide, et la Barberie*, 345.

(23) Thévenot, *The Travels of Monsieur de Thévenot into the Levant*, I, 244.

(24) Wansleben, *Nouvelle Relation en forme de Journal, d'un Voyage fait en Egypte en 1672 et 1673*, 228.

(25) Ray, *A Collection of Curious Travels and Voyages*, II, 151.

(26) Simaika, *Catalogue of the Coptic and Arabic Manuscripts in the Coptic Museum, etc.*, xxi.

(27) Sicard, *Lettres Edifiantes et Curieuses...*, III, 182.

(28) Granger, *Relation du Voyage fait en Egypte, en l'année 1730*, 179.

(29) Sonnini, *Travels in Upper and Lower Egypt*, 364.

(30) Browne, *Travels in Africa, Egypt and Syria from 1792-1798*, 42-43.

(31) Andréossy, "Mémoire sur la vallée des lacs de Natroun," 291.

(32) Cureton, *The Festal Letters of Athanasius*, xii.

(33) Taylor, *La Syrie, l'Egypte, la Palestine et la Judée*, 107-110.

(34) Curzon, *Visits to the Monasteries in the Levant*, 84-85.

(35) Wüstenfeld, *op. cit.*, 111.

(36) Platt, *Journal of a Tour through Egypt*, I, 273.

(37) Wilkinson, *Modern Egypt and Thebes*, I, 387.

(38) Tischendorf, *Travels in the East*, 52.

(39) *Cf.* J.R. Pacho, *Relation d'un voyage dans le Marmariques, le Cyrenaique, et les oasis d'Audjelah et de Maradèh*, Paris, 1827.

(40) Cureton, *Festal Letters of Athanasius*, v.

(41) Brugsch, *Wanderung nach den Natronklöstern in Aegypten*, 25.

(42) Stock, *The History of the Church Missionary Society*, I, 227-8.

(43) Lansing, *Egypt's Princes*, 389.

(44) Chester, "Notes on the Coptic Dayrs...," 105 f.

(45) Murray, *op. cit.*, II, 365.

(46) Butler, *The Ancient Coptic Churches of Egypt*, I, 316.

(47) Isambert, *Itinéraire de l'Orient*, 440.

(48) Baedeker, *Egypt*, 1892, 348.

(49) Strzygowski, "Der Schmuck der älteren el-Hadrakirche im syrischen Kloster der sketischen Wüste," 357.

(50) Gayet, *L'Art Copte*, 177-185.

(51) Lewis, "Hidden Egypt," 755.

(52) Falls, *Three Years in the Libyan Desert*, 87.

(53) Tyndale, *An Artist in Egypt*, 102.

(54) Flury, "Die Gipsornamente des Der es Surjani," 71-81.

(55) Johann Georg, *Streifzüge*, 30-36.

(56) Hatch, "A Visit to the Coptic Convents in Nitria," 99.

(57) Johann Georg, *Neue Streifzüge durch die Kirchen und Klöster Aegyptens*, 44-45.

(58) The Fast of Jonah which is observed on the Monday, Tuesday and Wednesday of the second week before the Fast of Heraclius or the Pre-Lenten Fast. The Fast of Heraclius is observed during the week before Lent, and together with Lent comprises fifty-five days of fasting. The Eve of the Nativity of Our Lord, and the Eve of the Epiphany are days of fasting.

Chapter 9: Dair Anbâ Samwîl

(1) Till, "Koptische Heiligen und Märtyrerlegenden," 55-71.

(2) Meyer, *St. Athanasius: The Life of St. Anthony,* 33.

(3) Evetts, B.T.A., *Abû Sâlih,* 205.

(4) Wüstenfeld, *Maqrizi,* 99.

(5) "From about the middle of the 7th century on, the influence and the fame of the Monastery of al-Qalamûn begins first to approach and then to surpass that of Naqlûn." Abbott, *The Monasteries of the Fayyum,* 38.

(6) Cyrus, Bishop of Phasis in the Caucasus was appointed archbishop of Alexandria by Heraclius.

(7) For the persecution of the Copts by Cyrus, *cf.* Butler, *The Arab Conquest of Egypt,* 168-193.

(8) Peterson, "The Paragraph Mark in Coptic Illuminated Ornament" in *Studies in Art and Literature for Bella da Costa Greene,* 310-2.

(9) *HPEC,* II, I, 45 f.

(10) Budge, *The Miracles of the Blessed Virgin Mary, etc.,* 75-83.

(11) *HPEC,* II, III, 387.

(12) Evetts, B.T.A., *op. cit.,* 207.

(13) Wüstenfeld, *Yacut,* II, 687.

(14) Anbâ Kîrillus VI, the 116th Patriarch served as hegoumenos of St. Samuel's though he identifies himself with the Monastery of al-Barâmûs.

(15) Wüstenfeld, *Maqrizi,* 100.

(16) Quatremère, *Mémoires Géographiques et Historiques sur l'Egypte,* I, 472.

(17) Fakhry, *The Monastery of Kalamoun,* 72. Shammas Nassif Fanus states that the monastery was inhabited until the 15th century. Fanus, *Tâbîkh al-Qiddis al-'Azim al-Anbâ Samwil bî Dair al-Qalamûn,* 35.

(18) Belzoni, *Narrative of the Operations and Recent Discoveries in Egypt and Nubia,* 433.

(19) Cailliaud, *Voyage à Méroe,* I, 33.

(20) Wilkinson, *Modern Egypt and Thebes,* II, 356.

(21) Schweinfurth, "Reise in das Depressionsgebiet im Umkreise des Fajum," 96 f.

(22) Liernur and Moncrieff, *Notes on the Wady Rayan,* 13.

(23) Beadnell, *The Topography and Geology of the Fayyum Province of Egypt,* 20.

(24) Smolenski, "Le Couvent Copte de Saint Samuel à Galamoun," 204-207.

(25) Johann Georg, *Neueste Streifzüge,* 12-15.

(26) Giamberardini, "II Convento dell'Anba Samu'il e i miracoli della Vergine," 140 f.

Chapter 10: Dair al-Muharraq

(1) *Matthew* 2: 13-15.

(2) *Hosea* 11:1.

(3) In all Coptic-Arabic documents Salome is a cousin of the Virgin and often accompanies Mary and Jesus. She is with them at the burial of Elizabeth, it is she

who brings Mary the sad news of the crucifixion of Jesus, walks with her to Golgotha and follows her to the sepulchre.

(4) For a detailed account of the travels of the Holy Family in Egypt, *cf.* Meinardus, *In the Steps of the Holy Family.* Cairo, 1986.

(5) Cf. 6th of Hatûr.

(6) Synax., *P.O.* III, 491 f.

(7) Monneret de Villard, *Deyr el Muharraqah,* 27.

(8) *Ethiop. Synax.,* Ter 5, Budge II, 453.

(9) Graf, *Gesch. d. christl. arab. Lit.,* II, 455.

(10) Evetts, B.T.A., *Abû Sâlih,* 227.

(11) Wüstenfeld, *Maqrizi,* 101.

(12) Cerulli, *Etiopi in Palestina,* II, 353.

(13) *Information from Brother Nicholas, a friar of San Michele Murano given in writing,* in Crawford, *Ethiopian Itineraries 1400-1524,* 129.

(14) Francesco Suriano, *Treatise on the Holy Land,* 195.

(15) Wansleben, *Nouvelle Relation en forme de Journal...,* 361.

(16) Jomard, "Description des Antiquities de l'Heptanomide," IV, 301.

(17) 'Abd al-Masîh Salîb al-Mas'udî al-Barâmûsî, *Tuhfat al-Sâ'ilin fi Dhikr Adyurat Ruhban al-Misriyîn,* 107.

(18) Watson, *The American Mission in Egypt,* 186.

(19) Rohlfs, *Drei Monate in der libyschen Wüste,* 41-52, and Zittel, *Briefe aus der libyschen Wüste,* 23-26.

(20) Jullien, *L'Egypte Bibliques et Chrétiens,* 249-250.

(21) Wilbour, *Travels in Egypt,* 480.

(22) Hafiz Naguib, (1878-1946), a Muslim *alias* Ghali Girgis, Mabrûk, Baron de Schneider, Abûnâ Ghabrîâl Ibrahîm, Abûnâ Fîlûthâûs. He was educated at the Military Academy, Cairo, and the Academy for Military Engineers in Paris. He served as a French spy in Germany. Caught and imprisoned in Germany, he escaped and returned to France and then to Cairo. Lived the life of a *bon-vivant,* accused of stealing, several times imprisoned and escaped. *Cf. L'iterafat,* Cairo, 1946.

(23) Monneret de Villard observes that the structure of the church resembles that of several mosques. For further details on his arguments, Monneret de Villard, *op. cit.,* 20 f.

(24) There was also the Ethiopian Church of St. Takla Haymanot.

(25) Evetts, B.T.A., *Abû Sâlih,* 227.

(26) Al-Hâfiz, 11th Fatimid Caliph, 1074-1149.

(27) The qasr is 16.5 m. high; the ground floor is 10.53 m. by 10.1 m.; the terrace is 9.6 by 8.8 m.

(28) The Pachomian Castle was built and named after Qummus Bakhûm I, (1905-1928) hegoumen of the monastery.

Chapter 11: Dair Abû Mînâ

(1) The problem of the historicity of St. Menas has been discussed by Drescher, *Apa Mena,* i-x, Delehaye, "L'invention des reliques de Saint Menas à Constantinople," Wiedemann, "Die Menas-Legenden, Ihre volkskundliche und Literarische Bedeutung." Three possible views are put forward. Either St. Menas

was an Egyptian and lived and died in Egypt, or he was a Phrygian martyr, or there were two Ss. Menas, the one Egyptian, the other Phrygian, and they were confused by the hagiographer. Sir W. Ramsey asserts that St. Menas is merely the Phrygian god Men in a Christianized form. *Journal of Hellenic Studies,* 38, 151 f., 166 f. Miedema postulates that St. Menas' cult resembles those of Horus, Osiris, Anubis, and Amen. *De Heilige Menas,* v.

(2) Synaxarium, *P.O.,* III, 293-298; "The Encomium of Apa Mena by John, Archbishop of Alexandria," Drescher, *Apa Mena,* 128-149. *Ethiop. Synax.,* 15 Khedâr, Budge I, 246-249.

(3) Blackman, *The Fellahin of Upper Egypt,* 248-9.

(4) Mosconas, personal correspondence, December 28, 1959.

(5) The number of the soldiers varies according to the source. The "Encomium" speaks of 1,200, an Arabic text (Simaika, *Cat. of the Copt. and Arab. MS. i. Copt. Museum,* I, 1063) has 12,000, and Budge's Ethiopic text 123,000.

(6) Kaufmann, *Die Heilige Stadt in der Wüste,* 13.

(7) *Cf.* Czetsch-Lindenwald, "Das Wasser des Abu Mena."

(8) Antoninus Martyr, *Of the Holy Places Visited,* 35.

(9) Butler, *The Arab Conquest of Egypt,* 177. Amélineau, *La Géographie de l'Egypte à l'Epoque Copte,* 319-21, Paris, *MS.* Arab., 139-97.

(10) SS. Cyri et Joannis Miracula, *Patr. Graeca.* 87. 3, c. 3596.

(11) "Une vie inédite de St. Jean l'Aumonier," *Analecta Bollandiana,* XLV, 1927, 24.

(12) HPCC, *P.O.,* V, 119-121.

(13) HPCC, *P.O.,* X, 410-468.

(14) Creswell, *Early Muslim Architecture,* II, 231.

(15) HPCC, *P.O.,* X, 512-514.

(16) *HPEC,* II, I, 3.

(17) *HPEC,* II, I, 50-60.

(18) Al-Bakrî did not visit N. Africa himself, but compiled his book from other writers, mostly of the first half of the 11th century. Creswell, *op. cit.,* I, 328.

(19) The name was given to the ruins of Abû Mînâ by the Bedouins, Karm Abû Mînâ means "Vineyard of Father Menas."

(20) The locality was also known as Bumna, so named by a Bedouin tribe of Abûm Dair.

(21) Qasr al-Qatâgî, 35 km. south of Abû Mînâ. This locality also had a church, and it is very likely that this building belonged to the fifth century, when it was used as a place of worship for the Christian pilgrims on their way from Alexandria to the Shrine of Abû Mînâ and further south to the Monasteries of the Wâdî 'n-Natrûn. De Cosson, "The Desert City of El-Mûna." Pacho, *Voyage dans la Marmarique,* 10.

(22) Junkers, *Reisen in Afrika,* I, 25, 96.

(23) To-day, we know that the pilgrims filled their flasks with the holy water from the source of St. Menas.

(24) The site of Abû Mînâ was actually identified by Mr. Ralph Carver early in 1905, and Kaufmann reaped the benefit of this discovery. (*Cf. Egyptian Gazette,* Jan. 17, 1940.)

(25) For the literature on the excavations of the Shrine of St. Menas, *cf.* Kaufmann, *Die Ausgrabung der Menas-Heiligtümer in der Mareotiswüste* (1906), *Zweiter Bericht über die Ausgrabung der Menas-Heiligtümer in der Mareotis-wüste*

(1907). *Dritter Bericht über die Ausgrabung der Menas-Heiligtümer in der Mareotiswüste* (1908), *Der Menastempel und die Heiligtümer von Karm Abu Mina in der Mariutwüste* (1909), *Die Heilige Stadt der Wüste* (1921).

(26) Grossmann, Peter, *Abû Mînâ, A Guide to the Ancient Pilgrimage Centre*, Cairo, 1986, 7. Also for the archaeological preliminary reports, p. 28, 29.

Chapter 13: Monasticism in the Fayyûm

(1) Budge, E.A.W., *The Book of the Saints of the Ethiopian Church*. Cambridge, 1928, I, 263.

(2) *Ibid.*, 167.

(3) Amélineau, *La géographie de l'Egypte*, 101.

(4) Amélineau, E., *Les actes des martyrs de l'Eglise Copte*. Paris, 1890, 69-71. Budge, *op. cit.*, II, 559.

(5) Budge, *op. cit.*, II, 563.

(6) Synaxarium *P.O.*, XI, 663.

(7) Budge, E.A.W., *Egyptian Tales and Romances*. London, 1931, 247-63. Amélineau, E., *Contes et romans de l'Egypte Chrétienne*. Paris, 1888, I, 109-143.

(8) Abbott, *The Monasteries of the Fayum*, 22-66.

(9) 26 Baûnah (Coptic), 26 Sanè (Ethiopian).

(10) Evetts, *Abu Sâlih*, 203, n.3.

(11) Abbott, *op. cit.*, 50, n.101.

(12) *Ibid.*, 39-40.

(13) Crum, W.E., *Catalogue of the Coptic Manuscripts in the British Museum*. London, 1905, 281, no. 590.

(14) Evetts, *op. cit.*, 205-206.

(15) Budge, *The Book of the Saints*, II, 559.

(16) Wansleben, *Nouvelle Relation*, 274-75.

(17) For Anbâ Abrâm of the Fayyûm cf. Leeder.

(18) The feasts in honour of St. Gabriel are held on 13 Hatûr (22 November), 22 Kihak (31 December), 30 Barmahât (8 April), 13 Baûnah (20 June), 26 Baûnah (3 July), and on the 22nd day of each Coptic month.

(19) His *vita* was written by St. Sarapion of Thmoui (cf. MS 112, Dair Anbâ Antûnîûs, Red Sea).

(20) Isaac of Tiphre (6 Bashons), who suffered martyrdom during the Diocletian persecution.

(21) Evetts, *op. cit.*, 210.

HPCC = "History of the Patriarchs of the Coptic Church", in *Patrologia Orientalis*, vols. I, V, X.

HPEC = *History of the Patriarchs of the Egyptian Church*, Attiyâ, A.S., 'Abd al-Masîh, Y., KHS-Burmester, O.H.E., Cairo, 1943, 1948, 1959.

BIBLIOGRAPHY

Abbott, Nabia. *The Monasteries of the Fayum.* Chicago, 1937.

'Abd al-Masîh Salîb al-Mas'ûdî al-Barâmûsî. *Tuhfat al-Sa'ilin fi Dhikr Adyurat Ruhban al-Misriyin.* Cairo, 1932.

Abudacni, Joseph. *Historia Jacobitarum seu Coptorum in Aegypto, etc.* Lubecae, 1733.

Amélineau, Emile Clément. *La Géographie de l'Egypte.* Paris, 1893.

Amélineau, Emile Clément. *Histoire des Monastères de la Basse-Egypte, vies des Saints Paul, Antoine, Macaire, Maxime et Domèce, Jean le Nain.* Paris, 1895.

Andréossy, Antoine-François. "Mémoire sur la vallée des lacs de Natroun." *Description de l'Egypte, ou Recueil des Observations et des Recherches,* I, 279, f. Paris, 1809-1822.

Antoninus Martyr. *Of the Holy Land Visited.* London: Palestine Pilgrims' Text Society, II, 1896.

Assemanus, Stephanus Euodius et Joseph Simonius. *Bibliothecae Apostolicae Vaticanae Codicum Manuscriptorum Catalogus.* Paris, 1926.

Attiyâ, 'Aziz Suryâl. *The Crusade in the Later Middle Ages.* London, 1938.

Attiyâ, 'Aziz Suryâl. *The Arabic Manuscripts of Mount Sinai.* Baltimore, 1955.

Attiyâ, 'Aziz Suryâl, Yassâ 'Abd al-Masîh, O.H.E. KHS-Burmester. *History of the Patriarchs of the Egyptian Church,* I, II, & III. Cairo, 1948, 1959.

Azadian, Hug, Munier. "Notes sur le Ouady Mouellah." *Bulletin de la Société Royale de Géogr. d'Egypte,* XVIII, 51-54.

Basset, René. "Le Synaxaire Arabe Jacobite." *Patrologia Orientalis,* I, III, XI, XVI, XVII.

Baumstark, Anton. *Die Christliche Literatur des Orients.* 2 vols. Leipzig, 1911.

Beadnell, H.J.L. *The Topography and Geology of the Fayum Province of Egypt.* Cairo, 1905.

Becquet, Th. "Les Monastères du Ouadi Natroun." *Irénikon,* 12, 351-371.

Belgrave, C. Dalrymple. *Siwa, the Oasis of Jupiter Ammon.* London, 1923.

Bell, H. Idris. *Egypt from Alexander the Great to the Arab Conquest.* Oxford, 1948.

Belon de Mans. *Les Observations de plusieurs singularitez et choses mémorables, trouvées en Grèce, Asie, Egypte, Arabie et autre pays étrangers redigées en trois livres.* Paris, 1555.

Belon de Mans. "Peter Belon's Bemerkungen auf einer Reise von Cairo durch de Sinaitischen Strich vom Petraeischen Arabien nach Palestina." Paulus, *Sammlung* I, 200 f.

Belzoni, Giovanni Battista. *Narrative of the Operations and Recent Discoveries in Egypt and Nubia.* London, 1821.

Besse, J.M. *Les moines d'Orient antérieurs au concile de Chalcédoine.* Paris, 1900.

Blaue, Willem Janszon. *Nova Aegypti Tabula.* Amsterdam, 1662-1665.

Blomfield, R.M. "St. Menas of Alexandria." *Bulletin de la Société Archéologique d'Alexandrie,* 6, 1904, 56-73.

Bonne. *Carte de l'Egypte ancienne et moderne.* Lattré, 1762.

Bourguet, Pierre du. "Saint-Antoine et Saint-Paul du Désert." *Bulletin de la Société Française d'Egyptologie,* 7, June 1951, 41.

Boussac, M.H. "Deirs et Nécropoles de la Chaine Arabique." *Revue hebdomadaire,* Oct. 1908.

Boussett, Wilhelm. "Das Mönchtum der sketischen Wüste." *Z. Kirchengeschichte,* 5, 1923, 1-41.

Breccia, Ev. *Alexandrea ad Aegyptum.* Bergamo, 1922.

Bremond, Jean. *Pèlerinage au Ouadi Natroun. Une oasis du désert monastique.* n. p., n. d.

Bremond, Jean. *Les Pères du Désert.* 2 vols. Paris, 1927.

Breydenbach, Bernard de. *Les Saintes Pèlegrinations de Bernard de Breydenbach* (1483). (Ed. F. Larrivaz). Cairo, 1904.

Brown, Robert. *The History and Description of Africa and of the notable things therein contained by al-Hassan ibn Mohammad al-Wezaz al-Fazi, a Moor, baptized as Giovanni Leone, but better known as Leo Africanus, done in English in the Year 1600 by John Pory.* 3 vols. London, 1896.

Browne, W.G. *Travels in Africa, Egypt and Syria from 1792-1793.* London, 1799.

Brugsch, Heinrich Karl. *Wanderung nach den Natronklöstern in Aegypten.* Berlin, 1855.

Budge, E.A. Wallis. *One Hundred and Ten Miracles of our Lady.* London, 1933.

Budge, E.A. Wallis. *The Wit and Wisdom of the Christian Fathers of Egypt: The Syrian Version of the Apophthegmata Patrum.* London, 1934.

Burkitt, F.C. "The Monasteries of the Wadi 'n-Natroun." *The Journal of Theological Studies,* XXVIII, 320-5, XXXIV, 188-192, XXXVI, 105-107.

Burmester, O.H.E. KHS. "On the date and authorship of the Arabic Synaxarium of the Coptic Church." *The Journal of Theological Studies,* XXXVIII, 240-53.

Burmester, O.H.E. KHS. *A Guide to the Monasteries of the Wâdî 'n-Natrûn.* Cairo: Société d'Archéologie Copte, n.d.

Burmester, O.H.E. KHS, Yassâ 'Abd al-Masîh. *History of the Patriarchs of the Egyptian Church.* II, I. Cairo, 1943.

Burmester, O.H.E. KHS. "The Consecration of the Holy Myron (Chrism) and the Kallielaion (Oil of the Catechumens)." *Eastern Churches Quarterly,* XI, 1954, 32-43.

Burmester, O.H.E. KHS. "Rite of the Initiation into Monasticism." *Eastern Churches Quarterly*, XI, 1954, 217-229.

Burmester, O.H.E. KHS. *A Guide to the Ancient Coptic Churches of Cairo*. Cairo, 1955.

Butcher, Edith Louisa. *The Story of the Church of Egypt*. 2. vols. London, 1897.

Butler, Alfred J. *The Arab Conquest of Egypt and the last thirty years of the Roman Dominion*. Oxford, 1902.

Butler, Alfred J. *The Ancient Coptic Churches of Egypt*. 2 vols. Oxford, 1884.

Cailliaud, Frederich. *Voyage à Meroe, au fleuve blanc au delà Fasoql*. Paris, 1826.

Campenhausen, Hans v. *Die Askese im Urchristentum*. Tübingen, 1949.

Carré, Jean Marie. *Voyageurs et Ecrivains Français en Egypte*. Le Caire, 1932.

Cauwenbergh, Paul V. *Etude sur les moines d'Egypte*. Paris, 1914.

Chaine, A.S.J. "Le couvent de Saint Antoine." *Le Rayon*, 9, 1936, 246-249.

Chaine. M. *La Chronologie des Temps Chrétiens de l'Egypte et de l'Ethiopie*. Paris: Librairie Orientaliste Paul Geuthner, 1925.

Chaleur, Sylvestre. "La Devotion a Saint Antoine." *Les Cahiers Coptes*, 7-8, 1954, 1-5.

Chaleur, Sylvestre. "Le Culte de Saint Antoine." *Bulletin de l'Institut des Etudes Coptes*, 1958, 31-41.

Chester, Greville J. "Notes on the Coptic Dayrs of the Wady Natroun and on the dayr Antonios in the Eastern desert". *Archaeological Journal*, 30, 1873, 105-16.

Clarke, Somers. *Christian Antiquities in the Nile Valley, a contribution towards the study of the ancient churches*. Oxford: Clarendon Press, 1912.

Cogordan, George. *Relations du voyage fait au couvent de Saint-Antoine, dans le désert de la Basse Thébaide... au mois de Novembre de l'an mille neuf cent un*. Paris, 1903.

Coppin, J. *Relation des Voyages fait dans la Turquie, la Thébaide, et la Barbarie*. Lyons, 1720.

Cramer, Maria. *Das Christlich-Koptische Aegypten einst und heute*. Wiesbaden, 1959.

Cramer, Maria. "Monastische Liturgie in Koptischen Klöstern." *Jahrbuch f. Liturgiewissenschaft*, 14, 1938, 230-42.

Crawford, O.G.S. *Ethiopian Itineraries Circa 1400-1524*. Cambridge, 1958.

Creswell, K.A.C. *Early Muslim Architecture*. Oxford, 1940.

Crum, Walter E. "Hugh Evelyn White." *Journal of Egyptian Archaeology*, 10, 1924, 331-332.

Crum, Walter E. *Catalogue of the Coptic Manuscripts in the John Rylands Library, Manchester*. Manchester, 1909.

Cureton, William. *The Festal Letters of Athanasius*. London, 1848.

Curzon, Robert. *Visits to the Monasteries in the Levant*. London, 1847.

Czetsch-Lindenwald, H.V. "Das Wasser des Abu Menas." *Die Pharmazeutische Industrie*, 20, 1958, 284-5.

D'Anglure. *Le Saint Voyage de Jérusalem par le Baron d'Anglure en 1395*. Paris, 1858.

D'Anville, B. *Egypt called in the Country of Missir*. R. d'Anville, 1765.

Davis, M.H. "The Life of Abba John Khame." *Patr. Orient.,* XIV.

Debanne, Nicolas J. "Le Mouled de Sitti Dimiana." *Bull. de la Soc. Roy. de Géogr. d'Egypte,* viii, 1917, 75-78.

Defrémery, C. and B.R. Sanguinetti. *Voyages d'Ibn Batoutah.* 4 vols. Paris, 1893.

De Goeje, M.J. *Bibiotheca Geographorum Arabicorum.* VII. Kitâb al-a'lâk an-Nafîsa VII, Abû Ali Ahmed ibn Omar ibn Rosthah, et Kitâb al-Boldân, Ahmed ibn Abî Jakûb ibn Wâdhih al-Kâtib al-Jakûbî. Lugduni Batavorum, 1892.

Delehaye, H. "L'invention des reliques de Saint Ménas à Constantinople." *Analecta Bollandiana,* 29, 1910, 117 f.

Delisle, Guillaume. *Carte de l'Egypte, et al.* Paris, 1707.

De Vries, Wilhelm. "Das Problem der 'communicatio in sacris cum dissidentibus' im Nahen Osten zur Zeit der Union (17. und 18. Jahrhundert)." *Ostkirchliche Studien,* VI, 1957, 2-3 81-106.

De Winton, W.E. "List of Mammals obtained by the Hon. N. Charles Rothshild and the Hon. R. Henley in the Natron Valley, Egypt." *Novitates Zoologicae,* X, 1903, 279-285.

Doresse, Jean. "Monastères Coptes aux environs d'Armant en Thébaide." *Analecta Bollandiana,* LXVII, 327-349.

Drescher, James. *Apa Mena. A Selection of Coptic Texts Relating to St. Menas.* Cairo, 1946.

Drescher, James. "St. Mena's Camels once more." *Bulletin de la Société d'Archéologie Copte,* VII (1941), 19-32.

Drescher, James. *Three Coptic Legends: Hilaria, Archellites, the seven Sleepers.* Cairo, 1947.

Du Bernat. *Nouveaux Mémoires des Missions de la Compagnie de Jésus dans le Levant,* Vol. II. Paris, 1717.

Du Bernat. "Brief des Pater Du Bernat, Missionaire von der Gesellschaft Jesu, in Aegypten and des Pater Fleuriau von derselben Gesellschaft." *Paulus, Sammlung,* IV, 233-288.

Dulaurier. *Chronique de Matthieu d'Edessa.* Paris, 1858.

Dümichen, Johannes. *Die Oasen der Libyschen Wüste.* Ihre alten Namen und ihre Lage, ihre vorzüglichsten Erzeugnisse und die ihrer Tempeln verehrten Gottheiten. Strassburg, 1877.

Ethiopian Synaxarium. *The Book of the Saints of the Ethiopian Church.* Transl. E.A.W. Budge, 4 vols. Cambridge, 1928.

Evagrius. *History of the Church from A.D. 431 to A.D. 594.* London, 1854.

Evelyn-White, Hugh G. *The History of the Monasteries of Nitria and of Scetis.* New York, 1932.

Evelyn-White, Hugh G. *The Monasteries of the Wâdi 'n-Natrûn.* New York, 1933.

Evetts, B.T.A. (ed. & transl.) *The Churches and Monasteries of Egypt and some neighbouring countries, attributed to Abû Sâlih, the Armenian.* Oxford, 1895.

Evetts, B.T.A. (ed. & transl.) "The History of the Patriarchs." *Patrologia Orientalis* I, V, X.

Evetts, B.T.A. "Le rite Copte de la prise d'habit et de la profession monacale." *Revue de l'Orient Chrétien,* 2, 1, (11) 1906, 60-73, 130-148.

Falls, J.C. Ewald. "Ein Besuch in den Natronklöstern der sketischen Wüste." *Frankfurter Zeitgemässe Broschüren,* 25, 1905, 61-85.

Falls, J.C. Ewald. *Three Years in the Libyan Desert.* London, 1913.

Fakhry, Ahmed. *The Monastery of Kalamoun.* Le Caire, 1947.

Fakhry, Ahmed. "Wadi el Natroun." *Annales du Service des Antiquités,* XL, 839-848.

Fedden, Henry Romilly. "A study of the Monastery of St. Anthony in the Eastern desert." *University of Egypt, Faculty of Arts Bull.,* 5, 1937, 1-60.

Felix Fabri. *The Book of Wanderings,* I & II. London: Palestine Pilgrims' Text Society, VII-X, 1893.

Flaubert, Gustave. *Voyage en Orient, (1849-51).* Paris, 1925.

Flury, Samuel. "Die Gipsornamente des Der es Surjani." *Der Islam,* VI, 71-87.

Fontaine, A.L. "Le monachisme Copte et la montagne de Saint Antoine." *Bulletin de l'Institut des Etudes Coptes,* 1958, 3-30.

Forbin, Count de. *Travels in Egypt in 1817-18.* London, 1819.

Fowler, Montague. *Christian Egypt, Past, Present and Future.* London, 1901.

François, Baron de Tott. *Memoires sur les Turcs et les Tatars.* Paris, 1784.

Frescobaldi, Gucci and Sigoli. *Visit to the Holy Places of Egypt, Palestine and Syria in 1384.* (transl. Bellorini and Hoade). Jerusalem, 1948.

Galland. "Mémoire des observations que l'on peut faire dans les voyages de Levant, remis à M. Galland, lors de son voyage, par M. Colbert," in Omont, *Missions Archéologiques Francaises en Orient aux XVIIe et XVIIIe siècles,* I, 207.

Garrido, Julio et Sylvestre Chaleur. "Quelques icônes du monastère d'Anba Bishoî." *Les Cahiers Coptes,* 10, 1956, 26-34.

Gasalee, Sir Stephen. "Bibliography of Christian Egypt." *Journal of Egyptian Archaeology,* 1-3, 1914-16.

Gasalee, Sir Stephen. "The Psychology of the Monks of the Egyptian Desert." *Philosopher,* 10, 1932, 73-81.

Gayet, Al. *L'Art Copte.* Paris, 1902.

Giamberardini, Gabriele. "Il Convento dell'Anbâ Samû'îl e i miracoli della Vergine." *La Voce del Nilo,* XVII, 5, 140-155.

Giamberardini, Gabriele. *S. Antonio Abate, Astro del deserto.* Cairo, 1957.

Glanville, S.R.K. *The Legacy of Egypt.* Oxford, 1942.

Golubovich, Gerolamo. *Biblioteca Bio-Bibliographica della Terra Santa e dell Oriente Francescano.* Quaracchi, 1927.

Goldschmidt, Lazarus and F.M. Esteves Pereira. *Vida do Abba Daniel do Mosteiro de Sceté.* Lisboa, 1897.

Graf, Georg. "Zur Autorschaft des arabischen Synaxars der Kopten." *Orientalia,* 9, 1940, 240-3.

Graf, Georg. *Geschichte der christlichen arabischen Literatur.* Citta del Vaticano, 1944.

Granger. *Relation du Voyage fait en Egypte, en l'année 1730.* Paris, 1745.

Graul, Karl. *Reise durch Egypten.* Leipzig, 1854.

Gravit, Francis W. "Peiresc et les études coptes en France an XVIIIe siècle." *Bull. Soc. Arch. Copte*, IV, 1938, 1-21.

Grebaut, S. "Le Synaxaire Ethiopien." *Patrologia Orientalis*, IX, XV.

Grossmann, P. *Abu Mina. A Guide to the Ancient Pilgrimage Center.* Cairo, 1986.

Guidi, Ignazio. "Le Synaxaire Ethiopien." *Patrologia Orientalis*, I, VII.

Gunther, John. *Inside Africa.* London, 1955.

Habashi, Labib. "Al-Adyirah al-Sharqiah wa'd Dair-al-Muharraq." *Al-Rahbânat al-Qibtiah*, 46-53.

Habashi, Labib. *Fi Sahrâ al- Arab wa' l-Adyirâ al-Sharqiah.* Cairo, 1929.

Harnack, Adolf v. *Monasticism, its Ideals and History.* London, 1901.

Hasselquist, Frederick. *Voyages and Travels in the Levant in the Years 1749-52.* (ed. C. Linnaeus). London, 1766.

Hatch, William Henry Paine. "A Visit to the Coptic Convents in Nitria." *American School of Oriental Research Annual,* 6, 1924, 93-107.

Hatch, William Henry Paine. "The Apostles in the New Testament and in the Ecclesiastical Tradition of Egypt." *Harvard Theological Review,* 21, 1928, 147-59.

Heussi, Karl. *Der Ursprung des Mönchtums.* Tübingen, 1936.

Hoogstraal, H., Kamal Wassif and M.N. Kaiser. *New Mammal Records from the Western Desert of Egypt.* Cairo, 1955.

Horneman, Frederick. *The Journal of Frederick Horneman's Travels from Cairo to Mourzouk.* London, 1802.

Horner, George (ed.). *The Coptic Version of the New Testament.* Oxford, 1898.

Hyatt, Harry Middleton. *The Church of Abyssinia.* London, 1928.

Ibrahim-Hilmy. *The Literature of Egypt and the Sudan from the earliest times to the year 1885 inclusive.* 2 vols. London, 1886.

Jaeck, Joachim Heinrich. *Taschen-Bibliothek der wichtigsten und interessantesten Reisen durch Aegypten,* 2 vols. Nürnberg, 1828.

Jarvis, C.S. *Three Deserts.* London, 1936.

Jennings-Bramley, W. "A Journey to Siwa in Sept./October 1896." *Geographical Journal,* X, 6, 597-608.

Johann Georg, Herzog zu Sachsen. *Streifzüge durch die Kirchen und Klöster Aegyptens.* Berlin, 1914.

Johann Georg, Herzog zu Sachsen. *Koptische Klöster der Gegenwart.* Aachen, 1918.

Johann Georg, Herzog zu Sachsen. *Neue Streifzüge durch die Kirchen und Klöster Aegyptens.* Berlin, 1930.

Johann Georg, Herzog zu Sachsen. *Neueste Streifzüge durch die Kirchen und Klöster Aegyptens.* Berlin, 1931.

John, Marquis of Bute (transl.). *The Coptic Morning Service for the Lord's Day.* London, 1908.

Jones, William J. "The Coptic Monasteries of the Wadi Natroun." *Metropolitan Museum Bull.*, 6, 1911, 19-29.

Jones, William J. "Monasteries of the Wadi Natroun." *Metropolitan Museum Bull.*, 7, 1912, 84-91.

Jullien, Michel. *Voyage au déserts de Scète et de Nitrie.* Lyons, 1882.

Jullien, Michel. *Voyage dans le désert de la Basse-Thebaide aux couvents de St. Antoine et de St. Paul.* Lyons, 1884.

Jullien, Michel. "Traditions et Légendes Coptes sur le Voyage de la Sainte Famille en Egypte." *Missions Catholiques,* XIX, 1886, 9-12.

Jullien, Michel. *L'Egypte. Souvenirs Bibliques et Chrétiens.* Lille, 1891.

Junkers, Wilhelm. *Reisen in Africa 1875-96.* vol 1. Wien & Olmuetz, 1889.

Kabès, Jean. "La dévotion à la Sainte Vierge dans l'Eglise Copte." *Les Cahiers Coptes,* 2, 1952, 4-7.

Kadloubowsky, E. & Palmer, G.E.H. *Early Fathers from the Philokalia.* London, 1953.

Kammerer, Winifred. *A Coptic Bibliography.* Ann Arbor, 1950.

Kaufmann, C.M. *Die Ausgrabung der Menas-Heiligtümer in der Mareotiswüste.* Cairo, 1906-8.

Kaufmann, C.M. "Neue Funde in der Menasstadt (Karm Abu)." *Römische Quartalschrift für Christliche Altertumskunde,* 20, 1906, 189-204.

Kaufmann, C.M. *Der Menastempel und die Heiligtümer von Karm Abu Mina in der Mariutwüste: Ein Führer durch die Ausgrabungen der Frankfurter Expedition.* Frankfurt, 1909.

Kaufmann, C.M. *Zur Ikonographie der Menas-Ampullen mit besonderer Berücksichtigung der Funde in der Menasstadt, nebst einem einführenden Kapitel über die neuentdeckten nubischen und aethiopischen Menastexte.* Cairo, 1910.

Kaufmann, C.M. *Die Menasstadt und das National-Heiligtum der altchristlichen Aegypter in der Westalexandrinischen Wüste, Ausgrabungen der Frankfurter Expedition am Karm Abu Mena 1905-1907.* Leipzig, 1910.

Kaufmann, C.M. "Menas und Horus-Harpokrates im Lichte der Ausgrabungen in der Menasstadt." *Oriens Christianus,* 1, 1911, 88-102.

Kaufmann, C.M. *Die Heilige Stadt der Wüste. Unsere Entdeckungen, Grabungen und Funde in der altchristlichen Menasstadt und weiteren Kreisen in Wort und Bild geschildert.* Kempt, 1921.

Keimer, Louis. "Quelques détails oubliés ou inconnus sur la vie et les publications de certain voyageurs Européens venus en Egypte pendant les siècles derniers." *Bull. Inst. d'Egypte,* XXXI, 1949, 121-173.

Keimer, Louis. "Les voyageurs de la langue allemande en Egypte entre 1800 et 1850 ainsi que leurs relations de voyage." *Cahiers d'Histoire Egyptienne,* V, March, 1953.

Keimer, Louis. "Les Coptes Catholiques à travers les relations de certain voyageurs." *Les Cahiers Coptes,* 10, 1956, 13-16.

Keimer, Louis. "Les Prosternations pénitentiaires des Moines du Couvent de St.

Paul dans le désert de l'Est." *Les Cahiers Coptes,* 11, 1956, 21.

Kersting, A.E "The Coptic Monasteries of Wadi Natrun." *The Bulletin,* July 1949, 9-15.

Kirchner-Demecini, E.I. *Oasen der Glückseligkeit.* Graz, 1949.

Kopp, Clemens. "Aus Vergangenheit und Gegenwart der Koptischen Kirche." *Theologie und Glaube,* 21, 1929, 305-15, 482-503.

Labib, Pahor. "Fouilles du Musée Copte à Saint-Ménas." *Bulletin de l'Institut d'Egypte,* 34, 1951-52, 133-138.

Laorty-Hadji. *L'Egypte.* Paris, 1856.

Lansing, Gulian. *Egypt's Princes. A Narrative of Missionary Labour in the Valley of the Nile.* Philadelphia, 1864.

Lapie. *Carte Historique, Physique & Positique de l'Egypte.* Paris, 1828.

Larsow, F. (ed.). *Die Festbriefe des heiligen Athanasius von Alexandrien.* (Klöster der Nitrischen Wüste). Leipzig & Göttingen, 1852.

Leake, W.M. *Map of Egypt.* London, 1818.

Leeder, S.H. *Modern Sons of the Pharaos.* London, 1918.

Le Gouz de la Boullaye. *Les Voyages et Observations du Sieur de la Boullaye-le Gouz, etc.* Paris, 1653.

Leroy, Jules. *Moines et Monastères du Proche Orient.* Paris, 1957.

Letts, Malcolm (transl.). *The Pilgrimage of Arnold von Harff Knight... in 1496-1499.* London, 1946.

Lewis, Agnes Smith. "A visit to the Coptic Monasteries of Egypt." *Cambridge Antiquitarian Society,* 10, 1898-1900, 210-215.

Lewis, Agnes Smith. "Hidden Egypt." *Century Magazine,* 68, 1904, 745-58.

Lucas, Paul. *Voyage du Sieur Paul Lucas fait en 1714 par ordre de Louis XIV.* Vol. III. Rouen, 1744.

Ludovico Di Varthana. *The Travels of Ludovico di Varthana in Egypt, Syria, Arabia Deserta and Arabia Felix, in Persia, India and Ethiopia, 1503 to 1508,* ed. J.W. Jones. London, 1863.

Madden, R.R. *Travels in Turkey, Egypt, Nubia and Palestine.* 2 vols. London, 1829.

Maillet. Benoit de. *Description de l'Egypte.* Paris, 1735.

Malan. S.C. (transl.). *The Divine Liturgy of St. Mark.* London, 1872.

Malan. S.C. (transl.). *A short history of the Copts and their Church.* London, 1873.

Malan. S.C. (transl.). *The Calendar of the Coptic Church.* London, 1873.

Masri, Iris Habib. *The Story of the Copts.* Cairo, 1978.

Massaia, G. *I mei 35 anni di missione nell'Alta Ethiopia.* Roma, 1886.

Meyer, Robert. *St. Athanasius: The Life of St. Anthony.* Westminster, 1950.

Michalet. *Les Déserts d'Egypte, de Thebaide d'Arabie de Syrie & etc. ou Sont exactement Marquez les Lieux Habitez Parles les Sainctes Pères des Déserts.* Paris, 1693.

Mingana, A. *Catalogue of the Mingana Collection of Manuscripts.* 3 vols. Cambridge, 1936.

Minutoli, Heinrich Freiherr von. *Reise zum Tempel des Jupiter Ammon in der Lybischen Wüste.* Berlin, 1824.

Monceaux et Laisné. "Mission de MM. de Monceaux et Laisné voyages de vaillant en Orient (1667-1675)," in Omont, *Missions Archéologiques Françaises en Orient aux XVII et XVIII siècles,* I, 35.

Monks of Dair as-Suriân. *Sirat al-Anbâ Yuhannis Kame, Tarikh Dair as-Suriân.* Wâdi 'n-Natrûn, 1951.

Morton, H.V. *Through Lands of the Bible.* London, 1938.

Munier, H. "Les Monuments Coptes d'après les Explorations du Père Michel Jullien." *Bulletin de la Société d'Archéologie Copte,* VI, 1940, 141 f.

Niccolo di Poggibonsi. *A Voyage Beyond the Seas.* (transl. Bellorini and Hoade.) Jerusalem, 1945.

Nigg, Walter. *Vom Geheimnis der Mönche.* Zürich & Stuttgart, 1953.

Norden, Frederick Lewis. *Travels in Egypt and Nubia.* 2 vols. London, 1757.

O'Leary, de Lacy. *The Saints of Egypt.* New York, 1937.

Omont, Henri. *Missions Archéologiques Françaises en Orient aux XVII et XVIII siècles.* 2 vols. Paris, 1902.

Pacho, M.J.R. *Relation d'un Voyage dans la Marmarique, la Cyrénaïque et les oasis d'Audjelah et de Maradèh.* Paris, 1827.

Palladius. *The Paradise or Garden of the Holy Fathers being Histories of the Anchorites Recluses Monks Coenobites and Ascetic Fathers of the Desert of Egypt between 250 and 400 A.D. circiter compiled by Athanasius Archbishop of Alexandria: Palladius Bishop of Helenopolis, St. Jerome and others.* (transl. E.A.W. Budge). London, 1907.

Paulus, H.E.G. *Sammlung der merkwürdigsten Reisen in den Orient.* 7 vols. Jena, 1792.

Pauty, Edmond. "L'Archéologie Copte et l'oeuvre du comité de conservation des monuments de l'Art Arabe, de 1933 à 1935." *Bulletin de la Société d'Archéologie Copte,* VII, 81-86.

Pero Tafur. *Travels and Adventures 1435-1439.* London, 1926.

Pereira, F.M. Esteves. *Vida do Abba Samuel Mosteiro do Kalamon.* Lisbon, 1894.

Perkins, J.B. Ward. "The Shrine of St. Menas." *British School of Archaeology in Rome,* 17, 1949.

Philostorgius. *The Ecclesiastical History.* (transl. Ed. Willford.) London, 1875.

Piankoff, Alexander. *Two Descriptions by Russian Travellers of the Monasteries of St. Anthony and St. Paul.* Le Caire, 1943.

Piankoff, Alexander. "Les Peintures de la Petite Chapelle au Monastère de Saint Antoine." *Les Cahiers Coptes,* 12, 1956, 7-16.

Piankoff, Alexander. "Deux peintures de Saints Militaires au Monastère de Saint Antoine." *Les Cahiers Coptes,* 10, 1956, 17-25.

Piankoff, Alexander. "Peintures au Monastère de Saint Antoine." *Bulletin de la Société d'Archéologie Copte,* 14, 1950-1957, 151-163.

Pieper, Karl. *Atlas Orbis Christiani Antiqui.* Düsseldorf, 1931.

Pietro Della Valle. *Voyages de Pietro della Valle dans la Turquie, l'Egypte, la*

Palestine, la Perse, etc. 8 vols. Rouen, 1745.

Platt, *Journal of a Tour through Egypt, the Peninsula of Sinai, and the Holy Land in 1838, 1839.* 2 vols. London, 1841.

Pococke, Richard. *Carte de l'Egypte et le cours de Nil.* Covens et Mortier, 1746.

Pococke, Richard. *A Description of the East and some other countries.* London, 1743.

Quatremère, M. *Mémoires Géographiques et Historiques sur l'Egypte.* Paris, 1811.

Quatremère, M. *Histoire des Sultans Mamlouks de l'Egypte.* 4 vols. Paris, 1845.

Queffelec, Henri. *Saint Anthony of the Desert.* New York, 1954.

Renaudotius, Eusebius. *Historia Patriarcharum Alexandrinorum Jacobitarum ad Marco usque ad finem saeculi XIII.* Paris, 1713.

Richard, Marcel. "Les Ecrits de Théophile d'Alexandrie." *Le Muséon,* 52, (1939), 33-50.

Richter, Julius. *A History of Protestant Missions in the Near East.* Edinburgh, 1910.

Robinson, Forbes. *Coptic Apocryphal Gospels.* Cambridge, 1955.

Rocco da Cesinale. *Storia della Missioni dei Cappucini.* Vol. III. Rome, 1873.

Roger, Eugene. *La Terre Sainte ou Description topographique très particulière des Saints Lieux, et de la Terre de Promission.* Paris, 1664.

Rohlfs, Gerhard. *Drei Monate in der libyschen Wüste.* Cassel, 1875.

Russegger, Joseph. *Reisen in Egypten, Nubien und Ost-Sudan.* Stuttgart, 1843.

Saint-Génois. *Les Voyageurs Belges du XIIe au XVIIe siècle.* Bruxelles, n.d.

Saint-Génois. *Les Voyageurs Belges du XVIIIe au XIXe siècle.* Bruxelles, n.d.

Sandys, George. *Sandys Travells.* London, 1670

Savary. *Lettres sur l'Egypte.* 3 vols. Paris, 1786.

Schefer, Ch. (ed.). *Le Voyage d'Outremer de Jean Thenaud, 1512.* Paris, 1884.

Schefer, Ch. (ed.). *Le Voyage de M. d'Aramon, Ambassadeur pour le Roy en Levant, escript par noble homme Jean Chesneau, l'un des secrétaires dudict seigneur Ambassadeur.* Paris, 1887.

Schmitz, Alfred Ludwig. "Die Welt der aegyptischen Einsiedler und Mönche." *Römische Quartalschrift für christliche Altertumskunde,* 37, 1929, 189-243.

Scholz, Augustin. *Reise in die Gegend zwischen Alexandrien und Paraetonium, die libysche Wüste, Siwa, Aegypten, Palaestina und Syrien in den Jahren 1820 und 1821.* Leipzig, 1822.

Schultz, B. Weir. "Christian Antiquities in the Nile Valley, a contribution towards the study of the ancient churches by Somers Clarke." *Journal of Egyptian Archaeology,* I, 1914, 301-3.

Schweinfurth, Georg August. "Reise in das Depressionsgebiet im Umkreise des Fajum im Januar 1886," *Gesellschaft für Erdkunde, Zeitschrift,* 21, 1886, 96-149.

Schweinfurth, Georg August. *Auf unbetretenen Wegen in Aegypten.* Hamburg, 1922.

Schwitz, Stephan. "Geschichte und Organisation der pachomischen Klöster im 4. Jahrhundert." *Archiv für katholisches Kirchenrecht,* 81, 3, 5, 1901, 461-90, 630-49.

Sicard, Claude. *Description de l'Egypte*. Paris, 1845.

Sicard, Claude. "Brief des Pater Sicard an den P. Fleurian über eine Reise in die Wüsten von Thebais und die dortigen Klöster." Paulus, *Sammlung*, V, 126-157.

Simaika, Marcus. *Catalogue of the Coptic and Arabic Manuscripts in the Coptic Museum, the Principal Churches of Cairo and Alexandria and the Monasteries of Egypt*. 3. vols. Cairo, 1939.

Simon, Jean. "Saint Samuel de Kalamon et monastère dans la litterature Ethiopienne." *Aethiopica*, I, 1933, 36-40.

Simon, Jean. "Le culte des XI martyrs dans l'Egypte chrétienne." *Orientalia*, n.s. 3, 1934, 174-6.

Simon, Jean. "Le monastère Copte de Samuel de Kalamon." *Orientalia Christiana Periodica*, i, 1935, 52-56.

Smolenski, Thadee. "Le Couvent Copte de Saint Samuel à Galamoun." *Egypt: Service des Antiquités*. Annales 9, 1908, 204-7.

Somigli, Teodosio. *Etiopica Francescana*, in Golubovich, *Biblioteca Bio-Bibliografica della Terra Santa*... III. Quaracchi, 1928.

Sonnini de Manoncourt, C.N.S. *Travels in Upper and Lower Egypt*. (transl. H. Hunter). 3 vols. London, 1799.

Spiegelberg, Wilhelm. *Koptisches Handwörterbuch*. Heidelberg, 1921.

Steindorff, Georg. *Durch die Libysche Wüste zur Amonoase*. Leipzig, 1904.

Stock, Eugene. *The History of the Church Missionary Society*. 3 vols. London, 1899.

Stocker, Otto. *Das Wadi Natrun*. Vegetationsbilder, 18. Reihe. Jena, 1927.

Strothmann, R. *Die Koptische Kirche in der Neuzeit*. Tübingen, 1932.

Strzygowski, Joseph. "Der Schmuck der älteren el-Hadrakirche im syrischen Klöster der sketischen Wüste." *Oriens Christianus*, I, 1901, 356 f.

Strzygowski, Joseph. *Koptische Kunst*. Vienna, 1904.

Täckholm, Vivi. "Report on the Botanical Excursion of the Desert Institute to the Red Sea Coast and the two Galalas in Spring 1956." *Bulletin de l'Institut du Désert d'Egypte*, VI, 2, July 1956.

Thévenot. *The Travels of Monsieur de Thévenot into the Levant*. London, 1637.

Till, Walter. "Koptische Heiligen und Märtyrerlegenden." *Orientalia Christiana Analecta*, 102, 1935, 55-71.

Tischendorf, L.F.C. *Travels in the East*. (transl., W. E. Schuckard). London, 1847.

Tousson, Omar. *Etude sur le Wadi Natroun, ses moines et ses couvents*. Alexandrie, 1931.

Tousson, Omar. *Cellia ses Couvents*. Alexandrie, 1935.

Tyndale, Walter. *An Artist in Egypt*. London, 1912.

Villamont, de. *Les Voyages*. Arras, 1606.

Villard, Ugo Monneret de. *Les Eglises du Monastère des Syriens au Wadi el Natroun*. Milan, 1928.

Wadell, Helen. *The Desert Fathers*. London, 1936.

Walters, C.C. *Monastic Archeology in Egypt*. Warminster, 1974.

Wansleben, Johann Michael. *Nouvelle Relation en forme de Journal, d'un voyage fait en Egypte en 1672 et 1673.* Paris, 1677.

Wansleben, Johann Michael. *The Present State of Egypt, or a new Relation of a late voyage into that Kingdom, 1672 and 1673.* London, 1678.

Watson, Andrew. *The American Mission in Egypt, (1854-1896).* Pittsburgh, 1904.

Wiedemann, A. "Die Menas-Legenden, Ihre volkskundliche und literarische Bedeutung." *Zeitschrift d. Vereins für rheinische Volkskunde,* 26.

Wilbour, Charles Edwin. *Travels in Egypt, December 1880 to May 1891.* Brooklyn, 1936.

Wilkinson, Gardner. *Modern Egypt and Thebes: A Description of Egypt.* 2 vols. London, 1843.

Wüstenfeld, F. *Maqrizi's Geschichte der Copten.* Göttingen, 1845.

Wüstenfeld, F. *Al-Sinaksari: Synaxarium, das ist Heiligen Kalender der coptischen Kirche aus dem arabischen übersetzt.* Gotha, 1879.

Wüstenfeld, F. *Yacut's Geographisches Wörterbuch aus den Handschriften zu Berlin, St. Petersburg und Paris.* Leipzig, 1924.

INDEX

Index of Individuals

Index of Places